THE FRAGRANT PATH

The Fragrant Path

A Book about Sweet Scented Flowers and Leaves

BY LOUISE BEEBE WILDER

ILLUSTRATIONS BY SIA KASKAMANIDIS

Hartley & Marks
PUBLISHERS

Published by
HARTLEY & MARKS PUBLISHERS INC.

P. O. Box 147	3661 West Broadway
Point Roberts, WA	Vancouver, BC
98281	V6R 2B8

ISBN 0-88179-125-3

Designed and typeset by The Typeworks
Set in CENTAUR

Printed in the U.S.A.

To the Memory of Balderbrae
A Lovely Garden

I sing of smells, of scents, perfumes, odours, whiffs and niffs; of aromas, bouquets, and fragrances; and also, though temperately and restrainedly, I promise you, of effluvia, reeks, fœtros, stenches, and — stinks.

DAN MCKENZIE, "AROMATICS AND THE SOUL."

PUBLISHERS NOTE TO THIS EDITION

Tampering with the content of a classic book such as Mrs. Wilder's Fragrant Path is fraught with all sorts of difficulties and leads inevitably to the committing of sins. But they are sins that we have consciously chosen to commit so that we might make her book once again a useful companion as well as a delight to read.

We have removed minor material that was particularly topical to the 1930s such as reports on what were recent flower show awards at that time. Much more significantly, we have updated plant species and variety names. In general, we have left the old name in square brackets [ ] where it appears after the changed name. For example, the entry for Heliotropium peruvianum has become Heliotropium arborescens [*H. peruvianum*] or the entry for *C. praecox*, has become *C.* x *praecox*. We have also updated the lists of recommended peonies (page 40), irises (page 41), and roses (page 43) to cover fragrant varieties that are generally available to be purchased at today's nursery.

I would like to thank the following people who have spent much time and effort in this quest to make *The Fragrant Path* available and once again, a book relevant to the needs of the "passionate" gardener who wishes to create their own fragrant path. Thank you to editor Heather Culliford, Doug Justice for the technical read-through, John Ross of the Vancouver Rose Society, C.D. Yeoman, and the many others who were so generous with their time and advice, and where necessary, criticism.

ACKNOWLEDGMENT

Many friendly persons have generously contributed the testimony of their noses to the making of this book. I am especially indebted to my friend and neighbour Magdalen Bartlett who did a great deal of the necessary research and whose keen and discriminating sense of smell was of the greatest value to me. Also I offer grateful acknowledgment to Lester Rowntree who kindly supplied me with accurate lists of sweet scented California wild flowers. Among others who sent me news of fragrant flowers are Mrs. C. S. McKinney, Helen M. Fox, Grace Sturtevant, Ethel Anson Peckham, J. Horace McFarland, B. Y. Morrison, Richardson Wright, Edward Porter St. John, T. H. Everett, Herbert Durand, Carl Purdy and D. M. Andrews.

Thanks are also due to Mrs. Emily Morgan who assembled the bouquet of fragrant flowers that is our frontispiece, and to Hobart Nichols, N. A., who gave it such charming semblance.

For the rest I would say in the pompous words of Henry van Oosten in his preface to *The Dutch Gardener*, or *The Compleat Florist*:

> I've weigh'd all that has been written or said upon that Subject, and borrow'd from other Authors what I found agreeable to Reason and Experience; taking Care to fetch in and bundle up what I found stragling in their bulky Writings, and not easy to come at. Not that this Performance is only a Collection; tho' I should not be troubled if the World thought so, since 'tis not Vainglory, but the encouragement of Florists that I have in view. He who considers it narrowly, will find that Collection was not my only Task, and that I have pointed to such things as are not to be met with elsewhere.

LOUISE BEEBE WILDER

July, 1932

INTRODUCTION

This book makes one realize how much pleasure is to be derived from one's own sensations, from smelling, tasting and noting the delicate variations in the colors and forms of the flowers; besides it is so full of delightful memories which a gardener harvests as he follows the flowery path that it stirs the desire in us to exchange experiences.

If we garden as Mrs. Wilder has we slowly come to notice more of the tenuous beauty in flowers. We see the exquisite harmonies or contrasts in color between the anthers and the corolla, the variations in green stems and leaves to suit the color of the petals and other delicate touches more subtle than any human artist could devise.

Monsieur Forestier, the great garden architect of modern France, used to tell a story of how one evening he was strolling between hibiscus, palms and oleanders in a garden along the African shores of the Mediterranean accompanied by a young Arab. As they walked along he noticed the Arab had a rose tucked behind his right ear, the blossom falling down on his dark cheek, and when they reached the end of the walk and turned to come back the Arab took the rose and placed it behind his left ear. So Monsieur Forestier asked him, "Why have you changed the rose from one ear to the other?" and the Arab answered, "Because the breeze is now on our left and this way I can continue to enjoy the perfume of the rose."

In our puritan land almost everything we do is through a screen of some kind. We read about love in novels and go to China or the South Sea Islands via the Movies and seldom have actual adventures and experiences to call forth our innermost deepest emotions. In southern lands especially in Latin countries it is quite different, as we have often experienced. One evening in Tours where we were spending the summer, as all American children, ours wanted to go to the Movies; so we went to the little theatre, and as we looked in we saw that except for the proprietor's family it was quite empty, and we asked the wife who was taking the entrance fees why this was and she answered, "Ah, Madame, it is so beautiful an evening, the lindens are all in flower and *tout le monde* has gone down to walk on the banks of the Loire under their perfumed branches."

There are many gates into the world of reality and gardening is one of them. As we dig and plant we sweat and strain our backs and get deliciously tired and when we go to bed we sleep so soundly that we do not hear the rain pattering on the roof, but upon awakening in the morning, with our first conscious breath we smell the sweet, clean air, and when we hurry down into the garden, all sunny and dewy it gives us a real thrill to see each little plant, still carrying raindrops in its leaves, standing up straight and strong, having imbibed nourishment from the moist earth we had enriched, made porous and crumbly for them.

Although most amateur gardeners begin tentatively and with gloves on it is pleasant to see how they slowly change until the love for growing plants and arranging them artistically takes complete possession of them and the whole world is colored over with the hue of their hobby. Although they do not go into gardening with the object of improving themselves, yet shy people become friendly and stiff ones thaw out, and the most unsuspected talents for combining colors both indoors and out are manifested, as is the ability for making and recording scientific observations. The further one goes along the road the more branches and related subjects one finds opening off from it and one has no idea whither these little side paths are going to lead. One thing is certain, however, that the people one meets as one travels along the garden path are delightful, remarkably generous and invariably genuine. Their eyes are bright, their faces bronzed, their hands are full of callouses, and their hearts are brimming over with the love of plants.

HELEN MORGENTHAU FOX

July, Foxden, Peekskill, N.Y.

CONTENTS

PART I

Sweet perfumes work immediately upon the spirits for their refreshing; sweet and healthfull ayres are speciall preservatives to health, and therefore much to be prised.

"A TREATISE OF FRUIT-TREES,"
— RALPH AUSTEN, 1653.

CHAPTER I

Pleasures of the Nose

Man only doth smel and take delight in the odours of flowers and sweet things.

WILLIAM BULLEIN, 1562

A GARDEN FULL OF sweet odours is a garden full of charm, a most precious kind of charm not to be implanted by mere skill in horticulture or power of purse, and which is beyond explaining. It is born of sensitive and very personal preferences yet its appeal is almost universal. Fragrance speaks to many to whom colour and form say little, and it "can bring as irresistibly as music emotions of all sorts to the mind." Besides the plants visible to the eye there will be in such a garden other comely growths, plain to that "other sense," such as "faith, romance, the lore of old unhurried times." These are infinitely well worth cultivating among the rest. They are an added joy in happy times and gently remedial when life seems warped and tired.

Nor is the fragrant garden ever wholly our own. It is, whether we will or no, common property. Over hedge or wall, and often far down the highway, it sends a greeting, not alone to us who have toiled for it, but to the passing stranger, the child skipping to school, the tired woman on her way to work, the rich man, the careless youth. And who shall say that the gentle sweet airs for a moment enveloping them do not send each on his way touched in some manner, cheered, softened, filled with hope or renewed in vigour, arrested, perhaps, in some devious course?

In mediaeval times there was a widespread belief in the efficacy of flower and leaf scents as cures or alleviations for all sorts of ills of the flesh, but more especially of the spirit, and as a protection against infection. This belief is testified to again and again in early horticultural and medical works. "If odours may worke satisfaction," wrote Gerard, "they are so sovereign in plants and so comfortable that no confection of apothecaries can equall their excellent virtue." In the "Grete Herball" it is written, "Against weyknesse of the brayne smel to Musk." The scent of basil was thought stimulating to the heart and "it taketh away melancholy and maketh a man merry and glad." The fragrance of sweet marjoram was deemed remedial for those "given to over much sighing." The smell of violets was thought an aid to digestion, and of rosemary it was written, "Smell of it and it shall keep thee youngly." "As for the garden of mint," wrote Pliny, "the very smell of it alone recovers and refreshes our spirits, as the taste stirs up our appetite for meat." To smell of wild thyme was believed to raise the spirits (and does it not?) and the vital energies, while the odour of garlic preserved those who partook of it or carried it about with them from infection.

Nor need we peer back into the dim past for corroboration. We all know persons who are affected for better or for worse by certain odours. A woman once told me that the smell of White Lilac revived her no matter how low she might feel in mind or body. My father was made actively ill by the scent of blossoming Ailanthus trees and he carried on a small but animated feud with a neighbour who had two in her garden and refused to part with them quite unreasonably, thought my father. To me the smell of clove pinks is instantly invigorating, while that of roses (the true old rose scent such as is possessed by the lovely dark red rose 'Etoile de Hollande') is invariably calming. Over and over again I have experienced the quieting influence of rose scent upon a disturbed state of mind, feeling the troubled condition smoothing out before I realized that roses were in the room, or near at hand. The soothing effects of lavender preparations are well known, and certain flower odours have an opposite effect, causing headache or nausea, even to the point of catastrophe, especially in a close room.

Miss Rohde ("Old English Gardening Books") quotes from the writings of a Dutch gentleman who traveled in England in 1560. He wrote of the English people that "their chambers and parlours strawed over with sweet herbes refreshed mee; their nosegays finely intermingled with sundry sorts of fragraunte floures, in their bed-chambers and privy rooms, with comfortable smell cheered me up, and entirely delyghted all my senses." Perhaps we do not realize that so fragile and subtle an influence as a pleasant fragrance in our living rooms and gardens has the power to cheer us up and delight all our senses. But it is true. "For smell often operates powerfully not only in surreptitiously enriching and invigorating the mental impression of an event but also in directing the flow of ideas into some particular channel independent of the will."[1]

But the subject is full of indistinctness, for a perfume that is a delight to one individual may be a horror to another. Memory, imagination, sentiment, a weak or strong stomach, are

[1] *McKenzie. "Aromatics and the Soul."*

inextricably involved in our reactions. But do not many of us know from experience that a chance whiff from a hayfield, a pine grove, the wayside bramble, the sea, often changes the mood of a whole day? A very old man once told me that whenever he smelled freshly sawed wood he felt instantly young and vigorous for a time. His youth had been passed in a New England village where there was a large saw mill and the acrid odour of fresh-cut wood was so strongly associated in his mind with youth and its abounding energy that it affected him physically.

Of course some persons are far more sensitive to such influences than others. Some there are, sadly enough, who are partially, or totally, anosmic, or nose blind, and to these a whole world of sensation and experience is closed. But there is undoubtedly a close and intimate connection between the sense of smell and the nerve centers and it is probably not fully understood how far reaching and profound is the influence of odour upon our mental state and physical makeup. Montaigne wrote:

> Physicians might in mine opinion draw more use and good from odours than they doe. For myself have often perceived that according unto their strength and qualitie, they change and alter and move my spirits and worke strange effects in me which make approve the common saying that the invention of insense and perfumes in churches, so ancient and so far dispersed throughout all nations and religions, had a special regard to rejoyce, to comfort, to quicken, to rouse, and to purify the senses, so that we might be the apter and readier unto contemplation.

In early times living-rooms, banqueting halls, churches and police courts were strewn with sweet scented herbs and flowers to disguise the odours arising from filthy and unsanitary conditions, and dandies and great ladies hung about their necks gold and silver filigree baubles filled with fragrant gums to preserve their delicate nostrils from the vile effluvia arising from the piles of garbage and filth rotting in the streets. Today we are proud of our sanitary conditions but are not our noses assaulted by almost as vile effluvia, the reek of gasoline and oil that pollutes the air of our cities and even rises triumphant above the delicate scents of the countryside? Perhaps it may again become fashionable to carry about with us little perforated balls of gold or silver filled with precious sweet smelling gums and resins to offset the unpleasant olfactory contacts that assail us.

Ancient books teach that the smell of many plants, rosemary among them, strengthens the memory, but none that I have come across calls attention to the trick that perfume sometimes plays us of suddenly calling up out of the past a scene, an episode, a state of mind, long buried beneath an accumulation of years and experience. How often the scent of some flower – honeysuckle, jasmine, lilac – stealing upon our senses in the night, causes the darkness to flower in visions of hallucinatory vividness. "Smell," wrote

E. F. Benson, "is the most memoristic of the senses."

Fragrance, perhaps, speaks more clearly, however, to age than to youth. With the young it may not pass much beyond the olfactory nerve, but with those who have started down the far side of the hill it reaches into the heart. "No other of the five senses is more subtle in its suggestions than the sense of smell or more unmistakably reminiscent of a time and state in which one was something else and possibly something better."[2] More than once I have seen eyes suddenly clouded with tears at the scent of some flower whose like may have grown in the dooryard of the old home, or about which cluster precious memories of a country-spent childhood. In the delightful letters of Robert Southey, one of whose own books, John Rea's "Flora," with his name inscribed in faded brown ink upon the fly leaf, is in my library, one reads that the poet was constantly reminded of his early childhood by the peculiar fragrance of decaying walnut leaves, while the scent of barberry brought to his mind the memory of a certain bush that grew in a garden where many of his happiest days had been spent.

The gardens of my youth were fragrant gardens and it is their sweetness rather than their patterns or their furnishings that I now most clearly recall. My mother's rose garden in Maryland was famous in that countryside and in the nearby city, for many shared its bounty. In it grew the most fragrant roses, not only great bushes of Provence, Damask and Gallica roses, but a collection of the finest teas and noisettes of the day. 'Maréchal Niel', 'Lamarque' and 'Gloire de Dijon' climbed high on trellises against the stone of the old house and looked in at the second-story windows. I remember that some sort of much coveted distinction was conferred upon the child finding the first long golden bud of 'Maréchal Niel'. Once a week, on Friday, a great hamper of freshly cut roses was loaded into the back of the "yellow wagon" – its physical aspect in no way bore out its sprightly name – and with Tom in the driver's seat we fared into the city and distributed to the sick, the sad and the disgruntled, great bunches of dewy fragrant roses. We children loved these "Friday Rose Days" as we called them, and would strive between stops for the privilege of jumping down and running up the clean marble steps to deliver the offering to the poor and the needy.

The box bushes grew tall in my grandfather's garden in Massachusetts, which has been little changed in outline for more than a hundred years. Their sharp scent seemed to bring about a special atmosphere of apartness and mystery, and when mingled with the simpler scents of herbs and the old time roses, after a shower or an early frost, the odours of this lovely old garden would be raised to such a pitch of oriental richness that one felt transported straight out of green and white New England to the glamorous East. And to a small person creeping through the white gate to play, the usual game of young matron tidily keeping house beneath the grape vine and

[2] *Somers. "The Garden."*

competently managing a large family of dolls, seemed no longer fitting. Instead a distraught lady out of the Arabian Nights glided with lissome grace up and down the straight paths, a fantastic head dress of hollyhocks masking pigtails, a lily scepter in her hand.

In the old Clark garden, Greenlea, in Delaware, ripe in years of gracious hospitality, lavender flourished, and there were sweet white violets in the grass and honeysuckle by the fence, while in the full summer the frosted plantain lilies scented all the air. And a child might play in these old gardens hours on hours secure from interruption, absorbing their gentle simplicity, storing up their sweetness, their still contentment, against the lean years sure to come. Precious memories these, invaluable and indelible.

GARDENIA
(*Gardenia jasminoides*)

Why do garden makers of today so seldom deliberately plan for fragrance? Undoubtedly gardens of early times were sweeter than ours. The green enclosures of Elizabethan days evidently overflowed with fragrant flowers and the little beds in which they were confined were neatly edged with some sweet-leaved plant – thyme, germander, lavender, rosemary, cut to a formal line. The yellowed pages of ancient works on gardening seem to give off the scents of the beloved old favourites – gilliflower, stock, sweet rocket, wall flower, white violet. Fragrance, by the wise old gardeners of those days, was valued as much as if not more than other attributes. Bacon said immortal things about sweet scented flowers in his essay, "Of Gardens," as well as in his less known curious old "Naturall Historie." Theophrastus devoted a portion of his "Inquiry Into Plants" to odours, chiefly floral and leaf odours. Our books of today make sadly little of the subject.

Our great-grandmothers prized more highly than any others what they called their posy flowers, moss rose, southernwood, bergamot, marigold, and the like. Indeed it would seem that save in that strangely tasteless period of the nineteenth century, when all grace departed from gardens and hard hued flowers were laid down upon the patient earth in lines and circles of crude colour like Berlin woolwork, geranium, calceolaria, lobelia, and again geranium, calceolaria, lobelia, no period has been so unmindful of fragrance in the garden as this in which we are now living. We have juggled the sweet pea into the last word in hues and furbelows, and all but lost its sweetness; we have been careless of the rose's scent, and have made of the wistful mignonette a stolid and inodorous wedge of vulgarity. We plan meticulously for colour harmony and a sequence of bloom, but who goes deliberately about planning for a succession of sweet scents during every week of the growing year?

In England I have seen more than one scented garden. These were usually very charming and well carried out, a square or rectangular enclosure bound about with sweet-leaved briers, or a hedge of box or yew. Paved paths, the joints of which bulged with thymes and low-growing mints, separated the little beds in which grew all manner of plants with sweet scented flowers or leaves. And there was always a comfortable seat, for the English plan to sit and enjoy their gardens; they are seldom merely for interest or display. And a fragrant garden especially invites the sitter. One might quite happily make a gathering of fragrant plants on either side of a winding path. Here would be space for great bushes of magnolias, honeysuckles, lilacs, mock oranges, bush roses, all manner of sweet scented herbaceous plants and annuals, and along the verges broad patches of low-growing things, sweet violets, mignonette, lily-of-the-valley, cowslips, sweet woodruff, with clematis scrambling into the trees and other climbers supported on posts.

But interesting as collections always are to the collector and to those of like mind, it is more generally satisfactory to grow the sweet scented plants throughout the garden, as many as may be found room for, a precious leaven for the whole, and with special attention paid to those with sweet smelling leaves, for these are delightful for use in making nosegays.

A few agreeably scented foliage plants that should be grown in gardens for use in bouquets are the following:

apple mint
basil
bay
bergamot
Cedronella canariensis
C. triphylla (tender)
lavender
lemon geranium (tender)
lemon verbena (tender)
micromeria
old woman
orange mint
rose geranium (tender)
rosemary (tender)
southernwood
sweet marjoram
thymes

For the most part fragrant flowers are light in colour or white. Brilliant flowers are seldom scented, though now and again there is an exception to prove the rule. There are more white scented flowers than any others and perhaps the purples and mauves come next. Some of the sweetest scented flowers are dull in colour, brownish or a sad purple. Flowers of thick texture are often heavily scented – the magnolias for instance, gardenias and those of the citrus tribe.

The perfume of a plant is not always found in its flowers. Sometimes it is in the root, sometimes in the seeds, the bark, the gum or oils, often in the leaves and stalks. "The daintiest Smells of Flowers are out of those Plants whose Leaves smell not; as Violets, Roses, Wall-flowers, Gilliflowers, Pinkes, Woodbines, Vine-flowers, Apple Blooms, Lime-tree Blooms, Bean blossoms." Certain plant families are especially gifted with perfume. This is true of the mint family, which embrace lavender, rosemary, the mints and thymes and micromerias, as well as many a coarse growth found by the wayside, the waterside, or in the fields, the odour of which is not always agreeable. The scents of these plants are in their leaves; only in a few cases have the blossoms any odour (rosemary flowers are fragrant) and like all herbs, save the pennyroyals, are what Bacon called "fast of their smells," and must be bruised before they will give up their sweetness. Sweet violets, lily-of-the-valley, hawthorn, heliotrope, lilac, many lilies and some roses are among those that release their sweetness spontaneously to the air.

Gardens are sweetest when the air is mild and full of moisture. In periods of extreme drought and heat it will be noticeable that the fragrant ethers are appreciably lessened. Frost, too, sets free latent fragrance, as does a shower of rain in many cases.

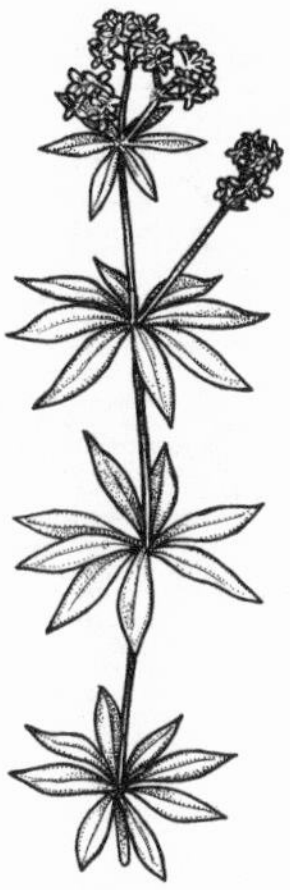

SWEET WOOD RUFF
(*Asperula odorata*)

A nosegay of sweet scented flowers is always an acceptable gift to visiting friends, especially if they hail from the city, and a guest is invariably complimented by such a bouquet upon her desk or dressing table. And it is pleasant to make up the nosegay with the character of the guest in mind. Honeysuckle and loose white rugosa roses make a delicious combination and possess a delicate poetic beauty; and I am fond of white petunia with sprigs of aromatic apple-scented mint. Mary Howett's "Poor man's Sunday nosegay" was composed of moss rosebud, white pink and mignonette – a rich regalement for the nose. A man will like nasturtium and sprays of southernwood, or a posy of hot-scented marigolds.

On the Island of Monhegan which lies, a gray shoulder shrugged out of the sea, some twenty restless miles out from Boothbay Harbor, on the coast of Maine, a delightful custom is followed. The tiny gardens on the island appear like encrustations of brilliant jewels dropped carelessly down anyhow upon the uneven ground, amidst the swart protruding rocks. Every cottage has one, and when your stay is spent and you stand upon the little jetty awaiting that small nimble boat that bobs like a cork upon the swelling waters, all those whom you have met and who feel friendly towards you, come to see you off, each carrying treasure trove from one or other of the gardens. You may have as many as ten or fifteen bouquets so that the little boat appears to be laden with a cargo of popular prima donnas – a charming picture against the blue sea with the stark heights of Manana looming in the background and the gulls flashing this way and that in the unbelievably sparkling air.

The most memorable bouquet among those that came to me was composed entirely of fragrant flowers and leaves, twenty-five different kinds, including sprigs of sharp-scented creeping juniper, characteristic growth of the Island, and there called trailing yew, and native bay, the whole bound about with sweet grass from the marsh. It came from the garden of Sidney Baldwin, delightful writer of children's stories, and I know I never had a gift of flowers that so delighted me.

Especially should small gardens, I think, be full of sweet scented flowers; it gives them a lovable intimate quality. And then if one thinks again, is it not just such endowment that a large garden has crying need of to make it more personal, more possessed, less aloof? On June 10, 1795, Horace Walpole wrote from Strawberry Hill, at "Eleven at Night":

> I am just come out of the garden on the most oriental of all evenings, and from breathing odours beyond those of Araby. The Acacias, which the Arabians have the sense to worship, are covered with blossoms, the Honeysuckles dangle from every tree in festoons, the Seringas are thickets of sweets, and the new cut hay in the field tempers the balmy gales with simple freshness.

Poets have ever known how to turn to gentle remedial things in times of stress, to draw from simple sources healing balms and assuagements. The scents of flowers and leaves are without doubt among the most potent sources of such alleviation. In Mary Webb's lovely book, "Poems and the Spring of Joy," she puts it beautifully:

> A thousand homely plants send out their oils and resins from the still places where they are in touch with vast forces, to heal men of their foulness. They link the places that humanity has made chokingly dusty with the life-giving airs of ambrosial meadows – bringing women's heads round quickly and setting people smiling.

CHAPTER II

Earliest Scents

"Jonathan," I said over our coffee, "have you noticed the weather today?"
"Um-m- pleasant day," he murmured abstractedly from behind his newspaper.
"Pleasant! Have you felt the sunshine? Have you smelled the spring mud? I want to roll in it!"

"THE JONATHAN PAPERS"
— ELIZABETH WOODVILLE

WHAT DAVID GRAYSON calls a downright good nose is a blessing to its possessor at all seasons in a garden, but never more so than in the spring. If our sense of smell is sluggish spring will lag for us until the strong scented flowers of May and June force themselves into our consciousness, and we shall have missed more than half the ecstasy. We shall have missed, for instance, that winter day in January, or February, when we step out of the door and suddenly smell the spring. In all external things it is still winter, snow lies about us, the air is cruelly sharp; but something new has crept into the world over night and the nose detects it. It is the best scent of the year. All sweet things seem to be in it, all things young and fresh and uncloying. But whence in reality does it come? From rising sap? From straining buds? Or is the earth breathing deeply, released from the bondage of the frost?

"After Candlemas," (February 2) says an old saw, "the sun lies on a hot stone." Perhaps in this we have the secret – some "strange alchemy of light" working with the earth and the frost and the rain to bring forth a pure fine scent, a scent which might happily be called essence of fertility, an intoxicating, soul stirring scent that affects one unaccountably. Filled with sudden urgency

for action we hasten forward the seed lists and, if we are of the feminine sex, buy an unnecessary gown; if masculine we indulge in an unrestrained tie or two and a new set of golf clubs. That first whiff of pure spring is nearly always expensive.

And how good the earth smells when first we go questing about and poking among the leaves. There is richness in it and something cool and fruity that appeals to us as wholesome and reviving. The old apothecary, William Coles, wrote:

> If a man want an Appetite to his Victuals the Smell of the Earth new turned up by digging with a Spade will procure it, and if he be inclined to a Consumption it will recover him.

Bacon tells of a certain "great Lord" who lived to a great age, that he had every morning immediately after sleep, "a clod of fresh earth laid under his nose, that he might take the smell there of."

A few flowers have this earthy scent, notable among them the old double daffodil. Press its wad of crumpled green-gold petals to your nose and, wherever you may chance to be in the flesh, your spirit will be transported to moist and greening pasture lands, or to gardens where the brown mould has lately swallowed the last of the Snow. It is a good smell.

Some noses go seeking scents in the early garden as eagerly as eyes seek flowers. Mr. Bowles, whose nose is a sensitive one, says in one of his books, "I have a strong conviction that the first real breath of spring that I inhale in the garden comes from *Iris unguicularis*"(*Iris stylosa*). And the scent of this flower with that of *Crocus imperati* he characterizes as "pure spring." In mild-mannered England this iris blooms freely out of doors in winter, as it does in California. In my cold garden it lives in a frame and gives its lovely blossoms only in favoured winters. A pot in a greenhouse is the safest place for it north of Washington. *Iris reticulata*, however, a bulbous species with purple and gold blossoms possessing a perfume much like that of violets, has lived in my garden for many years and blooms early in April. Lovely *Iris persica*, white & green & black, with a good scent, also stands our inclement winters in the rock garden and blooms very early.

But *Crocus imperati* blooms at an incredibly rash date – often in February. Its perfume is fine but so ethereal that I must bend to catch it. There is always a race between this Italian crocus and a colony of Mr. Elewes' snowdrop that lives under a red pine at the back of the garden, facing south. The race is nearly always to the snowdrops for they never seem to sleep, taking advantage of every relenting moment to edge upwards, the green spears often sticking through snow and ice for weeks at a time, waiting for a soft day when they will quite suddenly hang out the little frosty bells. "How beautiful are the Snowdrops," wrote Mary Pamela Milne-Holm, in "Notes from a Border Garden," a charming book about an old Scotch garden, "a perfect sheet of white, nodding their heads and literally scenting the air." Their scent is a fragile one, however, and it takes many hundreds of them growing together to scent the air. I have only patches here and there but it is no hardship to go with a bent back in February if by so doing one may catch a good scent.

The spring snowflake, *Leucojum vernum,* has a more marked fragrance and blooms almost as early as the snowdrops. Another small bulbous thing with a fine spicy perfume is *Puschkinia,* a relative of scilla. Both to see it and to smell it to the best advantage, the little arching spike of white blue-veined bells should be held in the hand. *Crocus vitellinus* blooms in winter and is fragrant. *Crocus versicolor* and *C. sativus* are also sweet scented and bloom before the Dutch varieties, and *C. biflorus,* called the Scotch crocus, has a delicate honey-scent. A sweet scented blue flower is not often met with, indeed the only one that comes to mind for the moment, save the English bluebell, is the grape hyacinth known as 'Heavenly Blue', a variety of *Muscari armeniacum* [*M. conicum*]. This little bulbous flower that was introduced by Messrs. Barr & Son of London from Trebizond, casts its rich fragrance upon the air with lavish generosity and when it is at the full of its bloom you take note of little else in its neighbourhood. The late Rev. Joseph Jacob described its scent as a mixture of the "real old clove carnation and of the ecclesiastical odour of the night-scented stock."

WINTERSWEET
(*Chimonanthus praecox*)

'Heavenly Blue' seeds freely and if you begin with a handful of the little bulbs you will soon have two hands full and so on to great riches. But you must not disturb the slender grass-like seedlings which you may mistake for young garlics and be disposed to root out. Weed the 'Heavenly Blue' neighbourhoods by hand, do not admit the hoe.

The musk hyacinth, *Muscari muscarimi* [*M. moschatum*], as its name indicates, has a musky odour, and for this reason a handful or two of the bulbs may be tucked away in a by-place. It has little beauty to recommend it, its dense globose clusters of greenish purple flowers offering little to the eye, but a few spikes in a glass on your writing table give pleasure to the nose. *Hyacinthoides non-scripta* [*Scilla nutans*], the English bluebell, that makes a blue mist in English woodlands, may lay claim to being one of the few sweet scented blue flowers. It has a pleasant honeylike sweetness that is noticeable on damp days quite a distance from the plantations. This flower belongs to May.

But I have not yet named the first flower scent of my garden, nor am I now quite sure that it is rightly so designated, but odour it is, the curious sweet dusty exhalation of the Chinese witch hazel, *Hamamelis mollis,* and of a vaguely agreeable character. A branch of it brought in from the cold February garden will quickly make itself known in a warm room. In milder climates than that of New York the delicious wintersweet, *Chimonanthus praecox* [*C. fragrans*], may be enjoyed at a very early date out of doors. A friend in Washington once sent me a few twigs by the post in February, and the queer make-believe-looking brown and yellow blossoms scented my study for more than a week. But this desirable scent-diffusing shrub is only for mild localities; even in Washington its blossoming is sometimes cut short by frosts.

Perhaps the first definite seeking fragrance of the year comes from the mezereon, *Daphne mezereum*, a member of an almost universally fragrant tribe. The purplish or white blossoms of this little erect shrub are not by any means "fast of their smell," but pour it out upon the cold spring air so that far down the garden path it greets you and you know that the mezereon is again at its work of distilling perfume. This, in the locality of New York, will usually happen to you in March, but I have known a mild spell in February to charm the little bush into flowering. A sheltered and partially shaded situation should always be given the mezereon.

Often the same breeze that carries the perfume of *Daphne mezereum* is also lightly freighted with violet, for it takes only a few mild days in February or March to bring the first sweet violets into bloom. Alas, these are not our own blue violets which, while they are well enough, cannot compare with the English violet for scent or earliness. "Without the violet," wrote Richard Jefferies, "all the bluebells and cowslips would not make spring." And one calls to mind the sweetness of the English spring with these three famous scent purveyors in charge.

It was after I had read a slender book called "A Year in a Lancashire Garden," by Henry Bright, that I determined to have an abundance of sweet violets in my garden, and for that matter, many another old-fashioned flower of which the author writes with great charm. The little book is long out of print, but if you are lucky you may find it upon the dusty shelves of some dealer in second-hand books, and if you are wise you will not come away without parting with the very small sum that will be asked for it. "We have violets in abundance," wrote Henry Bright, "and they scent all the air as we pass through the garden door. Even in winter a faint fragrance lingers among the leaves – a shadowy memory of a perfume which haunts them even when no single flower can be found."

My winter-bound nose was by this so intrigued that I straightway searched through catalogs until I found one that listed *Viola odorata*. Fifty plants were ordered, no great number, but how mightily they throve and increased! They were set out along the edge of a bed on the north side of the path which bisects my garden from east to west, connecting the Primrose Path with the region of the rock garden. In this bed grows a strangely assorted company – plum trees and currant bushes, two dwarf apples, lusty clumps of old double daffodils, gay parrot tulips, lavender, marjoram, sweet Mary Ann and lovage, York and

Lancaster roses, chives and what not. Across the path a bank rises steeply to a higher level of the garden. Now the violets carpet their own bed and have leapt the path and swarmed up the bank to the top, crowding unmercifully the plants that were put there to take the place of grass which objected to its steep incline, and thence have found their way all over the garden. One of the excitements of spring is the finding of new patches of sweet violets in unsuspected corners. My old Dutch gardener, van Oosten (1711), says that violets "love a lean ground under hedges," and this would seem to be true for they spring up luxuriantly close beneath the hemlock hedges and bloom there as nowhere else in the garden. If an abundance of blossoms is wanted in the place of lush foliage the hint about lean ground should be heeded, for fatness with violets goes to foliage and much sweetness is lost. I feel sure that this is the explanation of so many complaints concerning the non-flowering of the English violet in American gardens. We are too generous with its food.

There are pure white sorts among my violets now, as well as various tints of mauve and the deep purple. I keep an old steamer chair in the tool house and when a mild spell in March starts the violets to blossoming I drag it forth and lie by the hour in the sunshine inhaling the delicious fragrance. I feel sure Heaven can offer no greater felicity.

FEBRUARY DAPHNE
(*Daphne mezereum*)

Reading about violets takes one into pleasant and often eminent company. Shakespeare and Bacon and Miss Jekyll, dear Mary Mitford and old John Parkinson and Mrs. Ewing, Alcaeus and Mohammed ("As my religion," wrote the prophet, "is above all others, so is the excellence of the odour of violets above all other odours. It is warmth in winter and coolness in summer"). Napoleon loved them and liked to find a bunch of them on his desk. They were the favourite flowers of Queen Elizabeth. All the poets sang of them and are still singing. Who indeed that has ever taken pen in hand (unless it be some of our modern novelists and playwrights whose turbid ink could never form the simple word) has ever laid it down finally without having mentioned this universally loved flower, whose "littlenesse thereof in substance is noblye rewarded in greatnesse of savour and of vertue."

But of all that has been written about violets I like best the praise of them in the Herbal of old John Gerard, 1597, which offers one more proof of the high esteem fragrant flowers were held in by the gardeners of old.

> March Violets of the Garden have a great prerogative above others, not onely because

> the minde conceiveth a certaine pleasure and recreation by smelling and handling of these most odoriferous Flowers, but also for that very many of these Violets receive ornament and comely grace: for there bee made of them Garlands for the head, Nosegaies and Posies, which are delightful to looke on, and pleasant to smell to, speaking nothing of their appropriate vertues; yea Gardens themselves receive by these the greatest ornament of all, chiefest beautie and most gallant grace; and the recreation of the minde which is taken hereby, cannot be but very good and honest; for they admonish and stir up a man to that which is comely and honest; for floures through their beautie, variety of colour and exquisite forme, doe bring to a liberall and gentlemanly minde the remembrance of honestie, comeliness and all kinds of vertues. For it would be an unseemly and filthy thing (as a certain wise man saith) for him that doth look upon and handle faire and beautiful things and who frequenteth and is conversant in faire and beautiful places, to have his minde not faire, but filthie and deformed.

To early gardeners the violet was a chief flower of delight and usefulness. Tusser (1580) includes it in his list of Seeds and Herbs for the Kitchen, his Herbs and Roots for Salads, his Strewing Herbs, and his Herbs for Windows and Pots. It must have been found in every garden in the land, as well as in every hedgerow, copse and meadow. By the manner in which these plants seed and multiply in my garden, springing up and flowering prodigally in the most unlikely places, I feel sure that there is no reason why they may not be naturalized in our own wild to lend a richer glamour to the spring.

Dozens of recipes appear in old cookery books and medical treatises in which violets have a part – salads, potages, wines, sweetmeats, plates, liqueurs, many cosmetics and sweet waters also, and remedies for disorders, chiefly of the spirit. That sad affliction "the dumps" yields to a decoction of violets, roses, feverfew, capers, saffron, rosemary, sweet apples, scordium, wine, tobacco, and cider. A characteristically optimistic Gaelic recommendation runs:

> Rub thy face with Violets and goat's milk and there is not a prince in the world who will not follow thee.

Arabis alpina is noticeably reminiscent of almonds on a warm day in early spring and the stock-like spikes of the double form smell very like heliotrope, and make a fine show hanging from a ledge of rock or a wall pocket. Hyacinths are delicious in the early borders and I like them best when they have lost their first fleshy opulence and have gone a little thin and wan, as they do after a year or two of border life. The husky, rough scent of primroses should be part of the spring in every garden. In sheltered places they may be looked for in the neighbourhood of New York as early as the middle of March and they often flower again in the autumn. To be able to gather primroses and violets in November, even a very small nosegay, is a delightful experience and a quite possible one. Cowslips also frequently give a second flowering and their scent is bland and pleasing. The root of the cowslip is said to smell like anise. Cowslip wine must have been much used, for rules for its making are found in all old cookery books, and one would not have to have a very large patch of cowslips to make this pleasant beverage. It was much used to cure insomnia.

The oxlip has little or no odour but the polyanthus, *Primula* Pruhonicensis hybrids, like the bunch primrose, have a warm sweetness. An early writer thus expounds the often little understood difference between the cowslip, the oxlip and the polyanthus:

> Cowslips come like polyanthuses, but all looking down the contrary way. Polyanthuses come in umbells or heads of so many flowers on the top of one stalk and every flower looking up. The oxlip, which is a hybrid between the cowslip and the primrose, comes with the guard flowers or outside flowers of the head looking down and the centre flowers looking up, or half way between the two parents. All these are of more colour than one.

The auricula grows early in the year and has a most agreeable fragrance and displays many uncommon combinations of colour. I like best the yellow ones whose leaves are thickly coated with meal – dusty miller they are called. Other old names are bear's ears and tanner's apron, and in "A Dictionary of English Plant Names," that repository of so much interesting information, I find the name "Reckless" applied to *P. auricula.* I do not remember ever to have seen this name given to any other plant, though many deserve it more than does the Dusty Miller. Miss Jekyll notes that the scent of *P. auricula* has a "pungency and at the same time a kind of veiled mystery that accords with the clouded and curious blendings of many of the flowers." Wall flowers of course add deliciously to the spring mélange of odours, but in our cold climate they do not live out of doors over the winter. They may, however, be brought on under glass and planted out when danger from frost has passed. Theirs is a perfume with depth and richness – it seems as velvety, so to speak, as the texture of the flowers.

On a sunny hillside in a neighbour's garden grows a little plant which is seldom seen but which is very welcome in March because of its almond-scented blossoms. This is *Petasites fragrans,* the winter heliotrope. "Weed!" I can hear those of my readers who know it, murmuring, and the allegation cannot be refuted. Weed it undoubtedly is and not a retiring one, for the great leaves though they stay close to the ground take up a deal of room and are not ornamental, nor are the tousled blossoms that appear first. But the questing nose takes pleasure in it on a cold day in early spring so it is worth a corner in a byplace. The winter heliotrope though native in Southern Europe has naturalized itself in some sections of the country.

The narcissus tribe offers a great variety of scents and all of them good to my nose, though Miss Jekyll, who has a pleasant chapter on "The Scents of the Garden," in her "Wood and Garden," thinks that daffodils must be classed among flowers of rather rank smell. And there is perhaps always a hint of that wet earthiness about their scent that is so marked in the old double daffodil. But this to my thinking is a vivacious quality and always stimulating and refreshing, especially indoors. I love to keep a bowl of daffodils on my writing table and enjoy equally their perfume and their glowing beauty.

The most odorous of the narcissi are from the *poeticus* and the *jonquilla* divisions. To some delicate noses these may seem too strong and searching even in the garden, while indoors they may be quite insupportable. The double *poeticus* or gardenia-flowered narcissus is an old fashioned variety not often seen today. My stock of them came from an old farmhouse garden in Rockland County, N. Y., where they grew strongly in the dooryard. They have increased tremendously and I now have many hundreds from those first bulbs and have given away as many more. This variety is not a success in all gardens, the buds often blighting before they mature. The reason for this is too light a soil and too little moisture. All the *poeticus* varieties thrive in a rich retentive soil, black and fertile, and they love sunshine. 'Sweet Nancy' is a pretty old name of the double-flowered *Narcissus poeticus.*

The new Poetaz group of cultivars with their clusters of waxen flowers, from cream to yellow, are very handsome. They are the result of a cross between *N. poeticus* and *N. tazetta,* the tender bunch-flowered narcissus, and they inherit over much of the latter's somewhat too overpowering odour – the only narcissus scent I do not like.

The big and little jonquils concentrate much sweetness in their rich-hued petals. They are single and double varieties of *N. jonquilla* and of *N.* × *odorus,* the Campernelle jonquil. The flowers are borne in clusters and are delightful for cutting, the foliage is stiff and rushlike. They like a sheltered situation in full sun. Two other narcissi belong to this section; they are the tiny *N. assoanus* [*N. juncifolius*], happy in the rock garden and powerfully sweet for so small a thing, and *N.* × *tenuior* [*N. gracilis*], latest of all the tribe to flower, tall and pale and of an especially fine scent. The jonquils belong to May.

The daffodils on the contrary begin to bloom in sheltered places very early indeed. The wee *N. asturiensis* [*N. minimus*] is faintly sweet, the only slightly taller *N. minor* is richly fragrant. These bloom in the rock garden in March. All the daffodils, as I have said, have a good smell to my nose, but if you go about your garden on a mild and sunny day sniffing the different kinds you will perhaps like some and not others, certainly you will find a great deal of variety. The old bicolor 'Victoria' smells strongly of vanilla. 'Horsfield' has a scent very like magnolia; the gay 'Will Scarlet' to my nose smells exactly like a ripe pear; the little 'W. P. Milner' has the delicate transparent perfume of cowslips. 'Duke of Bedford' has a fine keen fragrance and *N. pseudonarcissus* ssp. *moschatus,* sometimes listed as *N. albicans,* smells agreeably of musk. Most of the *N.* × *incompara-*

bilis hybrids [the Leedsii tribe] are sweet, graceful, pale-colored creatures, delightful in the borders, in grass and for cutting. The blood of *N. poeticus* courses in their veins, whence comes their fine perfume and their sturdy physique. I have found these hybrids, or star daffodils, the most satisfactory and permanent, after the poeticus varieties, for naturalizing. Mr. Ellwanger in "The Garden's Story" describes the scent of the tender 'Grand Soleil d'Or' as a mingled essence of pineapple, orange and banana.

Several shrubs should be mentioned in this chapter on early scents. *Lonicera fragrantissima* and *L. standishii*, the two most fragrant bush honeysuckles, are very like each other and I think are sent out rather indiscriminately by nurseries, but the former is the better shrub if you can get it. It is called the twin-flowered honeysuckle because the creamy flowers come in pairs. Both shrubs grow to be five or six feet tall and as much in girth, so they require space and they should not be crowded into congested shrubberies, but allowed room to develop their natural grace. A south-facing wall provides an encouraging situation for them and here they will bloom in February and March, according to locality, and scent the garden for yards about their abiding place with a rich and fruity fragrance. If I could have but half a dozen shrubs, *Lonicera fragrantissima* would without doubt be one of them.

And I dare say *Magnolia stellata* would be another. It is one of the delights of the early season and blooms so prodigally while still very young that the small bushes seem overburdened with their thick-petalled starry flowers. In the garden of my old Maryland home grew huge bushes of *Magnolia conspicua* (now called *M. denudata*), the yulan. This is a native of China and more beloved by that flower-loving people than any other of their shrubs. We find this flower reproduced in their embroideries, their beautiful porcelains, on their screens and paintings of the most ancient periods. To them it is the lily tree and it is given the most conspicuous and honoured positions in the gardens of their temples, public buildings and dwellings. The fragrance of the great creamy blossoms is rich and fruity. Large bushes of *Magnolia* × *soulangiana* also greeted the spring in our Maryland garden with creamy blossoms flushed with rose-purple. These two bloom perhaps two weeks later than *M. stellata*, and so escape the vagrant snappish frosts that sometimes blacken the pure petals of the latter.

There are no flowers more delightful to plant near dwellings than magnolias, for their perfume, blown into the rooms on those rare early days when it is warm enough to open the windows, is delightful. It is worth while to give a good deal of attention to the placing and planting of these fine shrubs for few make so rich a return in beauty and fragrance. They should never be jammed into crowded shrubberies, but allowed full space for their development, and they prefer a soil that is not parched and hungry. A cool, deep and nourishing humus is the best for them and they are happiest where they are protected from strong winds. Mr. E. H. Wilson says: "In Northern gardens the best time to transplant magnolias is late in the spring. They may also be successfully moved in late August but they must not be allowed to suffer for lack of moisture at either season and it is always advisable to mulch them with well decayed manure." If you have an estate plant magnolias by the hundred. If a mere plot is all your landed possessions be sure to have at least one and it had better be the lovely star magnolia. It will be worth a dozen from the genera *Deutzia* and *Weigela* to you.

It is impossible to leave the subject of early scents without mention of that humble shrub, the yellow-flowering Missouri currant. It is quite out of fashion and is somewhat straggly of habit, but as a perfume distillery it is not to be surpassed. "A shrub will perfume a garden, a bunch of it a hall," wrote Mr. Ellwanger, "and its bouquet is as spicy as that of the yellow St. Péray wine, which I fancy it resembles, the favorite of Dumas pérè. The bees crowd around its yellow blossoms and its honey should be worth its apothecary weight in gold." It is one of the shrubs I like to plant beneath my chamber windows. It is delicious to waken to its spicy morning greeting.

"Whither do all men walk," wrote old Gerard, "for their recreation but where the earth has most beneficially painted her face with flourishing colours? And what season of the year more longed for than the Spring, whose gentle breath enticeth forth the kindly sweets and makes them yield their fragrant smells."

CHAPTER III

The Sweets of May

It is now the time of Laylock,
White Thorn, Musk, Florence Iris,
Lady's Smock and White Violets.

— JOHN RICHARD ANDERSON

DURING THE MANY years I lived in the hill country of New York I was glad every year when May came round that just beyond my chamber window grew a white hawthorn tree. It made an entrancing event of awakening, for its perfume entered the room with the first morning breezes. Not everyone cares for the scent of hawthorn. Walter de la Mare in one of his poems has called it a deathly smell and many find it stuffing or over sweet, but to me it is one of the young year's best perfumes, though perhaps more to be enjoyed when caught from the back of a hoyden breeze than when held directly under the nose.

In this country, strangely enough, this lovely tree, the common English hawthorn, *Crataegus laevigata* [*C. oxyacantha*], is comparatively little seen, but in England, as all know who have known an English spring, it is on every hand and the air is burdened with its sweetness. It is indigenous to that land and from ancient times has been employed to fashion the close-woven hedges that are so characteristic a feature of the countryside, and one often sees, too, venerable specimens standing apart that have not known the pruner's knife and have grown dark and gnarled with the passing of the centuries, and gray with lichen, but that still answer the mysterious urge of the vernal season and deck their ancient limbs with snowy beauty.

That the use of the hawthorn for hedging is of most venerable origin is proven by the fact that the name of the tree in Anglo-Saxon is "haeg-thorn," the hedge-thorn. It makes the most impenetrable of barriers against man and beast. It is called whitethorn to distinguish it from the blackthorn, *Prunus spinosa,* though just why these names should have been given is not known, as the wood of the hawthorn is not white, nor that of the blackthorn black. But the popular name of May is easily understood for in early summer, in May to be exact, the crooked branches are lost in a cloud of fragrant bloom. The transformation of the tree from its stark winter state to spring beauty is very sudden, and was noted by Spenser in his "Shepheardes Calender," thus:

> Seest thou not thilke same hawthorne studde
> How braggly it begins to budde
> And utter his tender head?

May Day, once a universal holiday, is still observed in very rural neighbourhoods in Britain, but the movies, the radio, the dance-hall have largely taken the place of such simple and innocent modes of self-expression. It is pleasant to think of the sombre grey London thoroughfares on those May Days of long ago with the doorways all decked with branches of the May and the young men and maidens dancing joyously in the streets, while every village green echoed their laughter and their song.

My hawthorn tree has a story. On a day many years ago the woman who lived in our old farmhouse before it came into our possession was driving to market with her husband in the jolting farm wagon. He was a harsh and uncompanionable man and she, while she was still young, had turned for warmth and beauty to flowers. She had gathered together quite an amazing collection of fine plants in the narrow dooryard between the low white house and the picket fence bordering the road, tending them with devotion in her rare moments of leisure. And each plant, as I found out when she went over her treasures with me as she was leaving, had its story of how it was acquired, how it prospered or languished, what it had meant to her. On this particular day of which I speak, the husband, growing churlish over some imagined grievance, told his wife that she could get down from the high seat of the wagon and await his return from the market by the roadside. As she sat miserably through the long day in the dusty grass she noticed lying near her a branch to which clung a few shriveled berries. Hardly realizing what she did, she took it in her hand and when she reached home planted the berries in tin cans and cared for them lovingly. Finally in one can appeared a pair of leaves. That winter and the next the little plant lived on the kitchen window ledge and stood out during the summer on the narrow porch with the other house plants. Finally it was entrusted to the earth out of doors and carefully protected from encroaching coarse growths. It grew lustily and one May day after a number of years she found the little tree full of buds, and soon white blossoms lay along the dark branches like new fallen snow, and she caught their quick scent. When we bought the farm from the old couple, then grown too infirm any longer to strive against the hardships of farming in that rocky county, she asked me especially to look after her bride tree, as she called it, not knowing its proper name, and almost every May she managed somehow to get back to see it in bloom and to carry away with her a white-wreathed branch. I think the hawthorn had made up to her for a good deal that she had missed – as flowers have a way of doing.

In America it is the lilac chiefly that scents the May world, and while nowhere does any species of *Syringa* grow naturally within the boundaries of our country, it is perhaps the most frequently encountered shrub in all sections where it will grow at all. Particularly do lilacs seem to prosper in old gardens and frequently when the house has fallen into decay and the garden been long abandoned to weeds, the lilacs continue to thrive and to keep faith with the idea of home and homely ties. To drive along country ways during lilac time is to enjoy a continual bath of fragrance, and next to box and wild grape it seems to me the most memory stirring of all fragrances. "The first whiff of their fragrance in the garden," wrote E. V. B., "is as the very heart and soul of memory."

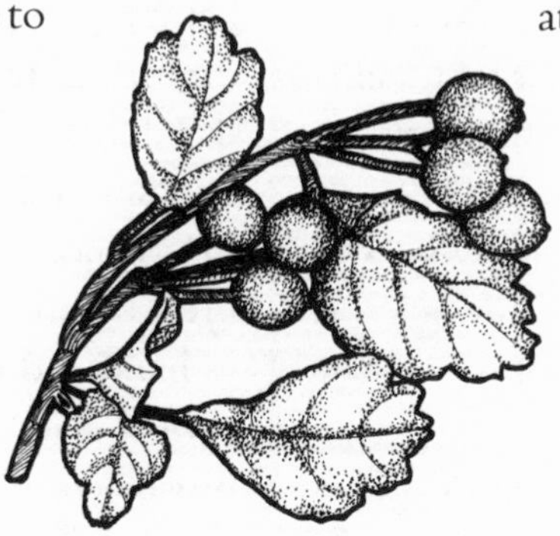

In the dooryard of my Rockland County home the lilacs grew so tall that the purple and white plumes looked in at the second-story windows. I remember one May evening as I leant upon the white gate before my door, listening to the many night sounds of that hill country, a heavy truck drew up before the gate and a tall young man in clean blue jeans climbed down and came shyly forward.

"Lady," he said, cap in hand, "would you give me some of them Lilacks?" I began at once drawing down the branches nearest me and breaking off the great purple trusses, but he interrupted me. "The white ones, please. They are for my wife. She's terrible sick in the horspital." And then looking away from me, "She makes me think of white Lilacks."

ENGLISH HAWTHORN
(*Crataegus laevigata*)
'Gireoudi'

I noticed then that his young ruddy face was strained and anxious and sent him off with an armful of white lilacs and a secret prayer for the safety of his wife who had inspired his soul with poetry. A week later I was again standing beside the gate at the twilight hour when the truck came rumbling by from the direction of the village. The young man dexterously manipulated the wheel with one hand, the other was about the shoulders of a fair young woman whose head rested against his broad blue shoulder and whose arm cradled a small pink bundle. They did not glance in my direction but I noticed as they passed that cocked over the ear of the young woman, like a victorious plume, was a spray of white lilac. I like to think it was one of mine.

The common lilac, *Syringa vulgaris*, is a very old plant in gardens. A native of the mountains of Bavaria, it is said to have been introduced into England in 1560 or thereabouts. Lord Bacon spoke of the "Lelach Tree" as one of the beautiful things blowing in his garden in April. The oldest common name for the lilac seems to have been blue pipe tree "because the stalks and branches are filled with soft pith which can be easily removed." It is said that in Turkey pipe stems are usually made of this wood. Other old names for the lilac were duck's bill, laylock and lily oak, the last two being corruptions of the Persian word lilag.

To me the scent of lilacs, though it varies greatly in the different kinds, is never heavy or cloying and I love to go from bush to bush drawing down the branches and burying my nose in the great bunches of bloom. There is a faint spiciness always present that prevents the odour from being too sweet. I thought all the world loved the smell of lilacs but F. A. Hampden in "Flower Scent" says that to him "there is something faintly unpleasant but indefinable which detracts from their fragrance."

White lilacs have the more delicate perfume and it would seem that the deeper and richer the colour the deeper and richer the scent. Some of the dark red-purple French hybrids are especially strong scented. I have heard it said however that there is a tendency today to breed lilacs that are less sweet scented than the older varieties. This is deplorable indeed, for like the rose and the carnation and the violet, the lilac is beloved chiefly for its fragrance. If any of the scentless or ill scented species are used in hybridization the inevitable result would be a lessening of the normal amount of fragrance. It is a danger to be looked out for and avoided at all costs.

Although the common lilac is an old inhabitant of gardens, it was only recently that it drew the attention of the hybridists. Our garden lilacs have largely been originated from two species, *S. vulgaris* and *S. persica.* It is not much more than seventy-five years ago that French and German hybridists took the lilac in hand and there are now many hundreds of hybrid lilacs for us to choose from. "The improvement of the lilac dates only from 1843," the late Professor Sargent tells us, "when a nurseryman at Liége in Belgium raised a plant with small double flowers. Nothing is now known of the origin of this plant but as it was called *Syringa vulgaris azurea plena,* it was probably a seedling of the common lilac and not a hybrid. It was this plant that Victor Lemoine chose as the first plant in his initial attempt to improve the garden lilacs, fertilizing it with the best lilacs of the day and with *Syringa oblata,* which was found by Robert Fortune in a Shanghai garden. The crossing of these sorts produced a plant known as *S.* x *hyacinthiflora,* characterized by early and very fragrant flowers." This was the beginning, the end is not yet in sight, but the work of Lemoine and other lilac hybridists has filled the temperate world with a vast number of splendid kinds. Many of the modern lilacs have immense trusses of bloom and though in my own garden I prefer the single-flowered kinds, it is not to be denied that many of the double varieties are very magnificent and richly fragrant.

CHAPTER IV

Gilliflowers

But what shall I say to the Queene of delight and of Flowers, Carnations and Gilliflowers, whose bravery, variety and sweete smell ioyned together, tyethe every ones affection with great earnestnesse both to like and to have them.

— JOHN PARKINSON, 1629.

AMONG FLOWER NAMES none in the language is softer or sweeter than gilliflower, and hung about it is a wealth of tradition and sentiment. It is sad that it has almost passed into disuse. In the old days gilliflower seems to have been a sort of pet name bestowed by flower lovers, not upon a single flower but upon several to show the esteem in which they were held, and there was usually a distinguishing prefix. Thus there were clove gilliflowers (carnations and pinks), stock gilliflowers (stocks), wall gilliflowers (wall flowers), queen's gilliflowers (sweet rockets, *Hesperis*), and a number of others, but nearly all that bore the pretty name had in common the gift of fragrance. The carnation, however, we are assured by Dr. Prior, was the gilliflower *par excellence* of early times, the favourite flower of high and low.

In old works we find the name spelled impartially Gylofre, Gillofloure, Gely flower, Gelouer, or Gelefloure, July flower, and so on, and by it was usually meant *Dianthus caryophyllus.* The name gilliflower is a corruption by way of the French giroflée from caryophyllum, a clove, "referring to the spicy odour of the flower, which seems to have been used in flavouring wines to replace the more costly clove of India" *Syzygium aromaticum* [*Caryophyllus aromaticus*]. But today the fragrant flowers sold on the streets of Paris as giroflées are wall flowers. The name carnation is said to have come into use about the middle of the sixteenth century and was usually written "coronation" because of the general use of these flowers in chaplets and coronels.

The wild carnation with its five rose-crimson petals may be seen by travelers in France growing in wild rocky places and upon the walls of many an ancient chateau, but nowhere so riotiously as at Chinon, the majestic ruin towering above the placid Loire. On the summer day when my children and I climbed the narrow stairway which leads steeply upwards from the huddled village to the castle (the same stairway that the famous Maid followed when she made her momentous call upon the skeptical French king) the walls above us were sprigged all over with tufts of wild carnations which seemed actually to spray us with spicy incense.

I was most anxious to secure some seed and easily induced the small son of the caretaker, who gravely informed us that he was making a collection of American coins, to clamber up the crumbling walls to gather some for me. When he returned from his somewhat hazardous expedition, which he accomplished, however, with dexterity and aplomb, one bright black eye fastened upon us as he gyrated in midair, my son held out to him a handful of small change with the question, "How much?" The young man with lightning speed picked out all the silver coins, amounting to considerably more than a dollar, and disappeared with a whoop among the ruins. We thought him a very practiced collector indeed.

The seed thus dearly bought was not, however, ripe and though I tried to dry it with great care as we went about our journeying, it came to nothing. A sad disappointment! The wild carnation is also naturalized in parts of England, especially on the walls of old Norman-built castles, such as Dover, Cardiff or Rochester, perhaps accidentally introduced, as Canon Ellacombe suggests, with the Normandy (Caen) stone of which parts of these castles are built. Or perhaps they were brought there by the Norman conquerors as a pleasant reminder of their old homes.

No one grows the wild carnation, so many and so enchanting are its descendants, but I should like very much to have had a tuft of it from those ancient walls to grow in my young garden. Just when this simple flower began to receive the special attention of florists is not known, but it was a long time ago. There is a portrait of Edward IV of England painted in 1463 in which he is shown holding a red carnation in his royal hand. It was probably the first of what we call Florist's flowers, the first upon which hybridization was practically performed. In any case it was the first flower to have an entire book devoted to it. This was "Le Jardinage des Oeillets," published in Paris in 1647, and this treatise was quickly followed by another – "Nouveau Traite des Oeillets," showing that new varieties were being introduced and new standards forming even at that early date. Turner in his Herbal refers to the gilliflower as a "flower made pleasant and sweet by the work of man."

In Shakespeare's time pinks and carnations were so many and so various that Gerard says, "A great and large volume would not suffice to write of everyone at large and in particular, considering how infinite they are, and how every yeare every climate and countrey bringeth forth new sorts, and such as have not heretofore bin written of." A writer of the time assures us that "Solomon in all his Princely Pompe was never able to attayne to this beautie. Some glittered with a perfect crimson dye, some with a deep purple, and some with a passing beautiful Carnation." Gerard wrote gratefully of a "worshipful merchant of London" who brought him from Poland gilliflowers of a yellow colour and gave them to him to grow in his garden, the which he said had never before been seen or heard of in England. Is it not pleasant to think of these gardeners of early times sharing their treasures as we do today and deriving keen delight out of being able to supply a fellow enthusiast with some long wanted plant?

The simple and sweet flower enjoyed universal popularity. In John Parkinson's "speaking garden," his great "Paradisi in Sole" (1629), he devotes several pages to gilliflowers and the illustrations therein show them to have been almost as opulently many-petalled as those we admire today. William Lawson, that accomplished gardener of the seventeenth century who wrote of his flowers in such a delightfully human way that his little book, "The Country Housewifes Garden," provides enchanting reading for any modern worker among flowers, admired gilliflowers extravagantly, calling them the King of flowers "(except the Rose), and the best sort of them are called Queen-July flowers." Lawson said he had "nine or tenne severall sort of them and divers of them as big as Roses; of all flowers (save the damask rose)" he adds "they are the most pleasant to sight and smell."

A famous grower of gilliflowers of the late sixteenth and early seventeenth centuries was one Master Tuggy whose garden was in Westminster. He was the friend of both Gerard and Parkinson and was described by the latter as "the preseuer of all natures beauties." Parkinson in turn preserved for us the names of some of Master Tuggy's creations and over them he waxes very eloquent indeed. There was the 'Princess', which Parkinson says was the "most beautifull that I ever did see," and Master Tuggy's "His Rose Gillofloure," which he describes as "being different sort from all other in that it hath round leaues without any iagge at all on the edges, of a fine stamell colour, or rather much like unto the Red Rose Campion, both for forme, colour, roundnesse, but larger for size."

Elizabethan gardens must have been very sweet with the rows upon rows of gilliflowers blowing along the trim borders. All the old books include long treatises on their culture and some of them give very curious directions as to how to make the flowers come double. One of them (Leonard Meager by name) instructs his readers to "take a Bean and hollow it; put into the seed of a single Gilliflower, and stopping the hole with a little soft wax, set it in proper ground, and a Gilliflower will spring out of it and be double and large." And another wily old experimenter says if you want your gilliflowers to give forth "divers smels or odours, you may also with great ease, as thus for example: If you will take two or three great

Cloves and steepe them foure and twenty houres in Damaske Rosewater, then take them out and bruise them, and put them into a fine Cambricke ragge, and so bind them about the roote of the Gilliflower neere to the setting on the stalke, and so plant it in a fine soft and fertile mould, and the flower which springeth from the same will have so delicate a mixt smell of Clove and Rose-water that it will breed both delight and wonder." As if the scent of the gilliflower alone were not enough for the delight of any nose! I wonder if any of these old tricks were ever really put to the test, or if they were simply conjectures on the part of imaginative gardeners.

By the time John Rea began to write (1665) the gilliflower was securely in the grip of the florists who were working their will upon it and multiplying the varieties with great rapidity. Rea's "Flora" was the first book to treat of flowers from the standpoint of beauty alone. Of their physical properties he says little or nothing. If I were going to make a really old fashioned garden I should use his book as a guide. But Rea was a practical florist and though he loved his flowers he regarded them less romantically than did the earlier writers. Of all flowers he admired most the carnation, or gilliflower, but it is strange and a little prophetic that while he discoursed for many pages upon their charms, their kinds and their culture, he did not once mention the chiefest of their qualities, their warm and spicy fragrance. He was the forerunner of those florists, of whom James Maddock was later typical, who split hairs about infinitesimal points and bred flowers to rule and measure. It was the beginning of the long tyranny of the greedy sense over the less assertive one, the triumph of the eye over the nose. Happily the green fingered flower necromancers have recently had a change of heart and it is good to read of gold cups being offered for the best scented carnation at recent London shows – "not the best Carnation with a scent but the Carnation with the best scent!"

The finest gilliflowers of old came from the Netherlands, a "multitude" of them being brought over to London every year and there "sold at mean rates to Gardeners," who, according to Rea, sold them again to other flower lovers "commonly for Twelve pence a layer; but the truth is" – he whispers a confidential aside to his readers – "most of these mercenary Fellows about London are very deceitful and whoever trusts them is sure to be deceived, as I myself have been, even by such of them as I had by many benefits obliged." The Dutch gilliflowers were large, thick and double, the more ordinary sorts of one colour, but those most prized by the fanciers were "well striped, flaked, or powdered upon white or blush, with darker or lighter red, crimson or carnation, sadder or brighter purple, deeper or paler scarlet," and so on, until the simple flower was less a flower than a mathematical problem. But through all it never lost its characteristic spicy sweetness, which cannot be said of many flowers which have had the misfortune to become the favourites of the florists.

It would be interesting to know who first

started work upon the simple wild gilliflower, but upon this point history is silent. We know that the early botanists distrusted and derided the work of florists in doubling the petals of flowers and called the flowers so worked upon "Monsters." Thus Linnaeus: "Such by an over-great study and assiduous inspection have discovered such amazing wonders in flowers as no man, the most clear sighted in the world, could discern, but those who are versed in this study. The grand Objects of their attention are the most beautiful flowers, such as Tulips, Anemones, Hyacinths, Ranunculus, Pinks, Carnations, Auriculas, and Polyanthuses. To the hidden varieties of these flowers they have given such pompous names as excite wonder and astonishment and are really ridiculous. These men cultivate a science peculiar to themselves, the mysteries of which are only known to the adepts; nor can such knowledge be worth the attention of the botanist; *wherefore let no botanist ever enter into their Societies.*"

Just so outraged I felt when I first saw a double lilac, fat and befuddled. Some flowers are, I am sure, intended by a wise God to remain single. The hyacinth doubled, for instance, is a fat abomination. But while we may think single roses the loveliest it is to the many petalled kinds that we turn for fragrance, and this is true also of wall flowers, stocks, violets, rockets, pinks and carnations. To the florists who have doubled their petals we owe our gratitude for the heightened fragrance.

As with roses, the deep red and crimson carnations are the best scented, the yellow kinds the least. In ancient times it was the red clove gilliflower which, because of its strong sweetness and the "gallant tincture" it imparted to a "Syrupe," was alone of all the varieties used in physicke shops and was accounted the most "cordial."

So far as I can find, the popularity of the carnation has never seriously waned since those early times. Its history has been a series of triumphs and the gay and fragrant flower never for long lost its hold upon the hearts of flower-loving mankind. There was a period, after 1850, according to Nicholson ("Dictionary of Gardening"), when they were for a time quite neglected and some of the older sorts were lost to cultivation. This temporary slump in their popularity was very likely brought about by the fact that the hair splitting and exactions concerning points became so extreme as finally to be insupportable to the very men who had instituted them. A flower belonged rigidly in a class. It was a "Flake" or a "Picotee" or a "Bizarre," and its every fleck and marking must conform to the rules and regulations laid down for these classes. To quote Thomas Hogg, whose slender "Treatise on the Growth and Culture of the Carnation," 1820, lies before me, "A flower possessed of all the properties called for by the Rules and Regulations laid down in the Societies, where they are exhibited for prizes, is seldom or never met with. Art is called in to the assistance of nature and the skillful hand of the Florist dexterously extracts the self-coloured and defective and over-crowded leaves, and sometimes even will insert others, and arranges and adjusts the whole with surprising nicety." Such artificiality could not long hold the interest of the public and it probably revolted.

Today there are carnation societies in all the leading countries of the world and carnation shows are of regular occurrence, while the sweet gay flowers are grown in millions for the market, in gardens and in private greenhouses. In the old days they were accounted no less sweet than the rose, no less beautiful than the tulip, and undoubtedly they still hold their own with these rivals. It has too the advantage of being comparatively cheap to grow commercially, and happily for those of us who are somewhat weak in what old Bodley called "purse ability," it may often be purchased at a fairly reasonable price.

A few years ago my children and I lingered on week after week in Quimper, held by the charm of the little Breton town and the comfort of the good Hotel de l'Épée, so pleasantly situated beside the softly sliding waters of the Odet. There is much in this quaint town and its environs to hold the interest of any lover of old scenes and old customs, but our chief delight was visiting the Cathedral Square on market day and returning literally laden with carnations which we had purchased for six cents the great fragrant bunch. There were always many flower-sellers in the market, indeed almost every woman who came in from the country with rabbits, hens, bits of lace or pottery, vegetables, butters and sardines (these last two commodities always lay in the basket side by side – and did anyone ever eat butter in Brittany that did not taste strongly of fish?) to sell, brought also many bouquets of flowers, for the Breton women are great gardeners and the tiny gardens with the queer turf walls are indescribably gay.

We always sought out one particular old lady whose face, despite it myriad wrinkles radiated a most sweet and contagious happiness from beneath her crisp fantastic cap. She arrived in one of those curious jumpy carts common to the country, driven by a small blue-smocked grandson, and she brought only two commodities for sale – five or six fierce looking black rabbits of formidable size, and bunches and bunches of carnations. The frantically struggling rabbits which she urged upon us we ignored as best we could, but we hung enraptured above the carnations – giroflées musquées, she called them. She had white ones and red ones and speckled ones, but the most ravishing to our attentive noses were a bright shrimp pink in colour. They were the sweetest I ever smelled, and the old lady always sold out to the last bunch.

In England hardy carnations are made much of in gardens but in America we seldom see them treated adequately. As a matter of fact they make charming beds, some of the strains blooming from June to frost and furnishing innumerable bouquets. Chabaud, the French grower, has a magnificent strain of border carnations that will bloom out of doors for many months if started in February under glass. But they are not hardy over the winter. However, they are easily raised from seed, which if started in a greenhouse or hotbed, or even a sunny window, in flats of light soil, transplanted to thumb pots when large enough to handle, and planted outside when settled weather arrives, will bloom all the summer and autumn. But they will not stand crowding or even the close proximity of very hungry plants, indeed they like well to grow in a bed or border to themselves or to be dotted about the spacious rose beds where they have full room to breathe and blow. Hardy carnations are not difficult to grow from seed but the impatient will prefer to buy them ready to set out. I am fond of the scarlet grenadin carnations which will bloom the first year from seed if started indoors early, and will last over the winter if lightly protected, and the improved forms of the marguerite carnation, which bear masses of clove-scented double flowers in many hues, are lovely, and if sown in February will begin to bloom out of doors in July and continue until frost.

Then there is Mr. Allwood's great race of carnation pinks, that bloom all the season and are beautifully coloured and scented. They should be given a sunny situation, sheltered if possible from strong winds but never overhung or hedged by hungry shrubs, and the soil in which they grow should be fat and *sweet.* Mr. Montague Allwood, I read, is of the opinion that the majority of carnation growers do not realize the fact that carnations love lime and *abhor* leaf-mold. And this is a pointer that we should not ignore, coming as it does from so authentic an authority.

The pink in early days was far less esteemed than the carnation. "They only served to set the sides of borders in spacious gardens and some of them for posies, mixed with the buds of damask roses," said our friend John Rea, and surely this would seem mission enough for any flower. But in those days the pinks, the plant we now know as *Dianthus plumarius,* but which was then known as *Caryophyllus sylvestris,* had another end to serve. It enjoyed a respected place in the domestic pharmacopoeia, being known to prevail against hot pestilential fevers, and to comfort the heart, being eaten now and then. With the carnation it was used to give a special flavour to wine, hence the same Sops in Wine, and the blossoms were also utilized in the compilation of salads, conserves and various sweets. But I am sure its most popular use must have been in "Nosegayes and to deck up houses."

A garden full of pinks "with spices in their throats," cannot but be a sweet and friendly one. Their modest beauty makes for informality, their fragrance reaches the heart, as well as the nose. The old mediciners when they declared it a sovereign heart remedy were not so far from fact. The richly fragrant fringy double white pink, so often found edging long sunny borders in English gardens, is *Dianthus fimbriatus.* You may obtain the seed from Thompson & Morgan, of Ipswich, England. And while you are sending your shilling for this send another for a packet of *Dianthus fragrans,* single, white and very fringy, and almost as sweet. But once you have got started you will never stop with these for your eye will be caught by the names of others –, 'Earl of Essex', 'Ipswich Crimson', – delicious and garbed in tones of pink and crimson, as well as that fat and sweet-smelling dame, 'Mrs. Sinkins', so beruffled that she more often than not manages to burst her "impalement," thus quite losing countenance.

One of the finest pinks I have seen is 'Annie Laurie'. It is a large single flower with deeply notched petals, the colour a clear orchid-pink with a circle of deeper colour at the heart. Like the new border pinks it is almost ever blooming and does not stop after its June display.

All these pinks deserve good culture, a rich sweet soil, free sunlight, room to breathe and stretch in.

Whenever I begin going over pink lists in seed or plant catalogs the lines under the letter *Q* in Mrs. Ewing's "Gardener's Alphabet" dance before my eyes:

> "Quaint, gay, sweet, and good for nosegays,
> Is good enough for any garden."

CHAPTER V

The June Garden

Where the noon is lovely with a hundred smells.

— STRUTHERS BURT

THE BOUQUET OF THE garden on a June day is rich and heterogeneous. Turn this way and that and the nose is accosted by wave after wave of sweetness from rose, iris, honeysuckle, mock orange, peony, pink, and besides these chief distillers, any one of which we should count as good for a month's allowance of perfume, there are many lesser alembics at work transmuting their juices into enchanting airs.

Hemerocallis, in many of its varieties, is endowed with the great gift. The yellow kinds have the best fragrance, the deep orange-coloured and tawny kinds the least, or none at all. *H. fulva,* the orange-tawny day lily, so often found colouring great stretches of the roadside, holding its own strongly amidst the coarse weedy growths, is scentless, as are its offspring; and such kinds as owe parentage to *H. aurantiaca* are commonly without perfume. The most richly gifted of all is the common old yellow day lily, called custard lily, in country districts, and which, according to William Robinson, earned the name of yellow tuberose from its fine scent. *H. citrina* is also very fragrant, as is also *H. dumortieri,* the latter being the earliest of the lemon lilies to flower, and a native of Siberia. Other kinds good to have for their perfume are 'Dr. Regal', 'Yellow Queen', 'Flava Major', 'Golden Bell', and many of the new Betscher hybrids that so richly increase our wealth of summer flowers. Other species and varieties have an agreeable aroma but these are the sweetest.

The fragrance of *Hemerocallis* is light and fine and a little fruity, never oppressive or fusty and so may be brought indoors with impunity. And what a splendid and sturdy race it is! One of the most satisfactory that we have in the garden, going about the business of growing and being beautiful without fuss or exactions, at once sturdy and graceful, and with the many new hybrids covering a blossoming period of many weeks of the summer.

Valeriana officinalis scents all the garden with its heliotrope-like breath but it is one of the odours into which one should not probe too deeply. Catch it from the breeze and it is delicious but draw too near and one is conscious of an underlying unpleasantness, a faint fetidness. The root has a loathsome odour when dried though it is much fancied by cats and, indeed, these animals will often dig around a plant until they have exposed the root and then go into transports of feline ecstasy, rolling and clawing until they have about destroyed the plant. Cats are also very partial to *Nepeta* and to the pretty little California baby-blue-eyes, *Nemophila mensiesii* [*N. insignis*], as well as to catnip. It is often very difficult to keep these plants in the garden because of the ardent preference of Pussy. Sowerby relates that rats also are attracted to the root of valerian and that would-be destroyers of these vermin use it to bait their traps.

In old times the garden heliotrope had many claims to fame. It was used as a pot herb by the poor, according to Gerard, who said that it was held in such veneration amongst them that "no broths, pottage, or physycall meates are worthe anything if Setwall were not at one end." 'Setwall' and 'Heal-all' were old names for it. Langham in his "Garden of Health," 1633, enumerates forty-one "griefs" that were thought to be relieved by various decoctions and applications of valerian. It is a charming and useful plant in the garden, lending grace and a welcome lightness to plantings of heavy-headed Oriental poppies or the June flowering plants of the genus *Anchusa.*

The red valerian that hangs from old walls in Europe and dazzles the eyes of trippers from this side of the water, filling the air with a honeylike scent, is *Centranthus ruber*. It will do as much for us here if we take the pains to establish it, although, alas, the crumbling walls, the happy home of so many treasures in the Old World, are not the heritage of our young country. There is a white variety of *Centranthus*, but it is less effective and I think less sweet.

'Sweet William', though belonging to the *Dianthus* tribe, lacks the spiciness of scent characteristic of so many of its kin. On the contrary it has a warm mild breath that some poet has called "its homely cottage smell." 'Sweet William' has long enlivened gardens with its round gay blooms and sturdy port. It grew in Gerard's garden as London Tufts and Parkinson called it pride of London. There were sweet Johns and sweet Williams in that day, the Johns having narrower leaves than the Williams but otherwise being similar. Parkinson lists sweet William not under *Dianthus* but under *Armeria.*

What a delicious place must Parkinson's garden at "Long Acre" have been, a very treasure trove of interest and beauty, for we know that he grew the greater number of the thousand odd kinds of "pleasant flowers" that he describes in his grand book, the grandest garden book ever written, "Paradisi in Sole, Paradisus Terrestris," which he dedicated to the young Queen Henrietta Maria, who is so quaintly styled upon her tomb at Lambeth "The Rose and Lily Queen." To read it today is to join in converse with one who knew and loved his plants well and spoke of them in simple and eloquent language. It is as full of the urge and push of growing things, as inspired with their sweetness as if of yesterday, indeed it is far more alive than many a book penned a short half century ago. He wrote, as someone has said of the early herbalists, as one who, as it were, "walked in holy places and spoke with something of the fragrance of a garden in their very speech."

DAY LILY
(*Hemerocallis*)

Parkinson's garden has long vanished, even its exact situation is in doubt, though it is thought to have lain in the neighbourhood where Covent Garden now rears its piles of inanimate bricks and mortar. It is strange to think that as late as the time of Charles I the teeming neighbourhoods of Charing Cross and Covent Garden had still a quite rural aspect and were only sparsely settled. "Parkinson lived to the grand age of eighty-three and is buried not far from the supposed site of his garden, in the beautiful old church of St. Martin's-in-the-Fields, the ancient register of that parish giving the date as August 6, 1650."

Fraxinella or bastard dittany, *Dictamnus albus* [*D. fraxinella*], is another plant of which the old master gardener spoke well. It has been cultivated in gardens for a period close on four hundred years and is a handsome plant with fine foliage and spikes of fringed flowers white or in a sort of low-toned rose colour. The late Mr. George H. Ellwanger, who had a very observant nose, said the odour of fraxinella suggests a blend of anise, sweet clover and lavender, and he thinks "you should plant it along your favourite walk with the lemon balm and the anise-scented giant hyssop, so that you may pluck a leaf of them as you pass by." My own nose detects a strong hint of turpentine as well and the flowers are supposed to exude a volatile and inflammable oil in hot weather. According to an English writer, "If a light be applied in the dusk of a summer evening the whole plant will be more or less enveloped in a bluish flame, which is however of very short duration." Repeated experiments here have failed of any spectacular results but I like the strong sweet resinous odour given off by the whole plant which is distinctly noticeable at some distance on a warm and humid evening.

Lupines give out a honeylike scent in the June garden (to Miss Jekyll's reliable nose they smell like a very good and delicate pepper) and many of the *Astilbe* are lightly sweet scented, a little suggesting newmown hay, as does the yellow flowered *Thalictrum flavum* ssp. *glaucum* [*T. glaucum*]. The meadow sweet, *Filipendula ulmaria* [*Spiraea ulmaria*], which grows wild in English meadows and is naturalized in our own, especially about Quebec and in our Northern States, has a strong scent not agreeable to all noses. Richard Jeffries writes, "Where ever the scythe has not reached the meadowsweet rears its pale flowers. At evening if it be sultry, on some days especially before a thunder storm, the whole mead is full of the fragrance of this plant. So heavy and powerful is its odour that the still motionless air between the thick hedges becomes oppressive and it is a relief to issue forth into the open fields away from the perfume and the brooding heat. But by day it is pleasant to linger in the meadow and inhale its sweetness."

Gerard reports that in his day the meadow sweet excelled all others in its use as a strewing herb in "chambers, halls and banqueting houses in the summer time; for the smell thereof makes the heart merrie, neither does it cause headache or loathsomenesse of meate." I have read that meadow sweet was the choice of Queen Elizabeth for "strawing" her private apartments and that the sharpness of the illustrious lady's nose was equalled only by that of her tongue.

The pretty dropwort, *Filipendula vulgaris* [*Spirea filipendula*], with leaves cut in the fashion of a fern, has creamy flowers with a light sweet scent; especially good is the double-flowered sort. Nor should we forget the great seakale, *Crambe cordifolia*, whose clouds of pale flowers emit a pleasant fragrance. This is a grand subject for the wild garden for its colossal leaves and five-foot stalk require a spacious setting. *Galium boreale* is a pretty little native that has long grown in my garden in out-of-the-way places and contributes its modest stems of creamy fragrant flowers to bouquets of scentless blooms. This is called the northern bedstraw.

Several columbines when investigated have most surprisingly proved to have a nice fragrance. Our beauty of the Southwest, *Aquilegia chrysantha*, has the gift, as has the Rocky Mountain columbine, *A. caerulea*. The little green-flowered *A. viridiflora* is quite sweet scented and I have found stray forms of *A. vulgaris* that were notably so. *A. suaveolens* is a rare Himalayan species said to be the sweetest of all. This kind may be the same listed by Nicholson as *A. fragrans*. The French honeysuckle, *Hedysarum coronarium*, is another somewhat fragrant plant of this prodigal month. It is not, I believe, a true perennial, but sows itself where it likes its surroundings. Country children find pleasure in sucking the honey from the reddish flower tubes.

The chief shrub of June for fragrance, as it is indeed one of the best of the whole year, is the mock orange, or *Philadelphus*. It is one of the oldest shrubs in cultivation, having been mentioned in books as far back as the sixteenth century. Like the lilac it was known of old as pipe tree, the white pipe tree, as the lilac was known as the blue pipe tree. "They had this name," Gerard tells us, "because the stalks and branches thereof when the pith was taken out, are hollow like a pipe." And both were enrolled under the name of *Syringa*. But quite obviously they did not belong to the same family and when Linnaeus began his great work of bringing order out of the chaos of botanical classification, he kept the lilac as the true *Syringa* and gave to the mock orange the name of *Philadelphus*. There remains until this day, however, some confusion between the two and many persons still refer to the mock orange as *Syringa*.

Like the lilac it was one of the first shrubs to be brought to this country and installed in the dooryards of the early settlers and there are many venerable specimens and their descendants throughout old New England neighbourhoods. It is a hardy and enduring shrub putting up with a deal of neglect and lasting in many old gardens long after all vestige of a dwelling has passed away.

While all the species and varieties, save the Mexican *P. coulteri*, which has purplish blotches on its creamy petals, bear white flowers, "ivory pure" according to the poet Cowper, there is great variety of height and habit among them, as well as in the shape and size of the blossoms. Also if you will go about among a large collection of mock orange bushes in June you will find an astonishing variety of scents.

MOCK ORANGE
(*Philadelphus* x *purpeo-maculatus*)
'Belle Etoile'

The late Mr. Wilson, Keeper of the Arnold Arboretum, records that people with an acute sense of smell can pick out a number of sorts by their odour alone and he is responsible for the following observations and comparisons. "The flowers of the small leafed *P. microphyllus* have a powerful odor of quince and melon fruits, delightfully mixed. The hybrid *P.* x *lemoinei* 'Erectus' emits a delectable perfume of pineapple and orange blossom combined. The Chinese *incanus* has an odor of hyacinth, whereas the flowers of the graceful *P. purpurascens* have the sweetness of sweet peas, and the odor of sweet vernal grass pervades the flowers of *P. sericanthus*. The quality of fragrance depends not a little on the weather and the time of day, being most pronounced in the morning and in the evening. The redolence is changeable, elusive, alluring, and a few *Philadelphus* bushes on a warm evening in June will fill the air with rich scents, conjuring up memories of nights in tropic lands." *P. subcanus* var. *magdalense* [*P. magdalense*] is a striking and floriferous shrub from China bearing masses of drooping bell-shaped flowers giving off the fragrance of sweet vernal grass, and visitors to the Arboretum in June may be introduced to a small straggling shrub with willowy stems clothed in saucerlike blossoms set in amethyst calices covered with grey hairs. This is *P. argyrocalyx*, a species introduced from New Mexico by Mr. Alfred Rehder. The flowers, according to Mr. Wilson, have the delicious odour of ripe pineapples. While many of the beautiful hybrid varieties are less fragrant than such of the species as *microphyllus* and *coronarius*, Dr. J. Horace McFarland, writing from his garden at Breeze Hill in Harrisburg, calls attention to a Lemoine hybrid called *P.* × *purpureo-maculatus* 'Belle Étoile', a variety which forms a "spreading shrub with graceful arching branches thickly set with enormous single flowers, with a lavender blotch at the base of each petal, the odor of which is that of gardenia and is so pronounced as to completely dominate a considerable area in its vicinity."

A small collection of mock oranges chosen for scent would include the following:

> *P.* × *lemoinei* 'Coupe d'Argent', single and very lovely; *P.* × *lemoinei* 'Erectus'; *P.* × *polyanthus* 'Mount Blanc', growing five feet tall; *P.* × *cycomus* 'Conquete', double; *P.* × *cycosma* 'Rosace', exquisite fragrance; *P. lemoinei* 'Candelabre', dwarf; *P.* × *lemoinei* 'Dame Blanche', semi-double, erect; *P.* × *polyanthus* 'Gerbe de Neige', large single; *P.* × *virginalis* 'Virginal', beautiful full double flowers of delicate not strong scent. The Rocky Mountain *P. microphyllus* is one of the most enchanting of small shrubs, with creamy, quince-scented blossoms, and grows less than three feet tall.

But many persons do not care for the perfume of the mock orange, whatever character it may have. Indeed there are those who cannot endure it at all. E. V. B. calls it "the best hated and best loved" of flowers and says that while many persons hail its blossoming with enthusiasm and break off sprigs to wear as they pass the bush, others will go the other way around to avoid passing near. Even Gerard objected to its aroma and tells of its "troubling and molesting the head in a very strange manner. I once gathered the flowers and laid them on my chamber window, which smelled more strongly after they had lien together some howers, with such a ponticke and unacquainted savour that they awakened me from sleepe so that I could not take any rest until I had cast them out of my chamber."

Certainly they pervade the air at the season of their blossoming and if you do not like this perfume you do not like it, and that is all there is to the matter. And in this case you have the option of planting some of the scentless, or soulless, species and varieties, of which there are not a few, most of them being Americans by birth. Among the beautiful and dumb are the following: *P. californicus*, *P. inodorus* var. *grandiflorus*, *P. hirsutus*, *P. inodorus* var. *laxus*, *P. lewisii*, and *P. lewisii* var. *gordonianus*. All are fine shrubs lacking nothing save scent – which is to say, from my point of view, that they lack everything essential to enable a mock orange to hold up its head among its gifted kin.

Most of the fine hybrid species that today embellish our gardens we owe to the skill and industry of one man, M. Lemoine of Nancy, France. His first creation saw the light in 1883 and bears his distinguished name. It was the result of a cross between the European *P. coro-*

narius and our delicious little Rocky Mountain species, *P. microphyllus*. It is an interesting fact related somewhere by Mr. Wilson that the double-flowered form of *P. coronarius*, 'Duplex', was known in Germany as long ago as 1613, and is one of the first double-flowered garden shrubs recorded as growing in Northern gardens.

The young leaves of the mock orange have a nice taste of cucumber and were used in Elizabethan times as an addition to salads. To keep *Philadelphus* bushes in good condition and blossoming freely, the old wood should be thinned out immediately after flowering so that the wood upon which the new crop of flowers will be borne shall have ample space to develop.

PEONY
(*Paeonia*)

Peonies, that are among the oldest flowers we grow in the garden, play a significant part in the omnium gatherum of June odours. At their best they may be said to have a coarse rose scent. In it is much of the sweetness and transparency of rose perfume, much of its refreshing quality, but back of this is something indefinable that is a little rank, a suggestion of something medicinal perhaps, which however seldom reaches a point, though it varies in strength in the different varieties, of being actively unpleasant. This curious sub-odour, so to speak, is most marked in the single and semi-double varieties, and it is said to be due to the strong, rather rank odour of the pollen that predominates over what little scent the petals may possess.

Peonies do not of course all smell alike and many of them have practically no smell at all. Few of the single kinds are markedly sweet scented, nor are those among the doubles of red colouring, save in a few instances. The purest and most delicious quality of scent is found in the various pale pink varieties and in the white and blush-coloured kinds. Several *Paeonia* species have fragrant flowers, among them the little red flowered *P. tenuifolia*, from the Ukraine, Russia, called the adonis peony because of the similarity of its feathery foliage to that of the adonis. It is a charming little species, suitable for and in harmony with the rock garden as well as for border life. It is the first of its race to bloom and after the flowering is past and seed has matured, the plant dies to the ground and is seen no more until the following spring. So mark well its dwelling that you may not injure it in digging about.

Paeonia wittmanniana, a Caucasian species with yellow flowers, has a light agreeable scent and the hybrids that have been derived from it by that great French wonder-worker, M. Lemoine, are extremely valuable in the garden, flowering early and bearing sweet scented, single flowers in the most delicate and lovely colours and foliage of a substantial texture that is a decoration in itself. *P. lutea* I have never seen but Mrs. Harding says, "In addition to its beauty this little peony is gifted with fragrance somewhat like a lily." It comes from the Yunnan Mountains in Southern China, has dark, deeply lobed leaves much like those of the tree peonies, and single deep yellow blossoms. *Paeonia lactiflora* [*P. albiflora*] has the rose scent in rather marked degree and is one of the most lovely for garden decoration.

Obviously it is not possible to mention here all the peonies that are gifted with scent so I will present a few that have seemed to me especially sweet. Some of them are still expensive, others are very much the reverse. They are all double flowered and among them are early and late blooming kinds.

'Angel Cheeks'. Some cameo-pink, with red freckles on the topmost petals.

'Avalanche'. Creamy-white with hair-line of red on the edges of the petals. Full crown type.

'Baroness Schroeder'. Charming rose-type, white, tinged palest pink.

'Couronne d'Or'. Semi-rose, milk-white with the odour of a waterlily. Late blooming.

'Edulis Superba'. Very double old-rose pink.

'Edwin C. Shaw'. Flesh pink, cupped shape. Late mid-season.

'Fairy's Petticoat'. A very soft pastel cream and pink. Ruffled.

P. lactifolia 'Festival Maxima'. Beautiful old peony of full rose-type, white-flecked with red.

'Festiva Supreme'. Beautiful white, fluffy double. Pearly white petals tipped in red at center.

'Gilbert Wild'. Huge two-tone rose-pink. Outstanding.

'Jeannot'. Delicate rose-pink overcast pale violet.

'Karl Rosenfeld'. Brilliant very deep red.

'Lamartine'. Full crown type, mauve-pink and white and very sweet.

'Le Cygne'. Enormous semi-rose flower, ivory tinted white.

'Madame Calot'. Exquisite flesh-tint. Early.

'Marie Lemoine'. Creamy-white almost transparent petals. Late.

'Mary Eddy Jones'. Huge light pink. Flowers large and cupped, center full. A beauty!

'Mons. Jules Elie'. Huge chrysanthemum-like bombs of deep silvery pink. Popular for all its 100 years.

'Mrs. F. D. Roosevelt'. Large flowers, broad soft pink petals.

'Phillipe Rivoire'. Early, dark crimson, rose-type.

'Pink Formal'. A soft even shade of mauve pink. Heavy stems.

'Pink Parfait'. A scrumptious treat. Rich dark pink edged in silver. Large, full rose type blossoms.

'President Wilson'. Rose-pink, paling as the flower opens. Spicy.

'Sarah Bernhardt'. Apple blossom pink with petals tipped silver. Red flecking adds a sparkling accent.

'Splendida'. Large globular blooms of flesh-white. Rather late.

'Therese'. Huge soft pink, glowing center. French classic.

'Top Brass'. Rounded ivory petals surround the full palest bomb with ivory and yellow center.

It has to be confessed that the old red "Piney" of our grandmothers' gardens, while it provides a most glowing bit of colour in the late May garden, rewards the nose with a rather rank and repellent odour. Mrs. Harding speaks of 'Marie Jacquin' as also offending in this way.

Sometimes the warm scent of the tall bearded irises hangs too heavily in the humid air of early summer days, especially where great numbers of them are grown; but it is an agreeable odour and one I do not object to indoors. There is a good deal of variety in the scents of these beautiful flowers, some being far better than others, and a few are actively unpleasant. Nor can I endure the odour of the old 'Alcazar'.

From Mrs. McKinney's perennially readable book, "Iris in the Little Garden," I take the following:

> Many irises add scent to their other attractions. It is particularly noticeable in the irises belonging to the pallida types and frequently to those influenced by *I. trojana*, and a distinct and delicious odour belongs to the variety 'Archeveque', which is imparted to a series of seedlings in a marked degree. 'Fairy' I have long considered the one iris whose fragrance was liked by all but only now I have heard of an Iris collector who cannot stand it. 'Caprice' is intensely pervaded by the fragrance of the vineyards. 'I smell ripe grapes,' cried a little freckle-faced boy standing near a planting of them in my garden.

In a letter from Miss Sturtevant she says, "The majority of irises that I grow are more or less delightfully scented, a few have (to me) a disagreeable odour and some have none. These days the iris novelties are apt to be crosses of hybrids and traits are so mixed that is difficult to place them in any class save by colour. I believe scent is an inherited character and I image I can tell by the odour from what species it has come. *I. cypriana* and *I. pallida* seedlings are almost always sweet and *I. variegata* includes most of the scentless ones."

A short list of sweet scented irises follows:

*Moonlight.

*Queen Caterina. One of the most delightful.

*Shekinah.

*White Knight.

*Zua.

'Acapulco Gold'. Brilliant tone of golden-yellow! Creates a most remarkable garden impact.

'Beverly Hills'. Exciting: Ruffled, lacy, vivid coral pink; free-blooming. An enchanting beauty.

'Blue Staccato'. Crispy flared plicata, sparkling white edged bright blue. Flowers are fluted and ruffled.

'Breakers'. A very ruffled, bubbly and

effervescent medium blue to deep blue. Superb. Glowing.

'Darkside'. Vivid rich shade of purple-black. Extremely ruffled. Ebony beards.

'Dusky Challenger'. Gigantic silky rich black purple. Well ruffled. Beautifully branched. Destined to challenge all comers.

'Eleanor's Pride'. Outstanding. A beautiful light powder blue.

'Honky Tonk Blues'. Novel blending of shades of blue and white. Blue-violet streaked with swirling white etching. Very ruffled.

'Jessie's Song'. Striking, ruffled violet plicata. Beard is lemon. Has charm.

'Laced Cotton'. Very heavily laced, immaculately clean pure white. Dainty. A new high in lace.

'Midnight Hour'. Magnificent ruffled dark blue self. Large and robust. An eye-stopper.

'Olympiad'. A champion. Palest blue-violet infused with deeper blue-violet markings. Ruffled, excellent substance.

'Royal Crusader'. Extra large flowers. Cloud blue. Deep blue. Nice contrast.

'Silverado'. Heavenly ruffled silvery blue white self. Tall and stately with good form and substance. A proud new achievement.

'Stepping Out'. Beautifully ruffled rich violet and white plicata. Strikingly picoteed, stunningly beautiful.

'Sultry Mood'. Exquisite cerise-purple. Sensational in every way.

'Thriller'. Nothing else like it. An exciting intense cerise claret accented by deeper purple beards. Uniform standout colour.

'Tides In'. Finest ruffled light celestial blue iris. Elegantly ruffled. Top notch. One of the best blues.

'Vanity'. Smooth, well formed and ruffled medium pink. Blooms heavy.

CHAPTER VI

Odours of the Rose

The scent of the Rose remains after it has fallen; the words of a good man remain after he has obtained mercy.

— KISUAHILI, EAST AFRICA

From E. V. B.'s "Ros Rosarium, Dew of the Ever-Living Rose"

FRAGRANCE IS THE RIGHTFUL heritage of the rose, and it is what we consciously or unconsciously expect of it. We cannot dissociate fragrance and the rose. If you doubt this, watch the visitors at any rose show bobbing forward automatically before each exhibit to inhale the fragrance and plainly registering by word or look pleasure or the reverse at the response they receive. Beautiful as is the rose it is only half appreciated by the eye; the nose has a great part in our delight in it and ever has had. In times long gone when the rose was a simple flower, not eclipsing the elegance of the Lily, nor the showiness of the Tulip, it was known as the Queen of Flowers, as it is today. Surely it was the lovely quality of its fragrance, with which no flower can compete, that gave it this prestige.

Of late there has been uneasiness among flower lovers because of the numbers of scentless, or nearly scentless, roses now appearing on the market. It is hard to believe that a scentless rose could have great vogue, but there is about them a chill and soulless beauty. A trend towards mere beauty of person in roses is greatly to be deplored.

What is meant by the pure odour of roses, and sometimes designated as the "true old rose scent," is the property of that famous trinity that once constituted the chief rose wealth of the western gardening world – *Rosa centifolia,* the cabbage rose; *Rosa damascena,* the Damask rose; *Rosa gallica,* the French rose. And there is no doubt that this rich and at the same time delicate rose fragrance is less in evidence today than it was at the period when nearly all garden roses had the blood of one or other of these old kinds coursing in their veins. This lovely scent is happily the inheritance of many a modern hybrid perpetual and of some hybrid teas.

Red roses, as a matter of fact, perhaps because they are close to those grand old varieties of early times, are usually the most richly endowed with fragrance. Pink varieties are next in point of sweetness, with yellow kinds the least scented, or wholly scentless, though some of the best of the so called fruity odours are found among varieties of yellow and cream colouring.

This true old rose scent, the scent that has charmed humanity from time immemorial, is assuredly the most exquisite and refreshing of all floral odours – pure, transparent, incomparable – an odour into which we may, so to speak, burrow deeply without finding anything coarse or bitter, in which we may touch bottom without losing our sense of exquisite pleasure. And this is far from being the case with all fragrant flowers. Inhale too long the perfume of the trailing arbutus and we come upon bitter almond; the scent of the peony is rose-like on the surface, but rather coarse and earthy if pursued past a certain point. And so with many flowers. But the perfume of the rose remains pure, uncloying and sweet to the last whiff, nor does it lose its sweetness in death. Dried rose leaves hold their scent for many months, even years.

But this *old* rose scent is not by any means the only fragrance that belongs to this versatile family. There are, as a matter of fact, many types and degrees of rose sweetness, as well as a complete lack of it in some varieties, and in a scant few an actually disagreeable odour. It is said that experienced rosarians are able to identify many kinds of roses in the dark, or with their eyes shut, which goes to show there are many distinct types of fragrance among them. "Indeed so capricious is the nature of this perfume and so extraordinary the complexity of its forms, it is claimed that not only in the whole list of roses are there no two that develop the same odour, but that in the same species, and even on the same plant, there are not to be found two flowers exactly identical as to odour, and yet further, that it is a fact well known among rose growers that at different times in the day, or of its development, an individual flower will emit a different perfume."

Warmth and moisture are important factors in rose fragrance, as with other flowers, though the presence or absence of either cannot be said to determine whether or not a specific variety is to be classed as especially fragrant; "but warmth does decide the rapidity with which the essential oil, which is the cause of scent, is generated in the cells of the petals and given off to the air." It will be noticed that on cool days, especially if the weather is dry, the perfume of the roses in the garden is perceptibly less strong than on warm ones, and it is well known that roses blooming under glass, or when brought into a warm room, are far more fragrant than those flowering in the open air, and more readily give off this perfume to the air. A still, moist and mild atmosphere is the most favourable to fragrance in any flower.

In periods of extreme heat and drought, however, to which our climate of extremes is prone, the perfume of roses grows appreciably less, and it has been noticed that before a storm the sweet odours will increase. Certain roses give off their perfume to the air with more facility than others; certain roses, too, seem to be more fragrant in the autumn than in the summer, having an almost piercing quality of sweetness as the season draws to a close. "And indeed," wrote Bacon, "the Nouember Rose is the sweetest, hauing beene less exhaled by the sun." And does it not always seem that the last rose, "wresting June from out the snows," is the sweetest of all the year?

Where roses are grown for the distillation of the attar they are gathered before they begin to open, a little before sunrise. Were they gathered later in the day, when fully expanded by the sun, the perfume, it is said, would be much stronger, but not so sweet, and the resulting essence of a poorer quality.

Among roses we find a great variety of scents testifying to their complicated and composite ancestry. Besides the true old rose scent that is present in so many hybrid perpetuals, we find the tea scent, the odours of spice and musk and of honey, even that of violets (the multiflora rose 'Eugénie Lamesch' has a faint scent of violets) and a whole gamut of fruity odours. The introduction from China in 1810 of the blush tea-scented rose, and a few years later from the same land, of the yellow tea-scented rose, profoundly influenced the fragrance of roses. These two little Orientals were forms of *Rosa* × *odorata* [*Rosa indica odorata*], the "*odorata*" distinguishing it from *Rosa chinensis* [*R. indica*], the China rose, which is not always fragrant. They were thought to smell like fine China tea. Originally they were brought to England but soon found a more congenial home in France where they were speedily taken in hand by the clever French growers, under whose skilled manipulation they became the progenitors of the great race of so called tea-scented roses. They were immediately popular, for though somewhat tender, their large delightfully fragrant blossoms, so freely borne in the autumn, were a new and delicious experience to rose lovers hitherto accustomed only to the short June bounty of the old kinds.

The tea rose crossed with the old musk rose brought into being the lovely and tender noisettes, exquisite of form and fragrance. In the Maryland garden of my youth we grew only teas and noisettes and I remember that splendid rose of the latter class, 'Maréchal Niel', that wound a vigorous wreath about the library windows, was called by us the strawberry rose, because its pointed golden buds so realistically suggested the pungent odour of ripe strawberries, and that the tea rose, 'Safrano', my mother's favourite, had distinctly the spicy breath of the Scotch pinks that edged its bed. Some varieties that possess in marked degree the true tea scent are 'Gloire de Dijon', 'Mrs. Foley-Hobbs', 'Anna Oliver', 'Lady Hillingdon', and 'Marie van Houtte'.

The crossing of the hybrid perpetual with the tea-scented rose toward the end of the nineteenth century resulted in the grand race of hybrid teas. The hybrid perpetual had been the result of earlier crosses between *Rosa chinensis* [*R. indica*] and the old Damask and French roses. Thus the cross fertilization of the hybrid perpetual with the tea tended to increase the tea element in the new class of roses and, though we gained immeasurably in the extraordinary perfection of form and the exquisite and infinite nuances and gradations of colour that make the hybrid teas the outstanding figures of beauty, there is no doubt that the "old rose scent" is less often present, in these beauties.

'Rosa Mundi'
(*Rosa gallica*)

Where the blood of the old musk rose has been used in hybridization, the perfume, while refreshing and delicious, is, it must be confessed, curiously unroselike; but these musk-influenced roses commonly have the pleasant faculty of the musk rose, of giving off their sweetness freely to the air, especially towards evening.

Few roses are wholly scentless, though many are only moderately sweet. There are a vast number of beautiful roses that are sweet scented and a fair proportion of these are quite deliciously scented. There is therefore no reason to include in our collections any that are without this lovely attribute. Climbers, it is true, are often very slightly gifted and it seems to me that we should beg of the wizard hybridists a race of more fragrant climbers. Certainly it is not beyond their skill to grant us this boon, and how much it would add to the delight of lingering in arbours and pergolas, and to the sweetness of our rooms beyond the casements of which clamber rose vines.

The perfume of the rose has long been believed to possess curative powers – "a Rose besides its beauty is a cure" – and old medical works and herbals abound in rules for making rose decoctions for the relief of every sort of disability, whether of flesh or spirit. You will recall those lines from Anacreon:

> The Rose distills a healing balm,
> The beating pulse of pain to calm.

And old Leonard Meager knew several hundred years ago what we still acknowledge today, that "Roses refresh the brain with their Sweet Odours and drive away Vapours from thence." A bowl of roses in the living room on a distressingly hot day does far more than please the eye and regale the nose; it distinctly enlivens the atmosphere and revives the occupants of the room. Even one fragrant rose in a slender glass vase will make a whole room sweet and fresh.

I am fortunate to be able to append here a list of especially fragrant roses.

FRAGRANT FLORIBUNDAS

'City of London'
'Courvoisier'
'Fragrant Delight'
'Margaret Merril'
'Radox Bouquet'
'Rosy Future'
'Sheila's Perfume'
'Valentine Heart'
'Sunsprite' (a.k.a. 'Korresia')
'The Fisherman's Cot'

FRAGRANT CLIMBERS

'Albertine'
'Cl. Etoile de Holland'
'Compassion'
'Gloire de Dijon'
'High Hopes'
'Mme. Alfred Carriere'
'Mme. Gregoire Staechelin'
'White Cockade'

FRAGRANT MODERN SHRUBS

'Aloha'
'Evelyn'
'Fruhlingsgold'
'Gertrude Jeckyll'
'Golden Wings'
'Graham S. Thomas'
'Heritage'
'L.D. Braithwaite'
'Maigold'
'Mary Rose'

FRAGRANT HYBRID TEAS

'Alec's Red'
'Alpine Sunset'
'Aotearoa – New Zealand'
'Audrey Wilcox'
'Barkarole'
'Baronne E. de Rothschild'
'Big Purple'
'Deep Secret'
'Double Delight'
'Fragrant Cloud'
'Fragrant Dream'
'Fulton Mackay'
'High Sheriff'
'Lady Mavis Pilkington'
'Mary Jean'
'Papa Meilland'
'Paul Shirville'
'Pink Peace'
'Prima Ballerina'
'Renaissance'
'Rosemary Harkenss'
'Royal William' (a.k.a. 'Duftzauber', 'Fragrant Charm')
'Valencia'
'Warm Wishes'

FRAGRANT BOURBONS AND HYBRID PERPETUALS

'Boule de Neige'
'Ferdinand Pichard'
'Gruss and Teplitz'
'John Hopper'
'Louise Odier'
'Mme. Isaac Pereire'

Most of the gallicas, damasks, albas. centifolias and noisettes are fragrant in some degree.

VARIOUS SPECIES AND VARIETIES*

Somewhere in his writings Eden Phillpotts says, "Our taste for the plump monsters of the Rose border is Mid-Victorian and we must struggle back to the more refined and distinguished species." Many of the rose species are indeed of a most appealing beauty and grace and we should do well to grow them freely. Our shrubberies would in particular gain by a more extensive use of the free growing bush roses, as well as of the old fashioned sorts that delighted the eyes and the noses of our forefathers. Single roses are not commonly as fragrant as are double ones. The "wylde" rose, proclaims an ancient writer, quoted by Miss Rohde "smellyth not so well as the tame, nother is it so vertuous in medicyn." But many of them have a delicate and individual scent that is very grateful to the nose. Wild roses are very generally distributed in the Northern Hemisphere and are of the summer's most comely decorations. Thoreau loved the wild roses that grew in New England and thought the season of their blossoming should be given some preeminence. He discerned a certain noble and delicate civility about them, "not wildness," and speaks of their rich colour, size and form, the rare beauty of the buds and their delightful fragrance. The following are sweet scented species:

Rosa x *alba*. The white rose. Though given a botanical name this lovely old garden rose is not thought to be a true species. By some authorities it is said to have been introduced into England in 1697, by others it is thought to be the white rose of the House of York. It has ever been a popular rose in cottage gardens and even in this day large bushes of it are sometimes to be seen in rural neighbourhoods. The flowers are semi-double and white, or in the variety 'Incarnata' ('Maiden's Blush'), a very pale pink, and they are very sweet. The foliage is bluish. A source of attar of roses.

R. arkansana. The prairie rose. A low-growing wild rose of the Central West that has grown in my rock garden for several years. It bears clusters of delicate pink single roses with a brush of golden stamens. Lightly scented.

R. arvensis. Field rose. Perhaps the most charming of the British hedge roses, blooming about ten days later than *R. canina*. "At midsummer *Rosa arvensis* needs no seeking, it forces itself into notice, being then one mass of flowers, pure white with a yellow base, golden stamens, and having a sweet scent peculiar to itself," thought by some to resemble that of mignonette.

R. banksiae. Banksian rose. A distinct species, native of China, a rambling individual climbing to twenty feet, evergreen and unarmed and bearing many-flowered clusters of small unrose-like blossoms, resembling more a double cherry blossom than a rose, white or straw-coloured, and violet scented. There are numerous forms. Flowers

*Editor's note: *Roses have undergone many changes in terms of cultivation and preferences in the years since Mrs. Wilder first wrote this chapter. Therefore much of the information is primarily of interest for historical reasons. However, we have updated the list on the previus page to include plants generally available at your local nursery. Opinions on the desirability of breeding for fragrance vary, but the emphasis today lies with breeding for health and vigor rather than fragrance.*

in May but is adapted only for mild climates.

R. beggeriana. A native of Afghanistan. A tall bush bearing small white flowers with a rather unpleasant odour.

R. bracteata. The Macartny rose. Native of China, Formosa and Northern India. A strong growing rose when happily established but too tender for any save mild climates. Half-climbing to twenty feet, with dark shining evergreen leaves and a profusion of large single white flowers set off by a profusion of golden stamens. The flowers possess a characteristic lemony odour. Naturalized in parts of this country.

R. brunonii. Himalayan musk rose. Beautiful milk-white rose that is at its best scrambling over low bushes or into trees. Flowers scented of musk. It is rather tender.

R. californica. Californian wild rose. This is common at low altitudes in California, a large bush bearing clusters of very fragrant pale pink flowers. Carl Purdy writes me that many of the western wild roses have the sweetbrier fragrance.

R. canina. Dog rose. This is Shakespeare's canker bloom, and is one of the most beloved roses of English hedgerows. Gray speaks of it as a casual escape from cultivation from Massachusetts to Tennessee, and thoroughly naturalized on river banks in Pennsylvania. The solitary bland pink blossoms have a light sweet scent. From the abundant hips Elizabethan ladies made a much prized conserve.

R. cerasocarpa [*R. gentilana*]. China. Partially climbing branches to twenty feet. Flowers white and fragrant in many-flowered clusters.

R. x *centifolia.* Cabbage rose. Provence rose. Hundred-leaved rose. "Delightful to the eye, delightful for its fragrance and most delightful for its associations," wrote Canon Ellacombe of this old rose. Certainly no rose surpasses it in fragrance. The moss rose is a form of the cabbage rose and has a peculiar sharp cordial odour very different from that of the type. The little de Meaux is also of this group.

R. damascena. Damask rose. The lovely old rose of long ago gardens with its rich velvet texture and grand fragrance. Thought to be oriental in origin. There are white and striped forms. The rose most esteemed for making rosewater, and a source of attar of roses.

R. ecae. A hardy rose from Central Asia growing five to six feet tall and bearing small yellow flowers. The leaves have the sweetbrier scent.

R. foetida (*R. lutea*). This rose belongs to the *spinossima* group of roses. The brilliant coppery flowers have a rather unpleasant odour, but the leaves are fragrant.

R. gallica. The French rose. The blossoms of the French rose are less fragrant than those of the Damask or the cabbage roses but their sweetness increases with drying. There are several other *gallica* roses.

R. helenae. A species from the mountains of Central China, with branches climbing to a height of fifteen feet. It is said that its clusters of white flowers perfume the countryside.

R. laevigata (*R. camelia*). The Cherokee rose. This charming decoration of our Southern States originally came from China, but is now widely and permanently naturalized where it is hardy. The foliage is evergreen and shining and the immense white single blooms have the rich fragrance of the gardenia.

R. majalis [*R. cinnamomea*]. Cinnamon rose. Candace Wheeler speaks of the cinnamon rose, "braiding its odors with those of the sweet white Syringa blossoms, quite undisturbed by a new generation of rose-lovers." It is a small, flat, tumble-headed pink rose of fine if faint spicy scent, often found flourishing by the dusty highway, or pressing its quaint blossoms through the broken palings of old and deserted gardens.

Rosa moschata. The musk rose. Mr. E. H. Wilson says that the true musk rose is lost to cultivation and that the name now applies to a vigorous climbing rose, *R. brunonii,* the Himalayan musk rose of Asiatic origin that has the fragrance of musk. In one of Mrs. Gaskell's stories ("Lady Ludlow"), she makes one of the characters say, "You remember the great bush at the corner of the south wall by the blue drawing-room windows – that is the old musk rose, Shakespeare's musk rose, which is dying out through the kingdom now." Canon Ellacombe wrote, "The scent is unlike the scent of any other rose, or of any other flower, but it is very pleasant and not overpowering; and the plant has the peculiarity that, like the sweet brier, but unlike other roses, it gives out its scent of its own accord and unsought, so that if the window of a bedroom near which this rose is trained is left open, the scent will soon be perceived in the room." Bacon placed the perfume of the musk rose next to that of violets. The late Rev. Joseph Pemberton in England produced numerous fine hybrid musk roses that are agreeably fragrant. The roses loved by Shakespeare and frequently referred to in his writings were the musk rose, the Damask, the sweetbrier or eglantine, the French rose, the cabbage rose, or Provencal rose, and the canker bloom. The musk rose was a favorite also of the poet Keats.

R. multiflora. The Japanese rose. Baby rose. China. Branches climbing or trailing and studded with small white fragrant flowers borne in many-flowered panicles. Its blood is in many of our garden roses.

R. multiflora var. *cathayensis* [*R. cathayensis*]. Half-climbing rose from China bearing scattered pink blossoms that are highly fragrant.

Rosa pendulina [*R. alpina*]. The thornless rose. The wild rose of European alpine heights, a slender, low, little-branched species bearing bright crimson-pink blossoms. Both flowers and leaves have a distinctive resinous odour. It is a parent of the Boursault roses.

R. pimpinellifolia [*R. spinosissima*]. Scotch or Burnet rose. Europe. Asia. A rather dwarf bushy species with small leaves and myriads of prickles. It is a parent of the Scotch Briers which are among the most delightful of bush roses and deserve greater appreciation than they receive in this country. It grows easily in any sunny position and should not be neglected for more showy novelties.

R. rugosa. The Turkestan rose. This is the hardiest and sturdiest of all roses. There are many fine hybrids noted for their sweet scent, which is very like that of the old *gallica* and Damask sorts. 'Rose à parfum de l'Hay' was considered by its creator, M. Jules Gravereaux, to be the sweetest of all roses, though its blossoms are not as fine in form as others of its class. In its veins flows the blood of *R.* x *damascena* and of 'General Jacqueminot'.

R. rubiginosa. Sweetbrier. Eglantine. It is in the leaves of the sweetbrier that we find the fragrance, and what a delicious fragrance it is, so clean and keen and uncloyingly sweet. "No true Rosarian," wrote Dean Hole, "can lightly esteem this simple but gracious gift." After rain this fragrance is especially freely diffused and the air of the garden where even one bush grows seems drenched with it. It has always been the favorite of the poets; it was Keats's "Pastoral Eglantine" and the "smelling Brere" of Spenser. To Lord Penzance we are indebted for the splendid hybrid sweetbriers with their delicate and exquisite colours and the characteristically scented foliage. They are rampant growers but well worth the space they occupy and one or two should find a place in every garden.

Doubtless the first sweetbriers to reach New England came over in the Mayflower, or soon after, for Harriet Keeler tells us that it bloomed in Pilgrim gardens long before the close of the seventeenth century. And now it has found its way out of safe garden enclosures and makes a home for itself in rocky pastures and along farm lanes in the most rugged and exposed localities, especially throughout New England. How pleasant it is to meet it in our walks afield, and catching its eager greeting of fragrance, to let our thoughts stray back in gratitude over the years, the centuries, that its keen sweetness has reached deep into the anxious heart of man with a message of courage or of contentment.

R. virginiana [*R. lucida*]. Dwarf swamp rose. A pretty low-growing rose that grows in bushy masses. It is probably the sweetest scented of our native wild roses. The blossoms are pink and single and Thoreau tells us of bringing home a few buds and placing them in water and that in the morning they scented his chamber. Miss Jekyll also somewhere notes the scent of this rose, calling it faint but very distinct.

Other wild roses that we meet in our walks about the countryside are *R. nitida,* the Northeastern rose, a low bushy species with small leaves; *R. blanda,* the early meadow rose and *R. carolina* [*R. humilis*], the pretty dwarf pasture rose. All have a delicate sweetness.

R. xanthina f. *hugonis* [*R. hugonis*]. The charming yellow flowers of Father Hugo's rose have a light sweet dog rose fragrance.

CHAPTER VII

Fragrant Annuals

Through the open door
A drowsy smell of flowers – gray heliotrope
And white sweet clover, and shy mignonette
Comes faintly in, and silent chorus leads
To the pervading symphony of Peace.

— WHITTIER

ANNUALS LABOUR UNDER the disadvantage of being annuals. They blossom, seed and die and next year we must begin all over again with them. But if they are fragrant they amply pay their way and the trouble we are put to in their behalf seems as nothing in comparison with the pleasure we have derived from them. Annual flowers with a sweet scent are not so many but that most of them might be included in a fair sized garden; some of them are indispensable to any garden. Who would be without the spicy scent of stocks, of mignonette, or the cool sweetness of the sweet pea?

But let us begin at the beginning of the catalog and take them alphabetically: The first is *Abronia umbellata,* the sand verbena, a little trailing plant from California, with bright rose-colored flowers, a little sticky, that are honey-scented especially towards evening. It likes sandy places and flourishes near the sea. It is sometimes used in hanging baskets.

And then we have *Alyssum,* sweet alyssum, it is called with good reason, *Lobularia maritima* [*Alyssum maritimum*], its little bunches of tiny white flowers smell exactly like new mown hay, particularly when the sun shines hot upon them or after a shower. It is good, as every gardener knows, as an edger or as a carpeter; and how the bees love it! Once let this little hardy annual into the garden and it is there for good; always there will be drifts of sweetness in odd corners and it blooms long and late. Last December I found a small wave of it beating against the base of the rock garden – where it had never been sown by hand – and scenting the winter air. In parts of England it has escaped from gardens and wanders about the countryside. The ordinary kinds grow about six inches high, but there have recently been introduced some very dwarf and compact forms. They should all be sown where they are to flower.

Though *Antirrhinum* (snapdragon) is counted a fragrant annual, it has to my nose what the old writers call a "stuffing scent," rather oversweet and cloying. But as its odour is not given off spontaneously in the open air it need not be annoying to one who does not care for it, and its beautiful hues, unsurpassed by those of any other flower, would make it desirable in any garden. Like its white perennial sister, the blue woodruff, *Asperula orientalis* [*A. azurea setosa*], it has a delicate pleasing fragrance. It is a very hardy annual from the Caucasus that will self-sow in the garden as long as a plant is allowed to mature seed. It grows a foot tall and is one of the annuals that may be admitted to the rock garden. Bees fancy it.

Under *Centaurea* we have the various kinds of sweet sultans, which are among the most fragrant of garden flowers. The thistle-like blooms, white, yellow, mauve or purple are borne on long stems fitting them for cutting, and they last a long time in water, though to some squeamish noses their scent is too strong indoors. An old garden flower originally from the Levant, the yellow sweet sultan, *Amberboa moschata* [*Centaurea suaveolens*], has an even stronger fragrance than the ordinary garden kinds and is a very handsome flower. To have success with it a dry situation where it meets the full force of the sun is necessary, and all the sweet sultans have a taste for lime. Parkinson names "Sultan's Flowers" as having been "but lately obtained from Constantinople, where because the great Turke, as we call him, saw it abroad, liked it and wore it himselfe, all his vassals haue had it in great regard, and hath been obtained from them by some that haue sent it into these parts." All the writers of early days mention the beauty of the sweet sultan but few speak of its fragrance, which is curious since this attribute is seldom allowed to go unnoted by the old writers when it is present in a flower. The cornflower (*Centaurea cynaus*) is an old inhabitant of gardens and older yet of cornfields. Parkinson describes it as "furnishing or rather pestering the Corne Fieldes." I must confess that until my attention was called to it by a more investigative person than myself I did not know that the cornflower, so beloved for its lovely blue colour, had any scented attractions. The next time you gather a bouquet of these flowers bury your nose in them and perhaps you will receive a surprise.

Candytuft. Who grows any but the fine hyacinth-flowered or spiral varieties? Few even know of the modest little sweet scented, unimproved kind, *Iberis odorata.* Get a packet or two and sow it in your poorest soil in full sunshine; it is sweetest when not pampered. It is a native of Crete whence it was brought to gardens not much more than a hundred years ago, but it has been quite superseded by the new varieties.

The very name *Datura* seems to send forth clouds of heavy perfume. There are several annual kinds offered, the familiar 'Horn of Plenty', *D. metel* [*D. cornucopia*], with its double white trumpets, marbled with purple, and Miss Jekyll recommends *D. ceratocaula,* with white flowers, the plant growing from two to three feet high, and *D. innoxia* [*D. meteloides*], that grows four feet high. All have the characteristic long trumpet-like flowers and are heavily fragrant. I do not greatly admire them for garden use; they appear too tropical and exotic for our northern atmosphere. As a child one of the few wild plants I disliked was the jimson (Jamestown) weed, *Datura stramonium,* that haunts heaps of rubbish or garbage, or other ill-favoured spots, and has won for itself, among other common names, nearly all uncomplimentary or sinister, that of stinkweed. It has a very unpleasant odour. My little "Flora Odorata" speaks well of thorn-apples, and says that they should be sown early out of doors in warm situations and the young plants protected with a hand glass or flower pot from stray frosts that may threaten.

STOCKS
(*Matthiola*)

Dianthus comes next but the annual pinks have little to recommend them in the way of fragrance. They try to make up for this serious defect by the gorgeousness of their raiment, but one has rather a grudge against them, notwithstanding. A pink should be sweet if anything. But there are some so-called annual carnations, hybrids between the scentless Chinese pinks and *Dianthus caryophyllus* that smell with the best. They are called Marguerite carnations, and they come in soft colours—white, pale yellow, pink, rose, crimson, with fringy petals and a fine spicy scent. A fair proportion of them comes double. I once had a lovely border edge of these Marguerite carnations that flowered within six months of sowing (seed having been sown in a box indoors in February) and bloomed until frost, furnishing innumerable bouquets the while.

There are many charming California annuals that are little known. One of these is *Limnanthes douglasii,* one of the many plants named for the young Scotch plant hunter, Douglas, who lost his life so tragically while in pursuit of his calling in the Sandwich Islands [the name given to Hawaii by Capt. James Cook]. Behind many a simple plant lies a brave tale of derring-do. Douglas was a Scotch botanist who explored the Pacific Northwest in the early part of the last century, introducing the Douglas fir to the gardening world and leaving his name to a genus of plants, *Douglasia,* as well as supplying the specific name to a great many, *Phlox douglasii,* and *Limnanthes douglasii,* among them. The last named little plant sprays about in a delicate pretty way, the six-inch stems bearing yellow blossoms, pale at the edges, which gives them a rather faded or fainting look. They are pleasantly fragrant and attract the bees in great numbers. *Limnanthes* should be sown where it is to flower and in succession, for it is soon over.

Annual lupins have the fresh scent of cowslips and are very delightful plants besides, possessing the beauty of leaf and flower-spike that is characteristic of the fine perennial garden varieties. Sutton of Reading, England, offers a dwarf yellow-flowered kind which is particularly rich in fragrance. The annual lupins transplant with ill grace. It is best to raise them in paper pots indoors, or to plant them in the garden where they are to flower. But be sure to thin them out to breathing distance – they want space and air.

Marigolds, with their rough, pungent scent, have their place in another chapter among the Nose-twisters, but *Martynia* comes in here – if you like it. I do not. Once I grew a great bed of it lured by the ingratiating description of its charms in a catalog, but I rooted them up before the season was over. Their odour was sweet beyond all bearing, and the plant (American born) a great coarse thing with heavy-lipped flowers, purplish and freckled. *Proboscidea fragrans* [*Martynia fragrans*] has a delightful sound, but heed it not. Much pleasanter is *Mirabilis*, that the French call belle-de-nuit. It is our old marvel of Peru, or four o'clock, not often seen now-a-days in fine gardens but still cherished in old fashioned neighbourhoods. It is a plant that will take you back to your country-spent childhood – if you are so lucky as to have had one. The little bushes are trigly symmetrical and gaily set forth with bright yellow, or crimson, or pure white flowers, round as pennies and smelling of oranges. On cloudy days the flowers open early and remain open all day, but under a warm sun they justify their name and remain tightly closed until four of the clock, or thereabouts.

Mirabilis is one of the flowers that grew in old Gerard's garden in Fetter Lane. The great Elizabethan gardener wrote of it with excitement and inaccuracy, for it was but lately introduced from the New World, whence so many wonderful plants were finding their way into England at that time. Gerard states that it remains open all day and closes at night, "and so perishes." He continues, "This marvelous variety doth not without case bring admiration to all that observe it; for if the flowers be gathered and reserved in several papers, and compared with those flowers that will spring and flourish the next day, you will easily perceive that one is not like another in colour, though you shall compare one hundred which flower one day, and another which flower the next day, and so on during the whole time of their flowering." By the time Parkinson wrote his "Paradisus" the excitement over the new plant had a little subsided and he is able to give a less imaginative account of it, though he is obviously greatly captivated by it. He calls it "Maruaile (Marvel) of the World" and devotes nearly two pages to a minute description of it. Parkinson notes the diversity of the colours, saying that you will hardly see two alike as long as they blow, "which is until the winters, or rather autumns cold blastes do stay their willing pronenesse to flower: And I haue often also observed that one side of a plant will giue fairer varieties than another, which is most commonly the Easterne, as more temperate and shadowie side."

Shirley Hibberd wrote, "A plant may have no history, and yet be full of fame. It is so with the mignonette, which was unknown to the authors of the best of our old English gardening books, and the history of which may be written on the thumb nail." Its story began but yesterday, but few flowers have attained to greater fame or been more beloved by high and low. Some one has said that as much has been written about mignonette as about Shakespeare. Its scent was its fortune for there was little to attract in the small grey and brown blossoms. Indeed, had it not been for its exquisite fragrance it would never have emerged from obscure weedhood. But how prophetic was the nose of the man who first sniffed its possibilities and brought it out of Egypt to its promised land. France received it with delight, calling it little darling – mignonette, and immediately it had a great and universal vogue. It was grown in fine gardens for the pleasure of the illustrious, and the grisette inhaled its sweetness from a box on her narrow window ledge. Soon the rumour of its fragrance carried it across the Channel to London where it was so much used in window boxes that a writer of the time said, "We have frequently found the perfume of mignonette so powerful in some of the better streets that we have considered it sufficient to protect the inhabitants from those effluvia which bring disorders with them in the air." The scent of mignonette seems somehow as appropriate to the grey old London streets as does that of lavender to an old lady's lace cap.

Many years ago when I came as a girl in the early spring on a visit to New York, I remember that I was made homesick for my Maryland woods by the scent of the trailing arbutus that was for sale on nearly every corner. Today even the most pervasive flower scent could not rise about the stench of gasoline that is the characteristic city odour.

The true scent of mignonette has never been caught by the skill of the perfumer; numerous perfumes have been called by its name but the keen sweet odour of this little flower remains for the enjoyment of those who would rather smell a flower than a handkerchief or a bottle. Some have compared the scent of mignonette to that of the vine flower, others to raspberries, but it is to my nose like no other flower scent. It is ethereal yet definite, with a cool, clean quality and a fine sweetness. No nosegay is so delicious as one made of mignonette and sweet peas, unless it be that other of my favourites – a bitter-sweet combination – moss rose and southernwood.

It is interesting to read that Cowper, that flower-loving poet, came to his majority in the same year that mignonette arrived in London to shower its perfume from window ledge and balcony. He could not but celebrate it:

the sashes fronted with a range
Of orange, myrtle, or the fragrant weed,
the Frenchman's darling.

There are many who will have it that the so-called improved varieties of mignonette are far less sweet than the earlier kinds, and indeed many of the stout trusses one meets with in florists' shops do not seem to carry the wild sweet fragrance that was their birthright. But some are certainly still very delightful, among them 'New York Market', 'Barr's Covent Garden Favorite', 'Parson's White', and 'Sutton's Giant', which grows eighteen inches tall, so requires plenty of space in which to develop. It may not generally be known that mignonette is more fragrant when grown in a poor soil. It flourishes in rich soil but its sweetness fails. Also it is a lover of lime. Where it does not prove a success and makes a sickly, poor-coloured growth, a generous application of lime will generally mend matters speedily. Its scent is strongest when the sun shines hottest.

Musk, once so stickily sweet, is still sticky but strangely has lost its fragrance, to the mystification of the horticultural world. It had a great vogue for use in pots and window boxes and was much worked over and "improved" by florists, and the elusive charm of fragrance is often lost when a flower suffers these attentions.

Nicotiana would come in here but is entreated in the chapter on Night-scented Flowers. Petunia is next, a close relative of the tobacco. The scent of petunia is not altogether pleasant save at night when it loses a certain coarseness of quality and becomes lighter and more transparent. Like the four o'clock it is a native of South America and though it is less than a hundred years since it came into prominence, it is now grown the world over. Florists have worked their will on the petunia and it has emerged from their ateliers in marvelous frills and ruffles. The wild plant would never recognize its sophisticated relation. The deep purple single kinds enrich the borders with both colour and fragrance, but the old single white is the best for sweetness, particularly after sunset.

Another plant for which the florists have done much is the sweet scabious, called also mournful widow, Egyptian rose and pincushion flower. Its flowers are honey-scented and are to be had in lovely and unusual colours – blackish-purple, cherry, cream, mauve, salmon, light lavender-blue, and the like, as well as pure white. They are fine for cutting, having long stems and lasting long in water. The sweet scabious is a biennial but in our severe climate must be treated as an annual, and raised from seed yearly, preferably giving the plants a start indoors and removing them to the open when large enough to handle.

The present day ten-week stock in its fine opulent beauty is little reminiscent of its humble forbear, the little plant with dusty leaves and single blossoms that clings to rocky declivities above the Mediterranean. But the sweetness is the same. Only with the doubling of the petals that has made the modern stocks like spikes of little roses the perfume also has been doubled. The development of the stock from wild-flowerhood to its present state we owe, according to Mrs. Louden, to the patience and skill of the weavers of Saxony. Whole villages were once devoted to this industry and it is said that but one colour was permitted to be grown in each village in order that the strains be kept pure. Once the weavers of Lancashire, England, had a like interest in growing carnations and pinks, and it is pleasant to think of men turning from the labours of the day to such fragrant tasks. Our industrial workers today are too intent upon getting to the movies or speeding in their new Ford cars from one hot-dog stand to another to concern themselves with such matters as stocks and carnations. But to every age its preoccupations.

Stocks like pinks have spices in their throats. Few flowers have a better scent and their colours reproduce those of old and worn chintzes – old rose, dim purple, delicate buff, cream, and so on. Raise them indoors or in a hotbed and plant them out when settled weather comes – and enjoy them for the rest of the summer.

Complaints are being registered against the modern sweet pea. It has lost, say the complainers, its original exquisite fragrance. Today growers talk of "poise" and "brilliance" in connection with this once simple flower, of "waves" and "frills," and there are those who claim that with every wave and frill some of the old sweetness took wing and that there are now many almost scentless varieties. I do not know. I think I never put any sweet pea to the test that disappointed me, though it may be true that the old grandiflora types are sweetest. At any rate let us insist that the name shall not become a misnomer and buy only those which we are sure have the old fragrance.

Do I imagine it or is it a fact that lavender and mauve and purple sweet peas have the sweetest fragrance? White and very pale pink varieties have a delicate "transparent" scent, the purest and most innocent of all perfumes, seemingly. How delightful it is to walk along the rows of sweet peas in the early morning when the dew is still upon them. It is then that they are the sweetest and most refreshing to inhale. It is then also that they should be gathered for the house. If not gathered before ten o'clock they should be left until evening.

The sweet pea is a Sicilian and was discovered in that sunny isle by an Italian monk, Father Francis Cupani, not much more than a hundred years ago, a little catching, clutching plant, with a dull purplish flower. One can imagine perhaps, as the good monk went his way, it caught at the sleeve of his cassock, and freeing himself from its frail clutch its ineffable fragrance caught his nose.* And so history was made. The first sweet pea bloomed in England in the garden of Dr. Uvedale at Enfield in 1813. In 1860 Carter of England

*Editor's note: *The sweet pea is very popular in England and the determined North American can order seeds from Sutton's. In North American garden centres, look for seeds marked 'Old-Fashioned Mixed' or 'Fragrant Mixed'. These older, more fragrant varieties have smaller flowers. To combine fragrance and show, plant some of the larger varieties with the fragrant ones.*

offered nine varieties. But it was not until the latter part of the nineteenth century when Mr. Henry Eckford in England, and Mr. Atlee Burpee in America, gave their minds to the development of the sweet pea, that it became the delight of the flower-growing world.

These are not by any means all the fragrant annuals to be had. A number more are mentioned in other parts of the book under special heads, and there are, besides, certain others that should not be wholly neglected. Among them, *Silene armeria* and *S. compacta* [*S. orientalis*], with spicy fragrance; *Erysimum perofskianum*, with rich orange-hued flowers and a fine wall flower scent; several gilias; the little Californian flower called cream cups, *Platystemon californicus*; *Clarkia breweri*, a charming annual with rose-coloured blossoms and a nice fragrance that comes early from seed and is attractive for beds and borders; and *Linanthus androsaceus*, a tiny, dainty annual that gives out a rich scent in the morning.

CHAPTER VIII

Summer and Autumn Scents

What cordials make this curious broth,
This broth of smells that feeds and
fats my mind?

"THE ODOUR"
— GEORGE HERBERT

AS THE SUMMER WITH ITS increasing light and heat advances fewer perfumes of definite character are noted, but the sultry air is burdened with an agreeable soft medley of odours sweeping in from the hayfields, from the plantations of resinous evergreens and from many kinds of flowers. Aside from the heavy lily scents and some of the elaborate exhalations of the night-blooming annuals, perhaps the most individual odours of the summer garden are derived from certain plants which persons of hyper-sensitive nasal organs may turn from in disgust. I call these plants Nose-twisters, because the rough and heady scent of nasturtium, which seems to have in it something bitter, something peppery, and a vague underlying smoky sweetness, is representative of them, and the name nasturtium, an old Latin word used by Pliny, was derived by him from *narsus*, the nose, and *tortus*, twisted, in reference to the supposed contortions of the nose caused by the hot pungent odour and taste of these flowers. Personally I am very fond of the odour of the Nose-twisters, marigold, calendula, chrysanthemum, tansy, and others of a like bitter pungence, and find it always invigorating and refreshing.

Possibly this taste is inherited for I am told that my Virginian great-grandfather was very partial to it and always insisted upon having a bowl of marigolds at his elbow when they were in season while he wrote his sermons, saying that to smell them cleared his brain. Even to look at marigolds we are told in some old books (and we can well believe it) serves to draw ill-humours from the head.

Calendula, the pot marigold of old days, has much the same scent and gust and its uses were manifold and various. It was famous in the cookery of bygone days when the palate shrank not from strong flavours and the stomach was a hardy and serviceable organ. "The double Marigolds being as bigge as a little rose, is good in stew," declared Lawson in his "Country Housewife's Garden," and all households kept on hand sacks of dried marigold flowers in readiness to meet domestic emergencies whether culinary or medicinal. "Put Marigold flowers in paper bags near the chimney," counsels one old writer, "until they pass the hazard of mouldiness," and when we read of their many important uses we do not wonder they were garnered and preserved with special care.

Steeped in wine marigold flowers were thought to be soothing to a "cold stomach" and surely they would be, and against the tremblings of the heart. They were good for toothache, or to remove warts and moles, and they prevailed against that embarrassing and somewhat mysterious, but seemingly prevalent affliction, "ear-worms." Strengthened by the juice of sage and rue they were good against pestilence. The leaves put into the nostrils cured a head cold and a dye was made from the flowers that "made the haire yellow." And we have hardly begun to recount the uses of this golden flower. The scent too was apparently liked by the fair sex, for Hyll reports that they were employed not only as ornaments of the garden but in "decking up Garlands, bewtifying Nosegayes and to be worne in the bosom."

I am always interested to know that certain flowers were admired by Parkinson. His taste was catholic but now and then he writes of a flower with more than ordinary enjoyment. Of the nasturtium he says it "is of so great beauty and sweetnesse withall that my Garden of delight cannot bee unfurnished of it." And again, "the whole flower hath a fine small sent very pleasing, which being placed in the middle of some Carnations or Gilliflowers (for they are in flower at the same time) make a delicate Tussimussie, as they call it, or Nosegay, both for sight and sent." Perhaps we should not today care for this combination but I can imagine that the two odours might be good together. Other plants which may be classed with the Nose-twisters, and which are spoken of elsewhere, are artemisias, fennel, tansy, rue and chrysanthemums. One old book says of tansy, somewhat ambiguously, that it has "a strong, disagreeable, peculiar, fragrant odour."

The most artificial of roses seems to me to have a sweet naturalness about it, the wildest of lilies to appear stiff and sophisticated. So the scent of the rose is ever refreshing and innocent and that of the lily languorous and decadent. I cannot say that I truly enjoy the scent of any lily; there is in all of them despite the sweetness something brooding and sultry that is enervating and vaguely unwholesome. Of course mingled with the odours of other flowers and diffused in the outside air it seldom becomes too apparent, but none of the scented lilies it seems to me should be brought indoors. In those days when the odours of many flowers were seriously believed to prevail as cures, or the reverse, that of the lily was deemed injurious. "Notwithstanding the sweet and delicious odour of the Lily of the garden," says one writer, "it becomes deleterious when freely inhaled in an apartment. Grave accidents and even death itself is reported to have resulted from individuals having remained exposed to the emanations of Lily flowers during the night."

In Langham's "Garden of Health," he says of the lily, "The flower is euill for the Plague." And this belief is borne out by van Oosten writing more than a hundred years later, "Lillies have a refreshing smell though many cannot endure it. It is said that in the time of Plague they must be avoided."

There is, however, to controvert this belief an old Romanian superstition which runs, "Show me a house where lilies grow and you'll show me a house where the plague cannot go." And it is only fair to remember that the "great white lily," the Madonna lily, the annunciation lily, has been perhaps the best loved flower of all times, and that long ago when only virtue in flowers and plants was truly esteemed, the white lily was loved for its loveliness. In 1578 Henry Lyte wrote in praise of the "white and sweet smelling Lillies," and earlier still Bartolomaeus (1495) said, "nothing is more gracious than the Lily in fairness of colour, in sweetness of smell, and in effect of working and virtue." And its virtues were many. It was believed to be a cure for Dropsy, dull ears, faint heart, "Byles, Fellons and Unecomes," and much more of a like serious and alarming nature. It was the root of the white "Lyllie" stamped usually in rosewater or honey that was made use of in many of these cases but the seeds and the flowers also had their importance.

Many lilies, particularly those of scarlet or orange colouring, have little or no scent and there are a few kinds that possess an actively unpleasant odour. Reginald Farrer with characteristic vigour called *Lilium pyrenaicum* "a stinking yellow horror" and added, "May dogs devour its hateful bulbs!" Miss Jekyll does not improve the case for this species by declaring that it smells like a mangy dog. Other lilies that are unfortunate in having a fusty, stuffy odour are *L. monadelphum* var. *szovitzianum*, *L. pomponium* and *L. sargentiae*, but none of these possess the virulence of *L. pyreneicum*, and indeed need not be fought shy of at all.

To me the strong unctuous scent of *Lilium auratum*, and even, though to a lesser degree, of *L. speciosum*, is almost as unpleasant as any of the foregoing but my prejudice is not generally shared. American lilies, many of them, especially the Eastern species, have little or no perfume and when this attribute is present it appeals to me as far more simple and ethereal than that of the European or the Oriental lilies. The southern swamp lily, *L. michauxii* [*L. carolinianum*], has a light and pleasing breath, rather refreshing. It is orange-colored with purple spots. Mrs. Fox, in "Garden Cinderellas," describes the wood lily of Northwestern California, *L. kelloggii*, as having a unique fragrance, a little like clematis. Parry's lily, that is found in Southern California and Arizona, has long chrome-yellow funnel shaped blossoms of which an admirer writes, "No lily of the wide world has a more delightful fragrance." The chaparral lily, *L. rubescens,* is freshly and quite keenly fragrant. The flowers are pale lilac upon opening but become rosy-purple as they age. And the beautiful white blooms of the Washington lily, *L. washingtonianum,* have a really fine and uncloying scent.

Among European lilies, *L.* x *testaceum,* a very hardy and easily grown kind, aside from its other good qualities, possesses an agreeable odour something in the way of the Madonna lily but less strong and penetrating. The perfume of the Madonna lily, *L. candidum,* and its "invariable six-petalled chalice of silver," is happily well known the world over. Mr. Bowles writes enthusiastically of the daffodil-yellow bells of *L. monadelphum,* which emit whiffs of blended essence of hyacinth and poet's narcissus, "almost too much of a good thing early in the evening when this lily seems to concentrate its efforts on advertising its presence."

And here are the Asiatic lilies:

L. auratum and its many varieties, heavy languorous scent.

L. brownii. One of the most beautiful of lilies. Sir Herbert Maxwell refers to the "delicious incense" of this species.

L. cernuum. Nodding purplish flowers with a light scent.

Cardiocrinum giganteum [*L. giganteum*]. I have never seen this great lily in bloom. It is a Himalayan species with immensely tall stems bearing heart-shaped leaves and great tubular white blossoms that pour out a fragrance that has been compared to honeysuckle and which carries to a distance of many yards.

L. hansonii. A handsome orange-coloured lily with a curiously indefinable fragrance. Mr. Ellwanger speaks of it as an Oriental odour and says you would know it came from Japan with your eyes shut.

L. japonicum [*L. krameri*]. A finely scented and lovely pink flowered lily whose scent is much like that of *L. regale,* though not so strong.

L. longiflorum, the Easter lily. Pure white with powerful fragrance.

L. nepalense. A lily of tender constitution that should grow in a greenhouse. The blossoms are scented.

L. philippinense, the Philippine lily. A low-growing kind with a long funnel that emits a rich and agreeable odour. White.

L. primulinum [*L. ochraceum*], the ochre lily. A note comes from B.Y. Morrison to the effect that this Burmese species has a delicious scent much like that of *Magnolia glauca* – and what could be better? It is a tender species fitter for a pot than the open ground.

L. pumilum [*L. tenuifolium*], the coral lily. The brilliant waxen vermilion flowers of this small species have a fine scent. Good in the rock garden.

L. regale, the regal lily. One of the finest and most easily grown of all lilies. The scent is powerful but has a slight spiciness which keeps it from seeming oppressive.

L. rubellum. An enchanting small lily good to

grow in the rock garden where it is happy in peaty soil among low shrubs. The clear pink flowers are very fragrant.

L. speciosum and its many varieties. Too strongly scented to be agreeable to me. Mrs. Fox quotes someone as saying "it has the sweet fragrance of petunia" – a rather mawkish scent.

L. sulphureum. Large fragrant funnel-shaped flowers, pale sulphur yellow in colour flushed claret and pink on the outside. Upper Burma.

L. wallichianum var. *neilgherrense* [*L. neilgherrense*] An Indian species with cream white tube-shaped flowers that are fragrant.

Notholirion thomsonianum [*L. thomsonianum*]. Funnel shaped rose coloured flowers that are sweet scented.

For a long season in summer the fragrance of the tall multicolored phlox dominates the garden. It is a warm sweet perfume that seems appropriate to the sultry heavy weather. And the hotter the day the stronger and more insistent becomes the breath of the phlox. I do not agree with Mr. Bowles' captious and somewhat too selective nose that the scent is a combination of pepper and pigstye. But it is one that I do not want too much of in a room. Nearly all members of the phlox family have a sweet scent though it is very faint in some. The chaste *P. maculata* 'Miss Lingard' is to my nose quite without fragrance.

The musk mallow, *Malva moschata,* is a charming flower of the summer that is fragrant in all its parts; the leaves as well as flowers have a soft musky odour. The plants grow about two feet tall, bushy and prodigally floriferous, bearing masses of satin-smooth flowers like small hollyhocks, white or mauve. They are good for cutting as well as for border decoration and have a long period of bloom. Miss Jekyll is responsible for the suggestion, delightful when tried, of planting the musk Mallows with steel-blue *Eryngiums,* sea hollies. *Malva moschata* grows wild in parts of Europe and in Britain and Gray notes it as one of the plants that has found its way from abroad into our own hospitable wild, but I have never happened to come upon it outside a garden.

Perhaps to ask of the delphinium more than caerulean colour is to be inordinately greedy, but when I discovered a few years ago that I had raised (from Thompson & Morgan's seed) some delphiniums that had the fragrance quite definitely of heliotrope I was enchanted. I know now that sweet scented delphiniums are not uncommon but I have so far seen no strain advertised as fragrant. How it would sell! For blue flowers with a sweet odour are not many. The Himalayan species, *D. brunonianum,* is a handsome plant with a spike of large blue-purple flowers that smell strongly of musk.

Several of the bush clematis add a honey-like sweetness to the blend of summer essences. *Clematis recta,* a good border plant, produces from June to August masses of small creamy white flowers that have a vanilla-like scent, much like that of the popular Japanese climber, *C. terniflora* [*C. paniculata*], but less penetrating. *C. heracleifolia* is a good summer border plant of spreading habit about four feet tall and woody at the base. The cold blue bellshaped flowers borne in profusion and for a long period "smell of ripe 'Greengages'" and the leaves when dying of newmown hay. Its fine variety, *C. heracleifolia* var. *Davidiana*, is perhaps a better plant and its flowers have a fragrance seemingly compounded of lemon and spices – a most pronounced and appetizing odour. I have news also of *C.* x *aromatica*, a hybrid of or allied to the climbing *Viticella*, a slender subshrubby plant four to six feet in height, semi-scandent, with solitary rich purple blue flowers having a delicate slightly aromatic odour.

From the various kinds of evening primroses come an assortment of pleasing scents; from the genus *Buddleja*, called summer lilacs, a richer aroma, honey-sweet and hanging sometimes rather heavy in the brooding steamy air. Where gorse (*Ulex*) is grown, and it is not often enough grown in American gardens, it fills the air with its young springlike sweetness. The sweetbrier makes itself known too, especially after rain, and from the pool the delicious scents of waterlilies seem to be the very breath of summer. Bergamot is in full flower in July and there are several kinds good to have, not only for the sake of their showy blossoms but for their aromatic leaves. The tall *Campanula lactiflora* belies its family scentlessness and gives off an agreeable sweetness, a little like newmown hay in quality. This is a fine plant to use in breaking the wheel-like regularity of the phloxes, and with its soft colours, cool blue or cream, takes the curse off their ubiquitous rosiness, though it does not quite last them out.

CLEMATIS
(*Clematis paniculata*)

A plant of old fashioned gardens is *Hosta plantaginea* var. *grandiflora* [*Funkia subcordata grandiflora*], the plantain lily, Corfu lily, or "old white" day lily. It is one of the plants that all who grew up in the country know well, for there were few gardens of a decade or two ago where this handsome tuberous-rooted Japanese plant was not grown in distressing round beds upon the lawn or set to fill dank situations at the edge of over-clogged shrubberies. My first recollection of it was in a deserted garden in Delaware persisting in the tangled grass beneath intensely tall high-branched evergreen trees of some sort, a garden that I used to steal into whenever happy chance offered, to play alone through the long summer days, as children love to do, at being a princess, a gypsy, a great actress.

To smell the old white day lily brings back those days and that enchanted old garden to me with poignant clarity. Doubtless the garden was long ago reclaimed or is lost beneath the inexorable march of some development scheme, but for me it will always live, enchantment, youth, high aspirations, and all, so long as the frosted white day lilies make their punctual appearance in my garden.

The plantain lily deserves a better fate than lozenge beds or dank shrubbery, indeed it makes one of the finest of border plants, neat and adequate at all seasons and bringing to the late summer, that somewhat lax and disorderly season, a certain prim seemliness and coolness of aspect that is grateful to the eye. Contrary to common belief it does not prefer to grow in dank shade, though it will endure there with the stoicism of its countrymen, but likes a place in the sun as well as most other plants, and only asks a soil that is not bone dry and is fairly rich.

In southern gardens the tender *Crinum* species, with handsome foliage and great umbels of beautiful lily-like flowers, white or pink, give off a delightful fragrance. In the North these same tender kinds may also be used and the roots taken up in the autumn and cared for as are dahlias. But *Crinum* x *powellii,* a hybrid, is hardy as far north as New York and a group of them makes an extremely handsome feature in the garden, with large pink, white or purplish flowers. The bulbs should be planted two to three feet apart and two and one half to three inches deep to the bottom of the bulb.

A hardy amaryllis-like plant with fragrant flowers is *Lycoris squamigera.* It is not as often seen as it deserves to be, for its great pinky-lilac lily-like flowers borne in a cluster at the top of a stem two to three feet high are very ornamental in the summer garden. The finest I ever saw were in the late Mrs. John Wood Stuart's lovely garden, Solana, at Northport, Long Island. *Lycoris squamigera* is a Japanese plant. It sends up its foliage in the spring but dies down in June and not until August does the flower stem make its appearance. It flourishes in shade.

A bed of heliotrope brings as much pleasure to the nose as anything that can be had in the summer garden. This plant, *Heliotropium arborescens* [*H. peruvianum*], to give its full title, was introduced to greenhouse culture from Peru in 1757. It sprang into immediate popularity because of its exquisite perfume and today is one of the most popular of bedding plants. But not by any means is all heliotrope fragrant and I have been disappointed more than once in sending for plants by mail to receive varieties that were practically scentless. Buy your heliotropes where you can smell them first. The odour of heliotrope is said to resemble that of cherry pie, hence its common name, but I have never been able to detect this likeness. In the garden heliotrope requires full sun and a rich soil. I always plant heliotropes in my rose beds and find the combination a pleasing one and apparently the two get along very well together.

And now it seems that through the skill and industry of Dr. Forman McLean of the New York Botanical Garden, we are actually to have fragrance instilled into the gorgeous gladioli, and this desirable occurrence is not to be "merely a pipe dream of optimistic gardeners" but a reality. Last winter while wandering about one of the plant houses at the Botanical Garden I came upon several flats of what appeared to be very slender and delicate gladioli, but sniffing them I decided that they could not be for they had the fresh sweet odour of freesias. However, gladioli they proved to be indeed, Dr. McLean's babies, as the attendant explained to me. Thirteen years it has taken to bring into being what Dr. McLean calls his sweetglads. They are still slender and soft colored but growing steadily in strength year by year. It is with the blood of certain wild species that this miracle is being worked. Several of the Cape species are sweet scented, among them *Gladiolus tristis*, a night blooming, night scented kind with soft yellow flowers borne on slender stalks that wave in the night breezes, scattering perfume like fairy censers. Other sweet scented species are *G. liliaceus* [*G. grandis*], *G. recurvus, G. maculatus, G. gracilis, G. tenellus,* and *G. alatus*. All of them are much more slender and fragile appearing than the splendours of the modern garden, but a little less splendour, dare I say it, and a little more grace would, it seems to me, be acceptable, and the sweetglads with their soft colours and delicious fragrance may be just what we have been longing for. Certain of the wild species are procurable in this country and would be interesting to experiment with, especially the night-flowering *G. tristis*. Some of the more slender species might be introduced into the rock garden.

Artemisia lactiflora is a Chinese plant introduced to gardens in fairly recent years and justly popular. It is very valuable as a tall summer-flowering border plant and its large panicles of fragrant milk-white flowers are always an attractive feature. *Adenophora lillifolia*, a relation of the campanulas, is valuable in the late garden both for its pyramids of pale lavender bells and for their agreeable fragrance. It is a native of Europe and Asia.

And as the autumn draws on, the sturdy *Caryopteris incana* [*C. mastacantha*], with masses of lavender-blue flowers, makes a pleasant haze of colour in the borders and regales us with a rich and pungent scent if we pinch its leaves. *C. mongholica* is a newcomer to my garden; it is a somewhat shrubby plant with the characteristic aromatic leaves, and lavender-blue flowers in broad heads. The Himalayan knotweed, *Polygonum polystachyum*, blooms in September and fills the air with sweetness until the first frosts cut short its exuberance. But beware of it, for under ground it is up to no good, and is weaving a tough network of rope-like roots almost impossible to eradicate once they are established.

There are scents abroad in the still autumn days whose composition it is impossible to analyze. Go out of doors on a dull November day and sniff the breeze. Brown leaves lie all about you, the garden beds are almost bare, yet the air is full of strange perfumes, stimulating and full of vitality. The tang of bitter-sweet chrysanthemums is there, the acrid fumes of wood smoke, the rich pungence of trodden walnut leaves, and now and then one catches a whiff of pure spring, perhaps caught by the breeze from the thready blossoms of the witch hazel that "by their color as well as fragrance belong to the saffron dawn of the year, suggesting amid all the signs of autumn, falling leaves and frost, that the life of nature, by which she eternally flourishes, is untouched."

Often I have followed a scent up the breeze on a sharp autumn day to find at the end of the quest a witch hazel thicket, or even a single tree, in its quaint regalia. When you draw near and thrust your nose among the blossoms you perceive little or no perfume unless you crush them, but withdraw and go about other affairs and the sweetest airs will overtake and envelop you. Sitting one Indian Summer's day this autumn in the lovely garden of Rollo Peters with several members of that delightful South Mountain group of craftsmen, we suddenly became aware of a distinct but intermittent fragrance. All about us were the amber and russet tags of the spent summer, no flower was in sight. We were curious and looked about and presently we saw bending over the near-by brook a crooked witch hazel in full flower. The fantastic little tree was sending us messages, remaining quiet for a time and then again seeking to get in touch with us. When we came close to it, it withheld its sweetness.

After the first frosts many odours are released to the world. From the herb garden especially comes a rich melange of scents; heliotrope is penetrating in its sweetness after a first nipping; from the roadside where wild grapes still hang comes a winy aroma, and from dying fern fronds that curiously heady odour of earth and herbage which is especially theirs. Our sense of smell seems to become keener with the sharpness in the air and we note the fragrance of the pine, the sweet resinous tang of the red cedar, and better still that of the savin juniper, which has a rich underlying bitterness that is most invigorating. And on the warm side of the arbor vitae hedge we catch a scent of ripe strawberries, and note that the scent of the Douglas fir is good close at hand and is also carried to a considerable distance.

And then there comes one day the peculiar sharp and penetrating fragrance of new fallen snow, the purest and most innocent of all scents, yet perhaps the most exciting. It fills the world and seems to penetrate our apathy, inciting us to work hard and to play hard until again creep into our consciousness those first disturbing aromas of a new order, those delicate airs that presage the coming of spring, that no barriers of brick or stone can keep out, no city stenches disguise, because they are generated in great part within ourselves.

I have today received these lines from Margaret McKenny, and she gives me permission to use them at the close of this chapter.

JANUARY DAWN

The snow still lies upon the ground,
And yet I feel
The shadow of the scent of flowers;
Breathless the firs against the gray—
So still the air
That hung upon a bare rose spray
Are drops of rain
Left there by midnight showers—

. . . . .

Black head atilt
A chickadee
Whistles the first love-notes of the year.

CHAPTER IX

Hardy Shrubs with Fragrant Flowers or Leaves

I will no longer permit the avid and eager eye to steal away my whole attention. I will learn to enjoy more completely all the varied wonders of the earth.

— DAVID GRAYSON

HARDY SHRUBS AND TREES possessing the attraction of fragrance are so many that there is no reason why our gardens, even small gardens, should not include a number, some being in evidence all through the growing season. In the following notes an attempt has been made to specify the exact degree of hardiness of each kind named but in general Washington may be regarded as the dividing line between north and south. Thus the shrubs listed in this chapter are suitable for use in gardens north of Washington, unless otherwise specified, though some will not stand out in the coldest localities.

Abelia chinensis. China. July, August. A neat and graceful deciduous shrub three to four feet tall bearing clusters of fragrant flowers during the summer and sometimes into the autumn. It is of doubtful hardiness north of New York save in sheltered locations. *A. grandiflora* is said to be somewhat hardier. It grows taller and its slender arching branches are sprigged with white rose-tinted blossoms continuously from June to September. Of garden origin. *A. triflora* is a compact evergreen shrub from the milder sections of the Himalayas that bears long clusters of lightly scented pink flowers in summer. It is not hardy north of Washington.

Aesculus parviflora. Dwarf buckeye. This little tree is a native of the Southeastern States. When well blossomed out with its feathery white and pink flowers, like those of a fairy horse chestnut, it is a charming sight. Slightly fragrant. Said to be hardy north.

Amelanchier asiatica. Chinese serviceberry. Japan, Korea and Manchuria. Unlike those of our American serviceberries, the misty white blossoms of this oriental species are delicately fragrant. The tree blooms later than our native species.

Andromeda (See *Pieris*).

Artemisia abrotanum. Southernwood. Lad's love. Old-man. A low growing hoary evergreen shrub with richly aromatic feathery foliage. Found often in old gardens and once played a part in every cottager's nosegay. Few sweeter are to be devised than southernwood and white moss rosebuds. The scent of southernwood is stimulating and refreshing and in times gone it was used to keep away moths. It gives its yellow blossoms only in hot summers. Hardy in New York.

Azalea (See *Rhododendron*).

Berberis. The barberries are valued chiefly for their pleasing forms and gay berries, but many of them bear distinctly fragrant flowers. The common barberry, *B. vulgaris,* that is so widely naturalized in the Eastern States as to seem a true son of the soil, bears quantities of hanging yellow flowers in spring, the odour of which close at hand is somewhat overpowering, though pleasant enough when borne on a wandering breeze from a little distance. *B. verruculosa* is a most delightful small evergreen with spiny leaves that turn a fine colour in autumn, and small richly scented yellow flowers. Hardy in New York and good for rock gardens. *B. buxifolia* (*B. dulcis*) grows to a fair height and presents a remarkably attractive appearance in April when hung all over with a vast number of little golden globes that fill the air with sweetness. According to Sir Herbert Maxwell it is one of the three shrubs that more than any others perfume the air of spring. The others are *Azara microphylla,* a Chilean as is the above, and *Erica arborea.* These are not hardy but *Berberis buxifolia* will stand the winter North if protected and given a sheltered situation. *B. dielsiana* is one of the new Chinese barberries. It is hardy, grows ten feet tall and bears quantities of dropping racemes of highly fragrant flowers.

Among other barberries with fragrant flowers are *B. actinacantha,* a deciduous shrub from the mountains of Chile, with crooked branches hung in spring with fragrant yellow flowers; *B. heteropoda,* Turkestan, growing six feet tall, with greyish leaves and yellow sweet scented flowers in spring, and certain species of *Mahonia. Mahonia japonica* is a charming shrub that smells like a whole bed of lily-of-the-valley when it blooms in early spring; *M. aquifolium,* our native Oregon grape of the Northwest, bears curious nubs of yellow flowers in early spring that have a peculiar but agreeable odour; *M. nervosa,* and *M. repens* are low-growing shrubs hardy in New England, and good for undergrowth, *M. nepaulensis* is a shrub of the Himalayas used in California and other mild climates. The mahonias are justly famous for their fine lustrous foliage. There are so many barberries of recent introduction that it is impossible to fully list them here.

Buddleja. The blossoms of many of these deciduous shrubs are exceedingly sweet scented. The kind most commonly seen in Northern gardens is *B. davidii* and its several varieties, known as summer lilac, or butterfly bush. About midsummer it hangs out a shower of honey-scented lilac blooms in long cylindrical tails, lasting over a long period.

Buxus. Box tree. The odour of box while stimulating to many is not by any means agreeable to all persons. Like the sweetbrier its shining leaves give off an especially keen fragrance after a shower of rain, when many persons find it oppressive and vaguely disturbing. Oliver Wendell Holmes thought it the most memory stirring of all scents. In "Elsie Venner" there is this passage: "They walked over the crackling leaves in the garden, between the lines of box, breathing its fragrance of eternity; for this is one of the odors which carry us out of time into the abysses of the unbeginning past; if we ever lived on another ball of stone than this, it must be that there was box growing on it." Long ago box was associated with holly and yew as festal decorations. Herrick says of the box: "It was once a time-honoured custom on Candlemas day to replace the Christmas evergreens with sprays of box, which were kept till Easter Eve, when they gave place to the yew."

Calycanthus floridus. Sweet shrub. Strawberry shrub. Carolina allspice. A wild shrub of the Southern States but long inured to garden ways. No garden of a generation ago but had its bush of sweet shrub near the door and children sought its little brown blossoms eagerly to tie tightly in the corners of small grimy handkerchiefs to take to school or Sunday school to regale their spirits with its good scent during the long hours of durance. Alice Morse Earle wrote of the scent of the *Calycanthus* blooms: "They have an aromatic fragrance somewhat like the ripest pineapples of the tropics, but still richer; how I love to carry them in my hand, crushed and warm, occasionally holding them tight over my mouth and nose to fill myself with their perfume. The leaves have a similar, but somewhat sharper scent, and the woody stems another; the latter I like to nibble."

Ceanothus americanus. New Jersey tea. Wild snowball. Mountainsweet. A pretty little native deciduous shrub with heads of small white flowers that appear in summer and are agreeably, though not strongly, fragrant. Said to have been used in the place of tea in Colonial times.

Cephalanthus occidentalis. Button bush or honey balls. A native shrub that haunts water courses in the Eastern States North and South and as far West as Arizona. It blossoms in summer, the small white tubular blossoms being borne in dense spherical heads. They remain in perfection for a long time and have a rich fragrance. Very attractive to bees.

Chionanthus virginica. Fringe tree. Old-man's beard. Southern Pennsylvania to Florida and Texas. A small round-topped tree that veils itself in loose panicles of white flowers, like fringe, in June. They are slightly fragrant. One of the most beautiful of our native trees. *C. retusa* is a Chinese species that thrives in moist soil of a peaty nature and prefers partial shade. The flowers are pure white and fragrant.

Cladrastis lutea. Kentucky yellow-wood or virgilia. Rarest of the trees of North America. Found principally on the limestone cliffs of Kentucky, Tennessee and North Carolina, but it is hardy in the North and rather extensively cultivated. The flowers are white, pea-shaped and borne in long terminal panicles. They are slightly fragrant and rival the blossoms of the lime in their attractiveness to bees. *C. sinensis* is a Chinese species, a tall tree bearing erect panicles of bluish white odorous flowers.

Clethra alnifolia. Honey-sweet or sweet pepper

bush. This lovely shrub is found chiefly in shaded lanes along the eastern seacoast. The white flowers borne in terminal spikes are so fragrant as to scent all the countryside during the period of their blossoming. About Gloucester, Mass., the sweet pepper is called "sailor's delight" because the men on incoming ships catch its sweetness when still far at sea. *C. acuminata* and *C. tomentosa* are other ornamental and fragrant members of this genus. When bruised, *Clethra* leaves emit a curious odour. *C. barbinervis* is a Chinese shrub of dwarf, spreading habit, bearing smaller terminal flower spikes than do the American species. *C. delavayi,* recently introduced from China, is said to be the finest of the genus. *C. arborea* is an evergreen species from Madeira cultivated in greenhouses. All are very fragrant.

HONEY-SWEET
(*Clethra alnifolia*)

Comptonia (See *Myrica*).

Corylopsis. Winter hazel. Very desirable shrubs from Asia, related to the witch hazels. They hang out nodding racemes of cowslip-scented and cowslip-coloured flowers before the leaves appear. All the species that I know are hardy as far north as New York City but will require protection and shelter in colder localities. The best are *C. pauciflora, C. spicata* and *C. glabrescens,* [*C. gotoana*], one of Mr. Wilson's Japanese discoveries. Good also is *C. sinensis* var. *calvescens.*

Cotoneaster henryanus. A semi-evergreen shrub growing to twelve feet with fragrant small flowers followed by clusters of red fruit. Not hardy north.

Crataegus laevigata [*C. oxyacantha*]. Hawthorn. May. The hawthorn is a beautiful and beloved feature of the English landscape. When the trees are decked with the white blossoms during May the whole countryside is sweet with them. Chaucer wrote:

> There sawe I eke the fresh
> hauthorne
> In white Motley, that so
> swete doth smell.

There are several forms of the above and those with pink or rose or white double flowers are very lovely. 'Paul's Scarlet' is not fragrant. The blossoms of some of the American thorns have a most abominable odour, among them *C. intricata* [*C. coccinea*] and *C. tomentosa.* But the Mount Sinai thorn, *C. azarolus* var. *sinaica,* of the Orient, and *C. tanacetifolia,* of Asia Minor, have very sweet scented blossoms in early summer.

Cytisus. The common broom, *Cytisus scoparius,* has become naturalized in many localities in this country, so that its golden honey-scented bloom is familiar to many. There are numerous varieties of it that are well worth growing, notably the 'Moonlight Broom', *C. scoparius* 'Sulphureus' and the yellow and russet *C. scoparius* 'Andreanus'. The white Portugal broom, *Chamaecytisus albus,* has a delicate fragrance, but the beautiful Warminster broom, *C.* × *praecox,* so lovely and so early to bloom, has a heavy stuffing odour. *C. purgans,* the auvergne broom, a native of the mountains of France, is a low bush bearing in April and May a cloud of yellow sweet scented flowers. The brooms might well be made more use of in American gardens for our conditions of heat and sunlight suit them, and their stems, bright green and effective all through the winter, are valuable in any scheme of winter gardening.

Daphne mezereum. Mezereon. The hedgerows are bare and the birds for the most part still silent when the mezereon begins to wrap its stiff branches in rosy bloom, flooding the cold spring air with sweetness of a rare kind. It is a little shrub, hardy and for a partially shaded situation. The genus is rich in fragrant plants. *D. alpina,* a small deciduous shrub, native of the European Alps, has slender downy twigs and highly perfumed white flowers borne in terminal clusters in spring. *D. blagayana,* a charming small evergreen, growing no more than a foot high, has deliciously sweet white flowers crowded together in terminal heads. *D. caucasica,* native in the Caucasus, bears richly fragrant white flowers. *D. cneorum,* the well-beloved garland flower, is evergreen and gives its pink flowers in May and frequently again in the autumn. *D. sericea* [*D. collina*] is also evergreen, but coming from Italy and Crete, is not as hardy as some of the other species. Its sweet scented purple flowers are borne in terminal heads. *D. genkwa,* one of the most enchanting little shrubs in my rock garden, is deciduous and a native of China and Japan. The flowers are like little lilacs and appear before the leaves. *D.* × *napolitana* is low and dense in habit, forming what Reginald Farrer calls comfortable-looking round puddings, two or three feet high, the leaves grey-green and the little bush covered in summer with heads of silky lilac sweetness. Of easy culture. *D. petraea,* says Mr. Farrer, "dwells high and far in the Southern Alps, confined to one small district, and there haunting hot and terrible cliff-faces of rose-grey limestone fronting the full radiance of the Italian sun." It is a small evergreen with small shining foliage and at the end of every shoot is a cluster of three or four "big waxy tubes of the most crystalline pure texture, the most brilliant clear colour, and the most intoxicating fragrance."

Elaeagnus angustifolia. Oleaster. Russian olive. Mediterranean region. A spreading somewhat spiny bush with whitish leaves and small very highly perfumed yellow flowers borne in the axils of the leaves in summer. The Portuguese call it the tree of paradise because of the rare fragrance of the flowers. Hardy in the coldest regions. *E. multiflora* [*E. longipes*] is a very desirable Japanese shrub with dark reddish twigs and dark green leaves that are silvery on the undersides, and yellowish white fragrant flowers. *E.* 'Quicksilver' is one of the most striking oleasters and the only species native in North America. It grows from six to ten feet tall and bears narrow tubular drooping flowers, silvery outside and yellow within, that exhale a fine perfume when they appear in May. Other oleasters with fragrant flowers are *E. macrophylla,* an evergreen from Japan and Formosa, with yellow flowers, that is hardy only in the far South; *E. glabra,* from Japan and China, a half climbing shrub to twenty feet, flowering in autumn; *E. pungens,* with variegated leaf forms, also flowering in autumn, but hardy only in the South and used in greenhouses; *E. umbellata,* a Japanese species, deciduous, flowering in May and June. All the oleasters have more or less showy fruits; that of *E. multiflora* is said to make delicious jams and jellies.

Forsythia. The golden bells have a delicate spring-like aroma.

Fothergilla. Little known American shrubs native

in the Alleghany Mountains and adjacent sections of the Southeastern States. They are close to the witch hazels and resemble them in foliage, but the flowers are quite distinct, consisting of "long erect white stamens tipped with yellow anthers crowded together in ovoid, rounded two-inch high clusters at the ends of innumerable naked branchlets. The whole inflorescence is fragrant and very conspicuous, resembling a bottle brush, and quite different from that of any other hardy northern shrub." The leaves assume a brilliant crimson in autumn. Three species are recognized, *F. gardenii*, slender and growing no more than a yard high; *F. major*, growing ten feet high, with glaucous leaves; *F. monticola*, not quite so tall and more spreading in growth. *Fothergillas* are hardy in Massachusetts and grow in any ordinarily good soil.

Franklinia alatamaha [*Gordonia alatamaha*]. This is the only species of this tropical and sub-tropical genus that is hardy north. A handsome shrub growing finally to a height of twenty feet, with bright shining leaves that turn a fine crimson in the autumn. The fragrant white flowers are three inches across and are set off by a fine bunch of golden stamens. It is one of the few shrubs that flowers in the autumn. Native in Georgia, but now known only in cultivation. Hardy in Massachusetts.

Fraxinus sieboldiana [*F. mariesii*]. This is one of the most beautiful of the flowering ashes. It is a deciduous tree reaching a height of about twenty feet and bears in May white or purplish flowers that are highly fragrant. It is native in Central China and not hardy north of Washington. *F. ornus*, the manna ash, belongs to southern Europe and Western Asia. It grows sixty feet tall and bears tassels of grey-white flowers that are sweet scented.

Genista hispanica. Spanish broom. A hardy and attractive broom bearing in profusion yellow honey-scented flowers. The Mt. Etna broom, *Genista aetnaensis*, though found in Sicily and Sardinia, is said to be one of the hardiest of the race and a good subject for poor sun-baked positions. It is a graceful shrub of tall, drooping habit, materializing showers of scented yellow blooms upon its almost naked green shoots in summer.

Halimodendron halodendron (*H. argenteum*). Salt tree. A not very attractive bush of irregular habit from Siberia, growing six feet tall with whitish leaves and stems and bearing in May short clusters of fragrant purple pea-shaped blossoms. Hardy north.

Hamamelis mollis is the handsomest and most fragrant of the winter blooming witch hazels. The scarlet and gold fringy blossoms exhale a dusty sweet scent that is perceptible at quite a distance from the little tree and it presents a gay appearance in the cold February garden. *H. japonica* and the native *H. vernalis* are less noticeably fragrant and less showy.

Leucothoe fontanesiana. Dog hobble. This handsome broad-leaved evergreen shrub is native in the Southern States but is hardy in the North, though requiring some protection as far north as Massachusetts. The drooping wandlike branches are clothed in thick shining leaves that redden handsomely in the autumn. The flowers are white and waxen, bell-shaped and open at the tips of the branches in May.

Lindera benzoin [*Benzoin aestivale*]. Spice bush. Benjamin bush. A charming little tree found in low ground and bending over water courses in the Eastern States and Canada from Maine to Ontario,

Michigan, Kansas and southwards. Bark and fruit and leaf are aromatic but the quaint fringy yellow blossoms, that offer us so sprightly a welcome in early spring, are scentless.

Liriodendron tulipifera. Tulip tree. One of the tallest and finest of our native trees, reaching a height of one hundred and ninety feet. The greenish yellow "tulips" that make the tree a most decorative object in May are fragrant and the petals are coated with a sticky honeylike substance.

TULIP TREE
(*Liriodendron tulipifera*)

Lonicera. The bush honeysuckles are not all gifted with sweet scented flowers but many of them are highly fragrant. *L. fragrantissima* and *L. standishii* are mentioned in the chapter on Earliest Scents. *L. angustifolia* is a deciduous shrub from the Himalayas growing eight feet tall and bearing pink and white fragrant blossoms in May and June. *L. alberti* is from Turkestan. It has narrow bluish leaves and sweet scented rosy-lilac blossoms and grows about four feet tall. *L. myrtilloides* is a deciduous shrub three to four feet tall, native of the Himalayas, with pinky-white fragrant flowers in May. Another Himalayan species is *L. rupicola,* a dense bush bearing profusely pale pink, very fragrant blossoms in May. The flowers of *L. syringantha* are lilac in colour and lilac-scented. It is a native of Tibet and blooms in May and June, a rather straggling shrub but indispensable because of its very fine scent. *L. syringantha* var. *wolfii* is a finer shrub than the type. Its flowers look and smell much like Persian lilacs. *L. maackii* is one of the best of the bush honeysuckles. It grows from six to ten feet tall, making an open bush and bears profusely creamy-white scented blossoms in pairs in the axils of the leaves in May and June.

L. nitida is slightly fragrant and *L. thibetica,* with lavender flowers produced in May and June on partly prostrate branches, is more so. *L. pileata,* the privet honeysuckle, with semi-evergreen leaves and almost prostrate habit, opens creamy fragrant flowers in April.

Magnolia. The flowers of many of these magnificent shrubs and trees are rich in fragrance. The best for scent among American species is *M. virginiana,* sweet bay, which in the North makes a large open bush but in the South grows to great proportions, eventually reaching a height of seventy feet. It has dark, lustrous leaves and bears during a long period in the summer small cup-shaped white flowers that give one of the best of outdoor scents – cool and fruity and sweet. (I read that the perfume of the sweet bay is not agreeable to all; that it sometimes causes uneasiness in the chest and a tendency to fainting.) It is hardy in Massachusetts and grows wild in low ground and swamps from Massachusetts to Louisiana and southern Arkansas. *M. acuminata,* the cucumber tree, is a handsome American tree found wild from western New York to Ohio and southwards. The small greenish yellow blossoms are only faintly scented. Hardy as far north as Hanover, New Hampshire. *M. macrophylla* is hardy in Massa-

chusetts though its natural home is in the Carolinas and southwards. It has the largest leaves of any magnolia and the huge creamy blossoms are from eight to twelve inches across and very sweet scented. It is a magnificent tree and worthy of greater attention than it receives. The earliest flowering native species is *M. fraseri,* a deciduous tree of open spreading habit that is hardy in Massachusetts, though of southern origin. The flowers unfortunately have an unpleasant odour as have those of the umbrella tree, *M. tripetala.* The former, however, makes a handsome tree for isolated planting. The blossoms are white and held well above the tips of the branches. May.

Earliest to flower of the hardy Asiatic magnolias is *M. stellata,* described in an earlier chapter. This is quickly followed by the stately Yulan, *M. denudata,* one of the most beautiful of flowering trees. *M. sieboldii* [*M. parviflora*] is a small deciduous tree from the forests of Japan and Korea. It bears slender egg-shaped buds that open out into snowy bowls five inches across with a rosette of crimson stamens at the heart and a lovely fragrance. It is one of the hardiest of the race and a most valuable shrub for northern gardens. It begins to flower in late May after the leaves are out and may continue to give a few blossoms until August. *M. salicifolia,* a slender pyramidal deciduous tree, native of Japan, bears its hairy buds and pure white flowers on naked shoots early in the spring. The flowers are four inches across. "The bark or young shoots when crushed give off a charming scent like that of *Aloysia triphylla* [*Lippia citriodora*] (lemon-scented verbena)." *M.* × *wiesneri* [*M. watsoni*] is a small deciduous tree of erect rather stiff habit. The leaves are leathery and long and slightly hairy beneath. The flowers are ivory-white, sometimes touched with rose on the outer side and with a rosette of crimson stamens, and they are richly fragrant of pineapple. The flowers appear in June when the bush is well leafed out. Of hybrid origin. The branches of *M. kobus,* a tall tree native of Japan, give off when young an aromatic scent something akin to camphor. It bears its carelessly assembled white flowers on naked branches early in the spring. Hardy.

No other genus of trees and shrubs is worthy of more devoted care and attention than the magnolias. According to Mr. Wilson the best results are obtained when they are protected from strong winds and are set in cool, deep soil, rich in humus.

Malus [*Pyrus*]. Crab. The blossoms of many crab trees have a delicate and elusive fragrance caught more readily from the breeze than when the nose is brought close to the crowding flowers. This is notably true of *M. floribunda* and allied forms. You pass them by thinking they are without fragrance but when you have gone a few paces you are suddenly enveloped by a cloud of fragile scent and you wonder whence it has come. Others of them, however, are definitely and deliciously perfumed. This is especially true of a number of American species. *M. ioensis,* the prairie crab, is very fragrant, and its double form, known as *M. ioensis* 'Plena', is one of the most delightfully scented of all flowering trees. The blossoms look like little hermosa roses and their perfume seems to be a mixture of roses and violets with a dash of spice. It is discernible many yards from the tree and like those of a rose the dried petals keep their fragrance for some time. The wild sweet crab or garland crab, *M. coronaria,* our eastern species, is a beautiful tree, sometimes thirty feet high, with a widespreading open crown. Its blossoms are pale pink and smell of violets. There is a fine form of the garland crab, known as Mathew's crab, which Mr. Wilson describes as having been found wild in Kentucky. Its clustered rose-pink blossoms are richly scented. *M. angustifolia,* the Southern crabapple, found wild from Virginia to Florida and Mississippi, but hardy in the North, is the latest to bloom. The blossoms are pure pink and very sweet. *Malus baccata,* Siberian crab, and its Manchurian variety, both with white fragrant flowers, pink in the bud, are desirable kinds, as is *M. spectabilis,* the Chinese flowering crab, or Asiatic apple, with large exquisitely fragrant semi-double pink flowers. *M. hupehensis* [*M. theifera*], another Chinese species, is also important among scented crabs. Of it the late Mr. E. H. Wilson said, "It is the very quintessence of crabapple loveliness."

It is a small tree with crooked branches spreading rather widely and when in bloom each branch is transformed into a "fragrant floral plume into which it is impossible to thrust a finger without touching a flower." *M. micromalus,* 'Kaido' and 'Eva Rathke', the weeping apple, are also gifted with sweet scented blossoms.

Myrica cerifera. Wax myrtle. Candleberry. A branching shrub four to eight feet high. It abounds along the Atlantic coast from New Brunswick to Florida and is also found in the Bahama Islands. The leaves have a delicious spicy fragrance. *M. gale,* the sweet gale, is lower growing, two to four feet, and bushy, and the wood and leaves are fragrant when bruised. It is a native of Great Britain as well as of Eastern North America. *M. pensylvanica* [*M. caroliniensis*], Northern bayberry, is common in sandy sterile soil near the coast. *Comptonia peregrina* var. *asplenifolia* [*M. asplenifolia*] is the sweet fern that borders all our dusty roadsides in the Eastern States and gives such a welcome regalement to our noses when we gather a handful of the leaves and crush them.

Oxydendrum arboreum. Sourwood. Sorrel tree. A slender tree with a rounded top found from Pennsylvania to Louisiana. The wood of the tree is slightly sour and the flowers are sweet scented prim white bells borne in spreading racemes in July and August. The leaves turn a fine scarlet in autumn.

Philadelphus (See Chapter V).

Pieris floribunda (*Andromeda floribunda*). A handsome native broad-leaved evergreen of compact habit. The foliage is thick and shining and the flowers are waxen and cream-white and borne in erect panicles five inches long. *P. japonica* is one of the finest of evergreen shrubs and very hardy. *Lyonia lucida* [*P. lucida*] is found in North Carolina and southwards. All have the fragrant waxen bell-shaped flowers borne in early spring, and are valuable where broad-leaved evergreens are called for.

Prinsepia sinensis. A dome-shaped bush from Manchuria, which is a lovely sight when, in early spring, the arching branches are closely set with clusters of yellow plum-like blossoms which diffuse a strong odour of almonds.

Prunus. Cherry. The blossoms of orchard cherries usually possess a fine sweet scent and many of the fine Japanese varieties also have this engaging attribute, though not all. The numerous forms derived from the sato-zakura group have pink or white sweet scented blossoms, many of them double. The type is a large tree. Mr. E. H. Wohlert sends me this list of fragrant Japanese cherries: 'Amanogawa', 'Asahiboton', 'Shirotae' ['Hosokawa'], 'Kirigayatsu', 'Ojochin' ['Momijigari'],

'Taizanfukun', 'Takinioi', 'Yedoensis' ['Yoshino'] and 'Ake-bono' ['Yoshino Daybreak'].

Prunus x *cistena,* a hybrid between the sand cherry and the purple-leaved plum, has sweet scented blossoms and reddish leaves. *Prunus mume,* the Japanese apricot, is one of the most delightful of early flowering trees. The pale pink delicately scented blossoms appear in profusion on dark naked branches producing a lovely effect. It is hardy as far north as Boston and is a most desirable tree.

RHODODENDRON
(*Rhododendron edgeworthii*)

Rhododendron. Section Azalea. Few flowers possess a more delightful and uncloying fragrance than do certain of the azaleas. It is much like that of honeysuckle but more delicate and transparent. Among native species, *R. arborescens,* found in open woods from Pennsylvania to Georgia and the Gulf States, ranks high. It is a tall shrub, reaching to a height of ten to fifteen feet and bearing in summer very fragrant white flowers with long scarlet stamens over a long period. *R. austrinum,* a Florida species, is of course not hardy in the North. This is the flame azalea of the far South and the blossoms vary from cream through various tones of yellow and orange to flame colour. They appear in early spring just before or coincident with the unfolding of the leaves. They are delicately scented. *R. calendulaceum* is the beautiful flame azalea found from Pennsylvania southwards. The flowers are orange-yellow to scarlet and slightly scented. *R. canescens* is the charming pink mountain azalea found from North Carolina to Texas. *R. periclymenoides* [*R. nudiflora*], the pretty pink and white Pinxter flower, is well distributed through the Eastern States, as is *R. occidentale* in the far West. This species haunts woodland streams and scents the air about with a fine fragrance from its many bunches of snowy or pink flowers. *R. serrulata* is native in the Southern States and bears white funnelform fragrant flowers on bushes that occasionally reach a height of twenty-five feet. The white swamp honeysuckle, *R. viscosum,* is found in low ground and bordering swamps from Maine to Florida and west to Ohio. The season of its blossoming is a delight to the wayfarer for it fills the countryside with sweetness. Other scented rhododendrons are *R. yedoense* (*R. yedogava*), with large lavender flowers; *R. schlippenbachii* with charming pink flowers; *R. mucronatum* (*R. ledifolium*), a lovely Chinese species, evergreen and with white flowers; *R. luteum* (*R. flavum.*) of Spain and Portugal, with clear yellow flowers, exquisitely scented and borne on a bush from ten to twelve feet high. The Ghent and Mollis azaleas smell deliciously of honeysuckle and run an entrancing scale of colours. They are superb for massing in the garden.

Section Eurhododendron. *R. falconeri* is a large shrub or small tree native in the Himalayas that bears in spring large creamy sweet scented flowers stained with lilac. *R. fortunei* is an evergreen species native in China that grows from ten to twelve feet tall and carries in spring lovely scented blush-coloured blossoms. *R. griffithianum* is also evergreen and grows tall enough to be called a small tree. The flowers are white touched with rose and lightly scented. It belongs to the Himalayas. *R. fortunei* ssp. *discolor* [*R. houlstonii*] is a charming species with pink flowers delicately and finely shaped, but its greatest attraction is its rich spicy odour. July. *R. decorum* from China bears pink and white spice-scented blossoms in May. *R. moupinense*, an evergreen native in the mountains of Tibet, bears large fragrant white blossoms spotted with pink very early in the spring. It is a low well-shaped bush. The pink flowers of *R. latoucheae* [*R. wilsoni*] a tall shrub native of Hupeh, China, are lightly scented.

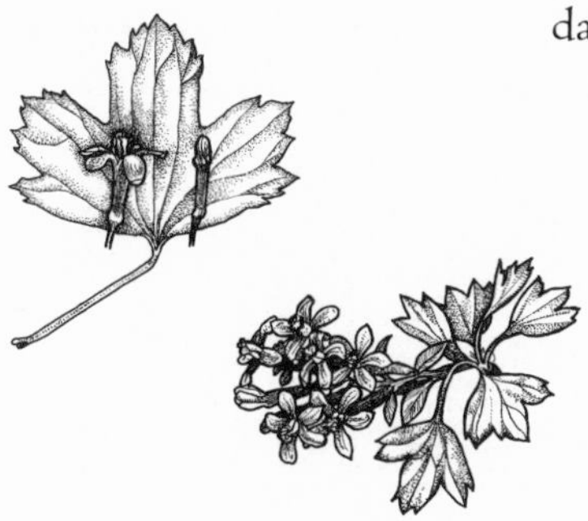

BUFFALO CURRANT
(*Ribes odoratum*)

Among other sweet scented rhododendrons may be mentioned *R. anthopogon*, an evergreen only one foot tall bearing flat yellow flowers, native in the Himalayas; *R. edgeworthii*, also of the Himalayas, with bell-shaped flowers white tinged with rose; *R. nuttallii* [*R. sinonuttalli*], an evergreen Chinese species reaching a height of ten feet and bearing pink bell-shaped flowers tinged with yellow.

Rhus aromatica (*R. canadensis*). Fragrant sumac. Lemon sumac. Polecat bush. Deciduous, low-growing, spreading, the leaves aromatic when crushed.

Ribes aureum. Golden currant. Buffalo currant. Missouri currant. Native of Central United States. A rather untidy straggling shrub but once the pride of door yards and still a treasure-trove of sweetness. *R. odoratum*, clove currant, is similar and often confused with it. *R. sanguineum* is less spicily fragrant but very showy when in blossom. British Columbia to California.

Robinia pseudoacacia. Black locust. Yellow locust. Ungainly, untidy tree bearing lovely dangling creamy panicles of blossoms in summer that scent the countryside.

Rosa (See Chapter VI).

Rubus odoratus. Purple-flowering raspberry. Thimbleberry. This scrambling shrub bears many large rose-purple blossoms in early summer. It is often to be found lounging against tumbledown stone line fences in the Eastern States, a beautiful shrub and one deserving greater use despite its habit of spreading from the root, often to the discomfiture of neighbouring plants.

Salix pentandra. Bay or laurel willow. Native of Europe and Asia. A large shrub or small tree the leaves of which when bruised have an aromatic fragrance like true bay.

Sambucus canadensis. Elder. The fragrance of the creamy flowers is not agreeable to all, but good and fragrant wine is made from both berries and flowers. The western red-berried elder has an odour that is almost fetid in its overpowering sweetness. The scent of the elders is not unpleasant when caught from a distance. It is only close at hand that it has what Dr. Hampden calls that black currant smell which easily deepens into the smell of cats and when very strong suggests a hot and perspiring crowd.

Santolina chamaecyparissus (*C. incana*). Lavender

cotton. Low hoary bushes from the Mediterranean region the foliage of which is pleasantly aromatic when brushed but strongly bitter when bruised. *S. rosmarinifolia* [*S. viridis*] has the same qualities.

Sassafras albidum [*S. officinale*]. Sassafras tree. This tree which is a native of many parts of North America is pleasantly aromatic in all its parts. Children love to nibble its pungent shoots and carry the fragrant leaves in their pockets. It belongs to the large tropical family of Lauraceae, among whose members are some of the most fragrant shrubs we have. Thoreau wrote that he was always exhilarated, "as were the early voyagers, by the sight of Sassafras. The green leaves bruised have the fragrance of lemons and a thousand spices."

Skimmia japonica (*Skimmia fragrans*). This is a low evergreen shrub from Japan, bearing scented white flowers in terminal clusters in May. *S. japonica* ssp. *reevesiana* [*S. fortunei*] from China, is not quite as tall as the foregoing. These plants are hardy in sheltered places as far north as Philadelphia. They like a sandy, peaty soil and dislike limestone.

Sophora japonica. Japanese pagoda tree. Chinese scholar tree. A graceful small tree from China and Korea hung in August with masses of long pendant panicles of yellow pea-shaped flowers that smell like honey and attract the bees in great numbers. A valuable summer-flowering tree.

Spartium junceum. Spanish broom. Weaver's broom. A tall shrub, reaching sometimes a height of ten feet, rather gaunt of aspect, but bearing in summer for a long period and in great profusion, racemes of fragrant yellow pea-shaped flowers, very sweet scented and attractive to bees.

Spiraea hypericifolia. Italian may. A trim little shrub native of many parts of the Northern Hemisphere. It bears greyish leaves and in April and May, pretty little white hawthorn-scented blossoms in small umbels along the whole length of the branches which curve gracefully to the ground.

Stewartia sinensis. A deciduous shrub or small tree, native in China, bearing white fragrant flowers in the axils of the leaves.

Styrax japonica. Japanese snowbell. A shrublike tree ten to twelve feet tall. The branches in mid-May are lined on the undersides with sweet scented white pendant bells in three or six-flowered clusters on long stalks. *S. hemsleyanum* is a vigorous widely branching shrub or small tree growing twenty feet tall and bearing in profusion white sweet scented flowers an inch across. One of E. H. Wilson's introductions.

Symplocos paniculata. Asiatic sweetleaf. Sapphire berry. A lovely little tree that is hardy in Massachusetts. It eventually reaches a height of thirty feet and bears panicles of creamy flowers in May and June that are followed by sapphire berries.

Syringa (See Chapter III).

Tilia. Lime. Linden. Both the American and the European lindens have one-sided heart-shaped leaves and bunches of yellow honey-scented blossoms that attract bees in great numbers. On summer nights towards the end of June the fragrance is very powerful and noticeable a long distance from the trees. The famed honey of Hybla was made from the blossoms of the European linden.

Ulex europaeus. Gorse. Furze. Whin. A spiny much branched evergreen shrub found growing wild on heaths and uplands and in waste places throughout the British Isles and over most of Europe. The yellow flowers have a curious and to me quite delicious odour, though it is thought by some to be oppressive. They begin to appear in May and their cheerful glint is often still to be seen in the dead of winter, "a token of the wintry earth that beauty liveth still." There is an old saying "When gorse is out of blossom kissing's out of fashion." Good to grow in gardens.

Viburnum carlesii. A beautiful native of the maritime areas of Korea, recently introduced and of the utmost value. Exquisitely fragrant flowers in broad heads, coral-colored in the bud and opening to pearl-white in April. Should be given a sheltered location to encourage early flowering.

Viburnum farreri [*V. fragrans*] was found by Mr. Farrer growing wild in a remote northern province of China. "All over China," he says, "it is probably the best beloved and most universal of garden plants." He describes it as forming "gracious arching masses ten feet and more across, whose naked boughs in spring before the foliage, become one blaze of soft pink lilac spikelets, breathing an intense fragrance of heliotrope." It blooms very early in the spring. *V. bitchiuense* is a rare Japanese species somewhat similar to the above but taller and more lax in habit.

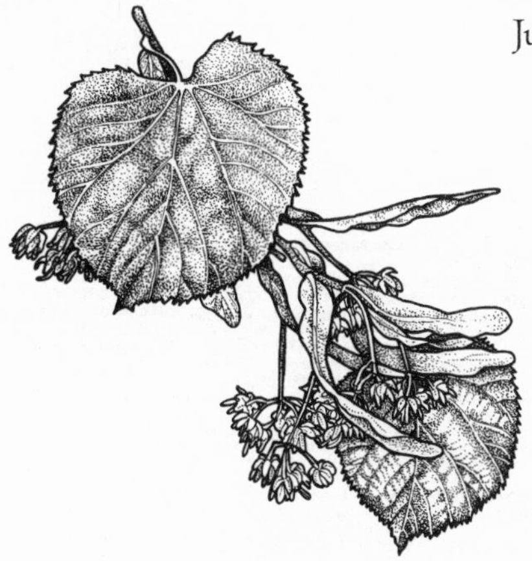

LITTLELEAF LINDEN
(*Tilia cordata*)

Viburnum japonicum grows four to six feet tall and bears white fragrant flowers in rounded cymes. Native of Japan. *V. lentago,* sheepberry, is a robust deciduous native shrub bearing creamy flowers in terminal cymes in May and June that are agreeably though not strongly perfumed. Other fragrant viburnums are *V. odoratissimum,* an evergreen native of China and Japan; *V. davuricum,* a hardy spreading shrub, six to eight feet tall, bearing profusely in early summer white funnel shaped flowers in small clusters followed by oval, fragrant berries; *V. opulus,* guelder rose, European cranberrybush, crampbark, June and July, white flowers suggestive in their fragrance of hawthorn. Good to grow by a pond. *Viburnum* x *birkwoodi* is a new broad-leaved evergreen with fragrant flowers.

Vitex agnus-castus. Chaste tree. Deciduous shrub native in the Mediterranean region, bearing pale violet fragrant flowers in one-sided panicled spikes five to seven inches long, in summer and early autumn. The leaves are strongly aromatic. Often kills to the ground in winter in the North but the roots survive save in exceptionally cold localities.

CHAPTER X

Climbers with Scented Flowers

Trailing odorous plants which curtain out the day with loveliest flowers.

— SHELLEY

IF IT COMES TO CHOOSING BETWEEN a climber with fragrant flowers and one that appeals only to the eye it would seem the simple part of wisdom to select one that yields a profit both to the sight and to the sense of smell. "A rose looking in at the window" is always a delight but if it be a sweet scented rose so much the more delightful. To veil our outdoor retreats with fragrant climbers, or to twine them about doors and windows, so that their sweet airs are carried into the rooms upon the wings of every breeze, is to thread our days with a subtle, gentle happiness, a happiness indefinable but profoundly felt. To sleep in a room beyond whose casement honeysuckle scrambles and to awake in the night to the exquisite fragrance that inspires the darkness is an experience of rare quality. Such things invade life's commonplace routine with an ecstatic pleasure.

There are many climbers with fragrant flowers other than the climbing roses. The clematis tribe alone offers a wide selection. The kind most commonly grown in this country is *Clematis terniflora*, a rampant Japanese climber smothered in late summer with clouds of small creamy flowers that emit a rich fragrance akin to that of vanilla and perceptible a long distance from the plant, informing all the garden in fact, and proving an irresistible attraction for the bees. A good deal in the way of *C. terniflora* but less effective and also less sweet scented, and also less floriferous, is the wild clematis that scrambles over our wayside hedge-rows and old walls. It is worth bringing into the garden only as a fast growing screen for some unsightly object. This is *C. virginiana.*

Woodbine. Leather flower. Virgin's bower. Devil's-darning-needle. It will grow from ten to eighteen feet in height in a very short time. The wild clematis of the Mediterranean region, which has been cultivated in English gardens since 1596, is *C. flammula.* It mounts to a considerable height, clothing arbour or trellis with a closely woven garment of slender stems and charming leafage almost lost beneath the thickly sprinkled clusters of pale stars that shine forth in the late summer and autumn, filling the air with the scent of vanilla. It has been called the fragrant Virgin's Bower, and Donald McDonald calls its perfume "the most spiritual, impalpable and yet far-spreading of all vegetable odours."

The clematis that is so lovely a feature in calcareous regions of England's richly caparisoned hedgerows is *C. vitalba,* the traveler's joy. It is a free growing woody climber, reaching a height of from fifteen to thirty feet, swinging in graceful festoons from tree to tree or scrambling over wall and bush and brake and filling the mild summer air with an almond scent from the small greenish white flowers. It is a loved feature of the English landscape and has earned innumerable folk-names testifying to the affection with which it is regarded. Old man's beard, from the feathery seed vessels that lie like a haze of smoke over its green expanse in the autumn, is one of the most common, and it is also called robin hood's fetter, snow-in-harvest, smokewood, withy-wind, love-blind, greybeard – and so on. All these small-flowered fragrant species are of great value in the garden, quick to hide unsightly objects, graceful in their habit, and they flower at a time when flowering climbers are few.

Clematis montana and its beautiful variety *C. montana* var. *rubens,* deserve a place in every garden, not only for their unusual beauty and flexuous rampant vigour but for the sweet perfume of the flowers which fills all the air about, during the period of their profuse blossoming in May. The flowers are the size and shape of a Japanese anemone, and the variety *rubens* has the delicate colour of *Anemone hupehensis* var. *japonica* [*A. japonica* 'Queen Charlotte']. This variety has proved quite hardy with me and I know a lovely garden on the bleak Palisades of the Hudson where it weathers the winter without flinching. It is said to be hardier than the white-flowered kind. Of its scent A. T. Johnson, writing in an English periodical, had this to say: "A large mass of the lovely *C. montana* var. *rubens* which has completely enveloped an old tree stump with its legions of blossoms, has this year been one of the most powerfully scented shrubs in the garden. Their extraordinary fragrance has even extinguished that of some azaleas close by. It has, especially towards evening, filled every room in the house and is almost too rich and sweet for any respectably middle-aged liver. I have been trying to define this peculiarly insinuating odour, but it evades the net like a wise butterfly. Does it recall the incensed joss-stick of some Oriental temple, or those vapours of sacrifice which rise from the flower altars of Grasse? I asked an amiable old gentleman whose nose I respect and he muttered 'Macaroons' and passed on. I asked a slip of a girl – one of the new voters who ought to know – and she said 'M, yes! Boiling toffee!' I asked my wife ('poor wretch') and she, unwilling to commit herself, said 'Those people who were here yesterday said it smelt like 'Daphne Snee-awrum mixed up with a ladies' hairdressing establishment.' Finally I put the problem to one cunning in the dark secrets of flowers but he only complicated matters by saying 'New bread, hot and steamy.' So mystery still shrouds the spicy aroma, cloying, sultry and heady, with which those rosy blossoms are haunting the garden to the fall of the last sun-paled sepal."

Which only goes to show how difficult– often impossible – it is to put a perfume into words. The scent of *Clematis montana* var. *rubens,* which has never been as strong and pervading in my garden, probably due to climatic differences, as described by Mr. Johnson, has to my nose the scent often found in greater or lesser degree in the clematis tribe, as well as in numerous others, a blend of vanilla and bitter almond, pleasant enough when not too strong but heady and disturbing at times.

Other clematis that are sweet scented are the following:

C. armandii. A Chinese species of vigorous habit and rapid growth suitable only for use in southern gardens. It is an evergreen climber with three-parted leaves and sweet scented white blossoms borne generously in loose clusters from the leaf axils, in the late spring.

C. x *aromatica.* (*C. coerulia odorata*). A sweet scented clematis said to be of garden origin. It is subshrubbery in character and grows not much taller than six feet. The flowers are small and reddish violet in colour. Mr. George Jackman of the Working Nurseries, Surrey, writes me that this kind, like *C. flammula* and *C.* f. *rosea purpurea* "all belong to the Paniculatae type and the scent resembles heliotrope to a marked degree."

C. calycina, of the Balearic Isles, is an evergreen, hardy in our Southern States, flowering in the winter from December until March, the blossoms white flecked with reddish purple. It is easily cultivated and a useful climber for balustrades and arbours.

C. campaniflora. A slender hardy European climbing species growing from eight to ten feet tall, that produces white or purplish, half expanded or bell-shaped, fragrant blossoms in July.

C. cirrhosa. A winter flowering species that was discovered by Clusius in Spain in the sixteenth century. The leaves are evergreen and the flowers bell-shaped, a pale greenish yellow in colour and fragrant.

C. connata. A deciduous climber from the Himalayas, flowers bell-shaped and fragrant in the autumn.

C. crispa. A charming native of our Southeastern States, sometimes called bluebell vine or blue jasmine. It is a slender deciduous climber, half woody with urn-shaped flowers, blue and with a light bergamot fragrance, that last in perfection a long time. This is an especially light and graceful little climber and quite hardy. August to October.

C. paniculata [*C. indivisa*]. The late Mr. E. H. Wilson called this species the most beautiful vine that New Zealand has contributed to gardens. It has shining, leathery, evergreen leaves and masses of milk-white fragrant flowers borne in axillary clusters. Save in the warmest parts of the country it must be grown in a greenhouse.

C. ligusticifolia. Western North America. Has small white fragrant flowers. The male and female flowers are on different plants.

C. nutans. An attractive Chinese species with pretty nodding flowers of a peculiar yellow-green colour having a pleasing fragrance of cowslips. It is especially valuable because it blooms in the autumn.

C. orientalis is of wide occurrence in Asia, a slender rampant climber reaching a height of fifteen feet, with attractive foliage and masses of lightly fragrant pale yellow bell-shaped flowers borne in the late summer, and followed in the clematis manner, by decorative silky seed vessels. It is in bloom in my garden as I write and is quite pretty enough for an odd corner or to trail over low bushes.

C. rehderiana. A Chinese kind, vigorous, deciduous and climbing to a height of twenty-five feet, bears masses of nodding primrose-colored flowers scented like cowslips in July and August. It is said to be especially fragrant towards evening. Useful to train over a wall or low tree.

C. reticulata (*Viorna reticulata*). A species found growing wild in dry soil from South Carolina to Florida and Texas. The flowers are urn-shaped, yellowish on the outside and pale violet within, nodding and solitary. The plant climbs to a height of about ten feet and the thickness of the leaves has earned for it the name of leather flower.

C. viticella. The virgin's bower of Southern Europe is the source of many of the most beautiful of the large-flowered hybrids that grace modern gardens. The flowers are from one to three inches across and lightly sweet scented. In Mr. Robinson's "Virgin's Bower" he says, "This kind comes as free from seed as furze, and with us sows itself in hedgerows where it comes in wreaths long after the May and the dog roses."

Chief among the large-flowered hybrid clematis that are fragrant is 'Duchess of Edinburgh', a beautiful double-flowered kind with a very delicate fragrance. Another is 'Fair Rosamond', said to exhale the scent of violets and primroses, and Maiden's Blush.

Raising clematis from seed is a very interesting and profitable enterprise, for in this country it is often difficult to buy the kinds we should like to have in our gardens. Seed germinates readily as a rule and the plants grow quickly. Practically all of them demand lime in the soil and hate acidity. When a plant is set out a generous amount of old mortar rubble, or slaked lime, should be incorporated with the soil. It should be remembered also concerning them that the majority are thicket or wood plants and that a degree of shade, particularly at the base of the plants, is necessary to their comfort.

Many have sung the praises of honeysuckle but none more eloquently than old William Bullein, who was born in the Isle of Ely early in the reign of Henry VIII. He was both physician and divine in that day when medicine and religion, sorcery and witchcraft, often formed a strange union. His great work, "A Bulwarke of Defense against all Sickness, Soreness and Wounds that doe daily assault mankind, which Bulwarke is kept with Hillarius the Gardiner, Health and the Phisician, with their Chyrurgian, to help wounded Soldiers, &c. with his Boke of Simples," was printed in London in 1562. It is full of delightful extraneous matter: "Oh how swete and pleasant is Woodbinde, in woodes or arbours, after a tender soft rayne, and how friendly doe this herbe, if I maie so name it, imbrace the bodies, armes and branches of trees with his long winding Stalkes and tender leaves, opening or spreading forthe his swete Lillis, like ladies' fingers, emog the thornes or bushes."

Bullein's woodbinde is the wild honeysuckle of Great Britain, *Lonicera periclymenum,* a climbing, wantonly scrambling shrub bearing in spring and early summer exceedingly fragrant yellowish white and red tube-like blossoms borne in terminal bunches. It is a lovely ornament of woodside and copse, wreathing hedgerows and trees to a height of twenty feet. There are several forms of it, among them the Dutch honeysuckle, so-called, *L. Penichymenum* 'Belgica', that blooms throughout the season. Parkinson says of the honeysuckle that "groweth wilde in every hedge"—"although it be very sweete yet I do not bring it into my garden but let it rest in his owne place to serve their senses that travell by it or have no garden." A lesson which vandal "nature-lovers" might well take to heart where this, as well as many other plants, is concerned.

Honeysuckle has what the old books call a fine quick scent; it is never over heavy or cloying and is one of those rare perfumes of which one can scarcely get enough. Of old, as were so many plants, it was endowed with medicinal virtues, supposed or real. Coles advises that a conserve of honeysuckle flowers be kept in every gentlewoman's house. The juice of the leaves was applied to bee stings by country people in the belief that it drew out the soreness, and in a very old treatise on herbs it is written, "If the bee-hives be anoynted with the jus of hir leaves, the been schalt not goo away; the housbondes kept hir swarmes in type of yere by suche anoyntynge." In fairly recent times a decoction of the stems was used for the gout, while an infusion of the flowers was held to be of healing value for sufferers from asthma. It was also one of the numerous remedies recommended for that seemingly very common affliction the "hicket," and one old writer asserts that "the flowers steeped in oile and set in the sun is good to anoint the bodies that is benummed and growne verie cold."

There are numerous kinds of honeysuckle that are good to have for their sweet scent.

L. x *americanum.* A hybrid form between *L. caprifolium* and the Italian woodbine, *L. etrusca,* with long oval leaves and yellowish purple flowers borne in whorls and with a very sweet scent.

L. caprifolium. Italian woodbine. Italian honeysuckle. Goat honeysuckle. Sometimes called American woodbine, though it is not a true native in this country but is naturalized from Europe and Asia. This species twines to a height of twenty feet, the leaves are bluish green on their undersides, the flowers white tinged with pink and borne in whorls. They are followed by orange-red fruit.

L. etrusca. A vigorous deciduous climber from

Mediterranean regions bearing immense clusters of large sweet scented yellow flowers suffused with red, that become clear yellow with age. It is perhaps the most beautiful and floriferous of all honeysuckles and blooms over a long period. Suitable only for mild climates.

L. flava. The yellow trumpet honeysuckle is a vigorous evergreen climber with thickish leaves, glaucous on both sides, and deep yellow tubular flowers borne in verticillate clusters in May and June. It is native in the mountains of North Carolina and Kentucky, Missouri, and the Southwest. It is quite hardy in the neighbourhood of New York.

L. japonica. A vigorous climber with long slender stems bearing pink and pale yellow fragrant flowers in the axils of the leaves during June and July, followed by black fruit. It is a native of China and Japan but has escaped from cultivation and is found twining up trees and over bushes from Connecticut to Florida. It has numerous forms, among them the familiar "gold and silver" honeysuckle, 'Aureoreticulata', and the very popular 'Hall's Prolific'. *L. japonica* is not to be confused with our native *L. sempervirens* which is scentless.

L. periclymenum. The common honeysuckle of Europe. The berries are said to be bitter and nauseous.

L. similis var. *delavayi.* A species from Yunnan bearing pale yellow perfumed flowers in the axils of the leaves. The leaves are covered with a grey tomentum on the undersides.

The honeysuckle is the true woodbine and was so named in the "Grete Herball," 1526, where it is spelled woodbynde. Turner spells it wodbynde. Other plants have shared this pretty and poetic name, among them the clematis, the wild morning glory, the ivy, and in this country the virginia creeper.

From time immemorial the jasmine has been a chief flower of delight wherever it could be grown. Sadly enough no species of sweet scented jasmine is hardy as far north as New York, though the hardy winter jasmine, *Jasminum nudiflorum,* which is quite scentless to my nose, is endowed with sweetness by some authorities. *J. mesnyi* [*J. primulinum*], of fairly recent introduction from China, is claimed by its sponsors to be fragrant but I have not yet been able to put it to the test. It is said to be much like the winter jasmine but with flowers "as large as a half dollar." It is reported hardy as far north as Washington, D. C. *J. humile* 'Revolutum' [*J. humile*] will live out of doors in Maryland and furnishes its bright yellow, deliciously scented stars in the late summer and autumn. It will climb twenty feet high and is a vigorous species of almost treelike habit, but with lax branches, and is probably the hardiest fragrant jasmine.

According to Gerard the common white jasmine, *J. officinale,* was in common use in his day in England, 1597, for covering arbours and trellises. And every poet seemingly has sung of it, while it lights Oriental poetry with a delicate radiance. Its origin is Persian. It has small dark leaves and "scattered stars" of purest white borne throughout the summer and autumn. It will live out as far north as Maryland. *J. officinale* f. *grandiflorum* [*J. grandiflorum*], the Spanish jasmine, is much like the common white kind but the flowers are larger and the habit of the plant is stockier and generally more vigorous. It is native in India but has become naturalized in Florida. The beautiful and delicious Arabian jasmine, or sambac, *J. sambac,* climbs only about five feet high, but it is delightful to grow in the open where it will survive the winters; it will endure ten or twelve degrees of frost. The perfume of the white flowers is powerful and refreshing, and there is a double form said to be even more strongly scented. This is the plant whose blossoms the women of India string into chaplets and necklaces for their adornment as they sit upon the house tops in the cool dusk.

POET'S JASMINE (*Jasminium officinale grandiflorum*)

In common with other jasmines the sambac is made use of in China for perfuming tea. About forty pounds of flowers are required to scent a hundred pounds of tea. Jasmine tea is a delicacy that may be had of the better grocers and it brings to the tea hour, with its delicate fragrance and flavour, a vague sense of the romance and the mystery of the East.

Ca. 200 species of jasmine are known; they belong to the hottest regions of the Old World (there are two species indigenous to South America), India, Arabia, the sun soaked islands of the tropics, and when grown in cooler climates the perfume is much etherialized.

In the Southern States jasmines are favourite climbing plants and their sweetness endows the gardens of the Gulf States with a rare charm. Several kinds are grown besides those already enumerated. *J. nitidum,* from the Admiralty Islands, is a slender, branched, twining plant with shining foliage and starry sweet white flowers. It is recommended for southern Florida and makes a fine greenhouse plant in the North. *J. multiflorum* [*J. pubescens*] is more shrubby in character but may be trained to a low trellis or fence. The blossoms are white and fragrant. *J. gracillimum,* the star jasmine, is close to this but differs in its very long hanging clusters of distinctly star-shaped flowers. *J. simplicifolium* is a tall climbing kind from Australia that has become naturalized in Bermuda. And there are others too numerous to name.

The Hindus gave the jasmine the poetic name of moon-light of the grove and the flowers of all kinds are said to exhale a richer fragrance at night. The blossoms of certain of them are much employed by perfumers and highly valued are the treasures they obtain

From timid Jasmine buds, that keep
Their odours to themselves all day,
But, when the sunlight dies away,
Let their delicious secret out.

Jasminum odoratissimum, a native of the Island of Madeira, is said to be one particularly valued by perfumers and the flowers have the advantage of retaining their delicious scent long after they are dried.

The scent of jasmine is unique, it is not the property of any other flower, nor has it been successfully imitated by artificial means. In the East jasmine flowers are rolled up in the well-oiled hair of the women when they retire at night to endow the hair and skin with alluring sweetness.

The cape jasmine is the gardenia and the wild jasmine of the Carolinas is *Gelsemium sempervirens,* called "Jasimer" in its native countryside. This is a wayward woody climber or scrambler, evergreen, with whorls of opposite leaves, dark and shining, and bright yellow deliciously fragrant bell-shaped blossoms in terminal cymes. It is a valuable plant for covering rough banks or for scrambling over low dense shrubs. I envy the climate that will suffer it. One encounters it in Pinehurst gardens and while winter still lingers and the nights are chill, the gilded flowers expand, making the air a delight to breathe. It is said to be hardy as far north as Washington.

Other climbers with fragrant flowers are the following:

Actinidia arguta. A vigorous climber, native of China and Japan, with dark shining leaves and greenish white odorous flowers that are attractive to cats.

A. deliciosa [*A. chinensis*] is exceptionally handsome but is not hardy in New England. It is a vigorous pushing plant with large roundish leaves and richly scented flowers that change from white to soft yellow as they age. *A. kolomikta* is another Chinese species with very fragrant flowers.

A. polygama. Silver-sweet vine. A climbing shrub with variegated leaves, and small waxy white flowers that emit a delicate fragrance. Not hardy. Japan, Korea, Manchuria and China.

Apios americana [*A. tuberosa*]. Wild bean. Potato bean. Indian potato. A little wild scrambler of our dampish copses that has no beauty or distinction save that in August when the small brownish-purple winged blossoms are fluttering about it, a most uncommon and delicious fragrance is perceptible at a considerable distance from the plant. Indeed the nose nearly always finds this little wildling before the eye spies it. One of its common names in certain localities is traveler's delight, which must have been given it because of the pleasure derived by the wayfarer from its freesia-like scent.

Akebia quinata. See Night Scented Flowers.

Aristolochia macrophylla [*A. sipho*]. A heavily leafed and heavily scented climber which is liked by some but which I find disagreeable.

Cionura erecta [*Marsdenia erecta*]. Slender climber from Southeastern Europe and Asia Minor, with numerous small, sweet scented white flowers in July.

Decumaria barbara. Climbing hydrangea. Wood vamp. A slender climber native of the Southern States but hardy in Massachusetts and useful for covering rocks or trellis work. It climbs by aërial rootlets to a height of thirty feet and produces in profusion feathery corymbs of white sweet scented flowers.

Dioscorea batatas. Cinnamon vine. Chinese yam.

Tall climbing from a tuberous edible root, shining leaves and cinnamon scented small white flowers in clusters. Leaves too scanty to make it an effective screen.

Hoya carnosa. Wax plant. Root-climbing plants to eight feet with fat shining leaves of a beautiful bronze tint when young, and clusters of waxen pink flowers edged with white that are especially fragrant at night. China. Australia. May be grown in a cool greenhouse.

Ipomoea alba [*I. bona-nox*]. The moonflower. Belle de nuit. A twining plant with large leaves and immense white ghost-flowers that open at sun-down and emit a rich fragrance, something akin to that of cloves. Covers large spaces in a short time; an annual in this country, which should be started indoors in early spring or winter. Other members of this family are scented, while still others have no trace of odour.

Mandevilla suaveolens. Chilean jasmine. A splendid woody deciduous climber from the Argentine with white or pinkish flowers not unlike those of the jasmine and scarcely less sweet.

Passiflora caerulea. The passion flower vine. Native of Brazil, with beautiful spectacular delicately fragrant flowers. This climber is usually a greenhouse subject but I remember that it was hardy in our Maryland garden though it was killed back to the crown every winter. It was an object of great awe amongst the children because of the dramatically revealed significance of the arrangement and shape of its parts by our nursemaids. "In an old Spanish tradition it was the passion flower that climbed the Cross and fastened upon the scars in the wood where the nails had been driven through the hands and feet of the Sufferer. The early fathers saw in its bud the Eucharist, in its half open flower the Star of the East, and in the full bloom the five wounds, the nails, the hammer, the spear, the pillar of scourging and the crown of thorns, in its leaves the spearhead and thirty pieces of silver, in its tendrils the cords that bound the Lord." The white-flowered variety, 'Constance Eliott', is very lovely and highly fragrant. Other members of this large tropical and sub-tropical genus have sweet scented flowers.

MADAGASCAR JASMINE
(*Stephanotis floribunda*)

Periploca graeca. Silk vine. A hardy, twining, fast-climbing deciduous plant, native of Europe. It is related to stephanotis but lacks its exquisite scent, the greenish-brown hairy flowers giving forth instead a most heavy and sickish odour. The milk that exudes from the stem of the plants is said to be poisonous and in its native countries it is thought to be inimical to health to breathe the air that carries its heavy breath. Flowers in July.

Schisandra chinensis. A deciduous climber to twenty or thirty feet, from the north of China and Japan, that bears pale rose-coloured scented flowers, each on a slender stalk, in May, followed by scarlet berries. The dried wood of the plant is aromatic. It is hardy in the north of our country and may be employed to clamber over rocks, fences, arbours, and the like.

Stauntonia hexaphylla. A handsome vine growing to a height of forty feet, with small oval leaves and flowers, white, in axillary clusters. Is very sweet scented in spring.

Stephanotis floribunda. Creeping tuberose. Madagascar jasmine. Bridal wreath. Chaplet flower. Waxflower. Floradora. One of the most exquisitely scented of all flowers and in great demand as a cut flower for bouquets in winter. The flowers are white, waxen, tube-shaped and borne in bunches, and they last a long time in water, often as long as a week, even in our tryingly heated houses. It is perhaps the finest of all hothouse climbers. Its home is in the Island of Madagascar.

Trachelospermum asiaticum [*T. divaricatum*]. Japan and Korea. A warm climate or greenhouse evergreen climber bearing orange-yellow flowers, small and very sweet, in slender terminal cymes, in July and August.

Trachelospermum jasminoides. Star jasmine and also called confederate and Malaysian jasmine, is somewhat less hardy. It is a useful greenhouse climber which Professor Bailey says may be grown in large tubs and trained to form bushes three or four feet high and as much through. The leaves are small and evergreen and the starry white flowers, borne in terminal cymes, are delicately and deliciously fragrant. It is a favourite in Italy where high walls are often covered with it.

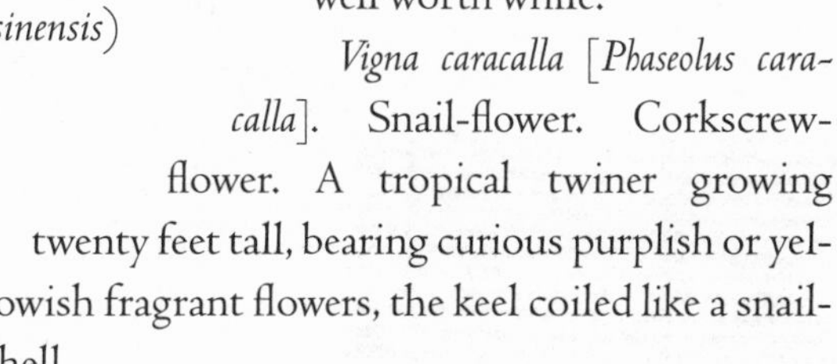

CHINESE WISTERIA
(*Wisteria sinensis*)

Tripterygium regelii. According to an Arnold Arboretum Bulletin this is "a twining vine native of Korea and Japan, where it often scales to the top of the tallest trees. . . . The flowers are borne in terminal thyrsoid panicles each from eight to eighteen inches in length. The individual blossoms are small, multitudinous in number, emit a fragrance of newmown hay and are speedily followed by white, bladder-like fruits. For its foliage, its flowers, or its decorative fruits, this climber is well worth while."

Vigna caracalla [*Phaseolus caracalla*]. Snail-flower. Corkscrew-flower. A tropical twiner growing twenty feet tall, bearing curious purplish or yellowish fragrant flowers, the keel coiled like a snail-shell.

Vitis (See Wild Scents).

Wisteria. The wisterias smell richly of honey and fill the air with their sweetness during the period when the branches are hung with the long panicles of pea-shaped flowers. The scent of the white *W. sinensis* 'Alba' is more delicate than that of its purple-flowered counterpart, as it is more exquisite in appearance.

CHAPTER XI

Night Scented Flowers

Then, with the falling of the dusk,
The scent of mignonette and musk
Will all the air enshroud,
And the new moon will slip its husk
Of sailing silver cloud.

— CLINTON SCOLLARD

TO NEARLY ALL PERSONS, however employed, the coming of evening brings leisure, an hour or two at least that may be freely spent. To the flower lover this is the time above all others to enjoy the garden. The day is full of activities and distracting contacts and, though some of these may center in the garden, their very nature fills the mind to the exclusion of much that is delightful. But when the gentle dusk creeps in and wisps of cool air come out of the shadows, tasks are laid aside and the mind is left open to impressions – and the nose as well.

Nothing so adds to the enchantment of the evening garden as fragrance. To follow the dim paths catching little secret scents like shy confidences as we go, or to sit beside the pool receiving the message of honeysuckle or stock are perhaps not exciting pleasures, as pleasures are counted today, but they are happy ones and tranquilizing. The busy man or woman, tired at night and with frayed nerves, will find in the peace and sweetness of a garden relaxation and refreshment undreamed by those who seek these assuagements in movie palaces or along the teeming roads. But to be truly potent it must be a fragrant garden. Without the fragrance the magic is not there. Colour disappears from the borders with the coming of dusk, the most splendidly wrought colour schemes are blotted out, marigolds, the flaunting poppy, sunflowers, retire into the gloom and only white flowers, or those of pale colouring, stand out, silvered in the moonlight or wraithlike in the thick darkness. They make of the garden a wholly novel place and happily most of these pale blooms have sweetness to offer as well as form.

It is a curious fact that many sweet scented flowers withhold their fragrance during the day and pour it out to the night. And it is these vespertine flowers, as someone has called them, that we chiefly enjoy at night, for there is a special poignancy in their sweetness not to be found in the simpler perfumes of the daytime hours.

Some day-scented flowers give out little or no perfume after sunset while others seem then to increase their emanations. Not infrequently too it is surprising to note that the fragrance given out by day is of quite a different quality from that given out by night. The aromatics of the honeysuckle by day and by night are not at all the same, and the white petunia, whose day-scent falls short of being agreeable, gives forth a refined and delicious perfume after sunset. "Some of the orchids show the elaborate specialization of their flowers by giving off different scents by day and night."

Pinks, sweet enough by day, are sweeter still and spicier under the stars. The ten-week stock is another that saves its choicest distillations for the evening, as does the tuberose. So much stronger is the scent of this flower at night that the enfleurage (the process of chemically extracting the perfume from the flower for commercial purposes) is nearly always carried on after dark. No garden planned for evening pleasure should be without this old-fashioned flower. Once it was in great demand for indoor as well as open air culture. Sentimental German ladies called it nachtliebste because of its night sweetness, and there were those who contended that in the darkness it shone with a peculiar luminosity, even emitting sparks of light. Thus the poet Moore:

> The tuberose, with her silvery light,
> That in the gardens of Malay
> Is called the mistress of the night,
> So like a bride, scented and bright,
> She comes out when the sun's away.

But the tuberose fell into bad odour, so to speak, when it became too popular as a funeral flower and it was presently no more cultivated in gardens and parlours. Today, however, it is not in fashion for these sad occasions and we may divest our minds of its gloomy associations and tuck in a few tubers of the kind known as 'The Pearl' beside the path that we are apt to follow at evening, or beneath the living room windows for the sake of its curiously moving perfume. It makes an extremely effective pot plant also for use on terraces and balconies among standard heliotropes, fuchsias and *Datura* species.

The true vesper flowers – those that withhold their sweetness from the day and give it freely to the night – are rather a curious company. Few have any daytime attractions, being either sad of hue, brownish, greyish or dull violet, or if white, as many of them are, seeming to lose countenance before the searching eye of the day, to droop and become dull and lusterless. But with twilight comes an extraordinary change. As if touched by a magic wand they lift their heads and become lovely, flooding the night breezes with a message of irresistible sweetness to the night-moths whose visits they must experience if they are to realize their potentialities.

The old bouncing bet, *Saponaria officinalis*, is one in which this change is notable. Dowdy and forlorn this onetime belle appears by day and with her pallid cheeks too often sullied by dust, but if you meet her by the roadside near some old garden in the twilight you will be surprised by her young freshness and the sweet breath with which she will entice you.

But perhaps the flower in which this eleventh hour rejuvenation is most conspicuous is the night-scented stock, *Matthiola longipetala* [*M. bicornis*]. This small annual presents a truly woebegone appearance during the sunny hours, its leaves dusty, its brownish purple flowers rolled up in little sulky balls. It is no plant indeed for any conspicuous place, but sow it about in patches along the edge of the shrubbery, or beneath the windows, for with the coming of dusk this small stock, once called the melancholy gilliflower, because of its sad daytime demeanor, lifts its head, expands its dim-hued blossoms and looses upon the mild evening air such clouds of sweetness as will cause you literally to take root beside it. "A veritable active volcano of the most delicious perfume," my friend the late Joseph Jacob called it and advised sowing it over the heads of departing bulbs. Several sowings should be made at intervals of ten days in order that its presence may be prolonged throughout the summer, and it may be thinned out to give each little plant ample space, but not transplanted.

Delicious also is the sweet white tobacco, "the dumb white nicotine" of Edna St. Vincent Millay's poem

> which wakes and utters her fragrance
> In a garden sleeping.

It, too, presents a poor figure by day, and we are apt to feel that it takes up a good deal of room. But with the coming of night the long creamy tubes freshen and expand and give forth their rich perfume and we are then glad we have so much of it. Once in the garden the white tobacco will always be there unless you take strenuous measures against it, for it is a hardy and free seeder and looks well to its posterity. It is perhaps not generally known that the tobaccos bloom well and thrive in partial shade. There are varieties with rose and crimson blossoms but they are not as sweet as the old white kind. There is a species, *N. sylvestris*, said not to close its blossoms by day but I have had no experience with it. If you have a small greenhouse a few plants of white tobacco will scent the house at evening.

Two other annuals that should be sown about near the windows, or in some inconspicuous place, are *Nicterinia selaginoides*, from the Cape of Good Hope, and *Schizopetalon walkeri* from Chile. The first is a small inconspicuous plant which during the day offers to the eye tightly closed blossoms like so many little brown buttons on the stem. At nightfall, however, these unfold to display "the most beautiful regular elongated heart-shaped petals of the purest white. They then give out a most delicious perfume reminiscent of jasmine and vanilla." This little annual may be sown early in heat if desired and transplanted later to the garden. It grows less than a foot tall. *Schizopetalon,* on the other hand, may not be moved, for it is impossible to disturb the delicate root system without injury. Sow it where it is to flower in rather poor soil and full sunshine. It is a small thing altogether but very pretty with blossoms "like little squares of white lace scented with almond." It is open only at night. White petunia may join these and the wild four o'clock of Colorado, *Abronia fragrans,* a trailing plant which though perennial is said to bloom the first year from seed sown indoors in March. The flowers are white and borne in large verbena-like heads, very fragrant at night.

My favourite among night-scented plants is sweet rocket, *Hesperis,* named for the evening star. Once it was very popular in gardens and known as the favourite of Marie Antoinette, that tragic queen who appears to have loved the simplest flowers. Perhaps it was encouraged in the gardens of the Hameau, the rustic hamlet adjoining the great gardens of Versailles, now so strangely still, where once the rash great folk played at being simple on the edge of desperation. It is easy to fancy its white stars gleaming about the Temple of Love and could we linger there at sunset the air would doubtless be sweet with its perfume.

Nowadays the sweet rocket must look after itself in holes and corners on the edge of respectability, and has even taken to the fields and roadsides in some localities. But it is worthy of serious consideration in the garden, both the white and the violet kinds, for few flowers so well offset the stodginess of peonies, whether in the borders or for cutting, and it creates a most welcome lightness among the heavy-headed June irises and oriental poppies. Of course it is biennial in duration and must be raised from seed annually, unless you give it a chance to perpetuate itself by self-sowing, which it is very ready to do.

Dame's violet and queen's gilliflower were old names for the sweet rocket, and Rea in his delightful garden book says it is to be found "growing plentifully in every countrywoman's garden, and by them called close sciences," a curious name which Parkinson tells us was manufactured by John Gerade out of Sciney, in turn a corruption of damascena – whence I suppose comes the name of damask violet. The sweet rocket has the advantage over many night-scenting flowers in that it does not lose its looks or its figure by day but appears always comely and fresh.

The double rocket was once even a greater favourite, especially in Scotch gardens where its culture reached a high state of perfection – for the double rocket, unlike its humble single sister, requires considerable skill in the growing. To keep it going it had continually to be transplanted to fresh quarters, or an increase maintained by means of cuttings. For four hundred years it was the boast of many a garden but today it has all but disappeared. I once saw double rockets in a Scotch cottage garden.

They were, as Mr. Bowles describes them, "whiter than the grey of an oyster and greyer than the greenish white of Lowestoft china," but I have never seen any in this country. Mr. Ellwanger in "The Garden's Story" several times mentions them, however, so doubtless they were once grown here. The scent of double rockets is faintly lemony by day but at night has the rich spiciness of the stock, and they have the appearance also of small double-flowered stocks.

Nicholson lists *Hesperis tristis,* a biennial, with flowers "whitish or cream-colored, or brownish red, or dark purple, and fragrant at night." This is a wild plant of Eastern Europe and Nicholson suggests that it be grown on old walls, ruins, and such like places where the seed may be sown in the crevices. Both these plants sound as if they would be very pleasant possessions, but so far I have not come across them in any seed lists. *H. tristis* however appears in the latest Kew List, so it must be somewhere about.

Silene and *Lychnis* a good deal resemble each other and both belong to the pink family, Caryophyllaceae. Though each genus has many scentless flowers, both contribute several species that are fragrant at night. The author of that delightful little work, "The Book of Old Fashioned Flowers," describes *Silene nutans,* a catchfly that is found in parts of England on limestone rocks: "This plant bears many large white flowers during June and July, each flower lasting but for three nights. At about seven o'clock of the first evening, the flower quickly opens and emits a strong scent as of hyacinths. Five of its stamens quickly develop, the pollen ripens and the anthers burst. At three o'clock in the morning, or thereabouts, the scent ceases to be produced, the five anthers wither and the corolla closes. During the following day the flower looks as though dead or dying. At the same hour as on the previous evening it again opens and again becomes fragrant. Five more stamens develop and ripen their pollen, after which the plant again closes as before. The proceeding is again repeated on the third night, the pistil however now developing instead of the stamens. The stigma having been fertilized by pollen brought by moths from another flower, the corolla closes as before, in the early morning and never again reopens."

Silene nutans has the name, in some quarters, of Nottingham catchfly because it was found growing plentifully in the walls of Nottingham Castle. That pleasant writer of the last century, Ann Pratt, described it as hanging in masses from the white cliffs of Dover where hundreds pass it daily without giving it a glance because the blossoms appear as if withered. "Yet by six o'clock in the evening the grassy spots seem whitened by stars and the perfume appears to the author to be more powerful than that of any other wild flower."

Silene noctiflora, the night-flowering catchfly, called by Parkinson "Morpheus' sweet wild campion" is an annual inhabiting sandy places and corn fields in Britain and certain localities here where it has become naturalized. The flowers are blush-coloured and fragrant only after sunset.

Silene latifolia [*Lychnis vespertina*], the vesper campion, or much less poetically the sticky cockle, a biennial, was once a garden plant in very good standing, especially the double form which was prized for cutting. Perhaps it is still to be found in some old fashioned gardens but I do not remember to have seen it since I was a child, that is in cultivation; one sometimes meets with it along the roadsides or hovering about the borders of cultivated fields where during the day you would not notice it. But at night the pale stars expand and it calls attention to itself by its sweetness. My book on "Farm Weeds" speaks of this erstwhile garden favourite quite cruelly as "a common impurity" in grass and clover seed and says that where it has gained a foothold in clover fields it is almost impossible to eradicate. Truly it has fallen upon evil days.

EVENING PRIMROSE
(*Oenothera acaulis*)

It is a pity that so many of these fragrant old garden flowers have gone out of fashion. We live in an age where display is over-emphasized and doubtless the inconspicuous night bloomer would be regarded as occupying space that might better be given to something of a more showy character. But the garden loses much of its magic by their absence and surely a few at least should be grown if they are to be come by. I have been looking over such catalogs as I have at hand but nowhere do I find the names of any of the night-flowering catchflies or the vesper campions.

Not infrequently when plants disappear from catalogs and garden books they reappear in Botanies and wild flower books. This usually means that fashion has turned its back upon them and the poor dears have fled for shelter to the wayside and fields and taken to a roving gypsy life. "Escaped" is the way their departure is usually described. Thus have gone many of the fine night-flowering plants whose day-time attractions are slight. If you look into Gray's "Botany" you will find the names of the night-scented campions and catchflies noted as "adventive from Europe" and it is only in our rambles about the countryside that we shall meet these flowers in the flesh. More than likely a patch of one or other of them is the source of the sudden lovely perfume that we sometimes catch as we pass on flying wheels through the summer darkness along some unfrequented country road.

The evening primroses (*Oenothera*), having quite showy flowers, have fared somewhat better and still appear, many of them, in accredited lists of garden flowers. It is altogether an American tribe, all the species being found in North or South America. Among them are annuals, biennials and perennials suitable for the borders, the wild garden, or the rock garden. They are all flowers of the sunshine, begging heat and light, and preferring a poorish, dry soil. Many of them are delicately scented but they are not all, despite their common name, evening flowering, though many are.

Perhaps the most deliciously scented of the evening primroses, and it may be thought the loveliest, is *O. caespitosa* (*O. marginata*). It is a low growing perennial from our Northwest that makes little tufts of grey-green leaves close to the ground, out of which arise on very short stems papery blossoms, over a long period in summer. A description of the opening of this flower from "The Garden," August 7, 1927, is worth giving in full: "The rough green buds prepare to open an hour or two before sunset when the pleated white petals begin to bulge out between the sepals and if they are plucked and brought into the house at this stage their flowering may be watched during dinner. The sepals under the pressure of the swelling petals suddenly spring apart and bending downwards about as fast as the minute hand of a clock, allow the petals to unfold into a great white chalice, some four inches across, tinted pale green at the throat and enclosing a green style and five delicately designed stamens looped about with ropes of sticky yellow pollen. All through the night the flower pours out the strong sweet scent, rather like that of *Magnolia grandiflora* but a trifle heavier (it has been compared to a combination of lemon and tuberose) till about eight o'clock the next morning when the petals begin to flush with rose, which deepens to bright pink as they fade limply an hour or two later."

A hot and sheltered locality on the rock garden should be given these fine plants in cold districts if they are to withstand the winter, or the roots may be taken up with the coming of cold weather and wintered in a frame. It is a pity to lose them. *O. acaulis* [*O. taraxacifolia*] is a beautiful and popular kind from Chile with leaves resembling those of the dandelion in a flat rosette and large scented white flowers opening with the coming of dusk and fading to pink with the dawn. "As seen at night a Chilean hillside covered with *Oenothera acaulis* in bloom appears to be strewn with innumerable round discs of white paper." In northern gardens this species requires the same treatment as the two before mentioned.

Oenothera tetraptera, a biennial species, found from Arizona to Texas and also in South America, is often spoken of as fragrant but though I have often watched the punctual unfolding of its white chiffon flowers in my garden just after sunset, I have never detected the least perfume. *O. elata* ssp. *hirsutissima* [*O. biennis*], American in origin, is now a weed the world over, and its so-called improved forms deserve no higher praise, whatever their sponsors may claim for them. During the day one is ashamed of the tall ungainly stalks hung untidily with tattered faded blooms that appear like louts at a gathering of elegant folk. But when the great lemon-coloured moons shine out against the gathering dusk and the light ravishing scent floats out upon the damp evening air, one is enchanted in spite of oneself. *O. odorata*, a Chilean annual, is much in the way of the foregoing and worth growing for its searching sweet scent and its evening illumination. Handsomer than either of these is a species that Margaret Armstrong says is found about the Yosemite, *O. elata* ssp. *hookeri*, whose blossoms begin to open as the mountain shadows slant across the valley until the meadows are strewn with "patens of bright gold."

A very beautiful species is *O. californica*, a rather rare plant of sandy stretches of interior Southern California with the characteristic wide silken blossoms, white in this instance, with a tangle of golden stamens, and exhaling a fragile but lovely perfume. *O. brachycarpa* (*O. howardii*) is from Colorado, a dwarf species with tufts of prostrate leaves and diaphanous, delicately scented flowers, each from three to four inches across, bright yellow in colour but changing to warm orange as they age.

The scent of the evening primroses is never heavy or cloying but always sweet and light though quite searching, and there is something exotic about it. Sniffing, one thinks of southern lattices and jasmine or orange flowers and the lovely stephanotis. Anyone may have this sweetness in his garden for the plants of the genus *Oenothera* are easily raised from seed.

Some writers credit the evening primrose with the power to give forth a mysterious phosphorescent light but though I have looked for it I have not seen it, nor have I heard the "silver burst of sound" that Mrs. Deland in one of her poems describes as accompanying the opening of the common wayside kind. Perhaps my senses are not keen enough to detect these delicate happenings and it is sad to think one's faculties may become dulled for want of exercise and many a lovely act of Nature be missed in consequence.

There are numerous other flowers that in a manner of speaking turn night into day. The little brown-flowered raisin vine is one of these. It gives to the night a spicy fragrance that it quite withholds from the day. This scent is associated with my earliest years, for the little climber wound a reveal of fragile luxuriance about the library windows of my Maryland home and at night mingled its spicy breath with the odour of dust and old leather characteristic of rooms where books have long accumulated. To smell the raisin vine brings before me more than one domestic scene dear to memory, but chiefly the picture of my father and mother sitting side by side in the soft light of the student's lamp reading through the long quiet evenings. Life offers us more distractions today, but as I look back upon those days they seem to have been very peaceful, very spacious and uncluttered, with time for much that was worth while that there is no time for today. Once a year, anyway, when the raisin vine blooms in April, I can go back to them for a fleeting moment.

The tall woolly mullein, *Verbascum phlomoides*, has a faint but searching odour on cloudy days and towards evening. Yuccas are sometimes surprisingly apparent to our nasal organs at night and the flowers of the sweet woodruff also exhale a delicate sweetness after the sun has set. Two night-scenting shrubs I have note of which are not personally known to me. *Genista cinerea*, of Southern Europe, makes a large bush, each branch of which is said to be wreathed in season with yellow pea-shaped blossoms that scent the air early in the morning and in the evening, and *Lonicera heckrottii*, a noble honeysuckle, with flowers deep rose without and buff within, is said to be delightfully scented, though only at night.

Mr. Bowles, whose keen nose I have had occasion to quote more than once in these pages, writes thus of the perfume of *Daphne laureola*: "It is strongest just after dark but sometimes one catches its fragrance at dusk. It is one of the scents that is borne on the air many yards from the plant and it is rather elusive, I mean you suddenly smell it and take a long breath to get more and lo! it has vanished. You go nearer the bushes but you cannot pick it up, then you pass them suddenly and get another whiff of it." Many fragrant plants thus play hide-and-go-seek with you. I often wander about the garden trying to track down some vagrant scent without success only to find it finally where I had passed many times. This is true especially of the witch hazel, that daring gay little tree that dons its fragile finery in the face of Winter's sure approach. Thrust your nose amidst the yellow blossoms and you can detect no perfume unless you crush them, but wander away indifferently and it will slyly seek you out and give you a rare treat.

Gladiolus tristis, a species that grows wild in South Africa, is delightfully fragrant at night. It grows in swampy waste land I am told and if you are walking home at sunset along the borders of a swamp you catch delicious whiffs of perfume, and there amidst the reedy growths gleam the pale yellow flowers of this gladiolus. *Tristis* is a usual specific name for night-scenting plants and means sad or dull in reference to the meek and often dingy colours so often worn by them. *Pelargonium triste* is a geranium with dingy flowers that fill room or greenhouse with rich perfume during the dark hours. Numerous greenhouse plants are night-scenting, among them the lovely white-flowered bouvardia, that smells like stephanotis, several from *Datura*, the night-blooming jasmine, *Cestrum nocturnum*, with creamy-yellow flowers, and *Nyctanthes arbor-tristis*, a small tree of India, sometimes called the tree of sadness because the beauty and sweetness of the pale flowers are for the night only, and before day dawns have fallen withered to the ground.

That astonishing waterlily, 'Victoria Regia', with its enormous platter-like leaves turned up about the edges and often seven feet or more in diameter, is one of the most magnificent of night-blooming flowers. The great blossoms, measuring from eight to fifteen inches across, open at dusk and remain open throughout the night. They partly close with the coming of light but open again the following night, the petals changing the while from gleaming white until by the third day they have become a deep purplish red. The fragrance of these great flowers is rich and pervading, strongly fruity, like pineapple in quality and perceptible many yards from the plants.

The lovely flowers of the lotus, *Nelumbo*, have also a richer fragrance at night. Brought into the house the delicate but exquisite sweetness, not unlike that of a magnolia but with a faintly bitter tang, finds its way through the darkness to all the rooms of the house. This is the noblest of all water plants and should be grown wherever conditions can be made to suit it. Someone has said that the lotus has its roots in the mud but its fragrance reaches the throne of God.

No record of night-scenting flowers would be complete without mention of the strange cactus, the queen-of-the-night, *Selenicereus grandiflorus* [*Cereus grandiflorus*], of the West Indies, whose bristling tortured stems give birth in the darkness to the most spectacular of blossoms. I remember being allowed to "sit up" when a little girl to witness the flowering of this strange plant in a neighbour's greenhouse. The huge flower began to unfold at about eight o'clock and at eleven was fully blown, its rich perfume seeming to fill the world. The calyx of the flower when fully expanded is nearly a foot across, brownish in colour without and bright yellow on the upper side, having the appearance of a great gilded star. The petals, snowy white and of a high lustre, gleam against this golden background and the vast number of stamens at the heart add to the splendid appearance of this flower. Probably no other flower equals it in sheer magnificence. But its hour of triumph is short. Before the cock crows the drama is played out and the beautiful blossoms fallen into decay.

Other night-scenting flowers are noted in the chapter on Annuals and in Additional Notes.

CHAPTER XII

Green Aromatics (Herbs)

When I pick or crush in my hand a twig of bay, or brush against a bunch of rosemary, or tread upon a tuft of thyme, or pass through incense-laden Cistus, I feel that here is all that is best and purest and most refined, and nearest to poetry in the range of faculty of the sense of smell.

— GERTRUDE JEKYLL

LEAF ODOURS, WHETHER sweet or bitter, are nearly all refreshing and stimulating. To persons who are unable to bear the heavy sweet perfumes of certain flowers the clean animating odours of aromatic leaves will be grateful. I find a nosegay of sweet herbs on my writing table a great pleasure both to sight and to smell. Lavender and southernwood is a good combination, or marjoram and winter savory. Nearly all leaves are what Bacon called "fast of their smells," they do not force themselves upon our attention, we must seek them out on the contrary and signify by a touch or gentle pressure that we desire them. They are like shy people who find it difficult to open their hearts save at the magic of a sympathetic touch. A sharp frost will bring their incense pouring forth, and sometimes a heavy rain, as in the case of box and sweetbrier. Goldsmith's familiar lines tell the story:

As aromatic plants bestow
No spicy fragrance while they grow,
But crushed or trodden to the ground,
Diffuse their balmy sweets around.

Leaves hold their perfumes far longer than do flowers, being sweeter often when in a dried state than when fresh, and they can impart this sweetness in such strength as to become a flavour. Many know the taste of mint, of sassafras, of sage, wintergreen or tarragon, who have no idea what the growing plants may look like.

More space was given in old fashioned gardens to sweetleaved plants than in ours today, and a sprig of southernwood with a moss rosebud, or a handful of lavender or lemon verbena, often passed from hostess to guest at parting with a friendly smile. Such a gift spoke a "dumb language" that was understood and appreciated by both donor and receiver. But plants that diffuse their sweetness through their bodies seldom have showy flowers; the blossom of the sweetbrier is inconspicuous, of the sweet geraniums negligible, of the sweet bay unnoticeable, and none of the sweet herbs has bright flowers. The gay bee balm is the exception that proves the rule, for even the pungent tansy's gold is tarnished, and when the sage family blossoms forth in scarlet raiment it has lost the potent tang for which its family is famous.

Today we place our dependence for charm in the garden largely upon colour and form, neglecting more subtle influences. But I know one lovely garden where the pleasant old parting custom is still observed. When you go reluctantly from Mrs. John Jay Chapman's garden, "Sylvania" on the Hudson, you carry with you a root of applemint to plant in your garden in memory of your sure-to-have-been memorable visit. One could not have a more potent reminder of the hospitality enjoyed beneath this gracious roof.

In "All's Well That Ends Well" there is this dialogue:

> CLOWN: Indeed, Sir, she was the Sweet Marjoram of the Salad, or rather the Herb of Grace.
>
> LAFEU: They are not Salad-Herbs, you Knave, they are nose-herbs.

The most famous of the nose-herbs is lavender whose flower spike, as modest in hue as a Quaker's bonnet, is highly fragrant as well as its dusty leaves. Indeed it is the flowers that are used in the many preparations in which this sweet herb plays a major part. We grew lavender in our old Maryland garden and the sheets in my mother's house always smelled of it. What sweet slumbers come to one between lavender-scented sheets! You will remember Isaac Walton's recommendation, "Let's go to that house for the linen looks white and smells of lavender, and I long to be in a pair of sheets that smell so."

Charles VI of France is said to have sat upon cushions stuffed with lavender, the scent of which perhaps helped to clear the poor crown-weighted brain. Lavender is indeed one of the cleanest and most invigorating of odours. Lavender water has for centuries been a mitigation for headache and the vapours. It "is renowned for a simple purity – a sweet fragrance and a subtle strength, it is the odour of the domestic virtues and the symbolic perfume of a quiet life."

Though lavender is native of the sun-drowned lands bordering the Mediterranean, it is in the moist air of England that it reaches its greatest perfection of strength and sweetness, and English lavender water and other lavender products are the finest in the world. In the south of England, about Mitcham, Hitchin, Canterbury and Bournemouth, lavender is grown on a large scale commercially, and the Mitcham Oil of Lavender is the finest made in any country.

In America this fragrant herb is little grown even in localities where it is quite hardy. This was not always so. I remember when a little girl in Baltimore the pleasantest corners of the great open markets, for which that city is justly famous, were the lavender stalls where the pale aromatic spikes lay piled in great bunches that were eagerly bought by the fastidious housewives of the city to strew in their linen presses. Lizette Woodworth Reese has preserved between the pages of one of her books of poems the memory of "The Lavender Woman" of the Baltimore market:

Crooked, like bough the March wind bends
  wallward across the sleet,
Stands she at her blackened stall
  in the loud market street;
All about her in the sun, full-topped
  exceeding sweet,
Lie bundles of gray lavender, a-shrivel
  in the heat.

I remember too that in the old Clark garden, "Greenlea," in Delaware, the lavender grew tall and rich scented, tended by my stately cousin Julia in her crisp lavender gowns of print or muslin, and in other gardens that I was familiar with in those days, it was always to be found. Perhaps it is still cherished in old fashioned southern gardens – but there are so many new names that sound in the ears one does not hear of it.

North of Philadelphia lavender is difficult to keep over the winter though it can be done. In the herb corner of my old Rockland County garden, against the stone wall of the garden house, facing south, I had for many years a narrow border of lavender and York and Lancaster roses that gave me infinite pleasure. The lavender plants originally came from Henry A. Dreer, of Philadelphia, and were a very narrow-leaved variety that seems to be hardier than the ordinary broad-leaved English lavender. Dwarf lavender, 'Munstead' or 'Compacta Nana', lives from year to year in the rock garden here with only a slight covering of leaves or salt hay. But it is safe only in a poor, light and perfectly drained soil.

Lavandula angustifolia [*L. vera*] is the true English lavender. *L. stoechas,* which is very finely scented, is called French lavender, though it grows much more plentifully in the mountains of Spain and Portugal, where it was once used to strew the floors of churches and dwellings on festival days. Ancient books wrote it Stichadoue. White flowered lavender is not nearly as pretty as the common kinds but it has the value that we place upon rare things. I had a little bush of white lavender once but a bitter winter claimed it. I read that Queen Henrietta Maria in her garden at Wimbledon had "great and large borders of rosemary and white lavender."

In the "Garden of Health," 1633, forty-five ills of flesh or spirit are named as curable by various decoctions of lavender, and just to smell it was said to "comfort and cleare the eyes." Lawson thought it the most "comfortable" flower for smelling, except roses.

Rosemary is hardly known in this country save as a legend. Even in salubrious England it is less common than lavender. Old Lawson wrote, "Rosemary, the grace of herbs here in England, in other countries common.... It becomes a window well. The use is much in meates, more in Physicke, most for Bees."

And in truth it does become a window well, it makes a charming pot plant, neat, svelte, with its dark, felt-lined leaves held sleekly against its sides. The smell of the leaves is keen and heady, resinous yet sweet with a hint of nutmeg, and the odour of the dried leaves is so lasting that the plant has become the emblem of constancy, or remembrance – "Here's Rosemary for Remembrance." In an Elizabethan song book is the following sentimental verse:

> Rosemary is for remembrance
> Between us daie and nighte,
> Wishing that I may alwaies have
> You present in my sight.

We who grow rosemary cherishingly in a pot on the window ledge can hardly visualize Parkinson's description of it – risen "unto a very great height, with a great and woody stem of that compasse that, being cloven out into boards it hath served to make lutes or such like instruments, and here with us carpenter's rules–" I never saw rosemary in England grown to any such size though I have seen many venerable bushes, hoary with years and gnarled. There is much of it in Miss Jekyll's garden at Munstead Wood trained against the walls where the sun draws out its sharp sweetness to greet you as you pass.

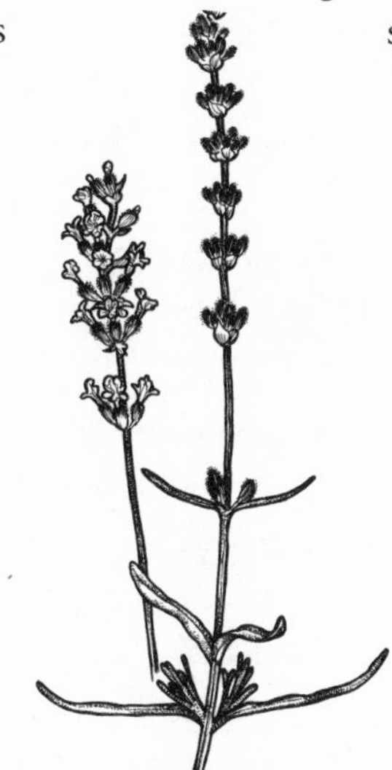

LAVENDER
(*Lavendula officinalis*)
'Provence'

In old days the odour of rosemary was deemed exceedingly potent; there was almost no evil seemingly that it could not be counted upon to ward off – even old age. "Smell it oft and it shall keep thee youngly," advised Banckes in his early sixteenth century "Herbal," which has as rhythmic a tempo as the Songs of Solomon. In Langham's "Garden of Health" he counsels to preserve youth make a box of rosemary wood and "smell to it."

Branches of rosemary placed beneath the bed insured against gruesome dreams; placed among clothes or books it protected them against the depredations of moths; boiled in water and partaken frequently it preserved against "all manner of evils of the body," and it was a famous cosmetic:

> Boyle the leaves in white wine and washe thy face therewith and thy browes and thou shalt have a faire face.

Rosemary is a native of Southern Europe and Asia Minor and there is but the one species – there are several varieties of *Rosmarinus officinalis,* meaning dew of the sea, one with variegated leaves more tender than the ordinary kind and not very pretty, and a charming prostrate form which scrambles over the rocks on the Island of Capri. The tiny downy, pale flowers are borne in great profusion along the stiff little shoots in spring and have a quite different sweetness from that of the body of the plant, and they are very free in casting it off upon the air. Bacon wrote of heaths of rosemary which he says "will smell a great way in the sea, perhaps twenty miles."

This pleasant old herb is easily raised from seed, or plants are commonly to be had of most nurseries. A sprig is delicious in the finger bowl, or you may like to try the French fashion of seasoning ragout of veal with it. North of the Carolinas it must grow in a pot.

All of the mint family have odoriferous leaves, though not all are agreeable; such as dead nettle, motherwort and the catmints, catnip and hoarhound are too coarse and medicinal in quality for enjoyment, though they are not actively unpleasant.

A small book might be written about the kinds and the many virtues of mints. Frances Bardswell has given them a whole chapter in her delightful book, "The Herb Garden." She enumerates ten kinds, including the powerfully odoriferous pennyroyal – one of the few herbs that floods the surrounding air with its searching aroma without encouragement – and the cat mints (*Nepeta*). Spearmint, *Mentha spicata* [*M. viridis*], is the kind we grow in our gardens to put in lamb sauce and innocuous summer drinks. Julep mint we used to call it in that far robust day when the breathlessness of summer Sunday afternoons was mitigated by shiny black trays of frosted glasses filled with crushed ice and amber liquid and sprouting sheaves of emerald mint. There is a tradition, I do not know if it be matter of fact, that spearmint must be transplanted every three years or it will lose its characteristic flavour and degenerate to the coarser peppermint, *M. × piperita,* which has an off smell of camphor that is slightly disagreeable, and which is widely naturalized in the United States in the neighbourhood of old gardens. It is from this kind that oil of peppermint is derived, and we have it to thank as well for the comforting menthol.

My favourite in this pungent family is the variegated apple mint that came to me from Mrs. Chapman's garden. It has a scent of both apples and spice, with a cool quality that is exceedingly pleasant. I often bring the long green and white branches, tipped with silvery inflorescence, indoors to fill an amber glass jar, on heavy summer days; besides being charmingly cool to look at, it seems to impart a subtle freshness to the sultry atmosphere. This mint is good to use as a variant to the garden mint in sauces and cold drinks of various kinds. Bergamot mint or orangemint, *Mentha × piperita* 'Citrata', is said to be very delicious also but it is not easy to come by – I have long sought it. It is one of the ingredients that endows Chartreuse with its exquisite, indefinable flavour and bouquet. Something akin to this is *Mentha* ×*gracilis* [*M. gentilis*], a pretty variegated kind with reddish stems.

All our mints are wayfarers from over seas but all of them have made a permanent place for themselves in our spacious wild, following streams or haunting low meadows and damp wood verges. If we are lucky, for it is not too plentiful, we may come in our wanderings afield upon the pleasantly scented watermint, of which Gerard wrote: "The Savour or smell of the watermint rejoyceth the heart of man." The coarser horsemint, *M. longifolia,* is more prevalent, as is the corn mint, *M. arvensis,* said by country people to keep milk from curdling. The pretty curly-leafed-mint, *M. spicata* 'Crispa' [*M. crispa*], is not scarce, and Gray enumerates several more.

Collecting mints would be a pleasant enterprise for they all have character and a good smell, but they grow too rapidly where they grow at all – which by the way they do not by any means always do, proving most unexpectedly intractable in some places – and require more space than most of us can allow them. If but two are to be grown the best indubitably are spearmint and applemint – and no garden should be without these. All the mints like moisture but are remarkably patient with only a modicum of it.

On my desk beside me as I write is a widemouth brown jar filled with sweet-leaved branches culled partly from my own garden and partly from that of the artist across the lane, who also has a nose for such simple delights, and who enjoys adding an unexpected flavour to her salads and other culinary adventures. Winter savory, *Satureja montana,* is there with its dark neat leaves, and quick warm sweet scent, much like that of thyme. It is a good and neat little perennial, ornamental in rock garden or border edge if you do not have an herb plot. The flavour of summer savory, *S. hortensis,* is superior, but this is an annual and so requires yearly thought. English cooks flavour their broad beans with savory, as they do their fresh green peas with mint; neither result is pleasant to my palate. Pot marjoram is anybody's plant, growing strongly in a sprawly way at the edge of any sunny border and producing in the late summer innumerable flat heads of tiny pinkish flowers set in reddish bracts. The scent of the dusty heart-shaped leaves is warm and rough and sweet. But Sweet or knotted marjoram has an even better scent with something vaguely resinous added to the other constituents. In a very savory little book called "Herbs, Salads and Seasonings," the authors mention another marjoram, *Origanum microphyllum,* "in which a hint of lemon is added to the curious, slightly cedar-wood scent of the type" and which they say is known as the eau de cologne plant. All the marjorams are easily grown from seed.

Sage is ornamental as well as virtuous. A friend of mine has a great bush of sage at the top of a dry wall where the slurred softness of its grey leaves, like grey duvetyn, shows to perfection, and when its violet flower spikes are in evidence it is a thing of real beauty. Sage is said to promote longevity and there is an old saying – "How can a man die who grows sage in his garden?" It is also thought to follow the fortunes of the house, dwindling when evil days befall and reviving miraculously when things are bright again.

As a flavouring sage is easily over-done. In stuffings of duck and goose the tiniest smitch only is admissible, more spoils the dish. Our forefathers relished sage cheese and were dosed with sage tea, but endurance is not what it was.

The two basils are here, sweet and bush, very neat to the eye and pleasing to the nose. Basil, says a sixteenth century writer, "used to bee set in the middest of Knottes and in windows, for the excellent savour it hath." But it was little employed in cookery of early days though in great demand for the manufacture of sweet waters, sweet bags, and to put into nosegays. A woman who keeps a roadside stand in Westchester County often has pots of basil for sale. I asked her what her customers used it for but she had not been curious enough to ask. I have grown one kind or another for many years, finding that chopped fine it adds interest and tone to a simple salad, and it is the source of an exciting flavour that animates a certain cocktail that is the specialty of a clever young artist of my acquaintance. The basils are from the East Indies, are hardy annuals and easily grown. An ancient writer reports Theophrastus as proclaiming that basil "prospereth best when it is sowed with curses." The seed of basil pounded fine and partaken will procure you a "merrie hearte."

Balm and bergamot and lemon verbena are all nose herbs of the first order with what might be termed an underlying likeness, one to the other, in their aromatics. Balm is a determined weed, too rampant to admit to the garden, but if you meet it in your country walks and draw it through your fingers you receive a delicious greeting. It has a fine lemony tang that was made use of by performers of old, but lemon verbena has now largely taken its place. John Evelyn writes of balm: "Balm, hot and dry cordial and exhilarating, sovereign for the Brain, strengthning the Memory and powerfully chasing away Melancholly." Lemon verbena makes a fine tidy plant in the summer garden or in a pot in the window, and its fragrant leaves with those of applemint and sweet geraniums are invaluable for nosegays, or the finger bowl.

Bergamot, *Monarda*, has a long past as a perfumery plant, not however in the most exclusive circles – chiefly among country belles who made a pleasant sweet water from its leaves and stalks with which to augment their charms. The true bergamot of the professional perfumer is derived from the rind of a small bitter orange, *Citrus bergamia*, a native of Southern Europe.

Wild bergamot, *Monarda fistulosa*, riots in pale and bloomy profusion along our country roadsides, and the grander kind, *M. didyma*, in its newest raiment of 'Cambridge Scarlet', is a prideful ornament of select gardens. An ancient great aunt, barely remembered, used to pin her faith upon a bath in which branches of bergamot had been steeped to ease the stiffness of her tired old joints. In "Daddy Darwin's Dovecote" there is a pretty passage between Phoebe and her shy young admirer about the red bergamot that grew in Daddy Darwin's garden. She had lost her meeting posy of old man and marigold and when young Jack offers to get another just like it Phoebe artfully angles for something better: "My mother says Daddy Darwin has red bergamot in his garden. We've none in ours. My mother says there's nothing like red bergamot to take to church. She says it's a deal more refreshing than old man, and not so common."

Our foremothers knew various innocent devices for palliating the tiresomeness of man's sermonizing. One, and not the least effective, was the Sabbath posy composed of stimulating and reviving herbs which they carried to church and held under their noses, or nibbled at, during the interminable discourses thundered from the pulpit. Various were the formulas for its assemblage, but favourite ingredients were southernwood (old man), marigold, bergamot, costmary, fennel, moss and cabbage roses, and sometimes heads of dill or coriander seeds.

Southernwood (*Artemisia abrotanum*) called also old man and lad's love, has a bland refreshing redolence and its grey feathery branches are the perfect accompaniment for white moss rosebuds.

The artemisias are a large family, all having odoriferous qualities, some nicer than others. Old woman, dusty miller, beach wormwood, *A. stelleriana,* is softly feathery and very good to smell. *A. frigida* is also agreeable and balmy. *A. annua* is a wayside annual weed naturalized from Europe, that is very sweet indeed. There are too many to name here but the weedy mugwort of deserted dooryards and run down fields is one that has a tonic breath and the sage brush of our western plains is another. In an old book I find the recommendation often made to keep clothes free from moths, "brush them over thoroughly well twice or thrice every year as they hang, with a brush made of wormwood tops."

TANSY
(*Tanacetum parthenium*)

Costmary and tansy belong together only because they are near relations, for as is often the case with those whom birth hath joined together they have little in common. Tansy, golden buttons, *Tanacetum vulgare,* is a tall, coarse, beautiful wayside weed, with lacelike leaves and heads of tarnished gold buttons in the late summer. A generation or so ago it was in high repute among us as a medicinal plant and tansy tea was a frequent affliction that had to be suffered by the young and helpless. There are recipes for it in all the old cook books, even as late as those of my mother's day. Tansy has a strong, bitter yet pungent odour which is more appreciated by the nose now that the palate need no longer fear it. In England tansy cakes were an Easter provision, whether in expiation of sins or as a reward I do not know, and there was a seemingly popular pudding to which the tansy lent not only its "sober green" but its truly terrible taste. What hardy stomachs must our forefathers have possessed!

Costmary, on the other hand is delicious, at least to the nose. The long flaccid green leaves have a scent that is like that of no other herb but is vaguely reminiscent of the taste of the "morning bitters" (whiskey with bitter herbs) that was a commonplace in many southern households a generation ago. It was a famous nibbling herb and played a part often in the Sabbath posy, or lay as a book-mark in the Bible or hymnal – hence its name of bible leaf. My country neighbours in Rockland County, N. Y., called it sweet Mary Ann. Its formal name is *Tanacetum balsamita,* and in old English works it is often referred to as Alecost because of its use in flavouring beer and negus. My root of costmary came to me from a very old Germantown garden and I value it highly.

The thymes of course have a high place among green odours but I have spoken rather fully of them in the chapter on fragrant plants for the rock garden. When the ancients wished to speak highly of an author they said he smelled of thyme.

Rue and hyssop have bitter odours and bitterer tastes but both are handsome enough to win a place in the flower borders on their looks alone. Rue was thought to prosper most when stolen from a neighbour's garden but if your skin is sensitive you will hardly escape detection for you will probably suffer a most disfiguring poisoning from contact with the leaves. That wildly conjectural, if elegant scientist of Elizabeth's spacious reign, the right Honorable Francis Lo: Verulam, Viscount St. Albans (Bacon), advances the curious theory that rue "doth prosper much and becommeth stronger, if it be set by a Figge-Tree: which (we conceiue) is caused, Not by Reason of Friendship; but by extraction of a Contrary Iuyce from the earth."

Of bitter hyssop I grow three kinds, blue, white and rose, none as pretty as the blue but the white was a pleasant find, for it is rare. The old books speak of gold and silver hyssop but these I have not come across. Hyssop, like the sweet-smelling germander, was used to edge the little beds or "knottes" of Elizabethan gardens and stood the necessary clipping with equanimity. Lavender cotton was also used for this purpose, as were rosemary, lavender, box, thyme and savory. There is a charming knot garden adjoining Queen Anne's Orangery at Hampton Court that is a faithful reproduction of those that flourished in the days of Elizabeth and James.

A few more herbs are in my brown jar that perhaps may claim a place in this chapter: tarragon, *Artemisia dracunculus,* the invaluable, that country people say can abide to grow in the same bed with but few other plants – and indeed it does seem squeamish, dying unaccountably. Chervil, so good a variant to parsley, and which is delicious chopped into romaine and lettuce salads. Lovage, a tall old fashioned "yarb" that I found in a tiny garden that clutched a mountainside with desperate finger-like little beds; it smells of celery and was thought sovereign for coughs and a consumption. The old woman who, after a deal of hinting and finally open pleading, gave me a root in exchange for some of my best "Pinys," called it levoce. Burnet, that Bacon admired but which seems to me to have an insipid smell and is less like cucumber in taste than is borage; fennel, tall, feathery and smelling like turpentine (once used as a dressing for fish), and the four important seed plants – anise, caraway, coriander and dill. These are of annual duration and come readily from seed, and you will find many uses for them if you have them in your garden. Dill I would not be without for anything, for a sprinkling of the seeds turns green apple pie into a quite celestial dish. And of course it is well known for its addition to cucumber pickles. But besides its condimental uses the seed of dill smelled "stayeth the hicket," that embarrassing and sometimes surprisingly sudden affliction, and the leaves of this potent plant chewed "aswageth the blasting and griping torment of the stomach."

Caraway seeds lift rye bread out of the realm of the commonplace and a few put into baked apples or pears give them a pleasant zest. Coriander is a delightful little plant with pale heads of lavender blossoms that look like the finest enamel work. The seed smells like a bakeshop when the trays of freshly baked good things have just been brought in. They also exert a subduing influence on "yeoxing or hicket." Gerard calls coriander "a very stinking herbe" but I cannot agree with him. I like its searching odour and I like also its taste when I meet it in curry powder. Anise gives to the cordial that bears its name its characteristic bouquet and flavour. It is used also by druggists and confectioners. The odour is a good deal like that of sweet cicely though somewhat less sweet. Sweet cicely is a tall plant with beautiful fernlike foliage and umbels of pale bloom borne in May, when they are very useful for decorative purposes. It is a famous old kitchen herb with good scent and flavour. The oil from the seeds is said to have been used in the north of England to polish the oak flooring, which gave it not only a fine gloss but a pleasant scent.

It is a pleasant and commodious provision – to use an expressive old word – to have all or many of these herbs scattered about the garden, if not in a plot to themselves. Many uses will be found for them, not the least of which is in providing fragrant and decorative foliage to combine with bouquets. Herbs belong to the common and homely things of life and for this very reason, and because of their long human past, they are endeared to us. They have the charm of quiet persons whose minds are yet charged with wisdom and their personalities endowed with the quality that comes of long and varied human experience. They are easy to grow – kindly and responsive in their attitude towards us. Room given them is never wasted.

CHAPTER XIII

Sweet Leaved Geraniums

And genteel geranium
With a leaf for all that come.

— LEIGH HUNT

ONE OF THE PLEASANTEST recollections of my childhood is of setting forth with my father on winter Sunday afternoons from the commodious old stone house where we dwelt, just beyond the then limits of the city of Baltimore, and making our way across the frozen fields and along a narrow lane to a small commercial greenhouse owned by an apple-cheeked old Englishman whose name was Unwin. My father had a small lean-to greenhouse off his library where he indulged his fancy for the genus *Abutilon*, fuchsias, and such like old fashioned greenhouse plants, but what brought us to Mr. Unwin's was to see and discuss his very fine collection of sweet leaved geraniums, or to speak more exactly, pelargoniums. It appeared that though Mr. Unwin's was a very modest establishment, this collection of fragrant leaved geraniums was very complete and enjoyed considerable fame among plant-fanciers about the city and its environs.

My part in these visits was a silent one and would no doubt to the youth of today seem an extremely dull manner of spending an afternoon. But it was far from being so to me. I followed the two flower lovers, the one so tall and straight, the other old and bent, up and down the narrow aisles between the benches of plants, pausing when they paused, moving slowly forward when they advanced, filled with beatitude by the warm sweet odours given off by the moist earth and the growing green things. No notice was taken of me and so, left to my own devices, I would snip as I went, a leaf here, a leaf there, until finally with my hands and pockets full of aromatic leaves I would subside on an upturned tub in a corner to sniff and compare the different scents to my heart's content. It was a very good game indeed, as well as valuable nose training. It always seemed amazing that just leaves could have such a variety of odours. Some had the scents of oranges and lemons, some were spicy, others had a rose-like fragrance, and many were vaguely familiar but tantalizingly elusive. One that specially ravished my youthful nose smelled exactly like the pennyroyal that grew in our woods. The leaves of this kind were large and soft and the bush was lax and ungainly in habit. I know it now for *Pelargonium tomentosum,* usually called the peppermint geranium. But my favourite was a little slender plant with small much-cut leaves that had the sharp refreshing scent of lemon, with something sweet behind it. It had the charm of lemon drops – acid and sweet – and always made my mouth water ecstatically. It was probably *P.* x *citriosum.*

Now what, I wonder, has become of the many varieties of sweet leaved geraniums that were once the pride of every plant fancier, whether professional or of the parlour variety. Early in the nineteenth century, it is said, there were over two hundred varieties to be had in England, and I dare say as many in this country. Great collections were assembled and played an important part in every horticultural exhibit. Today no notice is taken of them at all. In some catalogs we find two or three varieties offered but modern horticultural works ignore them utterly. To find out anything about them we must turn to old books – old numbers of Curtis' "Botanical Magazine," Andrew's "Botanical Repository," the "Floricultural Cabinet," or Sweet's great work, "Geraniaceae," 1820. And it is only in little rural greenhouses in the back country, or in cottage windows – growing more than likely in a tin can – that we find these one-time favourites still cherished.

The scented leaved geraniums are native of the Cape of Good Hope, whence they were brought to England chiefly, I read, through the medium of the British fleet, "when it was operating with the Dutch helping to uphold their supremacy at the Cape," about the year 1795. These novel plants sprang into immediate and wide-spread popularity. The cottager, the noble and the commercial grower found in them a mine of interest and opportunity. It was soon discovered that *P. capitatum* furnished a most plausible adulterant of the costly tatar of rose, and to this nefarious end it was widely grown in Southern France and Turkey and I believe is still cultivated for the same purpose and for use as a basis for many rose perfumes and for pot pourri.

The varieties increased rapidly. It is easy to imagine that hybridists found it fascinating to produce new scents by crossing the various species. And that this floral sport was rather carried to excess we know. In Curtis' "Botanical Magazine," Vol. 3, we read – "As a florist desirous of seeing plants distinct in their characters we would almost wish it were impossible to raise these foreign geraniums from seeds; for without pretending to any extraordinary discernment we may venture to prophesy that in a few years, from the multiplication of feminal varieties, springing from seeds casually, or perhaps purposely impregnated with the pollen of different sorts, such a crop will be produced as will baffle all our attempts to reduce to species, or even regular varieties."

Perhaps over-multiplication with its consequent confusion and satiation was what ultimately brought about the downfall of the sweet leaved geranium; but it seems more likely that the fickle fancy of the public, ever on the lookout for new sensations, was caught by the increasing noise of the zonal pelargoniums (the ordinary bedding geranium) whose great blossom heads were beginning to fill the exhibition benches with brilliant colour and the Victorian flower beds with solid blocks of scarlet, pink and white. (Miller says the leaves of the zonals smell exactly like scalded apples, but I have heard them called in rural neighbourhoods fish geraniums because of a fancied resemblance of their odour to that of fish.)

In competition with the gorgeous zonals the quiet hued, sweet leaved varieties stood little chance of holding their public. Their blossoms were small and inconspicuous and without scent, their leaves were their whole fortune and while these were cut and slashed and lobed in the most intricate manner, and deliciously scented, the eye is a much more insistent organ than the nose – and so the sweet leaved geraniums fell out of fashion and were little more seen or heard of.

But the wheel turns and fashions come round again, and after all like the old gardener in "Mary's Meadow," we all like to "feel a good smell." The sweet leaved geraniums offered us the best of scents, and in what immense variety! Old lists contain the filbert-scented, the nutmeg-scented, cinnamon-scented, almond-scented, lemon-scented, orange and apple-scented, anise-scented, rose-scented, pine-scented, musk-scented, violet-scented, lavender-scented, balm-scented, and many more. It is not at all beyond belief that we shall be again, and before long, collecting these old favourites, and the plants that have been hiding away in obscure greenhouses, in farm kitchens and shabby parlours, will be brought to light and once more slipped and exchanged, sniffed over and exhibited as of yore.

If we do not number a greenhouse among our possessions, a few pots of sweet leaved geraniums ranged along the window ledges of the living rooms will give pleasure. And if the taste is set down as Victorian so is a good deal else that is comfortable and agreeable. In the garden I find that most persons like to cull a fragrant leaf here and there as they make their way about, and if we can furnish them with an intriguing variety so much the better. I always put a few plants of rose geranium in my beds of hybrid tea roses. They make an uncommonly good combination and there is no sweeter nosegay than one made of such a fragrant rose (if there be any as fragrant) as 'Gruss an Teplitz' and a leaf of rose geranium. Tucked into the belt or through the buttonhole or carried in the hand on a warm day, it enlivens and refreshes one amazingly. Nasturtium and rose geranium also make a stimulating nosegay.

Once no bouquet was deemed complete

without a bit of this fragrant foliage and far from detracting from the sweetness of other flowers it has the faculty of enhancing it. The large cut leaves make a delightful frill for a bunch of sweet peas or stocks, and of course they are invaluable for use with flowers that have no scent of their own. White pinks and lemon geranium are delicious together and if you want a nosegay that is altogether "different" try rose geranium and a few sprays of mock orange.

In my youth during jelly making time the leaves of rose geranium were made use of to give point and flavour to certain otherwise rather insipid jellies, apple among them. A leaf was put in the bottom of each glass before the boiling syrup was poured in. It was not cared for by everyone but we thought it very delicious, and especially nice to serve with roast lamb in the place of the more usual mint sauce.

In a little known "Language of Flowers" illustrated by the quaint drawings of Kate Greenaway, the language of the sweet leaved geranium is thus interpreted:

lemon geranium – Unexpected Meeting
nutmeg geranium – Expected Meeting
rose geranium – Preference
oak-leaved geranium – True Friendship

Here is a short list of kinds that seekers after old-fashioned flowers may care to be on the lookout for.

P. capitatum – rose geranium
P. crispum 'Lady Mary' [*P. limoneum*] – lemon geranium
P. clorinda. Very sharp and refreshing
P. citrosum 'Prince of Orange' [*P. citriodorum*] – orange-scented
P. crispum 'Cinnamon' [*P. gratum*] – cinnamon -scented
P. fragrans. spice-scented
P. graveolens – nutmeg-scented
P. × *limoneum* 'Lady Mary' – spice-scented
P. odoratissimum [*P. odorata*] – apple-scented
P. radens [*P. radula*] – rose-scented
P. radens 'Dr. Livingston'. Skeleton geranium with strongly scented fern-like leaves
P. rapaceum ' Mrs. Kingsley' – mint-scented
P. quercifolium – oak-leaved geranium. Strong unpleasant odour
P. quercifolium 'Fair Ellen'. Large oak-leaved foliage rather pleasantly fragrant
P. quercifolium ' Pretty Polly' – almond-scented
P. tomentosum – peppermint geranium, odour of pennyroyal

CHAPTER XIV

Sweet Scented Flowers in the Rock Garden

The loveliest flowers the closest cling to earth.

— JOHN KEBLE

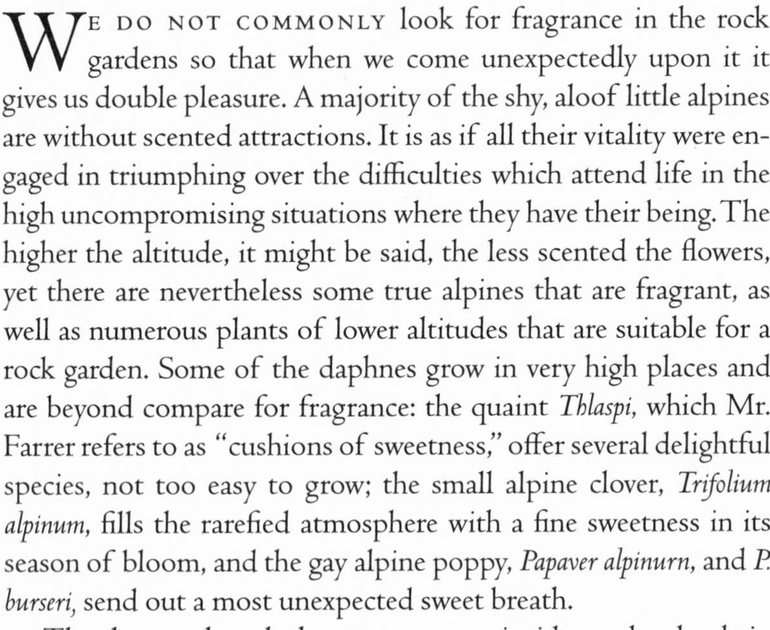

WE DO NOT COMMONLY look for fragrance in the rock gardens so that when we come unexpectedly upon it it gives us double pleasure. A majority of the shy, aloof little alpines are without scented attractions. It is as if all their vitality were engaged in triumphing over the difficulties which attend life in the high uncompromising situations where they have their being. The higher the altitude, it might be said, the less scented the flowers, yet there are nevertheless some true alpines that are fragrant, as well as numerous plants of lower altitudes that are suitable for a rock garden. Some of the daphnes grow in very high places and are beyond compare for fragrance: the quaint *Thlaspi,* which Mr. Farrer refers to as "cushions of sweetness," offer several delightful species, not too easy to grow; the small alpine clover, *Trifolium alpinum,* fills the rarefied atmosphere with a fine sweetness in its season of bloom, and the gay alpine poppy, *Papaver alpinurn,* and *P. burseri,* send out a most unexpected sweet breath.

The thymes that clothe many mountainsides and uplands in Europe are delicious and, if the different kinds are used, supply us with a great variety of good odours. Some have a lemony tang, others smell somewhat of camphor, and one at least has a strong odour of caraway seeds. There are many kinds of thyme but one seldom sees a representative collection. Most persons are content with one or two varieties and this is altogether too bad, for they all repay acquaintance in the most agreeable way and they make of the rock garden a pleasant place to work in, any little pressure sufficing to release the aromatic fumes, so that when we are weeding in their neighbourhood we are constantly reminded of their presence. Many of course may be grown in the open garden but for the rarer and more tender kinds the rock garden with its sunny sheltered nooks is the only safe place. The paved path and the dry wall also provide satisfactory homes for a wide variety of thymes and several will be required in the cook's garden, the common thyme and the lemon thyme especially. Sunshine they must have and for the rest a well drained soil in an airy position will keep them the most cheerful and happy of small creatures.

Thymus serpyllum is the European wild thyme, sometimes called mother of thyme. There are numerous forms of it. The most lovely is *T. serpyllum* 'Snowdrift', an absolutely prostrate creeper, clinging as closely to a stone, as someone absurdly said, as its own skin, and powdering itself all over in summer with myriads of white blossoms. I have encouraged great mats of white thyme in my rock garden so that I may have them to sit upon while weeding, for its scent when thus pressed is given off freely and is most heartening and reviving during this somewhat arduous task. There is also *Thymus serpyllum* 'Coccineus' which throws a dazzling crimson robe over earth and stones. The foliage of this kind is very dark and fine. The deliciously scented lemon thyme, *T.* x *citriodorus,* with its quaint "silver" and "gold" varieties, that Parkinson knew as "The Embroydered time that smelleth of pome citron," is also a form of *T. serpyllum,* as is the well-known woolly thyme, which is less fragrant than the others, and *T. caespititius* [*T. micans*], pineapple-scented, that is rather different in habit, forming "fragrant rounded heathery hummocks of ash-green."

The common thyme has several forms, an especially pretty one came to me as *T. vulgaris* 'Fragrantissimus'. It grows into a little eight-inch bush and its narrow pointed leaves have an especially keen scent. It is the earliest of the thymes to bloom in this garden. *T. nitidus,* a Sicilian species, is not so tall, an attractive little dusty-leaved bushling that has a very odd and pleasant perfume, a mixture of lemon and rose geranium.

A newcomer to my garden is *T. herba-barona* from Corsica. The tiny leaves are very dark in colour and it lies close to the earth. With me it has not bloomed but its charm is the strong scent of caraway that distinguishes it. It is sometimes called the seed-cake thyme. *T. zygis* comes from Spain and Portugal and is a low growing plant that smells rather like rosemary but more resinous, and is sometimes a welcome change in the stuffings of poultry from the ordinary thyme. *T. carnosus* is also a native of Spain; it is a diminutive shrublet that assumes a quaintly columnar form, growing finally, though very slowly, a foot tall. These three southerners will thank you for a sunny and protected corner and perhaps may not be hardy in the coldest parts of the country.

Many sweet leaved plants seem to flourish in Spain, the thymes among them. The latest to come to me was *T. membranaceus,* from an altitude of six thousand feet. It is described as a hardy plant for the rock garden, with white flowers, long and tubular, set in membranous cream-coloured bracts, the flowers having a sage-like fragrance and the leaves being aromatic when rubbed. I was enchanted with this mite, for it was a mite indeed, probably the smallest plant I have ever received, just two little shoots. But I lost it in the terrible rush of spring activities. It was too small to have been entrusted to the open garden but should have been cherished in a pot until it reached greater strength. I have heard also of *T. villosus,* said to be an improvement over the woolly thyme, of *T. striatus,* another Spanish species, of *T. capitatus,* of *T. pannonicus* [*T. marschallianus*], said to have narrow foliage and pink flowers, but these I have not known. *T. caespititius* [*T. azoricus*], a little invader from the Azores and one of my favourites, I was in danger of forgetting. It spreads itself out in the most engaging hummocks in the rock garden and in midsummer covers itself with a scarf of rich purple which lasts a surprisingly long time. It is one of the best scented and seemingly perfectly hardy. The leaves when rubbed give off a scent of tangerines.

Numerous micromerias have scented leaves and are low growing enough to make them suitable subjects for the rock garden. They are attractive shrublets whose leaves are variously odorous. Most of them come from sunbaked climes and are best pleased with a warm situation in the garden. The saturejas or savories, closely related to the thymes and calaminthas, may be put to the same uses and have very fragrant foliage.

SNOWDROP
(*Galanthus nivalis*)

We associate fragrance with the pink tribe but many of the alpine kinds are wholly devoid of this attribute. There are, however, plenty of subalpine and lowland kinds to fill the rock garden with sweetness during June. *Dianthus gratianopolitanus* [*D. caesius*] is richly and spicily fragrant, as is also *D. superbus,* with its careless ragged purple blooms. One of the sweetest is known to me as *D. petraeus,* either white or pink, a quaint buttonlike flower that everyone notices in the garden for its rich scent and attractive habit. *D. gallicus* flowers late and is rather a weedy and untidy plant which were it not for its very superior scent might not be included in a choice collection. *D. squarrosus* is white and fringy and very sweet and close to *D. superbus,* and there are several others given at the end of this chapter.

There are many primulas with fragrant blooms for use in the rock garden and its environs, more than a few sweet scented irises small enough to grace a situation in the restricted area of our miniature hills, numerous phloxes, erysimums, valerians, artemisias, and so on. The following list does not pretend to be exhaustive but it is sufficiently long to show that fragrance in the rock garden may be enjoyed by anyone who will take the trouble to fix it there.

FRAGRANT ROCK PLANTS

Abronia fragrans. Vanilla-like scent given off from white flowers that expand in the late afternoon.

Abronia latifolia [*A. arenaria*]. Honey-scented perennial with lemon-yellow flowers.

Abronia umbellata. Slightly fragrant rose-purple flowers.

Achillea erba-rota ssp. *moschata* [*Achillea moschata*]. Musk-scented leaves.

Acinos alpinus [*Calamintha alpina*]. Strongly aromatic leaves and small purple blossoms. *Acinos arvensis* [*C. acinos*], *Calamintha grandiflora* and *Clinopodium glabellum* [*C. glabella*] are also fragrant and desirable.

Aethionema grandiflorum [*A. pulchelum*]. Spicy odour. A charming pink-flowered alpine.

Allium inscubricum [*A. narcissiflorum*]. Said to have fragrant rose-colored flowers.

Alyssum spinosum. Small shrublet covered with delicate white or pink bloom over grey foliage.

Androsace chamaejasme. High alpine with delicious fragrance. *A. villosa* is also very sweet scented.

Anemone pulsatilla. A light sweet scent at certain stages of its development.

Anemone rivulatis and *A. sylvestris* are also lightly fragrant. Anemones are not commonly sweet scented.

Anthemis montana. Aromatic grey foliage.

Aquilegia vulgaris. Hay-like scent. *A. viridiflora,* small greenish flower of agreeable aroma. *A. chrysantha,* very fragrant yellow flowers. *A. scopulorum* var. *calcarea.* [*A. coerulea*] is also delicately sweet.

A. caucasica [*Arabis albida*]. Very sweet in early spring. *A. caucasica* 'Flore Plena' has spikes of double stock-like flowers that smell of heliotrope. *A. sturii* is also sweet scented.

Arctanthemum arcticum [*Chrysanthemum arcticum*]. Strongly aromatic foliage and white flowers in autumn.

Arnica. Golden flowers of Asteraceae with aromatic foliage. *A. montana* is the best.

Artemisia. Aromatic genus of Asteracea whose silver foliage is a decoration in the rock garden. Suitable kinds are *A. campestris* ssp. *borealis* [*A. canadensis*] (tall), *A. frigida, A. glacialis, A. ubelliformis* [*A. mutellina*], *A. rupestris.*

Astragalus danicus 'Albus'. Sweet white clover-like blossoms.

Cedronella cana. Aromatic leaves and pinkish red flowers.

Centranthus angustifolius. Delicate, fragrant, light rose flowers and grey foliage. Southern Europe.

Chimaphila maculata. Native plant with evergreen leaves and waxen white flowers having a rich oily fragrance. *C. umbellata* is also very sweet scented.

Coronilla valentina ssp. *glauca* [*C. glauca*]. Fragrant yellow pea-shaped blossoms.

Corydalis bulbosa. Very early flowering little plant with purplish sweet scented flowers. *C. nobilis* is much taller and has papery yellow and white flowers touched with black that have a rather heavy sweet odour.

Crocus. Numerous crocuses are sweet scented. Among the spring flowering kinds are *C. imperati, C. biflorus, C. chrysanthus*; autumn flowering species are *C. laevigatus, C. hadriaticus, C. longiflorus, C. sativus, C. speciosus* and *C. vitellinus.*

Cyclamen. Fragrant species among the hardy cyclamens are *C. balearicum, C. cilicium, C. purpurascens* [*C. europaeum*] (the most fragrant of all), *C. colchicum, C. repandum* and *C. libanoticum.*

Cypripedium. (See Additional Notes.)

Daphne. Many of this charming race are suitable for use in the rock garden; among those with fragrant blooms are *D. cneorum, D. rupestris, D. blagayana, D. striata.*

Delphinium bruonianum. A musk-scented species from India.

Dianthus. Fragrant species for the rock garden are *D. arenarius,* the sand pink, *D. fragrans,* rampant with fringed petals, *D. gallicus,* ragged and weedy but one of the sweetest, *D. monspessulanus,* kin to superbus and just as sweet, *D. petraeus, D. squarrosus,* Russia and Siberia, a neat edition of superbus, *D. monspessulanus* ssp. *sternbergii* [*D. sternbergii*], very sweet, *D. gratianopolitanus,* ragged mauve blooms with rich scent of orange blossoms, the cheddar pink, one of the most delicious, *D. petraeus* ssp. *integer* [*D. integar*], also very sweet. *D. sundermani* has a perfume very like jasmine and quite unlike that of most pinks.

Dicentra chrysantha. A California plant with a peculiar but agreeable fragrance. *D. cucullaria,* Dutchman's breeches is a pleasantly scented native plant.

Dodecatheon meadia. Shooting star. Has a strong spicy odour very like lilac with a dash of cinnamon.

Epigaea repens. Trailing arbutus. Delicious scent with a tang of bitter almond.

Epilobium hirsutum. Codlins and cream. Willowweed. Carmine flowers smelling of apple.

Erica odorata. A little white-flowered heath smelling of honeysuckle. *E. australis* is also scented.

Erodium. Storksbill. Heron's bill. Most of the species possess leaves that give off an agreeable resinous odour.

Erysimum heiraciifolium [*Cheiranthus alpinus*]. This species and *E.* x *allionii* [*C. allionii*] are less sweet than the border wall flowers but very effective in the garden.

Erysimum pulchellum and *E. helveticum* [*E. pumilum*] have a faint odour of wall flower.

Erythronium grandiflorum ssp. *chrysandrum* [*E. parviflorum*]. Mrs. Banghart says the meadows filled with this lovely trout lily give off an exquisite perfume.

Fritillaria pudica. A small western bulbous plant with nodding yellow flowers that are sweet scented.

Galanthus. All the snowdrops have a delicate sweet scent.

Galium boreale. Northern bedstraw. Hay-scented flowers and aromatic leaves.

Galium odoratum [*Asperula odorata*]. Sweet woodruff. Famous for its use in the German Maitrank. The leaves are hay-scented when dry.

Genista dalmatica. One of the most delightful of the little brooms. A faint scent.

Hemerocallis minor [*H. graminea*]. Dwarf graceful little plant bearing yellow lightly fragrant flowers in profusion.

Hosta minor. Scented like its taller prototype.

Iris. The following species are low growing and have sweetly scented flowers. Not all are hardy enough for outdoor culture in the north. Those marked * are hardy. *I. planifolia* [*I. alata*], fall-flowering, a gem for pots. Bulbous. *I. arenaria,** charming yellow flowers smelling of vanilla. *I. atropurpurea* [*I. atroviolaceae*],* very early, bright purple and fragrant. *I. bakeriana,* a charming bulbous species flowering early in the year. *I. barnumae* from Armenia, May and June, delightfully fragrant, Oncocyclus. *I. biliotti,** easy and delightfully fragrant, purple flowers. *I. bucharica,** 'Juno', ivory and gold and freshly fragrant. *I. cristata,** blue or white crab-scented blossoms, early in April. *I. dichotoma,** fragile flowers in August, opening at sunset and delicately fragrant. *I. ensata,** pretty, vigorous species with sweet, pale lavender flowers. *I. graminea,** smells like an Elberta peach. *I. histrioides,** a form of *I. reticulata,* with violet-scented blossoms. *I. hoogiana,** tea rose scent. *I. juncea,* Algeria, bulbous species with yellow, very fragrant flowers. *I. kolpakowskiana,* Kashmir, a bulbous species with reddish-purple flowers in March. *I. persica,** Asia Minor, lovely species with pale greenish flowers marked with black and a delicious fragrance. *I. reichenbachii,** and a number of the dwarf bearded kinds are sweet scented, among them, gracilis,* bluebeard,* bride,* commandant driant,* cyanea,* glee,* maia,* *I. statellae,** swerti,* *I. suaveolens.** *I. reticulata,** a deliciously violet-scented, bulbous species. *I. ruthenica,** smells of violets. *I. sindjarensis,** vanilla-scented. *I. unguicularis* [*I. stylosa*], winter-flowering, delicious primrose scent. *Gyandriris sysyrinchium* [*I. Sisyrinchium*], a bulbous species from Kashmir, delicately scented. *I. verna,** a native species as fragrant as a bunch of hothouse violets.

Jurinella moschus [*Jurinea depressa*]. Musk rose. An oriental thistle, blue and smelling like *Rosa moschata.*

Lavandula. Dwarf varieties, including *L. angustifolia* var. *delphinensis,* are very fragrant.

Leontopodium haplophylloides [*L. aloysiodora*]. Lemon-scented edelweiss. It has the odour of fresh limes.

Leucocrinum montanum. Sand lily. Star lily. Mountain lily. A very sweet scented plant from the Northwest, with white flowers.

Leucojum vernum. Pretty bulbous plant with white flowers early in the year. *L. aestiuum* bears green-tipped fragrant bells in May.

Cymbalaria pallida [*Linaria pallida*]. A small creeping plant with sweet scented lilac flowers.

Linnaea borealis. Twin flower. A tiny native shrub with bellshaped flowers scented of almonds.

Mentha requienii. Corsican mint. Powerfully fragrant microscopic mint, useful for carpeting dampish places. Other dwarfish species that may be admitted where there is space are *M. piperita* var. *citrata,* [*P. citrata*], the chartreuse-mint and *M. crispa,* the crested-mint.

Meum athamanticum. Aromatic umbellifer of low growth with exceptionally fine foliage and white flowers.

Micromeria. Low-growing fragrant-leaved shrubs. *M. chamissonis* [*M. douglasii*] of our Northwest is a flat carpeter that has a powerful fragrance. Its common name is yerba buena. Other more bushy kinds are *M. croatica; M. marginata* [*M. piperella*]; *M. thymifolia* [*M. rupestris*]. Clarence Elliott speaks of *Acinos corsicus* [*M. corsica*] as having the pungent scent of oysters and lemon juice and says that *M. chamissonis* is redolent of brown Windsor soap. All the species of *Micromeria* like sun and an airy situation.

Mitchella repens. Partridge berry. Running box. Two-eyed berry. A little native creeping plant with small white fragrant blossoms, followed by red berries.

Morina. M. longifolia, belonging to the East, has aromatic leaves that when broken exhale a strong lemon odour.

Muscari. Bulbous plants several of which are very sweet scented. *M. conicum,* heavenly blue; *M. moscarimi* [*M. moschatum*], delicious smelling Oriental species; *M. comosum,* tassel hyacinth; *M. neglectum* [*M.*

atlanticum], grape hyacinth with plumlike scent.

Narcissus. Certain small kinds are very highly fragrant. *N. minor, N. pseudonarcissus* ssp. *moschatus* [*N. moschatus*], *N. jonquilla, N. odorus, N. assoanus* [*N. juncifolius*], *N.* x *tenuior* [*N. gracilis*], *N. triandrus.*

Neofinetia falcalta [*Angraecum falcatum*]. A hardy little Japanese orchid producing large white flowers with a keen sweetness.

Nothoscordum gracile [*Allium fragrans*]. Greenish flowers scented of heliotrope.

Oenothera. Various low-growing species of evening primrose are sweet scented, among them *O. caespitosa, O. speciosa, O. triloba, O. pallida* ssp. *trichocalyx* [*O. trichocalyx*].

Olsynium filifolium [*Sisyrinchium filifolium*]. Pale maidens. From the Falkland Islands. Sweet scented chocolate-colored bells.

Onosma alborosea. Alpine plant with tubular white flowers that emit an almond-like fragrance; *O. tauricum,* the golden drop, is very fragrant of honey.

Origanum. Marjoram. Aromatic plants of the sage family growing in the Mediterranean region and the Orient. Suitable kinds for the rock garden are *O. dictamnus, O. pulchellum* [*O. pulchrum*], *O. calcaratum* [*O. tournefortii*].

Oxalis magellanica. Dainty plant for stepping stones with pretty foliage and sweet white flowers. Magellan Region.

Papaver alpinum. Delicate haylike scent. *P. fugax* [*P. caucasicum*] smells like ripe plums and has the most enchanting colour scheme of silver and apricot.

PRIMROSE
(*Primula auricula*)
'Duke of Cumberland'

Paradisea liliastrum [*Anthericum liliastrum*]. St. Bernard's lily. Small alpine "lily" that perfumes the high meadows with the scent of the Madonna lily. *P. liliago* is scentless.

Petrocallis pyrenaica. Fine alpine with lilac honey-scented flowers.

Phlox divaricata. Native wild phlox that has a modified scent of *Lilium auratum.* Where it grows in masses it is very sweet scented. Many of the dwarf phloxes are sweet scented, especially *P. stolonifera* [*P. reptans*].

Primula. This delightful race is rich in fragrant plants. *P. anisodora,* a bog plant from Yunnan, gives off from flowers, roots and leaves, a scent of anise. *P. vulgaris* [*P. acaulis*], common primrose, balmy scent. *P. auricula,* early and sweet. *P. chionantha,* sweet scented Chinese species. *P. deflexa,* also Chinese, *P. florindae,* tall-growing and very fragrant. *P. forrestii,* from Yunnan, with yellow flowers. *P. glutinosa,* a European species. *P. glycosma,* from Yunnan, *P. involucrata,* from the Himalayas, a lovely bog plant with intensely fragrant flowers. *P. kitaibeliana. P. marginata,* a fine alpine with silvered leaves and large fragrant lilac flowers. *P. sikkimensis* [*P. microdonta*], a bog plant with nodding sweet scented flowers. *P. veris* [*P. officinalis*], the cowslip of balmy breath. *P. flaccida* [*P. nutans*], from Yunnan. *P. palinurii,* an Italian species. *P. pinnatifida,* Western

China, *P. redolens. P. sikkimensis,* a very lovely bog species with nodding yellow flowers, *P. rufa* from Yunnan.

Puschkinia scilloides. Wintergreen. Shinleaf. A little bulbous plant with delicately spicy flowers.

Pyrola rotundifolia. Waxen flowers with lily-of-the-valley scent. *Moneses uniflora* [*P. uniflora*] has what Mr. Correvon calls a delicate and aristocratic perfume. This is sometimes called *Moneses grandiflora.* Other fragrant species are *P. americana, P. asarifolia, P. chlorantha, P. elliptica. P. media. P. asarifolia* var. *purpurea* [*P. uliginosa*]. Some have pink flowers.

Rhodiola rosea. Roseroot. Sweet scented roots.

Rosa pendulina [*R. alpina*]. A charming wee shrub with big rose-crimson fragrant flowers. *R. chinensis* 'Roulettii' [*R. rouletti*], according to Mrs. Banghart, is a little six-inch Rumanian species bearing semi-double sweet scented pink roses.

Santolina. (See Chapter 9.)

Satureja. Savory. These fragrant plants are near relatives of the thymes & micromerias. They make small dense aromatic bushesand are good to grow in the rock garden in full sun. *S. montana* [*S. pygmaea*]; *Micromeria thymifolia* [*S. rupestris*] are attractive kinds.

Sedum spurium. Pleasant hay-like scent.

Shortia galacifolia. Lovely native, liking acid soil; delicately sweet.

Sternbergia lutea. Autumn flowering bulbous plant with fragrant yellow crocus-like flowers.

Tanacetum. T. herderi is a dwarf aromatic bush with grey leaves.

Teucrium. Germander. Low growing labiates, some with aromatic leaves. *T. marum,* Cat thyme, is strongly aromatic. Not hardy in the North.

Thlaspi. Low creeping or bushy crucifers, some with scented flowers. *T. bellidifolium; T. cepifolium* [*T. cepifolium*]; *T. rotundifolium;* this one is honey scented.

Thymus. Thyme. Delightful small labiates with fragrant leaves. *T. caespititius* [*T. azoricus*], orange scent; *T. capitatus; T. carnosus; T. pulegioides* [*T. chamaedrys*]; *T.* x *citriodorus; T. coccineus; T. comosus; T. herba-barona; T. lanuginosus; T. pannonicus* [*T. marshallianus*]; *T. richardii* ssp. *nitidus; T. serpyllum; T. villosus; T. zygis.*

Trifolium alpinum. Little scented alpine clover.

Trillium sessile and several other species.

Ipheion uniflorum [*Triteleia uniflora*]. Small bulbous plant with white fragrant flowers.

Tulipa. Various species including *T. clusiana, T. patens, T. australis.*

Valeriana. Valerian. Certain small species have sweet scented flowers. *V. elongata; V. supina; V. celtica.*

Viola blanda. A little white-flowered native species that has faintly violet scented blooms. *V. canadensis* is lemon scented; *V. odorata,* rich scent; *Viola cornuta,* especially the white variety, has a very pleasant fragrance.

CHAPTER XV

Sweet Scented Shrubs and Trees for Southern Gardens

Awake, O north wind, and come, thou south; blow upon my garden that the spices may flow forth.

— CANT. IV. 16

WINTER AND SPRING ARE the seasons when southern gardens are at their best, and how lovely they seem to us who have fled the stark white realism of a northern winter! How delightful it is to find the sweet-leaved geraniums enduring out of doors in mid-winter, and roses blooming undiminished. Many of the shrubs are evergreen so that the gardens appear fresh and well furnished. Jasmines trail from the eves of the houses, or festoon the trees with their delicate foliage and exquisitely scented stars. *Michelia figo* [*Magnolia fuscata*], known in the North only as a greenhouse plant, lives out of doors all winter in the far South and gives to the air its exotic scent of banana. The sweet olives yield their ravishing tonic odour with a delicate reserve and the camphor tree "answers fragrantly the grasp of the hand." Myrtles are there with scented leaves and flowers, and the splendid large-flowered magnolias, pittosporums of refined fragrance, the perfumed oleanders, and the exquisite gardenia, these and many more.

The following is a selection of shrubs and trees suitable for growing in various parts of the South, or in mild sections of California, and many of them may be enjoyed in the North where they may have the protection of a greenhouse.

Acacia. Tassel tree, wattle or mimosa. Acacias are much grown in the warmer sections of the country. They are beautiful shrubs or trees native of mild countries. Some of the finest species come from Australia and New South Wales. Fragrant wood or flowers are characteristic of a number of the species. The wood of *A. pendula*, common in the interior of Australia and known as myall wood, has a strong odour of violets which it continues to give off as long as the wood remains unpolished. The wood of *A. acuminata* smells so strongly of raspberries that in Australia it is known as the raspberry jam tree. "Another species, *A. cambagei*, has so evil an odour that the Australians call it the stinking wattle. The smell is said to be particularly vile just before rain, and should be a boon to weather prophets." The species principally cultivated at Grasse and Cannes for the perfume trade is *A. farnesiana*, found in Texas and Mexico, as well as in Asia, Africa, and Australia, and originally naturalized in Europe in the Farnesian Gardens at Rome. The flowers of this species smell of violets. It makes a rather straggling bush with sensitive mimosalike leaves and profusely borne balls of yellow bloom with a penetrating fragrance. It is hardy in the far South, blooming in March.

Among other fragrant acacias are *A. dealbata*, the silver wattle, Australia and Tasmania; *A. odoratissima* and *A. pycnantha* of Tasmania. "It has been noticed that seeds and rootbark of these sweet-scented acacias when chewed taste and smell execrably of garlic and that the roots have an unpleasant smell" (*Odorographia*).

Adenandra fragrans. A small evergreen shrub bearing rose-coloured blossoms in May. Cape of Good Hope. Usually cultivated in greenhouses.

Adenocarpus hispanicus [*A. anagyrus*]. Low shrub from Teneriffe, bearing masses of yellow pea-shaped flowers that give off a ravishing fragrance. "It is essentially," says Mr. Bowles, "the smell of indoor plants, I think a mixture of *Genista* x *spachiana* [*Cytisus racemosus*] and tuberose or stephanotis."

Aloysia triphylla [*A. citriodora*]. Lemon verbena. This plant has long been famous among sweet-leaved plants. It comes from Chile and is herbaceous when cultivated out of doors but keeps its leaves the year round under greenhouse cultivation. Although not generally hardy in the North I know of bushes kept over from year to year out of doors where carefully protected. The leaves are deliciously scented and make a welcome addition to any bouquet. They keep their sweet odour when dried and "in Spain are often placed in the teapot to add their aroma to the tea."

Artabotrys hexapetalus [*A. odoratissimus*]. Climbing Ilang Ilang. Cinnamon jasmine. A choice flowering shrub recommended for Southern Florida, of half climbing habit, with broad glossy scented leaves and yellow flowers emitting a fragrance that has been compared to ripe bananas and pineapples.

Azara microphylla. Chile. A small-leaved evergreen shrub of semi-climbing habit that likes a wall facing east. The flowers are of small account to the eye, merely "a few yellow stamens bristling among the leaves" and on the under sides of the branches, "yet a blind man might know of their presence, so fragrant are they with the fragrance of Vanilla." This strong vanilla scent is noticeable many yards from the shrub. April. Hardy as far north as Washington, D. C. Sometimes cultivated as a greenhouse shrub.

Bauhinia purpurea. Mountain ebony. Showy small tree recommended for Florida street planting, with large two-lobed leaves that fall in the late winter, followed by a profusion of blooms that lasts for many weeks. The flowers are three inches across and come in pleasing tones of lavender, mauve, purple, and white, "resembling rare orchids," and are very fragrant. India.

Boronia megastigma. Scented boronia. Brown boronia. An Australian plant usually treated as a greenhouse subject but successfully cultivated out of doors in mild sections of the country. The foliage has a rue-like odour but the small yellow-brown flowers are among the sweetest smelling in the world. "One plant will make a full sized conservatory delicious and it is perhaps sweeter in the atmosphere and on the breeze than when smelt close at hand." There are several other fragrant species, among them *B. alata.*

CAMELLIAN
(*Camellia*)

Buddleja. Many of the buddlejas are sweet scented, especially those that must be grown in mild climates. *B. asiatica* is a choice Indian species with profusely borne tails of white flowers that have a very sweet fragrance, filling the corner of the garden where it grows with sweetness from September until the frosts. In the North it is much grown in greenhouses and employed by florists in bouquets. Another greenhouse variety is 'Farquhari'. *B. albiflora* is a vigorous Chinese species with the characteristic tails of bloom, pale lilac in colour with orange-coloured anthers. *B. officinalis* is a fragrant species of Afghanistan and Burma with long plumes of lilac flowers. *B. globosa,* the orange ball tree, is a native of Chile. It is a graceful deciduous shrub growing fifteen feet tall and flowering in round balls of golden bloom that smell strongly of heather honey and are highly attractive to bees. It is hardy as far north as Washington and though it may be cut to the ground in severe winters, will spring again from the roots. Deserving of a choice situation.

Camellia sinensis [*C. thea*]. Tea plant. Evergreen shrub eight to twenty feet tall, bearing many large very fragrant dull white flowers with yellow stamens. This is the tea plant of commerce. *C.* × *maliflora* [*C. sasanqua*] is native of China and Japan, a tree growing ten feet tall. The leaves dried in the sun have a very sweet odour; a decoction of them is made by the women of Japan in which they wash their hair, and they are also mixed with tea to give it a more agreeable odour. The flowers are not large but are very sweet scented. Successfully grown in South Carolina. The finest species of camellia have inodorous flowers.

Carpenteria californica. Tree anemone. Evergreen shrub allied to *Philadelphus.* Growing six to eight feet tall and bushy in habit, producing in June terminal clusters of large white fragrant flowers.

Populus × *jackii* [*Cedronella triphylla*], the balm of Gilead, has leaves that when crushed emit a most delightful odour. It is a half hardy shrub that would probably persist anywhere south of Washington in sheltered locations and is worth cosseting for the sake of its leaves. It grows about four feet tall, a square-stemmed herbaceous labiate, and bears little spikes of dullish flowers which are of no account. Native in the Canary Islands and sometimes cultivated in cool greenhouses. The lovely scent of the leaves has been described as a combination of lemon-leaf and camphor.

Cestrum nocturnum. Lady of the night. Night jessamine. A large rankgrowing shrub native in the West Indies, making itself known in the darkness by the intensely sweet muskiness of its small greenish flowers that open about sundown and send forth a ravishing fragrance, a fragrance of musk mingled with heliotrope, which can be distinguished at least twenty feet from the plant. Taken into the house a flowering branch will "send waves of perfume through the rooms while the night lasts." It is recommended for Southern Florida where it blooms at intervals throughout the year.

Murraya paniculata (Chalcas exotica). Orange jessmine. Satinwood. Chinese box. Cosmetic bark tree. A favourite greenhouse plant because of its panicles of white very sweet scented flowers, like orange blossoms, that frequently appear at the same time as the small bright fruit, making a very gay effect. It is a native of India, a small tree attaining a height of ten or twelve feet, sometimes used as a stock for citrus fruits. It is said to bloom several times a year. Recommended for Southern Florida in sandy districts. *C. floribunda* is an ornamental evergreen shrub from South America bearing sweet white flowers.

Chimonanthus praecox [*C. fragrans*]. The fragrant winter tree offers its curious fleshy yellowish blossoms in the dark days of winter and scents the air about it for a considerable distance. It is a shrub of some six feet tall, much branched, and generally treated as a wall shrub in gardens. The leaves fall in the autumn and the flowers form in the axils of the old leaves. They are made up of a large number of pale yellow waxy petals arranged in several rows and are about an inch in diameter. The delicious fragrance of these flowers has been compared to a mixture of jonquil and violet. It is hardy in sheltered places as far north as Washington, D. C.

Choisya ternata. Mexican orange. A charming evergreen shrub of the rue family with three-parted glossy green leaves that smell like eucalyptus when pinched, and lovely clusters of white starry flowers that have the scent of orange blossoms. It is a native of the Uplands of Mexico and will endure several degrees of frost, so that it may be made use of in many parts of the South. It blossoms in California at several seasons and makes a fine greenhouse shrub.

Cinnamomum camphora. Camphor tree. China. Japan. An evergreen tree used extensively for street planting in the Gulf States and where a high impenetrable hedge is desired. Said to be a common roadside planting in California also. Cultivated commercially for its camphor scented wood. For distillation the twigs are sheared twice a year.

Cistus. Rock rose. A genus of low shrubs peculiar for the balsamic odour given off by the leaves when bruised. The leaves of *C.* × *ladanifer,* the gum cistus, are said to be richly scented, especially early in the morning before the dew is off the plant. It is a native of Southern Europe and would be hardy as far north as Baltimore. A fine rock garden subject. The flowers are the shape of little single roses, white with a purple-red spot at the base of each petal. "In Andalusia where some of the hillsides are white for miles with the bloom of *C.* x *ladanifer,* they are brown by four o'clock afternoon, but under each bush is spread a yellow carpet of fallen leaves." (Sir Herbert Maxwell, "Flowers.")

Citharexylum spinosum. Fiddlewood. Zitherwood. A tree of the West Indies growing somewhat taller than twenty feet, bearing white sweet scented flowers in long spikelike racemes. From the wood certain musical instruments are made. Planted sparingly in California as an ornamental tree and in the far Southern States. *C. ilicifolium* is from Ecuador and also has white sweet scented flowers.

LEMON TREE
(*Citrus limonia*)

Citrus. Trees which flourish in all parts of the Tropics and in semitropical countries, yielding oranges, lemons, limes, citrons, etc., many of which have scented leaves, flowers and fruits. The sweet or Portugal orange is *C. sinensis;* its leaves and flowers are highly fragrant but in this respect quite inferior to those of the bitter orange, *C. aurantium,* which though its taste is extremely bitter, has rind, flowers and leaves deliciously sweet scented. *C. limon,* the mandarin lime, rangpur lime, lemandarin, is a native of India. There are now many varieties of lemon, the rind and fruits of some of them being very fragrant. "The lime is *Citrus aurantiifolia,* which grows wild in many tropical countries but does not flourish even so far north as the Azores. It is found wild and cultivated in Jamaica, Dominica and Tahiti, but among the most important plantations are those established on the Island of Mont serrat." The lime makes a bushy thorny tree with shining dark leaves which are so fragrant that they are universally used in the West Indies for perfuming the water of finger bowls. The small white flowers are like orange blossoms and their scent is equally delicious. *C. reticulata* [*C. nobilis* var. *deliciosa*] is the mandarin, so called because in China where this luscious variety has been raised it was commonly employed as a gift to the mandarins. The perfume of the flowers, leaves and fruit is delicately soft, and the taste of the pulp very sweet. *C. bergamia,* bergamot, is a small spiny tree grown in Europe for its sweet essential oil. *C. otaitensis,* otaheite orange, is a little bush of unknown origin, sometimes grown as a pot plant. The flowers are pink and very fragrant and followed by lemon-like fruits. The various citri produce valuable essential oils called nerolis.

Orange blossoms are used in the tea factories of Canton for perfuming the tea known as orange pekoe. For this purpose the flowers are gathered fully expanded and the petals when separated from the stamens are mixed with the tea. The dry tea and the undried sweet blossoms are allowed to lie together for twenty-four hours, when the blossoms are winnowed or sifted out, but sometimes a few remain and are easily detected when the brew is made. "The scent communicated by the flowers is very slight for some time but like the scent peculiar to the tea leaves themselves, comes out after being packed a week or two." Other flowers similarly used by the Chinese for scenting tea are *Osmanthus fragrans* [*Olea fragrans*], jasmines, and for their own use the petals of the rose. In John Evelyn's day the young tender leaves of oranges and lemons were employed to give an unusual flavour and savour to salads, being sprinkled over the other ingredients or used as a garnish.

Clerodendron. Glory bower. Handsome shrubs and subshrubs bearing showy fragrant flowers but often having ill-scented leaves. *C. philippinum* [*C. fragrans*], a half shrubby plant is a common ornament of gardens in China and Japan. It bears deliciously sweet white or blush flowers in compact hydrangea-like corymbs; leaves are ill smelling when crushed but it is a fine plant for the cool greenhouse. *C. trichotomum.* A slender erect subshrub four to ten feet high with large dark leaves, bears pale purplish white flowers that smell of honeysuckle, followed by blue fruits set in brown calices. Kills to the ground in the North but springs again with the coming of warm weather if the crowns have been protected. Japan. *C. trichotomum* var. *fargesii* [*C. fargesii*] is of China and bears white sweet flowers "followed by most beautiful azure fruits set in pink stars." *C. bungei* [*C. foetidum*] is only fetid so far as the leaves are concerned and then not actively so, the showy trusses of pink flowers are very sweet. Adapted to Florida and the milder sections of California.

C. paradoxa [*Colletia cruciata*]. Chile. A "spiny foreigner unlike anything else in my garden. The cruciform growth resembles rows of miniature anchors; the leaves are minute, few and far between; the flowers innumerable upon a successful specimen and make the plant white in October. They are sweet, but smell *Colletia* with care or he will stab you in a tender place." (Phillpotts, "My Shrubs.") Grown in Florida and California.

Corokia cotoneaster. Wire netting bush. Spreading evergreen shrub with small leaves suitable for outdoor planting in the South. Branches curiously directed, crooked and bearing small yellow sweet scented blossoms very freely. *C. buddleioides.* Korokio. Grows tall and has leaves two inches in length and yellow flowers with a warm fragrance. New Zealand.

Daphne odora [*D. indica*]. Winter daphne. A small evergreen shrublet with white or purplish flowers in January. "It is said it can boast of being the most powerfully fragrant plant in the world." As far north as Washington, D. C., it will persist over the winter if given a warm wall to sun its back against. *D. laureola,* spurge laurel, grows with great luxuriance in shrubberies where it is hardy. It often produces its small green flowers as early as January. A contributor to "Gardening Illustrated," April 6, 1929, says: "Now at this season from 7 to 8 P.M. onwards, my garden is filled with a delicious primrose scent from plants of *Daphne laureola.* Personally on a still evening I have often smelt the scent of this plant at a distance of thirty yards." The spurge laurel is an evergreen spreading bush three to four feet high. *D. pontica,* Southeastern Europe and Western Asia, has large evergreen leaves and small clusters of greenish yellow flowers borne in April that are highly fragrant at night.

Diosma ericoides. Breath of heaven. Buchu. South Africa. Heathlike evergreen shrub with small leaves. "A rather sombre little bush until spring gets into its blood when it bursts out into a myriad of tiny white stars of bloom.... But what really gives the plant permanent room in the garden is the entrancing fragrance released by the foliage at any time of the year upon having pinched or even brushed against it."[1]

Drimys winteri. Winter's bark. A small South American tree of the magnolia family, a beautiful evergreen with loose clusters of milk-white flowers in spring, scented like jasmine. The tree has knotty branches and the bark is thick, aromatic and pungent. "The leaves bitten are very pungent, stinging the palate like pepper." The hawthornlike flowers are followed by green berries containing aromatic seeds. The bark was once in demand medicinally but has now been superseded by quinine. *D. lanceolata* [*D. aromatica*], the pepper tree, from Tasmania, is also desirable.

Elliottia racemosa. Georgia plume. A rather rare deciduous shrub native of South Carolina and Georgia, where it grows in wet, sandy woods. It bears terminal racemes of white slightly fragrant flowers.

Eriobotrya japonica [*Photinia japonica*]. Loquat. Japanese medlar. Evergreen tree up to twenty or thirty feet. Flowers three to four inches across, creamy and packed in stiff terminal pyramidal panicles that have a strong scent of hawthorn. China and Japan. The loquat is much planted in the Gulf States west. It bears its white flowers from August until the approach of winter & ripens its clustered fruit in spring. South of Charleston it makes a fine lawn tree; in the North it is frequently found in greenhouses flourishing in a pot. Hardy as far north as Washington but does not fruit in that latitude.

[1] *C. F. Saunders. "Trees and Shrubs of California Gardens."*

Escallonia. Shrubs or small trees bearing very fragrant flowers, said to be half hardy as far north as New York. *E. bifida* [*E. floribunda*] has white hawthorn-scented flowers with yellow stamens. *E. illinita* (which has a rather horrid odour) and *E. revoluta* of Chile also bear white flowers, and *E. laevis* [*E. organensis*], of the Organ Mountains, Brazil, bears rosy-pink flowers. *E. rubra* var. *macrantha* [*E. macrantha*] has a gummy fragrance and is delighted in by bees. Chile.

Gardenia augusta [*G. jasminoides*]. Cape jessamine. A beautiful low broad-leaved evergreen shrub, two to six feet tall, with dark lustrous leaves and exquisite large white waxen flowers of enchanting fragrance. The double flowered form is famous as a buttonhole flower. It blooms from May to September in the South where it is often used for hedges. It is hardy as far north as Virginia.

Cystisus supranubius [*C. fragrans*]. A delightfully fragrant evergreen shrub for pot culture under glass that may be brought into bloom very early in the spring. "A few plants in a house in flower are sufficient to fill it with a delightful perfume which reminds one of the fragrance of lemon verbena." The flowers are yellow and freely borne. *Retama monosperma* [*Genista monosperma*] is a straggling shrub two to four feet high bearing milky white refreshingly fragrant flowers in early summer. Southern Europe and North Africa.

Illicium anisatum. Star Anise. Small tree or shrub native in Japan, it is a rather dull little evergreen but regarded with respect in its native land. The flowers are scentless but the leaves and bark are strongly aromatic. *I. floridanum* is a native of southern swamps and bears scented red flowers suggestive of the strawberry shrub and has the characteristic spice scented leaves. Florida to Louisiana.

Laurelia serrata. Huanhuan tree. Chile. Evergreen timber tree with leathery leaves that have a pleasant aromatic odour when crushed, and fetid wood.

Prunus caroliniana [*Laurocerasus caroliana*]. Carolina laurel cherry. A fine native broad leaved evergreen shrub with shining dark foliage and masses of small white flowers in close racemes that possess a fine fragrance. Recommended for hedges and shrubbery planting in southern gardens. Grows naturally from New England to Florida and Texas. *Prunus laurocerasus* [*Laurocerasus officinalis*], cherry laurel, a native of Southeastern Europe and Persia, is a low evergreen bush or small tree with very fragrant creamy flowers borne in racemes. It is much planted in the South and in California.

Laurus nobilis. Sweet bay. Poet's laurel. "This is the true laurel of the ancients, the one whose leaves are used to make crowns for triumphant heroes and wreaths for distinguished poets"– hence the name Poet Laureate. An evergreen aromatic shrub native in regions bordering the Mediterranean, it belongs to the family Lauraceae, a family famed for the great number of fragrant plants it embraces, among them the spice bush, sassafras, and camphor tree. "Of all growing things," writes Miss Jekyll, "there is nothing much more beautiful in detail than a little branch of bay, the leaves are so well set on the stems and their waved edges give a satisfying impression of graceful strength." The sweet bay is often grown in tubs and used for outdoor as well as indoor decoration.

Lawsonia inermis. Henna. A tall shrub native in South Africa and naturalized in the West Indies where it is known as mignonette tree and Egyptian privet. It yields a yellow dye used to colour the hair and nails. It is grown for ornament in Florida and California.

Luculia pinceana [*L. gratissima*]. A very beautiful evergreen shrubby tree from the temperate Himalayas, with large heads of pink richly scented flowers that have the virtue of remaining "pink, sweet and perfect for a month." Save in very mild climates it must be given the shelter of a greenhouse. In "Farrer's Last Journey" Mr. Cox says, "I should give it place as first of all flowering shrubs that I have ever seen." This is high praise.

Magnolia delavayi. A wide-spreading flat-topped evergreen species native in Yunnan, with creamy-white cup-shaped fragrant flowers that last only a day. *M. grandiflora* is the magnificent bull bay of the Southern States. The leaves are large and leathery and the immense cupped white flowers are deliciously fragrant and produced from June to September. *Michelia figo* [*Magnolia fuscata*]. Banana shrub. China. A greenhouse shrub with small foliage "whose fragrant stars are pale auburn, insignificant to the eye but so powerfully fragrant that one half-expanded flower affects the air of an entire house." In the air it is not unpleasantly strong.

Melia azedarach. Bead tree. Persian lilac. China tree. Chinaberry. Pride of India. Tropical Asia. Evergreen. Bipinnate, deeply serrated leaves and much branched panicles of fragrant lilac flowers in April, succeeded by an abundant crop of yellow translucent berries in the late summer. It is a quick growing tree to forty feet and has been naturalized throughout the South and as far north as Norfolk, Virginia.

Michelia champaca. A large tree found wild in the temperate Himalayas and widely cultivated in the East. It is allied to magnolia and has long shining leaves and flowers that are "not unlike a double narcissus." "This tree is celebrated for the exquisite perfume of its flowers, though some Europeans find it somewhat powerful and at night it becomes rather rank. The native women adorn their heads with the flowers for the sake of the perfume and for the elegant contrast of the rich orange colour with their black hair. The tree is highly venerated by the Hindus, who have given one of its names 'Tulasi' to a sacred grove of their Parnassus on the banks of the Yumuna. It is also dedicated by them to their god Vishnu" (Odorographia). It is said that the odour is so strong that bees seldom approach it.

SWEET OLIVE
(*Osmanthus fragrans*)

Myrtus communis. Myrtle. Found wild in the south of Europe on exposed rocks; extremely abundant in Italy, Southern France and Spain. By some it is believed not to be indigenous to these localities but only naturalized, having originally been brought from Western Asia, where at the present time it is found in a wild state as far east as Afghanistan. It grows in the form of a large bushy shrub from three to ten feet in height; "its small evergreen leaves, pointed and shining, respond to your gentlest caress with such a gift of fragrance as makes it a blessing in your garden." The modest white flowers are nearly always solitary and are delicately sweet. The myrtle hedges in Southern France and Spain are a beautiful feature of the gardens. In California and in the Gulf States myrtle is grown freely out of doors. I can imagine no more delightful possession than a hedge or even a single bush of this fine shrub. We in the unkindly North must enjoy it in a pot. It makes an excellent window or greenhouse plant.

Nerium oleander [*N. odorum*]. Sweet scented oleander. Persia, Japan, India. A charming shrub common in the gardens of upper India, bearing pink or white salver-shaped blossoms, with the scent of almonds, that perfume the air for many yards about the bushes. Much used for garden and greenhouse decoration, in the North grown in tubs. A cultivar, 'Lillian Henderson', has double white flowers that are said to have the fragrance of the old double white pink. Another perfumed oleander is 'Splendens'.

Osmanthus. Sweet olive. Evergreen shrubs or small trees belonging to Asia and Polynesia with one species in North America. The hardiest species is *O. heterophyllus* [*O. aquifolium*], which will stand out of doors as far north as New York. It is an evergreen rounded shrub bearing white fragrant flowers in the autumn. "It looks like a dark-leaved holly with an unusually graceful and sinuous habit.... After a fine summer, tufts of very fragrant little snow-white flowers peep from among the leaves." *O. delavayi,* a low branching evergreen shrub with leathery dark green leaves, shining and handsome, bears in spring masses of white flowers in the form of little waxen trumpets in small axillary and terminal clusters, that send forth a most delicious fragrance. It makes a fine subject for a rock garden where it will stand out of doors. *O. fragrans*, fragrant olive, sweet tea, tea olive, is popular in the North as a greenhouse shrub, and *O. armatus* and *O. fortunei* are also desirable by reason of their highly fragrant flowers. The former blooms in the autumn. *O. americanus* is the devilwood of the Southern States, a tall evergreen with lustrous leaves and white flowers.

Posoqueria latifolia [*Oxyanthus isthmia*]. Needle flower. A very handsome large erect shrub grown in gardens in Southern Florida, having broad evergreen leaves and bearing quantities of very long tubular flowers, six inches long and only one eighth of an inch through, that give out an intense and delicious odour.

Peumus boldus [*P. citriodora*]. Chile. A handsome shining evergreen for a shaded situation. The foliage is spice scented when crushed.

Omanthus decorus [*Phillyrea decora*]. Jasmine box. Mountains of Asia Minor. Distinct shrub with laurel-like leaves and a small white inflorescence of great sweetness, appearing in early spring. It will stand several degrees of frost. Likes half shade and a peaty soil. There are several other species of *Omanthus* that are valuable for their evergreen foliage and scented flowers.

Pittosporum. Hardy and half hardy evergreen shrub widely grown in California and the Gulf States. Several of the species make valuable hedge plants and nearly all have scented flowers. *P. undulatum,* called Victorian box, is a tree growing to a height of thirty feet. The whitish waxen flowers appear in January and linger sometimes as late as July. They are of a peculiarly penetrating fragrance, especially at night. *P. tobira* is a tall evergreen shrub native of Japan, with white flowers smelling like orange blossoms, making their appearance in early April and lasting for a long time.

Poncirus trifoliata [*Citrus trifoliata*]. Bitter orange. Trifoliate orange. This is a deciduous Chinese tree much used in the far South for hedges. Mrs. H. G. Lloyd writing in the "Bulletin of the Garden Club of America," says these hedges are "mule high, bull strong and hog proof." The small white flowers are very fragrant but the round bright golden fruits are its chief glory . . . "so delicious to slip in the pocket, to pinch and smell."

Prunus ilicifolia. Islay. Evergreen cherry. Mountain holly. Evergreen bush or small tree rarely exceeding twenty feet. San Francisco to Lower California. "Its pretty feathery white bloom has a bitter tonic fragrance that is a veritable call of the wild to the home-tied nature lover." (C. F. Saunders.)

Rhaphiolepis indica. Indian hawthorn. Low branching shrubs with thick roundish evergreen leaves and pale clusters of pink, sweet scented flowers. Requires rich soil. Recommended for Florida. *R. umbellata,* the yeddo hawthorn, is a Japanese shrub with evergreen leaves and sweet white flowers in dense pubescent panicles.

Sarcococca ruscifolia. A little evergreen shrub from China that decks itself in scented white bloom in January, a time when sweet flowers are at a premium, and which look very pretty peeping from among the dark leaves. They are followed by scarlet fruit. This attractive little shrub will thrive in the shade of trees. *S. humile* is a still dwarfer species, a good subject to use as an underplanting for taller shrubs. Hardy as far north as Philadelphia in sheltered places.

Styrax officinal. Storax. Shrub twelve to twenty

feet high. Northern Greece and Asia Minor. Allied to benzoin. This little tree presents a very lovely appearance in June by reason of the abundance of orange-flower-like blossoms that give off a very fragrant aroma. Said to yield a fragrant gum. *S. obassia* is a Japanese treasure and grows to a small tree in mild localities. "Its fragrant flowers are like snowdrops and hang with grace among the large leaves."

Umbellularia californica. California bay. Headache tree. California olive bay. Common in mountainous parts of California and the Pacific slope. A fast growing tree twenty to fifty feet tall with dark lustrous evergreen leaves that are highly aromatic.

Hebe cupressoides [*Veronica cupressoides*]. A very good imitation of a small cypress, a neat ornamental little shrub the leaves of which give off a balmy odour of cedarwood, with a hint of violet, especially on damp or dewy evenings or after a shower. It grows from two to four feet high and bears pale violet inodorous flowers in clusters at the tips of the shoots. Good for rock garden.

Viburnum odoratissimum. This shrub from the Khasia mountains in China is extremely handsome, possessing beautiful shining thick leaves and bearing pure white flowers in pyramidal panicles that have the scent of *Osmanthus fragrans.* Evergreen. Much grown in the Southern States as an ornamental feature of gardens. *V. tinus.* Evergreen laurustinus. A beautiful broad-leaved evergreen, hardy as far north as Philadelphia, especially near the coast. Its small sweet white flowers are borne profusely in winter. Sir Herbert Maxwell in "Flowers" says, "Every countrybred child has learnt to love the laurustinus . . . for the quiet gaiety of its blossoms in the dark days."

CHAPTER XVI

Bees and Honey Flowers

The bee is little among such things as fly; but her fruit is the chief of sweet things.

— ECCLESIASTICUS, 11.3

MANY OLD TIME GARDENS owed their charm to the simplicity and appropriateness of their accessories. In them beauty and utility, as so often happens, went hand in hand. There were the straight, direct paths, sometimes arched over by a grape arbour; the well with its stone curbing and picturesque peaked roof from which hung the oaken bucket; a dovecote of one kind or another and most decorative and useful of all, there were the rows of bee-hives. A garden thus furnished was a pleasant place indeed, livable, friendly, utilitarian in the best sense – what the old books called commodious.

Until fairly recent times almost every country dweller was a bee keeper and if we go far enough back we find garden literature teeming with apiarian lore that makes very fascinating reading. The gardeners of ancient times wrote almost as lovingly of their bees as of their flowers. "From the beginning," wrote Maeterlinck, "this strange little creature that lived in a society under complicated laws and executed prodigious labors in the darkness, attracted the attention of men." Aristotle, Cato, Pliny, Columnella, wrote of the bee and Virgil devoted to these busy insects his Fourth Georgic. For many centuries honey and bee's wax were simple ingredients of all sorts of household remedies, sweets, drinks, and cosmetics. Sugar when first discovered, according to Pliny, was used only in medicines. It remained a luxury until after the time of Queen Elizabeth and "as late as the days of Gilbert White's career at Oxford a sugar loaf was deemed a polite and valuable present." Honey was the sweet relied upon and old

household cookbooks and stillroom records abound in recipes in which its use is demanded.

Honey drinks have been popular since time immemorial. Mead is a beverage of ancient lineage. It was made of honey and water fermented and often with a sprig of sweetbrier added to give it flavour. A more elaborate rule for Mead, or Metheglin as it was called by the Welsh, had in it the flowers of elder, rosemary and marjoram, of each a handful, with cloves, ginger, cinnamon and pepper added to taste. The Hydromel of the ancient Teutons was a honey wine drunk by them for thirty days following marriage – whence comes the expression to spend the honeymoon. Attila, the Hun, is said to have partaken so freely of this honey wine at his wedding feast that he died.

Mel-roset, or honey of roses, was made of "faire purified honye and newe rede Roses," the latter chopped fine and boiled in the honey, and "when it is boyled enoughe ye shall knowe it by the swete odoure and the coloure." In Russia a drink termed "lipez" is made from the delicious honey of the linden. The Mulsum of the ancient Romans consisted of honey, wine and water boiled together, and a favorite drink of Chaucer's time was called "clarre" or "piment," and was made of honey and wine with the addition of spices. A similar drink was "bracket" for which there are rules in many old books and which was concocted with the wort of ale instead of wine.

"Honey nourishes very much and breedeth good Blood and prolongeth Life and Old Age," wrote Sir Jonas Moore. Undoubtedly it is the most wholesome of sweets and lacks the deleterious effects of sugar. In the unselfconscious, if unregenerate day in which I grew up, a mixture of rum and honey was the common remedy in many households for a cough. The prescription was simplicity itself – half and half, one part pure strained honey and one part sound Jamaica rum, well shaken and partaken in doses large or small, according to age or capacity, whenever a paroxysm seemed to impend.

Reading the writings of the early apiculturists it is impossible not to agree with the old husbandman, Worlidge, who wrote, "There is no creature to be kept about our Rural Seat that affords unto us so much variety of pleasure as the Bee." His dwelling is a decoration, his product is nectar, his droning machinery the very voice of the garden. Nor is bee-keeping a difficult or even an expensive matter. Certain attentions are required at definite times but "which need to be no hindrance to other business, but rather a delightful recreation amid the same," and for the most part these efficient creatures are able to look after themselves. As a matter of fact bee-keeping is, so to speak, a natural biproduct of gardening and orcharding.

"The fittest place for bees" wrote Thomas Hyll (1563) "is that which is in a garden, not farre or rather neare to the owner's house, which by that meanes suffereth not the windes, nor accesse of thieves or beastes." There was another reason for their being placed in the garden, other than for the sake of the store of nectar-filled flowers. Like the garden, the apiary was nearly always in charge of the mistress of the house and she liked to have it close at hand. William Lawson, a bee-master himself, in his advice to housewives says in part:

> There remaineth one necessary thing prescribed, which in my opinion makes as much for ornament as either Flowers or forme or cleanliness, and I am sure as commodious as any of or all the rest, which is Bees, well ordered. I will not account her any of my good House-wifes, that wanteth either Bees or skillfulness about them.

In my youth most of the people who dwelt in our countryside kept bees. We ourselves always had ten or twelve teeming hives, the ordinary wooden kind painted white that stood upon little wooden stools ranged beneath a row of ancient seckel pear trees at one side of the garden. Our bees were Italian by birth and said to be so amiable that they would not sting even an investigative child. But they did not always bear out this good character and we were fairly often stung and had the bruised leaves of balm clapped upon the afflicted part by our Irish nursemaids who were well versed in beelore from experience in the Old Country.

My father loved the rich dark buckwheat honey, which John Burroughs called the black sheep of this white flock, and always grew a field or two of buckwheat not far from the hives. But my mother preferred the fine white clover honey and so, being of an amiable temperament, my father also grew a field or two of white clover. The result of course was that our honey was neither the one thing nor the other, and moreover it was usually highly flavoured with mint, for just below the hives flowed a little brook whose banks were clothed in that pungent herb. And how the bees reveled in it!

Of course judged by all proper standards our honey was poor but it was the principal sweet known to us countrybred children, and whether spread upon paper-thin corn griddle cakes, or added to the last helping of spoonbread (alas – why can no northern cook ever be taught to make this delicious southern dish?) it seemed to us food for the most epicurean Gods.

The most prized honey in this country is the fair pale product of orchards and clover fields.

> White virgin honey comes from earliest flowers, White virgin honey in the market prized; From the white clover creeping in the field, From the orchard blossoms that the worker scours.

Later garnered honey is apt to be darker in colour and stronger of flavour. Some flowers give a distinct taste to honey. That from basswood blossoms lends a faint flavour of mint, and nectar gathered from hoarhound, pennyroyal and mint gives to the honey a distinctly aromatic tang. Nectar from the white tubes of the tobacco plant produces honey that is unfit for the table as does that gathered exclusively from wild asters. Bees love the blue-flowered borage but where it is their sole article of diet a dark and unpalatable honey is the result.

"Box," says an early writer, "maketh honie

of a bad smell and which troubleth their brains that eat it." The ancients believed that box produced honey, and that in Trebizond the honey issuing from this tree was so poisonous that it drove men mad. Corsican honey was supposed to owe its ill repute to the fact that the bees fed upon box. Numerous flowers secrete nectar that is supposed to be more or less poisonous, among them our lovely mountain laurel and the innocent appearing little annual snow-on-the-mountain. Several of the genera *Andromeda* and *Pieris* also bear this unwholesome reputation as well as certain rhododendrons.

The most important honey plants in the United States are white clover, sweet clover, basswood, buckwheat, tupelo, raspberry, milkweed, goldenrod, alfalfa, fruit trees of all kinds, acacia and mesquite. The author of "American Honey Plants," an exceedingly interesting book, says that catnip is a famous bee plant and if it could be grown in large fields like clover, catnip honey would doubtless appear on the market.

In California a delicious amber-hued and very fragrant honey is produced where the bees feed upon the orange blossoms. Alfalfa honey is mildly spicy in flavour. John Burroughs says that bees that have been pasturing in a field of buckwheat "bring the delicious odour of the blossoming plant to the hives with them, so that in the moist warm twilight the apiary is redolent of the perfume of buckwheat." It is said that where mignonette is grown in sufficient quantity to provide ample pasturage for the bees the honey has a most exquisite bouquet.

The honey most esteemed by the ancients was that of Mount Hybla in Sicily, said to be made from lime blossoms; and of Mount Hymettus in Attica, where the bees drew aromatic nectar from the thyme blossoms and other scented labiates, such as lavender and rosemary, for many months of the year. The far-famed Narbonne honey is pale and highly aromatic, and the little province of Gatinais in France has long been known for its sainfoin honey, made from the fodder plant of that name. And this is the most exquisite honey it has ever been my pleasant lot to taste. It tastes as white clover smells – and what could be more delicious?

Bacon wrote that "Honey in Spaine smelleth (apparently) of the Rose-mary or Orenge, from whence the Bee gathereth it." Orange blossom honey has a fine aroma. The honey that brings the highest price today in Europe is heather honey. It is a bright warm amber in hue and has a most unusual flavour, very agreeable when one grows accustomed to it. The aroma is very pungent and penetrating, "making itself manifest in a room where it is kept in a closed cupboard." "In my native village in Yorkshire," wrote A. J. Bean, "it used to be, and possibly still is, the practice for the beehives of the cottagers to be ladened on vans and taken every summer to the moors, ten or twelve miles away, for the bees to collect honey from the heather. They were brought back each autumn." [1]

[1] *In California the hives are carted many miles to the orange groves.*

In certain parts of Germany a honey nearly black in colour and rather rank in flavour is harvested from the pine forests where the bees feed upon the resinous blossoms of the pines. This is called Echter Honig and it is highly relished by noble German epicures, bringing a high price at all times. And in Palestine, the land flowing with milk and honey, the product of wild bees, especially in the wilderness of Judea, found in crevices between rocks, in hollow trees, and elsewhere, is a means of subsistence with many of the inhabitants.

When I became interested in writing something about bees, I began to look about in the shops in New York to find what kinds of honey were to be had. The result of my investigation was to me most surprising and I spent a winter sipping nectar from the flowers of all parts of the world. Besides the exquisite sainfoin honey and the dark pine blossom honey from the Black Forest, I found a most delectable kind made in Portugal where the bees feed upon the vine flowers. It was specially delicate and fragrant and was put up in a little pale green pot. Very good also was the peach blossom honey from Spain. Lavender honey (put up in a pretty grey jar) from Syria had a most agreeable and unusual flavour, and from Syria also came the products of the wild acacia blossoms, cactus and wild thyme.

There is a dark, rich and rather heavy honey made in Florida from the blossoms of the palmetto, and wild sage blossom honey, also rich and dark from our Southwest. Very fine buckwheat and orange flower honey also comes from this locality. There was Virgin honey, said to be made by young bees in the Holy Land, called Zohar, put up in squat two-pound pails with amusing handles; Spring Blossom honey from Dalmatia; a dark and very rich honey made from acacia flowers, from Budapest, Hungary, called Zita-mez, Dutch heather honey, dark and thick, gathered and put up in jars in Holland; Jewish honey from Hederah in Palestine, and of course the long famous Greek honey of Mt. Hymettus (in a smart yellow and black jar), as well as the illustrious product of Mt. Hybla. Each one of these possessed a distinct flavour and making acquaintance with it was decidedly a little adventure, an adventure that took one out of the humdrum daily round and transported one, in spirit at least, to Elysian fields.

We have many kinds of gardens today – rock gardens, rose gardens, herb gardens, iris gardens, and more, why not a bee garden forsooth? It could not but be a delightful place, homely and comely and rich in sweet odours, and the hives would lend "a new meaning to the flowers and the silence, the balm of the air and the rays of the sun." The bee garden might be situated in an angle of the house – if such there be – or in some other sheltered place, a neat pattern of little beds and borders overflowing with such flowers as are rich in honey, and flanked about with apple, pear, plum and peach trees "in which when they cast (swarm) they may knit without taking any far flight or wandering to find out their rest." The place should be "open to the South Sun and yet notwithstanding, neither exceeding in heat nor in cold, defended from windes and tempests, so that they may flie their sundrie and several waies to get diversitie of pastures, and so again may return to their little Cottages laden with their composition of honey."

Among the flowers for the bee garden there would be numbered some for nectar and some for pollen, for easily available sources of pollen are second only in importance to an abundant supply of nectar. There should be included many of the labiate tribe, those plants of modest blossoms that are so beloved of bees and especially adapted to their convenience, the ground ivy, the white archangel, catnip, cedronella, nepeta, the mints and thymes. Blue flowers there would be in plenty, for these are the favourites of the bees. How greedily they buzz about the cornflowers, the borage, the nigella, the anchusa, the larkspur, the blue salvias and the pretty phacelias. And there should also be sweet alyssum, sweet peas, sweet woodruff, sweet sultans – all the famous sweets in fact, and arabis, ambrosia, nemesia, coreopsis, bergamot, buddleja, zinnias, collomia, candytuft, viscaria, eutoca, gilias, bartonia, mignonette, lupines, angelica, cerinthe or honeywort, oenotheras, flowering currant, snapdragons, *Silene pendula,* schizopetalon, sunflowers, *Saponaria calabrica, Limnanthes douglasii,* clematis, stocks, wall flowers, poppies, sage, winter and summer savory, violets, pinks, basil, brooms and heathers of many kinds. "Aniseed sown near the Apiary is esteemed an extraordinary delightful food for bees" and Virgil recommends:

> About them let fresh lavender and store
> Of wild time with strong savorie to floure.

A very gay garden indeed this would be and one where the bees would find rich pasturage for many months of the year. Thoreau thought that the unsavoury flowers of the skunk cabbage were the first to be visited by the bees in spring. ("Lucky," he says, "that the flower does not flavour the honey.") But one having a garden knows that the bees find the snowdrops however early they may come forth and cling in the chilly bells almost numbed with the cold. They plunder the first yellow crocuses too, and the scillas, as well as the hepaticas, early primroses and cowslips, and we note that other popular points of call at this spare season are the catkins of the alder and pussy willow and the blossoms of the red maple, about which they swarm in great numbers. They visit also the flowers of the red bud and the serviceberry. Later flowering trees that are favoured by them are the hawthorn, all the fruit trees, locust, basswood and tulip. If you have walked beneath the "Immemorial Limes" at Trinity College, Oxford, where once paced the elder Pitt, you will remember the loud chant of the feeding bees in the scented blossoms over head. Honey from lime blossoms is regarded as the best flavoured and it is used exclusively in medicines.

Hives have been of many kinds. Hollow logs have been used and in Galilee and Bethlehem, where bee-keeping is extensively carried on, the hives are sunburnt tubes of mud about four feet in length. In very early times wicker hives were fashioned and daubed over with a mixture of cowdung and lime. William Lawson (1617) used hives made of straw, commending them for "nimblenesse, warmnesse and drynesse" as well as for the ease with which they could be moved about. The hives made of sweet wheaten or rye straw and bound with bramble, "large and deep and even proportioned like a Sugar-loaf" must have been very picturesque when set up in rows amid rioting flowers. But apparently they had their drawbacks. Gervase Markham, a bee-keeper and gardener of repute in the seventeenth century, states that the straw-hive "is subject to breed mice," and another early writer testifies that when they are old and loaded "they do usually sinke on the one side (especially if they take wet) and so break the combs and spill out the honey." Frequently wooden hives had a quaint peaked thatching over them which must have added greatly to their pictorial value. Such must have been the hives in the little Flanders village where Maeterlinck first saw an apiary and "learned to love the bees." Here the apiary was composed of twelve domes of straw, some of which had been painted a bright pink, some clear yellow, but most of them a tender blue, because the wise beemaster had noticed, "long before Sir John Lubbock's demonstrations, the bee's fondness for this colour."

But even the common wooden hives, painted white or in gay colours, are very decorative by reason of their very simplicity. And the picturesque straw skeps are procurable from any considerable dealer in apiarian supplies.

All work among bees, we are told, should be done gently but with decision. Any fumbling or apparent nervousness is apt to provoke a painful sting. Some bee-masters of old recommended drinking a cup of good beer before going among the bees, others "wash their hands and face therewith, which proves a good defence." Worlidge says he has "gone amongst them in their greatest Anger and Madness only with a handful of sweet Herbs in my Hand, fanning my Face, as it were to obscure and defend it. Also if a Bee do by accident buz about you, being unprovided, thrust your face amongst a parcel of Boughs or Herbs, and he will desert you." A bit of advice worth remembering, without doubt, in a distracted and terrified moment.

A country woman who once helped out in my kitchen had serene confidence in the theory that if you hold your breath a bee cannot sting you. And she was fond of demonstrating for the benefit of my children. But the experiment when tried by the trusting children was always a painful failure. If, however, your garden is properly set forth you will have many remedies at hand to use if peradventure you meet a bee in a mood "curst and malicious" and ready to sting spitefully. You may rub the wound with the leaves of balm, of marigold, hollyhock, houseleek, ivy, burdock or rue. Indeed if you go your way among bees anointed with the bitter juices of the herb o' grace, you will be quite safe, for no bee will come nigh you.

Science tells us that bees are not specially attracted to fragrant flowers and their marked preference for those of blue colour, that are so often scentless, bears out this contention. "In a long series of experiments von Frisch has found that the bees' appreciation of scent is very much the same as our own. They perceive the same smells that we do and with about the same acuity – he did not find any that were odourless to ourselves but scented to the bees."

Ancient bee-masters, nevertheless, rubbed their hives with balm and other sweet scented herbs which "causeth the Bees to keep together and causeth others to come unto them." Markham says, "before you lodge any bee in your hive you shall perfume it with juniper and rub it all within with fennel, hyssop and thyme-flowers, and also the stone upon which the hive shall stand." John Burroughs tells of smearing his bee-box, when out wild honey hunting, with the fragrant oil of anise, which he says "will attract the bees half a mile or more." But bees seldom notice the sweet scented blossoms of the lilac, heliotrope or rose, preferring the almost scentless cornflower or the wayside goldenrod and asters.

PASSION FLOWER
(*Passiflora*)

It seems, however, to have been very generally agreed that "ill smells" are very offensive to bees, so much so that Markham in his counsels to bee-keepers says that they should "refraine in a manner from all smelling meates, poudered meates, fryed meates, and all other meates that doe stinke, like as the Leakes, the Onions, the Garlicke, and suche like, whiche the Bees greatlye abhorre. Besides to be sweet of body and cleanly of apparell minding to come to their Hives, for in all cleanlinesse and sweetnesse the Bees are muche delighted."

Alexander Japp, in a book entitled "Hours in My Garden," wrote pleasantly of birds, bees and flowers, ponds, coppices and hedgerows. In it he points out that it is a mistake to suppose that bees hibernate the winter through. "On the contrary they are very wakeful, much more so than the bee-master wants, and in certain kinds of weather will give him a good deal of trouble and concern, being apt to steal out if the weather is mild at all and then to become so benumbed with the cold that they are unable to get back to the hive." The bee-master must prevent this by dint of various attentions, one of which is to slip a tube of honey into the hole of the hive. Mr. Japp also notes that bees, "like many other animals (and men too) who bear a high character for respectability" are apt to go on an occasional spree and get quite disgracefully tipsy. Certain flowers have this effect upon them and they show no mind to avoid these but on the contrary will sip the insidious nectar until quite incapacitated for industry and frequently unable to get home. That the burly humble bee is an offender in this way does not seem so surprising but one is quite shocked at such behaviour on the part of the svelte and elegant honey bee. Willow flowers are said to be intoxicating to bees and so are the

intricate blossoms of the passion flower, and the bright gauds of sunflowers, as well as the inconspicuous blossoms of the English ivy. And I think the eminently respectable hollyhock must be doing a little bootlegging, for I have often found a humble bee completely undone within the capacious cup – the morning after.

But I like the humble bee. I like his broad black back with its smart tawny bar, and his disposition is altogether more amiable than that of his more nervous and highly-bred relative of the hives. He is slow to sting and one cannot watch his comings and goings without knowing him to be a patient and kindly creature. Seldom does his hum become angry.

His labor is a chant,
His idleness a tune.

And one feels that his horizon is wide, he is not tied to the observance of small neat duties. He is a gentleman of the road with all the road's cheerful philosophy and good nature. But he is an indefatigable worker as well, rising, I have noticed, earlier than the honey bee and going to bed later. Often at dusk when I am going about among the flowers attending to one or two last matters I meet the humble bee. In the hushed sleepy garden his hum is very loud – a bit vainglorious perhaps – but I like his company and we often work sociably over the same plant. Sometimes the whip-poor-will chanting his strange vespers finds us both still there – choosing the society of our souls.

Familiar to all bee folk is the old rhyme:

A swarm in May
Is worth a load of hay
A swarm in June
Is worth a silver spoon.
But a swarm in July
Isn't worth a fly.

What then of a swarm in November? Last autumn during one of those balmy "backward looks" of the weather which we call Indian Summer, a swarm of bees appeared in my garden and "knit" upon a branch of the hemlock hedge. For three days with manifest excitement and much loud buzzing they made comb with unbelievable speed in the golden deceitful weather, and were extremely short tempered with any who ventured near them. Upon the fourth day the wind veered sharply to the north and gray skies poured forth a biting barrage of chill rain for three days. When I went out to look at the bees I found them in desperate and pitiable plight, and by another day they had all gone, whither I know not. The unfinished comb still clings to the hemlock branch in mute testimony to the fact that the wisest among us sometimes make grave mistakes. It would seem that instinct should have told these wise insects that their venture was doomed to disaster from the first.

The whole subject of bees is a fascinating one whether we approach it from a practical standpoint or if merely interested in old bee lore.

"The Bee is a little Creature," wrote Samuel Purchase, in 1657, "but God's smallest Springs prove at length main Oceans, His least beginnings grow into great works, great wonders."

CHAPTER XVII

Scents of Orchard and Berry Patch

Apples and quinces, Lemons and oranges, Plump unpecked cherries, Melons and raspberries, Bloom-down-cheeked peaches, Swart-headed mulberries, Wild free-born cranberries, Crab-apples, dewberries, Pine-apples, blackberries, Apricots, strawberries;-All ripe together In summer weather.

— CHRISTINA ROSETTI

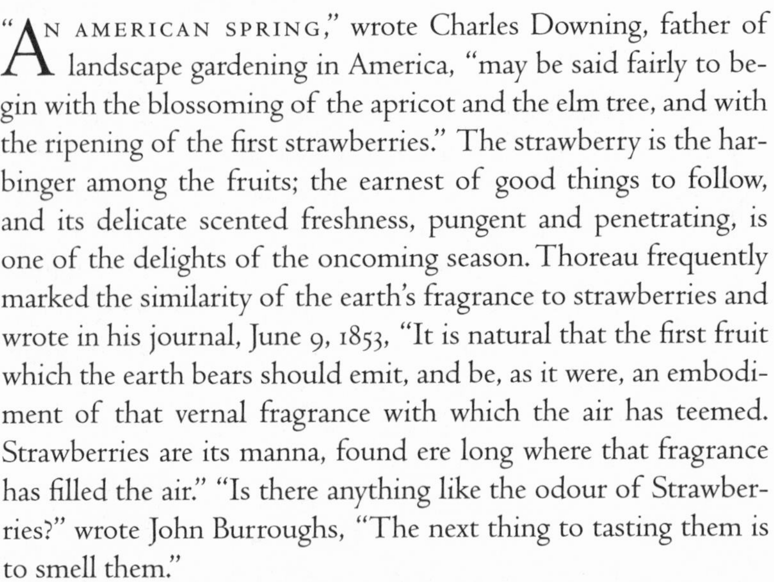

"AN AMERICAN SPRING," wrote Charles Downing, father of landscape gardening in America, "may be said fairly to begin with the blossoming of the apricot and the elm tree, and with the ripening of the first strawberries." The strawberry is the harbinger among the fruits; the earnest of good things to follow, and its delicate scented freshness, pungent and penetrating, is one of the delights of the oncoming season. Thoreau frequently marked the similarity of the earth's fragrance to strawberries and wrote in his journal, June 9, 1853, "It is natural that the first fruit which the earth bears should emit, and be, as it were, an embodiment of that vernal fragrance with which the air has teemed. Strawberries are its manna, found ere long where that fragrance has filled the air." "Is there anything like the odour of Strawberries?" wrote John Burroughs, "The next thing to tasting them is to smell them."

But those who have inhaled this aroma only when the fruit is served at table can form no idea of the wild racy sweetness of the small crimson fruits when gathered on some windy upland under the sky. The wild strawberry is far more aromatic than the cultivated varieties, though its blood courses in their veins. Often when walking in the country one is halted by the unmistakable odour of strawberries and guided to the place where they spread a bountiful repast beneath the smiling daisies or carpet some sandy hillside. Delicious and unspeakably pristine both in taste and smell is this "lowly but youth-renewing berry" in its wild state.

The cultivated strawberry of today is the result of a fusion between our American species, *Fragraria virginica,* and a Chilean, but "the wedding ceremony of the American immigrants was celebrated in England, and for some years the large modern fruits were known as 'English' in Continental countries." The hautbois, which is found wild in high places in France and is sometimes served to one in that country, had no part in the development of latter day varieties; it has a curious musky flavour and aroma, rather agreeable though unusual, that with the deep violet-red colour of the fruit serves to identify it at once. The alpine strawberry, particularly the white variety, has a quite exquisite bouquet and an especially delicate flavour, and the plants have the peculiarity of bearing fruit and blossoms at the same time and throughout the season. It was introduced to cultivation from Mount Cenis in 1754 and is known in France as "Four Seasons" because of its long fruiting period.

Little baskets lined with vine leaves and filled with wild strawberries often form a most colourful and acceptable accompaniment to French meals, and the French manner of serving strawberries with a sauce of Claret and sugar is an epicurean experience to be sought. The juice of strawberries was once deemed a fine cosmetic and ancient medical works prescribed it, or a distillation of the leaves, in hot and feverish afflictions because of their cooling and alleviating qualities. Strawberry cordial, strawberry shrub and strawberry wine are all good drinks. A rule for strawberry wine is as follows:

> Twelve gallons of bruised strawberries, ten gallons of cider, seven gallons of water, twenty-five pounds of sugar. Ferment, then add half an ounce of bruised bitter almonds, one half ounce of bruised cloves, and six ounces of red tartar.

Many poets, Spenser among them, have praised the scent of strawberry blossoms and it is said that those of *Fragaria lucida,* the California wild strawberry, are slightly violet scented. The "most excellent Cordial Smell" of dying strawberry leaves, which Bacon places second only to white violets and musk roses in sweetness, is said not to be discernible to the plebeian nose. Indeed the power to enjoy this fragrance is claimed as an hereditary faculty handed down from generation to generation in aristocratic families. This notion, however, when examined is proven to be pure fallacy, for under a hot autumn sun, or after a first sharp frost, the odour arising from a bed of strawberries is so pungent that the most indigent and upstart nose cannot fail to catch it – if it is a nose sensitive to odours at all.

In Shakespeare's day there flourished a belief that plants were affected by the neighbourhood of other plants to such an extent that they assumed each other's faults. Thus fragrant flowers were planted near fruit trees with the idea of improving the flavour of the fruit, and evil-smelling trees, like the elder, were carefully cleared away from fruit trees lest they be tainted. But the strawberry was deemed an exception to the rule and was said to thrive in the midst of evil communications without being corrupted. This alleged incorruptibility was naturally seized upon, according to Canon Ellacombe, by preachers and moralists generally as a text for many a discourse in which the gay little berry was likened to the innocent and pure in heart who are able to dwell without contamination amidst noisome influences and corrupt manners.

To wash strawberries spoils the fragrance of the fruit and thus despoils us of half our gastronomic pleasure. An old number of "Garden and Forest" informs us that sand may be removed from the berries without washing by bouncing them about in a damp cloth just before they are served.

Raspberries are ripening their rosy thimbles before strawberries have quite gone over and almost this exquisite berry, which Thoreau called the most innocent and simple of fruits, makes us forget our delight in the vivacious first fruit of the year. In early days, however, the raspberry was considered inferior even to the blackberry.

Unlike the strawberry, the raspberry has not lost under cultivation either fragrance or flavour and so in the large berries of today we have gained more than mere bulk. In taste and colour and aroma, as befits the warmer weather that brings them forth, they are altogether milder than strawberries, their colour softer, their fragrance richer and more flowery, their taste lacking the acidity that characterizes the strawberry. But the perfume of raspberries though bland is curiously penetrating. "In Canadian towns," writes Martha Flint in "A Garden of Simples," "during their season the air is redolent with the penetrating perfume of red raspberries, or scotch-caps, which women bring to market in great baskets of white birch."

The red raspberry is a product of rich alluvial soils in Europe, Asia and America. The American red raspberry is very hardy, much more so than its toothsome blackcapped sister; indeed it is one of the hardiest of fruits, flourishing far beyond the Great Lakes in this country and into Alaska. The raspberry found in eastern American markets today has been developed from this wild species, *Rubus strigosus.* The European red raspberry is *R. idaeus* so named by Pliny centuries ago because of its plenitude on Mount Ida in Greece. It will not endure a rigorous climate but is often grown in California. Early writers refer to raspberries as raspis and sometimes as hindberries, and in country neighborhoods hereabouts we hear them referred to as rasps.

Worledge in his "Systema Agriculturae," published in 1669, says, "Raspberries are not to be omitted out of a number of the most pleasant and useful Fruits which yield one of the most pleasant Juyces of any Fruit and being extracted and preserved will serve to tinge any other Liquor with its delicate Aromatick Gust." A pleasant wine used to be made of raspberries in rural neighbourhoods and perhaps still is, of which it has been said, "Of all homemade wines it is the most delicious to the taste; it lightly and pleasantly stimulates the nerves of the mouth and nose with a most agreeable smell and taste."

Raspberry vinegar was made in every home in my youth and when diluted with water and finely crushed ice is a most refreshing and innocuous summer drink.

A famous dessert that used to be served by the very eminent Filippini, who once presided over the gustatory triumphs of old Delmonico's, was Compote of Raspberries with Wine. Its preparation is in this manner:

> Place a quart of fresh raspberries in a bowl, season with two tablespoons sugar, one tablespoon of kirsch and mix well. Place in a small saucepan one and half gills claret, with one ounce powdered sugar and a half stick cinnamon. Reduce on the fire to half the quantity; let cool off, strain through a cheesecloth over the raspberries, mix well, transfer into a compotier and serve.

The blossom of the raspberry has little attraction for us for it is insignificant in appearance and lacks fragrance, but in localities where it is plentiful it is an important honey flower yielding a rich store to the bees. Langham in his "Garden of Health," 1633, says, "the flower stampt with hony and applyed, is good for the inflamation of the eyes and the shingles."

The blackberry too has its fragrance – rich, racy of the dark moisture-retentive soil from which it springs, distilled to winyness by the hot summer suns in which it revels. "Almost all the year round it is a treasure house of odours," wrote David Grayson, "even when the leaves first come out; but it reaches crescendo in blossom time, when indeed I like it least, for being too strong. It has a curious fragrance once well called by a poet – 'the hot scent of the brier' – and aromatically hot it is and sharp like the berries themselves." The blackberry is as hardy as the raspberry and is found in one form or another – dewberry, high-and-low-bush blackberry, loganberry, cloudberry, in all parts of the country save in the drought-ridden reaches of the Southwest, as well as in many parts of the world. "Of all the fruits," wrote Mary Webb, "the wimberry or cloudberry, should rank first. Its colour is the bloomy purple of distant hills. It tastes of Faery." All across the world in Arctic and Subarctic regions, the cloudberry embroiders the earth, creeping southward occasionally, as in Maine and New Hampshire, to overlay with its slender tracery the high and airy steeps of their mountains. "It will grow only in beautiful and mysterious places," we are told, yet the shy cloudberry is quite easily trained to acceptance of the counterfeit wildness of rock gardens – those regions which may often enough be characterized as mysterious though not always with truth beautiful.

The blackberry is the "Bramble Breer" of ancient times famed as a palliative or cure for innumerable ills of the flesh and not a few of the spirit. Nor is all its fame as a medicine of antique origin. I remember well the stone jug of blackberry cordial made by our great-aunt Mary, that always stood upon a high shelf in my mother's clothespress. The dark and aromatic liquid used to be spooned out when occasion demanded to the children of the family to soothe the "griping griefs" of our imprudent young stomachs, and very warming and ameliorating it was. It was made yearly by mashing and straining the fully ripe berries until there was a gallon of juice, then sugar and allspice and cloves were added to taste and the whole cooked until slightly thickened. When nearly cold a quart of good brandy was added. During the making and for days thereafter the whole house was redolent of its stinging aroma.

A superstition – or is it fact? – that snakes are inordinately fond of blackberries, has credence in some localities, and so, going a-berrying for me, that most wholesome and entertaining of rustic activities, was always attended by a tremulous fear of meeting more sinister pickers than the gingham-clad women and children of the countryside. True, I never met with any sort of snake among the tall canes, but bloodcurdling if somewhat vague tales were freely recounted during berry-picking time of those whose experience had been less fortunate and even fatal.

Blueberries, which someone has called celestial jelly wrapped in heaven-hued filament, purvey a curious woodsy odour, and so potent is a word to call up a scent, and a scent to reproduce a scene that the bare mention of the globose bloomy fruits serves to fill my nostrils with the curious acid fragrance of massed blueberry bushes and to frame a picture of the Cape Cod landscape where grow the largest and most luscious blueberries of my experience.

Apricots, plums, nectarines and peaches, those seductive warm-cheeked products of the mature summer, have each a different and distinguishing scent. The apricot, or abricocke, as it was known of old, came to us from gentle climates better suited to it than ours and we are seldom able to look upon its golden velvet coat at its best or to inhale its richest aromas. In America it is grown commercially only on the Pacific Coast and in a few of the Rocky Mountain states. In a few private gardens it is attempted but it is usually seen sallow, rather than golden, and sadly lacking in flavour and perfume. When fully ripened by an ardent sun the apricot has a smooth and mellifluous perfume and its flesh is then firm and juicy, but the specimens commonly presented to us for purchase by the green-grocer lack both flavour and aroma and I know a little boy who describes their texture well when he calls them "woolly peaches." Perhaps they have been picked too green.

E. A. Bunyard in his delightful book, "The Anatomy of Dessert," quotes "the ever famous Dr. Muffet" as saying, "Apricots are plums concealed beneath a peach's coat." In old days they seem to have had innumerable uses, chiefly medicinal, though Parkinson informs us that "They are also preserved and candid, as it pleaseth Gentlewomen to bestowe their time and charge, or the Comfit-maker to sort among their candid fruits." The French Liqueur, Eau de Noyaux, owes its flavour to the fact that it is prepared from the bitter kernels of apricots.

Few fruits display more lovely colours than do plums – golden, water-green, violet inclining to red, red inclining to violet, and that dark bloomy hue described by old writers as a "quick blacke," and always of a translucent quality that half reveals flickering golden lights through the thin skin. To enjoy to the full the perfume of the plum the skin must be broken, and then the quality of it varies; some are much sweeter than others, but the green gage I think is the most fragrant of them all. Plum blossoms are in most cases delightfully sweet and few fruit blossoms are more charmingly decorative, though they are very fleeting. The nectarine is grown commercially in America only in California and comes to eastern markets as a luxury. It is a delicious fruit, full of rich juices and with a fine full-bodied aroma much more distinctive than that of a peach. Thompson in "The Seasons" sings of the "ruddy, fragrant nectarine." Like the peach, the nectarine seems to have reached the Western World through Persia and indeed, though it was not always so considered, the nectarine is now generally classified as a variation of the peach. Dr. Bailey tells us that "Nectarines often come from the seeds of peaches and peaches have come from seeds of nectarines." Those who dislike the downy surface of the peach will appreciate the smooth cool cheek of the nectarine.

PLUM
(Prunus domestica)

But the peach unfailingly delights us, as that great French gardener of the last century, de la Quintinye, says, because of "its Beauty and Largeness, its lovely round Figure, the abundance of its Sugared Juice and its rich perfume." Our great peach orchards are among the most beautiful and wondrous achievements of man. To see the orchards of North Carolina and Georgia in bloom – mile on mile of diaphanous pink colour – peachglow – against the flawless sky is a sight never to be forgotten in this world, and hardly less spectacularly beautiful are they when in fruit. I once had the felicity of being on a North Carolina peach farm during the picking season. The air from the immense open packing sheds, where women and girls in clean print frocks and sunbonnets graded and packed the fruit with unbelievable speed and deftness, was almost intoxicating in its winy fragrance and pervaded the whole sun-saturated countryside, and the perfectly matched fruits seemed without doubt the most beautiful of the earth's products.

The peach as we know it today is nowhere known in a wild state. It has been cultivated for countless ages in most parts of Asia and seems to have been introduced to the Western World from Persia through Greece during the reign of the Emperor Claudius. It was then known as *Malus persica,* the Persian apple. Few states grow peaches in some quantity, though in the cold prairie states of the North and in frigid mountainous regions they are of course not largely grown.

To turn from the luscious perfumed peach to the quince is to leave enchantment for harsh reality, for the quince, the quoin of olden days, is a forbidding and cross-grained fruit, repelling us by its bitter acidity and ungiving quality, yet inviting us as it were, with its powerful pressing fragrance. In Shakespeare's time the quince was held in the highest repute and planted far more freely than it is today. Parkinson wrote, "there is no fruit growing in the land that is of so many excellent uses as this, serving as well to make many dishes of meat for table, as for banquits, and much more for their physical virtues." Sir Thomas Browne extolled it as "the stomach's comforter, the pleasing quince." And in that simple day for a man or woman to send a gift of quinces to one of the opposite sex was to proffer a love token. Quince wine was and still is a popular and flavorous beverage in rural neighbourhoods. I once long ago was regaled with quince wine and delicious seed cakes at a vine-covered vicarage somewhere in the south of England. I wish I could remember the names of the kindly clergyman and his sister who were so cordial to a dusty motorist discovered hanging entranced over their white gate gazing at the flowery enclosure within, for I should like to acknowledge here their gracious hospitality. How amazingly ready to be friendly are flower lovers always the world over, but more particularly, I believe, in England. A real love of flowers seems to be a passport universally accepted there.

The flushed shell-like blossoms of the quince are without odour but the fruit is highly scented, too much so for many, and Thomas Lawson, in his "New Orchard and Garden" warns us that "Quinces should not be laid with other Fruite for the scent is offensive both to other fruite and to those who keepe the fruite or come amongst them: therefore lay them by themselves upon sweet straw where thy have ayre enough." The perfume of the fruit of the Japanese quince, *Chaenomeles japonica* [*Cidonia japonica*], of our shrubberies, is even more agreeable, almost rose-like. Long ago as children we always kept a Japanese quince in the box with our little pocket handkerchiefs and thought the scent finer than any eau de rose that was ever bottled.

Early writers frequently celebrate the fragrance of the vine in all its parts; the blossoms – "that little dust, like the dust of a bent, which grows upon the cluster in the first coming forth," which Bacon so highly praised, the bloomy pendant clusters of fruit themselves, when ripe, and we have Chaucer thus testifying to the sweetness of the root, "Scorners faren like the foul toade, that may noughte endure the soote smel of the Vine roote when it flourisheth."

To drive through a grape-growing countryside when the fruit is ripe is to indulge in a most innocent Bacchanalian feast. Far and near the air is heavy with the fumes of potential wine, "the luscious liquor" of the grape. You can smell the vineyards long before you reach them. It is one of the richest and most stimulating of the year's odours. One vine indeed in a garden – and is there a climber of greater decorative value? – serves to perfume the whole enclosure and eloquently proclaims the prodigal generosity of the teeming earth. "Grapes!" exclaim the school children as they pass my home in September, though the grape arbour is nowhere visible from the lane.

But the favourite fruit of the American people is without doubt the apple. The apple, firm, wholesome and ingenuous, with its autumn tinted coat, russet, incarnadine, Indian red, roseate, green, amber; the apple with its diverse scents and savours, its manifold homely uses. Undoubtedly it was the first tree planted by the homesick colonists in the new land and it was the cheerful fruitful orchards arising about the new dwellings that first made homes of these stark erections. And the apple at once and whole-heartedly adopted America; it thrives here as nowhere else and our farflung orchards like our peach plantations are today among the wonders of the world. Who has seen and not marveled at the great orchards of the Northwest, running to forty thousand trees and more, and who but cherishes memories of those among the rockbound enfolding hills of New York State and New England? In all parts of the country it is the fruit of the people, of high and low, rich and poor, of young and old. The homely names bestowed upon it attest the affection with which it has long been regarded – sweet bough, spice sweet, gilliflower, wealthy, winesap, juneating, bellflower, greening, delicious, banana sweet – to name a few at random, so different from the grand cognomens worn by pears like worldly medals. This generous fruit has brought comfort and prosperity to many sections of the country and so grateful are the people for its largess that in certain localities monuments have been raised up in its honour. The 'McIntosh' is thus commemorated in Canada at Dundela, Ontario, the 'Baldwin' at Wilmington, near Lowell, Massachusetts, and the vigorous and flavorous Northern 'Spy', the 'Primate', the 'Wealthy', in other localities. If it has not already been accorded, the well-named 'Delicious' would seem to be ripe for such visible recognition from the inhabitants of the Chelan and Hood River districts of the Northwest, or perhaps from the State of its nativity, Iowa.

The cultivated apple owes its excellence to the skill and industry of man, for the crabapple is the only fruit of the kind indigenous to any country, and at some obscure time, by some means, all the apples we know today have been derived from the dour and forbidding crab. "As for Wildings and Crabs," wrote Pliny, "their taste is well enough liked and they carry with them a quicke and sharpe smell; howbeit this gift they have for their harsh sourness, that they have many a foule word and shrewd curse given them." But crabs nevertheless were much in use in old times, both medicinally and for cooking. A favourite dish was roasted crabs served with hot ale. The fruit of the crabapple is in most cases globose and broader than high, rather squat, and it hangs usually in little bunches on long slender stalks; sometimes it is very brightly coloured but more often green or pale yellow. It is very fragrant and often covered with a sticky secretion.

"Of all fruits the apple seems to have had the widest and most mystical history. The myths concerning it meet us in every age and country" and "When man emerges into history," wrote Harriet Keeler, "he has an apple in his hand and a dog by his side," and these two good companions of man seem never to have failed him. The apple has always been considered highly medicinal as well as so agreeably gustative. Many are the versions of the old couplet,

> Eat an apple going to bed
> And make the doctor beg his bread.

And there seem even today, when so many of our time-honored dietary beliefs are being wiped out, few voices lifted against the apple. Of old even the odour, which is well described in an old book as a "merry" scent, was deemed alleviating and curative. In Miss Rohde's "The Scented Garden" she quotes from the book of John Key, who was physician to Queen Mary and later to Elizabeth, concerning the wholesomeness of the smell of apples. The learned doctor counselled his patients when feeling weak after a dangerous illness to "smell to an old swete apple for there is nothing more comfortable to the spirits than good sweete odours."

In a most curious book called "A Thousand Notable Things," by one Thomas Lupton, 1650, I read, "The people of Astamores (as Plinie reports) have no mouth; and are clad with a woolly moss growing in India, and live only with smelling flowers and apples that grow in the woods which they carry with them in their long journies to sustain and nourish them with all, lest they should want thereof to smell." Schiller is said to have found his best inspiration in the winy smell of half rotten apples. "A rose when it blooms," wrote John Burroughs, "the apple is a rose when it ripens."

In farmhouses where the bins for fruit and vegetables are still in the cellar, the wholesome smell of apples pervades all the rooms and mingles with the fragrant steam arising from the catnip or chamomile tea kept brewing on the back of the stove in case of sudden need. It is a characteristic rural winter smell. Mrs. Earl relates that in rural communities not so long ago an apple stuck full of cloves was called a "Comfort Apple" and was sent to bereaved families as an expression of sympathy.

There is as much difference in the scents of apples as there is in their lovely blossoms or in their brisk flavours. Often the name of an apple describes its fragrance, thus the bergamot, the gilliflower, the spice sweet, the winesap. Many are warmly aromatic, highly spicy, others have a sweet flowery fragrance, sometimes they smell of raspberries, and there is always an underlying acidity which is stimulating to the appetite.

There was a custom followed in England up to a comparatively recent date, called wassailing the trees, which has been commemorated by Herrick:

Wassaile the trees, that they may beare
You many a Plum and many a Peare;
For more or lesse fruits they will bring
As you do give them Wassailing.

The ceremony commonly took place on New Year's or Christmas Eve when men and boys of the locality went about singing to the trees to encourage them to bear heavy crops and offering them the old toast:

Here's to thee, old apple-tree!
Whence thou may'st bud, and whence
thou may'st blow,
Hats full! Caps full!
Bushel-bushel-bags full!
And my pockets full too! Huzza!

Pitchers full of cider with roasted apples floating in it were then cast at the tree, but the simple rural ceremony did not it seems always end so innocently, for we find these lines in Milton's "Comus":

I should be loath
To meet the rudeness and swilled
insolence
Of such late wassailers.

Many palatable drinks have been made from apples from time immemorial. In Hogg's "Vegetable Kingdom" one is mentioned as being a very ancient English beverage. It was called Lamb's Wool, or earlier, Lamasool, being a contraction of La maes abhal, which in ancient British signifies the day of the apple fruit, from being drunk on the apple feast in autumn. It was composed of the pulp of roasted apples, highly seasoned with sugar and spices. But the most famous of course is cider, about whose composition whole books have been written and thousands of treatises. How richly burdened with fragrance is the air about a cidermill and how best of all is that amber liquid when drunk sweet and fresh from the dripping presses! Evelyn, however, thought otherwise. He says that "New Cider and all diluted and watered ciders, are great enemies to the Teeth and cause violent pains in them and Rheums in the Head." He also offers the information that "All Cider suffers Fermentation when the Trees are blossoming, though it be never so old; and Cider of very ripe fruit if bottled in that season will acquire a fragrance of the Blossom."

In England juniper berries are sometimes put into cider to give it a special flavour "as anise-seeds in bread, rather strange than odious." Other ways of improving or changing the flavour were also tried and William Lawson was of the opinion that if we hang "a poakefull of Cloves, Mace, Ginger, and pils of Lemmons in the midst of the vessel (in which the cider is kept) it will make it as wholesome and pleasant as wine." Another ancient work cautions that we must be careful in making cider not to mix early and late apples.

Cider shared the reputation of fresh apples as a healthful adjunct to the diet and Ralph Austen who wrote more beautifully of orchards than anyone has done before or since, said that "it will beggar a Physitian to live where cider and perry are of generall use." Mrs. Grieve ("A Modern Herbal," 1931) states on medical authority that in countries such as Normandy where unsweetened cider is the principal drink, cases of stone are almost nonexistent.

There was a belief in some countries that a twig of apple would do as well as a hazel rod in locating water, but I cannot find that this notion was ever held in America.

"Next unto Apples, the Pear challengeth his place." And the pear though not seemingly as old as the apple is far from being a new comer. It has been known and cultivated from a period of remote antiquity. As early as the time of Pliny the Romans were known to have possessed thirty-six varieties of cultivated pears. Today the list is long indeed and the pear has become a grand and sophisticated fruit. It has long been the Frenchman's darling and many pages of de la Quintinye's great book, "The Compleat Gardener," translated by Evelyn, are devoted to the culture and the description of pears. The cultivated pears as we know them today are derived from two species, the European *Pyrus communis* and the Oriental *Pyrus pyrifolia* [*P. serotina*], wild thorny trees whose thorns under cultivation, however, meekly turn to fruiting spurs, and though their fruit is harsh and uneatable unless cooked, it has a very pleasant fragrance.

Most of the fine pears of today are of French origin, but the 'Bartlett', the only kind save the unpalatable 'Kieffer' that is extensively grown in America, is a Britisher. This pear has many aliases. It is said to have been originated by one John Stair, a schoolmaster of the parish of Aldermason, near Reading, England, in 1770, and in that locality it is called after its creator, Stair's Pear. "Arriving in London a nurseryman, Williams, thought well to give it his own name, as did a certain Mr. Bartlett when it arrived in America." Well known is the svelte and lovely form of this luscious pear, with its thin perfumed skin, its pale cheek and its rose-red cheek, its juicy flesh between "breaking and tender," its rich flavour. It is a smoothflavoured delicious fruit. "I passionately love a little Smack of Perfume in my fruit," says de la Quintinye with Gallic enthusiasm, and of pears, "I esteem those that are pretty much perfum'd and well scented though I do not care this Perfection should be inclosed in a Pulp that is extreme hard, stony and full of dreggy Matter."

But the urbane pear has never, so to speak, made its way in America, has never become a popular dessert fruit; nor is it widely grown in comparison with the apple and the peach. We have originated the hard-bitten Kieffer, only fit for cooking, but a good winter keeper, and the succulent Seckel which has the disadvantage of keeping only a few days after it is gathered, seeming almost to dissolve in its own sweetness. In New England and in New York and west as far as the Great Lakes, the pear grows well and it is a hardy and long-lived tree, accepting conditions that the apple and the peach would disdain, and though slower to come to bearing will exist for centuries and still keep its health, vigor and productiveness. There is an old saying –

> He who plants Pears
> Plants for his heirs.

And I know many a venerable tree, dark with age and knotted, known to be well over a hundred years of age that still bears fair and fine fruit in great quantity.

And yet we do not grow pears on a large scale. Perhaps Thoreau summed up the American point of view towards this fruit when he wrote, "Pears are a less poetic though more aristocratic fruit than apples. They have neither the beauty nor the fragrance of apples but their excellence is in their flavor, which speaks to a grosser sense, they are *glout-morceaux;* hence while children dream of apples, judges, ex-judges and honorables, are connoisseurs of pears and discourse of them at length between sessions.... They are named after emperors and kings, queens, dukes and duchesses." Nor is the pear the friendly tree that we deem the apple. It has not its kindly generous spread, giving grateful shade to tired man and ruminating beast, and curving its boughs to fit the forms of children; it is a stiff and upright tree growing naturally in a self-conscious pyramid, proud and aloof. Yet a pear orchard in full blossom regalia is a beautiful sight. I was once well acquainted with a great pear orchard that covered a mountain hillside near my old home. In May it always made me think of a great concourse of proud and joyous brides veiled in their pale draperies setting out for a stupendous wedding ceremony. Pear blossoms bunched along the dark branches are beautiful enough to look at but their fragrance is not agreeable. Sniffing them you quickly pierce the light surface sweetness and reach something mawkish, almost fetid.

"The Pear tree bears almost its weight in Sprightly, Windy Liquor; sometimes one tree bears two, three, or even four Hogsheads per annum." This sprightly liquor is called perry and like cider it has long been a popular beverage, though I cannot find that it is much used today and I doubt if it was ever made to any extent in America. While the best apples make the best cider, the poorest pears seemingly make the best perry – pears of so harsh and uninviting a quality that "even a swine will not take them in his mouth." "Sharp and shrewish Pears," says one old writer, are the best for perry. And even then there is so little natural acidity in this fruit that crabapples are frequently crushed and their sharp juices added to cure the normally rather flat flavour of this drink and give it character.

CHAPTER XVIII

Plants of Evil Odour

Nature imitates all things in flower. They are at once the most beautiful and the ugliest objects, the most fragrant and the most offensive to the nostrils.

— THOREAU

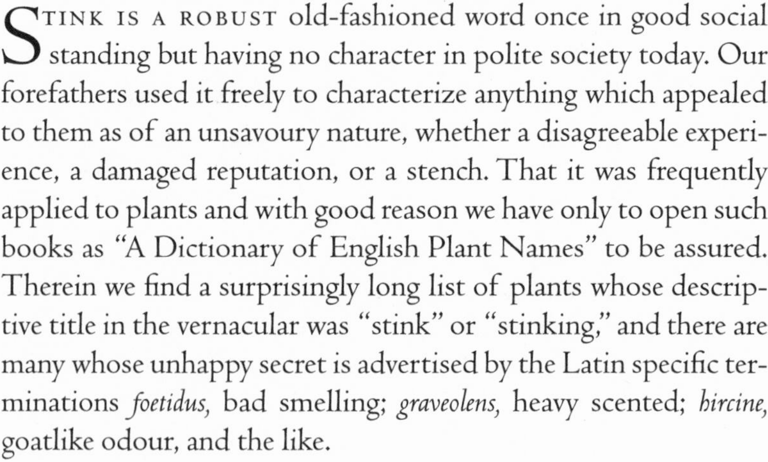

STINK IS A ROBUST old-fashioned word once in good social standing but having no character in polite society today. Our forefathers used it freely to characterize anything which appealed to them as of an unsavoury nature, whether a disagreeable experience, a damaged reputation, or a stench. That it was frequently applied to plants and with good reason we have only to open such books as "A Dictionary of English Plant Names" to be assured. Therein we find a surprisingly long list of plants whose descriptive title in the vernacular was "stink" or "stinking," and there are many whose unhappy secret is advertised by the Latin specific terminations *foetidus,* bad smelling; *graveolens,* heavy scented; *hircine,* goatlike odour, and the like.

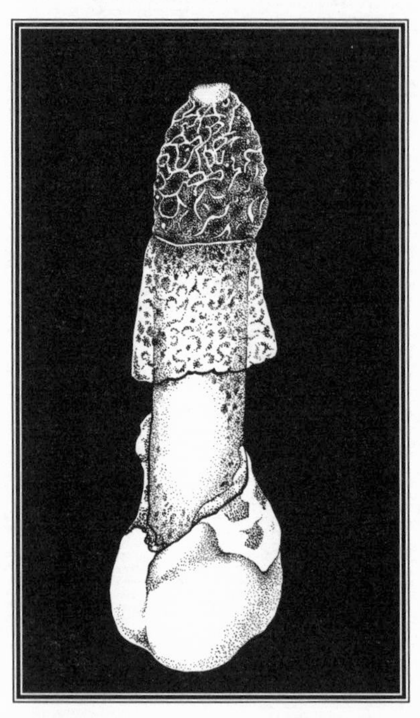

But happily for the nose of the world the ill-scented plants are distinctly in the minority. There can be in any event no hard and fast rule laid down between the sweet and the ill; certain plants that appeal to the susceptibilities of some persons as distinctly disagreeable may in another produce a quite opposite reaction. Most of the world agrees to the horridness of the released secretions of the skunk cabbage, yet I know a lovely and most ethereal young woman who finds this odour agreeable and invigorating.

The flowers of the hawthorn to which Walter de la Mare ascribes a "deathly smell" and which are unpleasant to many, seem to me among the sweetest of spring scents, eagerly awaited, and that great gardener of the last century, Canon Ellacombe, bears me out in my preference, for he speaks of the may tree as "loaded with a scent most delicate and refreshing." Moreover conditions of atmosphere and place as well as time have a distinct bearing on the odours of plants and flowers and our reactions to them. Under certain conditions the most agreeable of odours may become so exaggerated as to be intolerable. The scent of most lilies when brought indoors affects me unpleasantly and the luscious heavy sweetness of the paper white narcissus can easily become unendurable in an overheated room. Miss Jekyll in one of her books quotes her brother as writing from Jamaica of a large flowered jasmine: "It does not do to bring it indoors here, the scent is too strong. One day I thought there was a dead rat under the floor and behold it was a glass of fresh white jasmine that was the offender."

On hot and thunderous summer days I have known the scent of the tall bearded iris in the garden to seem positively hateful, especially when the season is about going over. The scent of certain plants when carried on the breeze may be delightful, when close at hand they may seem singularly less agreeable. This is true of hawthorn, valerian, elder, buckwheat, barberry and *Filipendula ulmaria* [*Spiraea ulmaria*], to name a few that come to mind. Many persons do not like the smell of elder and it is sometimes called stinking elder, but the wine made from both flowers and fruit has a delicate bouquet, and when the scent is caught as we drive along the highway it is very delicious and seems the very breath of summer. An old book, "Good's Family Flora," published in Cambridge in 1854 says, "the whole plant has a narcotic smell and it is not prudent to sleep under its shade." It was in great use in rustic medicine, however, as were many strong-scented plants; and in the same book elder wine is spoken of as "a powerful, warming and enlivening article for family use." The odour of *Filipendula ulmaria,* the meadow sweet, was also thought deleterious to health. A lady writer of the last century said, "but the powerful scent is not wholesome and I have heard of children who have kept a quantity of it in their little bed room being found insensible in the morning."

Our own mood too has a good deal to do with our reaction to certain odours. I once heard a woman say, "If I am worried about anything I simply cannot endure the odour of box, it affects me so that I want to scream. At other times I like it." And perhaps we have all known times when the scent of honeysuckle or lilac caught suddenly in the darkness affected us with the power of physical pain.

John Evelyn did not like the smell of box and referred more than once to the "unagreeableness of its smell," and in Hogg's "Vegetable Kingdom" the leaves are described as bitter and nauseous with a disagreeable odour, particularly after rain.

Mr. E. A. Bowles, who has written so many delightful garden books, has an experienced if somewhat crotchety nose. To him phloxes smell like a combination of pepper and pig-sty, most brooms of "dirty soapy bath sponge," hawthorn of "fish house," and meadow sweet of curry powder. He does not like *Philadelphus coronarius,* elder or *Aruncus dioicus* [*Spiraea arun-*

cus], but this is because they generally bring on a violent attack of hay fever. My father, a robust and far from fanciful man, was made positively ill by the odour of blossoming Ailanthus trees, and the scent of privet affects me as distinctly nauseating.

Miss Jekyll in "Children and Gardens" tells of her dislike of the odour of barberry. "There was one flower smell that I always thought odious, that of the common barberry. After a time when I learnt how the wind carries scent, I used to approach it cautiously from the windward side. The smell is not really very bad but of a faint and sickly kind but I remember years when to me it was so odious that it inspired me with a sort of fear, and when I forgot that the barberries were near and walked into the smell without expecting it, I used to run away as fast as I could in a kind of terror."

BARBERRY
(*Berberis verruculosa*)

It is curious how many persons turn in disgust from the odour of onion who relish greatly its taste. This has always been so even in that hardy age which we believe to have been so much less fastidious than our own. Old Bullein writes,

> It is a grosse kinde of medicine, verye unpleasant for fayre Ladies and tender Lily Rose coloured Damsels which often time prefereth sweet breathes before gentle words, but both would do very well.

There are many attractive members of the onion tribe that are useful in gardens, some indeed having sweet scented flowers, but brush the stems or dig up the roots and the cat is out of the bag, so to speak. The little sauce-alone or jack-by-the-hedge, *Alliaria officinalis* [*Erysimum alliaria*], a gypsy of British hedgerows, has the garlic odour in a very strong degree, and Ann Pratt tells us its name of sauce-alone was given from its uses, "for to some who cannot afford more costly condiments it is serviceable in adding flavour to the frugal diet."

The root and stem of *Ipheion uniflorum* [*Triteleia uniflora*] also has this penetrating onion scent and I find a note by Miss Jekyll telling of a border plant, something in the way of *Crambe cordifolia,* called *Peltaria alliacea,* which while it is good to look at is "undesirable" to handle, for when touched it gives off a strong smell of garlic, as is indicated by its specific name.

The leaves of certain familiar plants have to me a most unendurable odour. Chief offender among these is the pretty Herb Robert, *Geranium robertianum,* known sometimes as stinking cranesbill. It is a little wild plant introduced originally from Europe and often encountered in rocky, woodsy places. It sometimes makes its uninvited appearance in my rock garden and is so pretty and altogether amusing that I let it stay. Then presently I awake to the fact that my small area is positively overrun with Herb Robert and with the safety of choice treasures in mind it must be rooted out. It is a horrid task, for when bruised or broken it fills the world with expostulations in the form of a nasty odour which clings to clothing and hands for a long time. *Lamium maculatum,* the dead nettle, is another which it is unpleasant to have to weed because of its strong-smelling secretions, and clary, *Salvia sclarea,* is yet another. The leaves of *Mentha arvensis,* the corn mint, a gift of Europe to our spacious wild, when bruised smell like stale cheese. If you gather it because of its pretty dark rose-colored blossoms that appear in the late summer your regret will last until you reach home and can thoroughly wash your hands.

A few plants have ill-scented leaves and sweet-scented blossoms. This is true of the pretty little dogbane, *Apocynum,* and sometimes the reverse is true, as in the case of the California allspice, *Calycanthus occidentalis,* the leaves of which give off a pleasantly aromatic aroma but whose blossoms are ill-scented.

There are certain plants whose emanations affect everyone as noxious; these are the true stink-plants and chief among them are those that reproduce with horrid realism the odour of decaying flesh – the carrion flowers. Occasionally in walking through the countryside one is halted by a terrible and sickening odour and the thought immediately registers that some animal has crawled into the nearby thicket and died. But this stench more than likely arises from the small green flowers of *Smilax herbacea,* the carrion vine, a beautiful and decorative climber with heartshaped shining leaves that is frequently found in low ground scrambling over shrubs and fences. Thoreau said of the carrion vine, "It smells exactly like a dead rat in the wall, and apparently attracts flies like carrion. I find small gnats in it. A very remarkable odour. A single minute flower in an umbel, open, will scent a whole room." There are numerous species of *Smilax* in various parts of the country, nearly all with the distinguishing disgusting odour. Other plants have the same smell, among them *Cimicifuga racemosa,* one of our most lovely wild plants, with tall stems bearing a long fleecy inflorescence in summer. It makes itself known at a distance of many yards.

Stapelia, the carrion cactus, looks and smells as its name indicates. It is a curious fleshy plant of repellent appearance with large strangely formed and luridly coloured blossoms, thick, horrid, and emitting a noxious odour. There are many species of *Stapelia,* largely native of the Cape of Good Hope among which the characteristic odour varies in strength. It seems strange that these offensive plants should ever be regarded as desirable greenhouse subjects. Many of them are vividly pictured in Loddiges' "Botanical Cabinet" and they seem at one time to have been quite popular. Little mention is made of their foul odour and there seems generally a disposition among horticultural writers to leave out this bit of information concerning plants they describe. Not so Mr. Bowles, however. He writes of *Dracunculus muscivorus* [*Helicodiceros musci-*

vorus], the hairy or twist arum, as the most fiendish thing he knows, the sort of thing "Beelzebub might send to his mother-in-law." "The whole thing," he says, "is a mingling of unwholesome greens, livid purples, and pallid pinks, the livery of putrescence in fact, and it possesses an odour to match the colouring. It only exhales this stench for a few hours after opening, and during this time it is better to stand afar off and look at it through a telescope."

Dr. Hampden ("Flower Scent") describes the common stink horn, *Phallus impudicus,* a fungus, "whose horrible foetor can be smelt ten or twelve yards away and attracts blow flies in large numbers. These feed upon the foul smelling slime with which the cap of the fungus is covered and carry away with them and disseminate the spores that are embedded in it." Some of the species of *Aristolochia* also have this peculiarly atrocious odour. *Arum dracunculus,* the dragon arum, a hardy wild plant of Southern Europe, naturalized in parts of Britain, a near relative of our cheerful jack-in-the-pulpit, is said to possess a disgusting odour of carrion, "and yet," writes Miss Jekyll, "how fitting an accompaniment it is for the plant for if ever a plant looked wicked and repellent it is this, and yet like Medusa it has its own kind of fearful beauty."

A number of plants reproduce in their flowers or leaves the overwhelming and abominable odour of the skunk's defensive secretion. Chief among these is of course the skunk cabbage, which provides almost the earliest and certainly the most beautiful green of the year. In Rockland County, N. Y., where I lived for many years, the country people made a decoction of fresh skunk cabbage leaves and molasses which was fed to helpless children suffering from whooping cough. It was said to be an unfailing remedy. But how terrible! The crown imperial was a favourite flower in the gardens of the seventeenth century and I imagine there were few in which the splendid crowned flowers did not make their early appearance and flood the air with their strange and rather terrible odour. Apparently, however, it was not then regarded as terrible. Parkinson refers to it as "not unwholesome," and Gerard makes the astonishing statement that the flowers are "greatly esteemed for the beautifying of our gardens and the *bosoms of the beautiful!*" The italics are mine.

CROWN IMPERIAL
(*Fritillaria imperialis*)

Several other flowers have this strange skunk-like odour, indeed it seems rather common among plants. I remember one spring that I was certain a "wood kitty" was lurking somewhere in the near neighborhood of my garden, and it was not for several weeks that I discovered the source of the odour. It came from some plants of the pretty crosswort, *Phuopsis stylosa* [*Crucianella stylosa*] that edged one of the beds. It was much stronger in the morning than at any other time and permeated the whole garden. Walking in the Harvard Botanic Garden at Cambridge last summer I again encountered this unmistakable odour and this time traced it to the gay magenta blooms of the spider flower, *Cleome,* which tainted all the air about it for a considerable distance. Other flowers that possess this penetrating odour are various *Codonopsis* species, the skunk currant, *Ribes glandulosum* [*R. prostratum*], *Rhus trilobata,* and certain azaleas.

It would seem fitting and fair if poisonous plants advertised their baneful properties by an evil odour. But such is not by any means their invariable custom. Several dangerous fungi have a noxious odour, the pretty purple flowered nightshade, *Solanum dulcamara,* that is only mildly poisonous, possesses a heavy uninviting redolence, and the thorn apple or jimson weed, that loiterer about unsavoury neighbourhoods, rubbish heaps, railroad sidings and the like, pours a heavy narcotic odour from its great ivory trumpets as night descends, and its foliage when bruised gives off a most abominable stench. This plant introduced into England in Gerard's time from Constantinople and by him "dispersed through the land" has crossed the seas with other alien weeds and is now said to be found in every state of the Union. The odour is reputed to produce headache and faintness.

Two of the most poisonous plants we have do, however, sound an odoriferous warning which is heeded by birds and animals if not always by human beings. *Conium maculatum,* the hemlock, most virulent of a family most of whose members fall under suspicion, though it is a handsome plant, gives off a rank pestilential breath when bruised. It has been compared by some to the smell of mice and by others to the urine of cats. This hemlock is said to be the notorious Athenian state poison by which Socrates and other philosophers were put to death. It is widely naturalized in this country and still furnishes a remedy for certain disorders.

Less frequently met with in the United States is the black henbane or stinking nightshade, *Hyoscyamus niger,* an annual introduced from Europe. It is a most repellent plant to look at, hairy, sticky, crouching to the ground, and "its dingy cream-colored blossoms veined with lurid purple would confirm the impression made by the disagreeable and sickly odour of the whole plant." It is a dangerous poison and though it has always had and still has legitimate medicinal uses it must be handled with the greatest caution. Even to smell the flowers, according to Gerard, "causeth sleep."

In Turner's "Herbal" there is a curious recommendation concerning evil-smelling flowers: "If the pacient be too much slepi put stynkynge thynges unto hys nose to waken hym therewith."

LIST OF PLANTS OF EVIL ODOUR

Ageratum. Floss flower. Stale sweetish smell.

Ailanthus glandulosa. Tree of heaven. North

China. Leaves ill-smelling and flowers giving off a sickening odour. Tree fifty to seventy feet high. Much used in certain localities as a shade tree.

Amorphophallus rivieri. A remarkable aroid, native in China, having an immense calla-like inflorescence, reddish brown in colour, that is characterized by a most fiendish odour. It is sometimes grown under glass as a curiosity. In a recent number of "Horticulture" there was a picture of this strange plant showing it as considerably taller than the man who stood beside it.

Anargyris foetida. A deciduous bush or small tree native of the Mediterranean region, the leaves of which have a very disagreeable odour when crushed.

Anthemis cotula. Stinking chamomile. Common dog fennel. Native annual of Europe but widely naturalized in this country where it creeps about old barns and neglected dooryards and along roadsides. The small leaves are "cut and slashed into absolute formlessness" and are remarkable for their rank odour. One of the names of this plant is pigsty daisy and it may frequently be seen crowding against the palings of pigstys of the less cleanly order. Toads are said to be partial to this plant.

Apocynum androsaemifolium. Dogbane. Charming little wildflower found by the wayside in summer. The flowers have a pleasant fragrance but the leaves and stems exude a most disagreeable odour when crushed.

Dracunculus vulgaris [*Arum dracunculus*]. Black arum. Odour of carrion.

Borkhausia foetida. Stinking borkhausia. A wild British plant with drooping unexpanded flowers and hairy leaves. It frequents dry chalky lands in certain localities. Its common name is not undeserved for although at a distance the plant seems to have a faint odour of almonds when held in the hand for a minute the scent is most disgusting.

Calycanthus occidentalis. California Allspice. A deciduous shrub growing twelve feet tall found on shaded hillsides, and bearing from April to November small wine-colored blossoms said to have the most unpleasant smell, though the leaves when bruised give off an agreeable bitter-aromatic fragrance.

Castanea. Chestnut. Two Chinese chestnuts are most disagreeably scented. *C. henryi,* according to Mr. Wilson, has flowers of a most peculiarly unpleasant smell; *C. mollissima* is described as laden with evil-smelling white flowers. It is a tree growing sixty feet tall.

Cimicifuga racemosa. Black cohosh. Black snakeroot. Smells like carrion .

Clerodendron bungei [*C. foetidum*]. Dwarf spreading shrub three to six feet high that is not hardy north of Philadelphia. The flowers are not ill-smelling but the leaves are distinctly so.

Codonopsis ovata. A campanula-like plant with small velvet leaves and pretty blue bell-like flowers marked with orange. "The exquisite flowers smell not unlike the small cat house at the zoo." *C. viridilflora* is a climbing plant with unattractive and vile-smelling flowers. Skunk odour.

Conium maculatum. Hemlock. A poisonous plant of most abominable odour.

Crataegus pedicellata [*C. coccinea*]. White thorn. Scarlet haw. A low native tree forming a broad flat head and bearing corymbs of white flowers in May that have a most offensive odour. This is the thorn of old pasture fields, the haunt of nesting birds. *C. calpodendron* [*C. tomentosa*]. Black thorn; is a small tree with slender contorted branches that form a wide flat head. It flowers later than the white thorn but has a like fetid odour. Despite the unpleasant odour of many of the American thorns they are high in favour with the bees.

Crocus graveolens. According to Mr. Bowles this Crocus is a "little stinking beast" which he says would be recognizable anywhere ". . . by the abominable odour that is perceptible even at a distance of some yards when its small flowers are open on a sunny day." Said to smell like black beetles.

Cynoglossum virginaticum [*C. officinale*]. Houndstongue. A troublesome British weed naturalized in this country, with violet-blue flowers. The whole plant has an unpleasant odour suggestive of mice. Biennial.

Cytisus x *praecox.* A very beautiful hybrid broom with graceful bushy plant, bearing quantities of sulphur-yellow blossoms in April and May. Unfortunately the blossoms possess an unpleasant odour so that it should not be planted near the dwelling. *Cytisus purgans* also has a heavy fulsome aroma.

Datura stramonium. A heavy offensive odour, especially at night.

Escallonia illinita. Tender shrub whose flowers are said to smell like a clean pigsty, or to the nose of another gardener, of curry powder.

Fritillaria imperialis. Crown imperial. Smells of skunk.

Geranium robertianum. Herb robert. Leaves very unpleasantly odoriferous when crushed.

Helleborus foetidus. Stinking hellebore. Bear's foot. A handsome plant native of western Europe, grown in English gardens for the sake of its foliage, that remains green over the winter, and the early appearance in winter, or very early spring, of the panicles of large, round, apple-green flowers. The foliage is "many fingered" of a dark fine green and "as substantial as leather." The specific name has been given because when the leaves are bruised they give out a strong acrid odour. Ann Pratt says that honey made from this plant is reputed to be poisonous. Like so many ill-scented plants it was believed at one time to be of great medicinal value. The roots powdered and mixed with meal were said to destroy mice.

Hippocrepis comosa. Horseshoe vetch. A common annual or biennial plant that grows wild in Great Britain in limestone regions. The yellow flowers smell like cheese.

Hyoscyamus niger. Poisonous plant with an evil odour.

Ipheion uniflorum [*Triteleia uniflora*]. This pretty little South American bulbous plant, it is said, should be enjoyed while growing and not gathered, for the stalk when bruised gives forth a most unpleasant onionlike smell. Its chief value in the North is as a pot plant used for spring display. Hardy in the South.

Lamium maculatum. Creeping plant with leaves that give off a strong disagreeable odour when crushed. Much enjoyed by bees.

Lantana. Shrub verbena. A plant much used for bedding with heads of orange and scarlet small flowers that give off a strongly pungent odour on a hot day of full sun. The smell of the shrub verbena is not disagreeable to all persons but I have known those who were made actually ill by it.

Lardizabala biternata. Shrubby evergreen climber from Chile with brownish purple flowers in winter and spring, said to emit an unpleasant aroma of vinegar.

Ligustrum. Nearly all the privets have a heavy objectionable odour. *L. ovalifolium* is perhaps the worst offender. The emanation is of a sickly sweetish character and seems to be a drawing card for all sorts of insects. The privets seems to me particularly unpleasant at night and on damp days.

Lilium. Ill-scented species, *L. pyrenaicum, L. pomponium, L. sargentiae.*

Mentha arvensis. Corn mint. Strong disagreeable odour that has been compared to decaying cheese. This is one of the commonest mints and one of the few that has not an agreeable fragrance. Adventive from Europe where it grows commonly in corn fields.

Nicotiana tabacum. James Stuart, King of England, wrote a book against the use of tobacco in which he characterizes it as "a custom loathsome to the eye, hateful to the nose, harmful to the brain, dangerous to the lungs, and in the black stinking fume thereof nearest resembling the horrible Stygian smoke of the pit that is bottomless."

Nuphar advenna. Spatterdock. Brandy bottle. Ill-scented aquatic.

Onion. The flowers of *Allium ursinum* are known as stink lilies.

Ononis arvensis [*O. hircina*]. Rather a pretty little plant with rose or white flowers that have a curious flat stale odour. *O. cristata* [*O. cenisia*] is said also to have an offensive odour.

Orchis mascula. Early purple orchid. Said to suggest the odour of cats when faded but smells of vanilla while fresh.

Papaver somniferum. Opium poppy. Nearly all poppies possess a rank heavy odour which detracts from the beauty of their lovely flowers.

Passiflora foetida. Running pop. Wild water lemon. A species of this usually sweet-scented family, the leaves of which when bruised are exceedingly unpleasant to the nose. West Indies.

Peltaria alliacea. Onion odour.

Phallus impudicus. Common stink horn. A fungus growth with the horrid odour of carrion.

Phuopsos stylosa [*Crucianella stylosa*]. Crosswort. Smells like skunk.

Podophyllum peltatum. The odour of the little may apple is distinctly unpleasant to some, pleasant to others.

Polemonium viscosum [*P. confertum*]. A western wildflower. Is said to have the aroma of stale beer.

Pontederia cordata. Pickerel weed. This beautiful but troublesome aquatic has an unpleasant odour.

Primula. It is difficult to think of any of these lovely and usually sweet scented flowers as belonging to this chapter, but *Primula parryi* is said to have a rather offensive odour, and Mr. Farrer says, "The one disadvantage of *P. hirsuta* [*P. latifolia*] is that it does stink. It stinks very markedly with a rancid hircine odour."

Putoria calabrica. Cliffs of Spain and Greece. Shining leaves and wax-pink flowers that emit an unpleasant odour.

Ribes americanum. American black currant. The leaves have a very heavy unpleasant odour. *Ribes nigrum,* European black currant, possesses a particularly foul odour suggestive of cats. *Ribes glandulosum* [*R. prostratum*] has the self explanatory common name of stink currant.

Rhus trilobata. An ill-scented species of sumac ranging from Illinois westward. Its common name is skunk bush. *Toxicodendron vernix* [*Rhus vernix*], the poisonous sumac, grows often to the height of a tree but is usually seen in a more shrubby form. Its greenish grey fruit emits a curious sulphurous odour. "This," says Harriet Keeler, "is the most poisonous woody plant of our flora. Its juices and the effluvium exhaled by it under a hot sun are extremely poisonous to some persons. There are those who are absolutely immune, others so sensitive that they cannot pass the bush with impunity. . . . The poison shows itself in painful and long continued swellings upon the surface of the body, usually the face and hands."

Rosa. Those who press the pretty golden blossoms of *Rosa foetida* [*R. lutea*] to their noses in the expectation of enjoying fragrance are disappointed. The curious odour of this rose has been compared to raspberries and bugs.

Salvia sclarea. Clary. The soft large leaves of this old-fashioned plant, once deemed a sovereign cure for coughs and colds, have an extremely rank and disagreeable odour to my nose, but the oil distilled from them has a strong grapy aroma that is distinctly pleasant and stimulating.

Schizanthus. According to Miss Jekyll the charming flowers of this pretty and popular annual are "redolent of a dirty henhouse."

Scrophularia nodosa. Stinking Christopher. A dull weed with flowers and leaves that have a sickening odour not unlike that of elder.

S. jacobaea. The common ragwort or stinking willie. The tarnished yellow flowers of this plant are familiar to most people in the country. The whole plant including the root has a most unpleasant odour. Naturalized in this country from Europe.

WAKE-ROBIN
(*Trillium*)

Serissa foetida. A swamp plant common throughout the East under the name of *Lycium japonicum.* "The odour of this Japanese boxthorn," comments Eden Phillpotts, "is most afflicting."

Skimmia laureola. Low evergreen shrub two to three feet tall, the leaves of which when crushed emit a heavy unpleasant odour as do the young shoots and flowers.

Symplocarpus foetidus. Skunk cabbage. The beautiful spring greenery of this plant often lures the uninitiated to disastrous contact with it.

Trillium erectum. A handsome native species remarkable for its nasty smelling reddish flowers.

Viola tricolor. The pansy has a warm sweet scent but the plant when broken or bruised gives off a curiously unpleasant odour, much like that of a peach kernel, due to the presence of hydrocyanic acid. This same odour is often perceptible on a warm day as one stands above a bed of pansies when the plants have grown old and rank. The juice of the pansy in old times was believed to have a wondrous power of increasing the affections, or as Shakespeare wrote,

Will make a man or woman madly dote
Upon the next live creature that it sees.

PART II

Additional Notes

A Compilation of Fragrant Plants Not Elsewhere Mentioned.

The sweetest air is wild flower air.

—RICHARD JEFFRIES

CHAPTER XIX

Wild Scents – Native and Naturalized

For it is a great pleasure to identify a friendly odour in the fields.

"GREAT POSSESSIONS."
— DAVID GRAYSON

THE CHARGE HAS SOMETIMES been made that our wild flowers on the whole are less fragrant than those of Great Britain, but I am inclined to believe that an examination of the facts does not bear out this contention. True, none of our violets can compare with the wild English violet for scent, nor have we the wood hyacinth filling the hollows of the copse with misty blue colour and a rich perfume; nor can we boast the hedges made of perfumed May; nor the wastes of golden gorse fuming into the ether their honey scent; nor are our meadows lined with pale balmy breathed primroses and cowslips. But we can, nevertheless, gather a more than passably fragrant bouquet from field or wood at any time of the growing year, though as John Burroughs has pointed out, our sweetest wild flowers are shy and must be searched for. Few wildlings have a more delightful bittersweetness than the trailing arbutus, and numerous others among our woodland blossoms offer much to the seeking nose. The *Chimaphila* and *Pyrola* species are unexcelled in sweetness, as are many of our orchids, and our snowy pondlily is one of the most beautifully fragrant flowers in the world, though its British prototype is scentless.

At the time of the blossoming of the elder, the honey locust, the blackberry, the wild grape, the air of the countryside is burdened with a rare sweetness. At certain seasons of the year too the various wild azaleas richly perfume whole tracts of country, and along the Atlantic coast in the late summer, the blossoming of the *Clethra*, the sweet pepper bush, not only bathes the land in intoxicating sweetness but sends a greeting far out to sea so that passengers on incoming ships are aware of it. When the *Clethra* blooms in my garden I can shut my eyes and smell the sea.

Or what more delicious airs could be breathed than those wafted from our far-flung orchards in May, or from our great forests of fir and pine, or the wide fields of clover, red and white, or from the hillsides of wild lupin or phlox? And what, I ask you, is more delicious than the tangle of wild roses and sweet fern in a New England lane?

And what of the shrewd scent of the bayberry that covers great sandy wastes along the coast, or of the many plants with aromatic or pungent-scented leaves, such as the mints, the bergamots, the *Monardella*, the *Artemisia* species, and the like, in which our wide country is especially rich? And out in the West there are hills misty with the fragrant blossoms of the wild lilac, the vast reaches covered with pungent sage brush, the meadows filled with *Erythronium*. But let us take them one by one and give to each its mete of appreciation.

The following list does not pretend to be exhaustive and when American wildflowers have been mentioned in any other part of the book it has not been thought necessary to include them in this list.

Abies balsamea. Balsam fir. Balm of Gilead. Thoreau says that the young shoots of the balsam fir when plucked and kept in the pocket for a few days emit the fragrance of strawberries, "only it is somewhat more aromatic and spicy." The balsam fir grows from Labrador to West Virginia and West to Iowa. Richard Jefferies says the odour of firs is variable, sometimes it fills the air, sometimes it is absent altogether and doubtless depends upon certain conditions of the atmosphere. A very small pinch of a fresh shoot is pleasant to the taste; these shoots eaten constantly were once believed to cure "chest disease." It is a common practice to fill pillows and cushions with the fragrant leaves of the balsam fir.

Abronia fragrans. White abronia of the Rocky Mountains. The large flowers grow in dense clusters and open at sunset when they give out a rich fragrance of vanilla. *A. salsa,* called sand puffs, is a delicately fashioned and softly tinted little plant found in sandy wastes in Utah. The foliage is greyish, the stems semiprostrate and the heads of pink flowers deliciously fragrant. It blooms in the late summer and autumn. *A. villosa,* the pink sand verbena, is a quite delightfully pretty little plant of sandy localities in Arizona, California and Utah. It has a somewhat careless habit, the stem trailing over the ground; the leaves are blue-green and the flowers, a good deal like garden verbenas, are a bright lilac-pink colour and very fragrant. *A. maritima,* a stout, sticky and rather coarse plant is found from Santa Barbara to San Diego. It has sweet scented magenta flowers. *A. umbellata* is another plant of the California seashore and as far north as British Columbia. *A. latifolia.* The yellow abronia is a plant of the sand dunes of the western coast from California to British Columbia. The bright clusters of yellow flowers appear in spring upon thick trailing grey stems and fill the air with the delicate fragrance of heliotrope.

Acanthomintha ilicifolia. Thorny mint. A tender annual with a good deal the appearance of ground ivy, growing about six inches high and bearing spikes of rosy-purple flowers. The whole plant is odorous. California.

Acer saccharum. Sugar maple. Rock maple. The blossoms of the sugar maple provide one of the earliest wild scents of the year. A few twigs brought into a warm room fill it with a keen springlike fragrance. It is only at a certain moment of their development that the small crimson blossoms are gifted with fragrance, as they age they give off a rather stale odour. Bees are grateful for the food offered them at such an early date by this wholesome and beautiful tree.

Achillea millefolium. Common yarrow. Milfoil. A common wild plant with white flowers in close heads and ferny foliage that has a strong pungent odour. There are forms with pink or rose-coloured flowers that are often cultivated in gardens.

Achlys triphylla. Vanilla-leaf. Sweet-after-death. An odd plant found in the woods of the Coast Ranges with one large leaf divided into three leaflets and a stalk one to two feet tall finished at the end with a long feathery spike of small white scentless flowers. The leaf is very fragrant when dried, hence the common names. Summer.

Acorus calamus. Sweet flag. A tall rushlike grass with decorative leaves having a curious scent, found growing on the margins of streams or ponds. It is widely distributed in Europe and Asia as well as in this country. "The root has been used in India from very early times and was known to the Greeks centuries before the Christian era. It has a pleasing odour due to an essential oil which is distilled from it. When powdered it was a common ingredient of the dry perfumes formerly used." In warm countries it develops greater fragrance than in this country. The whole plant has an aromatic and slightly acid taste. *A. gramineus,* an Asiatic species, grows only a foot tall.

Adenostoma sparsifolium. Ribbonwood. Redshanks. An evergreen shrub or small tree characteristic of the low mountains of the southwestern U.S.A. Its height is from six to twelve feet and it has the foliage and general habit of the heaths, with clusters of fragrant white flowers. It is recommended for southern gardens in dry localities because of its drought-resisting capabilities. In colder climates it will stand many degrees of frost.

Adoxa moschatellina. Muskroot. Moschatel. Townhall clock. A small tuberous-rooted perennial plant found in mossy woods and among damp rocks in subalpine and Arctic regions of North America. The flowers are greenish and carried in a loose cluster just above the foliage and emit a musky scent, especially towards evening when the dew falls. Sometimes grown in rock gardens.

Aesculus californica. California buckeye. A tree growing forty feet high and bearing in summer dense cylindrical clusters of fragrant white or pinkish flowers.

Agastache cana [*Cedronella cana*] and *Agastache mexicana* [*Cedronella mexicana*] are compact free-growing border perennials, sub-shrubby in habit and with aromatic leaves. *Agastache canna* is found in Northern Mexico and blooms from June to October, the leaves are small and minutely hairy and the flowers are reddish pink. It is hardy in New York. *Agastache mexicana* is rarer in cultivation, the flowers are bright pink. The leaves of these plants must be rubbed to bring out their agreeable sweetness.

Agastache foeniculum [*A. anethiodora*]. Anise hyssop. A tall plant of our west country with dark hairy leaves and feathery heads of pale violet flowers. The plant has a strong aromatic smell like anise. It is important as a bee plant and the honey made from it has a most agreeable taste.

Agrimonia eupatoria. Agrimony. A common wayside plant in the Eastern United States of America, of no special beauty but possessing certain scented attractions. Both the roots and the spike of yellow flowers are endowed with a pleasing fragrance not unlike that of ripe apricots. Our grandmothers valued the agrimony for many reasons: the root was considered a mild astringent tonic and valuable when made into a tea, in bowel complaints and fevers. The leaves were believed helpful in jaundice, scurvy and other complaints. A common name is stickwort because of its green bristly burs that adhere to clothing that comes in contact with it.

Ailanthus altissima [*A. glandulosa*]. Tree of heaven. Chinese sumac. Paradise tree. A Chinese tree that was brought to this country and rather widely planted about a hundred and fifty years ago. The leaves have a disagreeable odour when crushed and at the season when the greenish flowers are at their height the air is pervaded by what to many is a most sickening stench.

Amorpha fruticosa. Polecat tree. Bastard indigo. The polecat tree is an inhabitant of damp places in Florida and Texas. The reason for its name is self-explanatory – the leaves have the unpleasant odour of the "wood kitty." They appear in late winter and are soon followed by dense racemes of tiny blackish purple flowers whose rich and unusual colour is emphasized by yellow anthers. *A. californica* grows along mountain streams in Southern California. The leaves are sweet scented but rather sickening.

Androsace chamaejasme. This is the sweet-scented *Androsace* of the Selkirks and the Rocky Mountains. It is a most lovely member of this important rock garden family and its fragrance lends it added value. The small blossoms, carried in characteristic umbrella-like clusters, are cream-white with a yellow eye.

Androstephium caeruleum. A liliacaeus American herb growing from a corm to a height of eight inches. Flowers violet or lilac and sweet scented. It is a native of the Central West and is found as far south as Texas. Sometimes planted in wild gardens.

Pulsatilla hirsutissima [*Anemone patens* 'Nuttalliana']. Western pasque flower. Anemone is commonly a scentless race but the beautiful purple flowers of this species possess a mild and pleasing aroma.

Anemopsis californica. Yerba mansa. Apache beads. An erect aquatic plant bearing flowers that have somewhat the appearance of an anemone. The root has a pungent fragrance and pieces of it in the form of cylindrical beads, are strung into necklaces by the Indians of the Southwest and are used medicinally, in the form of an infusion, for malaria and other maladies. The plants are found in swampy places but the roots are gathered in the dry season in Mexico and sold in the local drug market.

Angelica atropurpurea. Alexanders. Masterwort. A stout plant with a dark purple stem found from Newfoundland to Delaware and westward. The root has a strong odour and a pleasant aromatic taste.

Anthemis nobilis. Common chamomile. A low growing plant of creeping or half trailing habit with finely dissected leaves and rather shabby little "daisies," borne on erect stems in the late summer. Chamomile is one of the oldest known remedies, popular in domestic medical practice from time immemorial. As a valued remedy it was brought from the Old World to the New and it is still popular in rural neighbourhoods, especially an infusion of it which is used to quiet fretful babies. The whole plant has a strong tonic odour but is extraordinarily bitter to the taste. In Elizabethan times the chamomile that we now regard as a weed was commonly planted at the edges of flower borders and paths so that being trodden upon the scent was set free to regale and invigorate the passerby.

The Camomile shall teach thee patience
That rises best when trodden upon.

Apocynum androsaemifolium. Common dogbane. A pretty little wayside plant found in many parts of the country, with small pinkish flowers very sweet scented. The roots have some medicinal value.

Aquilegia canadensis. The seeds are used by the young bachelors of the Omaha and Ponca Indians as a perfume, which is obtained by crushing them, usually by chewing them to a paste. This is spread among their garments, the fragrant quality lasting for a long time and being especially perceptible when dampened by dew or rain. The Pawnee Indians use these seeds also as a love charm, crushing them and rubbing them in the palms, then "the suitor contrives to shake hands with the desired one, whose fancy it is expected will then be captivated."

Aralia. Herbs, shrubs or trees with alternate leaves and small whitish flowers in clusters forming terminal panicles followed by berrylike fruits. Some of the smaller native kinds are made use of in gardens. *A. californica* is a tall pungent plant known as elk clover. It is found along streamsides of the Coast Ranges and fills the air with a peculiar odour. *A. nudicaulis,* the wild sarsaparilla, is found in moist woods from Newfoundland to Georgia and west to Colorado. It is a low herb, the long horizontal aromatic roots of which are used as a substitute for official sarsaparilla. *A. spinosa,* devil's walking stick, Hercules' club, is a spiny forbidding shrub growing finally to a height of thirty feet. The panicles of white flowers are inodorous but the leaves and bark possess a pleasing though peculiar odour. *A. hispida,* Bristly sarsaparilla, is a bristly herb or subshrub that is used medicinally. The whole plant has a disagreeable odour.

Arbutus menziesii. Madrone. A beautiful evergreen tree with polished leaves found from British Columbia to California, growing fifty feet tall, or more. In May and June it bears great panicles of waxen white bells that give off a pleasing fragrance of honey and are followed by scarlet berries.

Arctostaphylos manzanita. Manzanita. Parry manzanita. The flowers of this and other species are strongly fragrant. The manzanita is a crooked, branched shrub growing to a height of twelve feet and even taller, with white flowers often tinged with pink, carried in drooping panicles, appearing sometimes as early as Christmas. Lester Rowntree writes me that there is a species of *Arctostaphylos* for every locality in California save desert districts. Some of these are *A. bicolor, A. diversifolia, A. glauca, A. nummularia, A. pungens,* and *A. tomentosa.* The alpine cranberry, *Vaccinium vitus-idaea,* is found in Arctic

America and south to the summits of Maine and New Hampshire. My correspondent, Edward P. St. John of New Hampshire, wrote me early in August, "The alpine cranberry is out of bloom now but a month ago it was the loveliest plant of the Alpine Garden, and its fragrance, which is sweet and spicy, was as entrancing as the rose blush of its petals. I think that nothing on these mountain tops appeals to me more strongly."

Arenaria groenlandica (*Alsine groenlandica*). Greenland sandwort. A low mat-making plant, haunting high mountains from Greenland and Labrador to North Carolina. The decumbent or erect stems bear narrow leaves and three to five white flowers. The leaves have a pungent scent.

Artemisia. There are many of these fragrant leaved plants found in America, especially in the far West. The sage brush, *Seriphidium tridentatum* [*Artemisia tridentata*], so common a feature of the arid Western plains, is one of the most agreeably scented of the whole race. *A. californica,* California sage brush, is also very sweet and aromatic and *A. frigida* has a most agreeable rough scent. Other aromatic American species are *A. annua,* sweet wormwood, *A. arbuscula,* and the common mugwort, *A. vulgaris,* which has been naturalized from Europe.[1]

Asarum. Wild ginger. Dwarf creeping plants with large soft kidney-shaped leaves and curious little brown blossoms borne close to the earth. The leaves and the thick stolons are strongly aromatic, smelling, according to M. Correvon, of patchouli. *A. canadensis* is a common native variety. *A. caudatum* is the wild ginger of the Coast Ranges of Central and Northern California.

Asclepias. Milkweed. Silkweed. Swallow-wort. A genus of perennial plants blossoming in summer and autumn, most of which are native in North and South America and in Africa. Many are sweet scented and the blossoms are usually rather showy. A pretty little native is *A. quadrifolia,* found on dry wooded hillsides in the Eastern States, bearing its very fragrant pink flowers in June. *A. speciosa* is a handsome plant of canyon bottoms and streamsides in the West, growing four feet tall and bearing clusters of purplish flowers with woolly pedicels that give off a penetrating, though not always agreeable odour. *A. syriaca* (*A. cornuti*). The purplish flowers of the silkweed are extremely fragrant. This tall species is found from New Brunswick to North Carolina and Kansas in rich ground. *A. vestita,* the desert milkweed, grows eighteen inches tall and is woolly all over. The pinky-purple flowers are very sweet smelling.

Asclepiodora decumbens. Spider milkweed. A striking plant of the Southwest widely distributed on dry hillsides, with roughish dull green leaves and stiff rosette-like clusters of large greenish yellow flowers with incurved tips, a green stigma and brown anthers. Slightly sweet scented.

Asimina. Paw paw. Genus of shrubs or small trees found in open pinelands in the Southern States, usually in rich, moist soil. The leaves and bark when bruised give off a strong peculiar odour. The flowers are showy and are followed by large edible fruits in the autumn. *A. triloba* has proved hardy in Massachusetts.

Bejaria racemosa. Tar-flower. A slender evergreen shrub native in Southern Georgia and Florida,

[1] Artemisia dracunculoides, *called fuzzy weed, is used by the Winnebago Indians as a love charm. The root is chewed and put among the clothing both of wooers and of hunters.*

found in low places in sandy soil. The purple flowers are borne in racemes in early summer and are very fragrant.

Betula lenta. Sweet, cherry, or black birch. A graceful roundtopped tree with drooping branches that is very conspicuous in spring when hung all over with its showy staminate catkins. The bark is dark red and, when young, very aromatic and of a pleasant biting taste. The bark of the branches and the leaves is still popular in domestic medical practice and yields an oil similar to oil of wintergreen and useful for the same purposes. Birch wine was formerly popular in rural neighbourhoods.

Bigelowia graveolens. A low shrub densely tomentose when young, found in alkaline soils in Dakota and thereabouts. The leaves are malodorous, especially when drying.

Brickellia californica. Found along gravelly stream beds in Central and Southern California. The whole plant is fragrant and the flowers especially so at night.

Bumelia angustifolia. Saffron plum. This is a thorny shrub of the Florida Keys blooming in winter, with many tiny flowers that scent the air about for a great distance, followed by edible fruit.

Calandrinia cilata [*C. caulescens*]. Wild portulaca. Red maids. A pretty little succulent plant of spreading habit, bearing many satiny flowers of a deep magenta colour which open only in bright sunshine. They have a delicate somewhat musky perfume. From Lower California to Vancouver Island.

Calliandra eriophylla. Fairy duster. Mock mesquite. A shrub native of Western Texas and Mexico growing twelve inches high. It has pale grey spreading branches and finely cut foliage and the clusters of fragrant pink flowers have very long stamens.

Canella winterana [*C. alba*]. Wild cinnamon. A tree belonging to Southern Florida and the West Indies growing forty-five feet high. It is an evergreen with greyish bark and curious violet coloured flowers growing at the ends of the branches in clusters. The whole tree is very aromatic, especially the flowers, which, though they seldom open fully, perfume wide areas about the tree and when dried and softened again in water have the odour of musk. "Pigeons feed upon the berries and so strong is their peculiar aromatic flavour that it is said to communicate itself to the flesh of the birds." The bark is stripped from the trees and an oil somewhat similar to that of cinnamon is expressed from it.

Carya ovata. Shagbark hickory. The leaves of this native tree are strongly aromatic when crushed.

Cassia armata. Desert senna. A beautiful plant of the desert, growing in large clumps, with pale green leaves and long clusters of sweet scented orange-yellow flowers.

Catalpa bignonioides. Indian bean. Indian cigar. Smoking bean. A handsome tree native in the Southern States, bearing immense terminal panicles of trumpet-like white flowers purple on the exterior. The leaves are strongly scented. *C. speciosa* is the Western catalpa. The huge inflorescence, white spotted brown, is very fragrant. The individual flowers that make up the large panicles are shaped like foxgloves and have a fragrance something like that of sweet peas.

Ceanothus. Wild lilac. North American shrubs, particularly of the Pacific Coast. They are extremely ornamental, bearing for the most part in great profusion, dense panicles of small flowers, white or pale blue, some of which are very sweetly scented. The Pacific Coast species are not hardy in the Northeastern States but are much grown abroad. *C. arboreus* is a shrub or tree growing to twenty feet, with finely toothed leaves, tomentose beneath, and pale blue fragrant flowers. It is found on Santa Barbara Island. In the mountains grows the beautiful *C. integerrimus*, the deer brush, with plumelike sprays of scented white (sometimes pale blue or pink) flowers that "covers whole mountainsides with drifted snow in summer." One of the most abundant species is *C. cuneatus*, buck brush, which for miles covers dry hot ridges and exposed valleys, where it forms extensive impenetrable thickets. The leaves and twigs are spice scented. *C. thyrsiflorus*, blue blossom, is a small shrub or tree that bears shining evergreen leaves and large clusters of smoke-blue fragrant blossoms. It is abundant in the Redwood district. *C. velutinus*, tobacco brush, is found on high mountain slopes of Central and Northern California. Both flowers and leaves are scented, the latter of cinnamon. (For *C. americanus*, see page 71.)

Cephalanthera austinae. Phantom orchid. A strange flower of dense mountain forests in California. In the dim light the "flowers shimmer like pallid ghosts among the dark trees. They are translucent white throughout, stem and all, and the leaves have shrunk to white sheaths, an inch or two long." These ghost flowers are fragrant.

Cerastium arvense. Field chickweed. A pretty little scrambling plant found in many parts of the United States and cultivated in gardens. The leaves are slightly hairy and the abundant white blossoms, borne in spring, smell pleasantly of honey.

Ceratifolia ericoides. Florida rosemary. "On the wide stretches of Florida's dryest pine barrens this 'Rosemary' forms densely branched evergreen shrubs several feet in height which under a hot sun give out an aromatic fragrance. The leaves are narrow and the flowers minute and of a reddish color."

Chamaebatia foliolosa. Mountain misery. Bear mat. "In open places in the Sierra forests," says Margaret Armstrong, "the ground is often carpeted for acres with the feathery foliage of this charming shrub, sprinkled all over with pretty white flowers." The whole plant is covered with a strong smelling resinous substance which comes off on the clothes in a most disagreeable manner, the odour, which is something like Pond's Extract, lasting for a long time.

Chamaebatiaria millefolium [*Spiraea millefolium*]. A hardy and distinct shrubby *Spiraea*, native in California, a neat and attractive shrub that would repay use in our northern gardens, for it is said to be quite hardy. The flowers are white and the leaves are pleasantly fragrant. *S. salicifolia*, the bridewort, is a common shrub of the summer found blossoming in many parts of the country along roadsides or at the edges of meadows. It bears in great profusion bluntly pyramidal spikes of pinkish flowers with prominent carmine stamens. Close at hand, or where the plant grows as it often does in thousands, the odour of the flowers is insipid and even frankly unpleasant. But the scent from the single bush, that has sprung up uninvited beside the back door of my home, when it creeps into the rooms on the gentle night breeze, is mild and pleasant.

Chamaecyparis thyoides. White cedar. The wood of this Coastal Plain cedar is slightly fragrant.

Chenopodium ambrosioides. American wormseed. Mexican tea. Strong smelling weedy plant naturalized in the United States from Tropical America, thought to have medicinal properties. *C. botrys* (*Ambrosia mexicana*). Feather geranium. Jerusalem oak. Weedy plant with strongly odoriferous leaves and small white florets that are fragrant. The foliage smells like newmown hay and was once popular for use in bouquets. Found on uncared for lots and waste places.

Chilopsis linearis. Desert willow. A shrub of the American Desert with tall canelike stems bearing large fragrant bignonia-like blossoms, lilac-pink stained with yellow.

Chimaphila umbellata. Pipsissewa. Western prince's pine. A low plant of dry woods often among or near pines, found from Nova Scotia to British Columbia, south to Georgia and the Rocky Mountains, flowering in summer. The stems are extensively creeping and the numerous leaves evergreen. The flowers carried in a few-flowered umbel are waxen and vary from cream to pink in different localities, they are deliciously fragrant. *C. maculata* is very like it save that the leaves are conspicuously marked with white. The pipsissewas are almost the latest of the fragile woodland flowers to bloom. They often carpet wide woodland areas with their shining evergreen foliage. *C. menziesii,* little prince's pine, is a species of the Northwest and California, having much the same characteristics and sharing the delicious lily-of-the-valley fragrance.

Chrysothamnus nauseosus. An ill-smelling plant of the Asteraceae family, found on the borders of arid lands in California and northward to British Columbia.

Cleome platycarpa. Yellow cleome. A curious spring flowering plant bearing clusters of warm yellow flowers. The flowers are slightly sweet scented but the leaves emit an unpleasant odour. This plant is said to be conspicuous on the dreary mesas around Reno, Nevada.

Cleomella angustifolia. The yellow blossoms of the *Cleomella* are very fragrant. It is found from Nebraska to Utah and south to Texas, a plant of variable height growing much like sweet clover or mustard but forming a bushier top. It is an annual and no stock will eat it, but it is a good bee plant.

Cliftonia monophylla. Buckwheat tree. Titi. Ironwood. An evergreen shrub or small tree of ashen colour inhabiting damp peaty woods, or even swamps, from Florida to North Carolina and westward. The sweet scented white flowers are borne in nodding racemes and the fruit resembles buckwheat.

Calamintha coccinea [*Clinopodium coccineum*]. Southern calamint. A low shrub with aromatic foliage found in Western Florida, growing in sandy soil. The flowers are red and appear in August. *C. georgianum* [*C. caroliniana*] grows as far north as North Carolina. It is a low shrub with leafy branches and fragrant white or purple flowers.

Clitoria mariana. Butterfly pea. In dry soil and in many a mountain wood or on steep hillsides this fragile plant disputes its right of place among coarse-growing rhododendrons, wild mints and coreopsis. Its range is from Florida to New Jersey and westward. The lavender flowers are very charming, if examined, and possess a faint but very sweet fragrance.

Cneoridium dumosum. A stiff, twiggy, evergreen shrub of low stature, found on hills in Southern California. It bears in great abundance very fragrant flowers, pinkish on the outside and white within.

Cnicus pumilum (*Carduus odoratus*). Pasture or bull

thistle. Biennial plant of dry fields in the Northeast and as far south as Delaware. The "thistles" are purple, rarely white, and fragrant.

Collinsonia canadensis. Stoneroot. Richweed. Horse balm. This strongly scented plant, named for Peter Collinson, an early British botanist, is found from Quebec to Florida and westward in rich moist woods. The yellow flowers are borne in a slender panicle and are lemon-scented.

Comptonia peregrina var. *asplenifolia* [*Comptonia asplenifolia*]. Sweet fern. Sweet gale. This is a familiar plant along dusty roadsides where it is an ever welcome companion on our walks. The whole plant when bruised gives off a strong sweet resinous and spicy smell, one of the best scents of our countryside, especially delightful mingled with wild roses. An early American *Materia Medica* informs us that "a strong tea distilled from it and freely partaken of, and the leaves put in a cushion to sit on, and between sheets to lie on, has cured the St. Vitus dance."

Convolvulus arvensis. Field bindweed. A troublesome weed in gardens but a lovely decoration of fields and roadsides. The charming pink morning glories give off the scent of heliotrope. Once established, this plant is difficult to eradicate for the roots go very deep. For this reason it has earned the name of devil's guts.

Cornus nuttallii. The mountain dogwood is a handsome tree, handsomer even, some think, than the eastern species, *C. florida,* and it has the advantage, Margaret McKenny tells me, of a most agreeable honeylike fragrance. *C. amomum.* Kinnikinnick. Redstemmed dogwood. The inner bark is fragrant and is used by the Indians for smoking.

Cotula coronopifolia. Brass buttons. Butter heads. A lowly little weed naturalized from South Africa and now quite common along the coast of California. Its round yellow rayless flowers have given rise to its common names. The leaves when crushed give off a pleasant odour of lemon verbena and camphor.

Cowania mexican var. *stansburiana* [*C. stansburiana*]. Cliff rose. A wild shrub of the Southwest with small evergreen leaves and large sweet scented pale yellow flowers borne in long wands of bloom. It is one of the shrubs found in the Grand Canyon of the Colorado. The fragrance given off by the flowers is delicious, much like that of orange blossoms. Also found on mesa and canyon sides of Southeastern California.

Crinum americanum. Florida swamp lily. Southern swamp crinum. A beautiful member of the amaryllis family found in Florida and westward through the Southern States. It is usually found growing at the verge of a swamp, sending its white very fragrant "lilies" aloft on stems two feet high amidst narrow pointed foliage.

Cucurbita foetidissima. Calabazilla. Missouri gourd. Buffalo gourd. Foetid wild pumpkin. A plant with ill scented leaves found in sandy flats in Central and Southern California. The leaves are valued medicinally by the Indians.

C. origanoides [*Cunila mariana*]. Maryland ditany. Stone mint. An inconspicuous but strongly scented member of the mint family. It is a familiar feature of dry hills and roadsides in the Eastern States and west to Arkansas. Its small purple blossoms gleam faintly in the summer luxuriance but the leaves when bruised give out a warm greeting.

Cuphea lanceolata. A Mexican annual usually grown as a greenhouse subject. Purplish flowers.

The whole plant is sticky and possesses a strong fragrance.

Cupressus. A genus of Western American evergreen trees, very ornamental in growth and with foliage that possesses a peculiar balsamic sweetness.

Dalea [*Petelostemum*]. The prairie clovers are at home on dry barrens. The clustered stems with many finely cut leaves, bear pink, lavender or white cloverlike heads, which have a faint agreeable fragrance. Southern States and westward.

Dalibarda repens. Robin-run-away. False violet. A lovely little inhabitant of our northern woods, a diminutive member of the rose family, though to the casual observer looking more like a violet. The pure white flowers are delicately fragrant.

Datura wrightii [*D. meteloides*]. Tolguacha. A conspicuous plant found in sandy valleys in Central and Southern California with large spectacular funnel-shaped white flowers tinged with lilac on the exterior and heavily fragrant, "drooping like wet tissue paper in the heat of the afternoon." It is used as a narcotic by the Indians. *Brugmansia suaveolens* [*Datura suaveolens*], Floriponda or Angel's Trumpet, has large creamy pendulous flowers, fragrant at night.

Decumaria barbara. Climbing hydrangea. Wood vamp. A climbing plant of the Southern States found at the edges of swamps, clambering up the trees and rocky cliffs, clinging by aerial rootlets and bearing in June sweet scented white flowers in loose panicles. It is a scarce plant and very lovely.

Dendromecon rigida ssp. *harfordii.* Bush poppy. A handsome shrub growing sometimes to a height of ten feet, with grey leaves and a wealth of glowing poppylike flowers that bring light to the chaparral even on cloudy days. The flowers have a pleasant fresh smell like cucumbers and the plant exudes a bitter juice that has been thought good for warts.

Dicentra chrysantha. Golden eardrops. An attractive plant of the bleedingheart family with large divided leaves and a stout stem bearing a few pretty yellow flowers of characteristic shape. The plant has a strong narcotic odour. It is found in sunny dry places in the Coast Ranges. Both the squirrel corn, *D. canadensis,* and the dutchman's breeches, *D. cucullaria,* of our eastern woods are surprisingly sweet scented as are other members of this engaging race.

Dodecatheon. Shooting star. Mad violet. American cowslip. Decorative and distinctive plants belonging to the primrose family, with tufts of narrow leaves and stems five to eighteen inches tall, carrying a cluster of from five to fifteen nodding cyclamen-like flowers that have a curious but pleasing scent. *D. meadia* is our eastern species. In the West grow *D. jeffreyi, D. clevelandi,* with a scent somewhat like clove pinks, *D. pulchellum* and *D. radicatum* are somewhat fragrant. *D. hendersonii,* also a western species, is said to have blossoms with an odour strongly suggestive of a tannery.

Echinocereus pectinatus (*Cereus pectinatus*). A species of cactus native in Mexico in hot dry regions bearing in great profusion large pink flowers that are strongly fragrant.

Ellisia chrysanthemifolia. A plant found in shaded Coastal regions in Central and Southern California with strongly odorous foliage, not always thought agreeable.

Encelia californica. A shrubby plant abundant in Southern California. The large flowers are decorative, yellow with brown centers, but the leaves have a strong and not wholly agreeable odour.

Epigaea repens. Trailing arbutus. One of the earliest and perhaps the most beloved of our wild flowers. Often it is hawked about the city streets before the snow smell is out of the air and causes one to catch one's breath at the memories it evokes of wide still spaces under the sky, of winding paths soft underfoot with the long accumulation of pine needles, perhaps of the old home long left and of the dear ones in it. It is called in New England the mayflower and is said to have been so christened by the Pilgrims, who saw in the intrepid resurrection of the delicate leaves above last year's brown and withered foliage, an analogy of their own triumph over grim and bitter experience. In the fragrance of the small exquisite flowers is noticeable a hint of bitter almond. This is one of the plants that should be protected against extermination. Robert Lemmon is successfully raising it from seed and propagating it on a large scale. Plants thus raised are far more likely to succeed than those torn ruthlessly from their natural environment.

Eriodictyon californicum. Consumptive's weed. Yerba santa. A branching shrub of the dry mountain slopes of Central and Southern California, with inconspicuous white and lilac flowers that are slightly fragrant. The leaves of the plant are strongly aromatic when crushed and were used medicinally by the Indians – hence the name holy herb. *E. trichocalyx* belongs to the Chaparral Belt of Southern California. Both these herbs are used as a substitute for tobacco and hops.

Eriogonum fasciculatum. Sulphur flower. California buckwheat. An attractive little plant of the Southwest. From a tuft of grey-green leaves arises a downy reddish stem about a foot tall that separates into two or three branches, each carrying a close cluster of small, sweet scented, sulphur-yellow flowers. Found in sandy soil, blossoming in summer. *E. compositum.* A big plant with stout stems, one or two feet tall, slightly downy thickish leaves and pale yellow flowers in feathery clusters that smell of honey. Bare mountainsides in the Northwest. Summer. These are important honey plants.

Erodium circutarium. Red-stemmed filaree. Pin clover. A valuable native forage plant of the far West. Its seed vessels have the characteristic stork's bill shape. The smell of the foliage is sweet and agreeable and children chew the stems for the sake of their pleasant taste. *E. moschatum,* white-stemmed filaree, musk clover, is a coarser plant whose foliage has a musky scent, especially when wilted. It also is a valuable forage plant.

Erysimum asperum. Western wall flower. Delightful plant with glowing orange-coloured flowers forming a showy cluster. They are very fragrant. Hillsides and sandy wastes in California. *E. capitatum,* coast wall flower, is also of California and has flowers fragrant, but less so than those of the western wall flower.

Erythronium. Most of the western trout lilies have a pleasant light fragrance. Mr. Purdy writes me that *E. helenae* [*E. californicum* var. *bicolor*] has a quite pronounced perfume that is readily noticeable among other species. A lovely fragrance is said to be wafted from meadows where *E. grandiflorum* or *E. parviflorum* grow in quantities. Our Eastern species is not scented.

Fendlera rupicola. "Among the many beautiful plants to be found in the Grand Canyon," writes Margaret Armstrong, "one of the most conspicuous is the fendlera. It is a tall handsome shrub growing along the upper part of Bright Angel Trail, and in May is covered with charming white blossoms." The scent of these flowers is unpleasant though they are lovely to look at.

Fraxinus ornus [*F. macropetala*]. Flowering ash. This is described as an odd beautiful shrub growing on the ledges of the Grand Canyon, about as large as a lilac bush. The white flowers are carried in drooping plumes and are very fragrant.

Gaillardia lanceolata. Sweet gaillardia. This species of the blanket flower loves to grow in dry pine barrens from South Carolina to Florida and westward. The flowers are purple and yellow and have a curious scent.

Galium triflorum. Sweet scented bedstraw. At all times, but especially when drying, this little plant has a pleasant fragrance of vanilla. It is used by country people in bouquets and one of its names is lady's bouquet. An Indian name for it means woman's perfume, and the plant is used by Native women as a perfume, a handful of it being tucked under the girdle, where its scent increases as it withers. Found from British Columbia and Newfoundland southwards in rich soils. Also in Europe.

Gaultheria hispidula [*Chiogenes hispidula*]. Creeping snowberry. A diminutive spreading plant of the heath family that weaves a close carpet in Adirondack and other northern bogs. It has small white flowers followed by snow-white berries. The whole plant gives off a pleasant spicy odour and the leaves when nibbled taste like wintergreen.

Gaultheria procumbens. Wintergreen. Teaberry. A low evergreen plant with creeping stems and thick leathery oval leaves, found in woods from Newfoundland to Manitoba and Georgia. The white flowers are followed by scarlet fruit. Both leaves and flowers have a pleasant aromatic tang and produce an essence used in the manipulation of medicines. *G. Shallon*, called by its Indian name of salal in the West, is an attractive shrub, two to six feet high, with finely toothed leathery leaves and pink and white waxen flowers in panicled racemes. They are fragrant and the black pungent berries that follow are valued by the Natives of the Northwest as an important article of diet. Other species have aromatic berries.

Gaura coccinea. A perennial plant found from South Dakota to New Mexico, with spikes of small white, pink or red flowers in summer. Sometimes grown in garden borders. The fragrance is very sweet and intense.

Gentiana barbellata. The members of this family are commonly without fragrance but Mr. D. M. Andrews writes me that this rare perennial fringed gentian "has about the most delightful fragrance of any Colorado flower, not very strong but suggestive of strawberries and other aromatic things."

Geranium maculatum. Wild geranium. David Grayson, in "Great Possessions," tells of following an elusive odour until it led him to a sunny slope where the wild geranium was in bloom in quantity and there he sat down to enjoy it fully. The leaves of this native species are without the fragrance that characterizes a number of the family. The blossom is only faintly sweet but gathers body and volume where it is found in masses.

Gilia tricolor. Bird's eyes. A beautiful little spring flower of the Southwest. The plant grows six to twelve inches high and carries its sweet scented funnel-shaped flowers in clusters. It is common on low hills in California. *Leptodactylon pungens* [*Gilia pungens*]. The small prickly gilia is a woody summer flowering plant of low stature with semiprostrate stems clothed in needle-like leaves. The flowers are white or pale pink and very sweet scented. *Leptodactylon californicum* [*Gilia californica*] is an interesting and conspicuous shrub, "suggesting some kind of a small prickly pine or cedar, and known as prickly phlox." It forms large straggling clumps about two feet high with many woody stems and rich green foliage ornamented with numerous satiny bright pink blooms an inch wide, smelling of honey. *Linanthus androsaceus* [*Gilia androsacea*], according to Dr. F. A. Hampden, smells like pigs. *Ipomopsis aggreta* [*Gilia aggregata*], known as skyrocket, also has a most unpleasant odour.

Glechoma hederacea. Ground ivy. Gill-over-the-ground. Ground ivy is naturalized in many localities and is often to be found creeping about old fields or along the roadsides near deserted gardens. Formerly it was in great repute medicinally and like so many medicinal plants has an agreeable balsamic odour. "A Modern Herbal" states that "In America, painters used a concoction of ground ivy as a preventive of, and remedy for lead colic, a wineglassful of the freshly made infusion being taken frequently." In Saxon times it was made use of to clear ale – hence one of its names, "Alehoof."

Gnaphalium polycephalum. Fragrant everlasting. Of this Oliver Wendell Holmes wrote: "Perhaps the herb everlasting, the fragrant immortelle of our autumn fields, has the most suggestive odour to me of all those that set me dreaming. I can hardly describe the strange thoughts and emotions that come to me as I inhale the aroma of its pale, dry, rustling flowers. A something it has of sepulchral spicery, as if it had been brought from the core of some great pyramid where it had lain on the breast of a mummied Pharaoh. Something too of immortality in the sad faint sweetness lingering so long in its lifeless petals. Yet this does not tell why it fills my eyes with tears and carries me in blissful thought to the banks of Asphodel that border the River of Life." This plant is common in old fields and woods in many parts of the country. *G. ramosissimum* is a fragrant pink flowered everlasting of the Coastal hills.

Grindelia robusta. Gum plant. The gum plant occurs in the states west of the Rocky Mountains. It is a branching plant covered with a resinous substance that gives it a varnished appearance. The leaves are pale green and leathery and the branches terminate in yellow flowers. The whole plant has a balsamic odour.

Hastingsia alba (*Schoenolirion*). Reed lily. An attractive marsh plant of the Northwest growing three feet tall, with long swordlike leaves and white scented flowers, forming a long fuzzy wand of bloom which has a pretty silvery effect and looks interesting at a distance, but is not very striking close by as the flowers are too colorless. Summer.

Helianthemum canadense. Frostweed. American sunrose. The leaves of this very attractive little native sunrose give off the strong scent of balsam when bruised. Maine, southward and westward.

Heliotropium convolvulaceum [*Euploca convolvulacea*]. Wild heliotrope. A plant of the Rocky Mountains possessing a rich heliotrope-like fragrance.

Hepatica triloba. This beloved flower of the spring is not always fragrant but it quite certainly sometimes is. Whether it is that occasional individual plants have this gift persistently or whether the flowers of any plant may have it at definite moments of their development I do not know. Certain it is that now and again you will find in them a delicate and ethereal perfume something akin to that of the wild sweet English violet.

Hesperocallis undulata. Desert lily. A beautiful desert plant, much like an Easter lily, with narrow bluish leaves. The "lilies" are about three inches long and delicately scented. They become curiously transparent as they wither. Miss Armstrong says that in dry seasons they do not bloom at all but the slightest moisture will cause them to send up a stout stem, crowned with exquisite blossoms, which look very extraordinary on the arid desert.

Heteromeles arbutifolia or *Photinia arbutifolia.* Christmas berry. Toyon. An evergreen shrub native in California and Lower California and planted there for ornament and used in holiday decorations. The white flowers have much the fragrance of hawthorn. They are followed by bright red or yellow berries that persist throughout the winter.

Hibiscus denudatus. A plant of the mallow family found on mesas and canyon sides of Southern California, the leaves of which are fragrant after rain.

Hololiscus discolor or *Spiraea discolor.* Creambush. Ocean spiraea. A handsome and conspicuous shrub, growing eight feet high, found on hill and mountain sides of the Coast Ranges. The tiny white flowers borne in plumy clusters in summer suggest the odour of slippery elm.

Hulsea nana. A plant of the mountain peaks of Northern California, the foliage of which is balsam scented.

Hymenocallis. Spider lily. Amaryllis-like plants with large funnel-shaped flowers grown in greenhouses North but suitable for outdoor culture in the South where the bulbs flower year after year if given reasonable care. The spider lilies are among the most unusual and beautiful of our native southern flowers and they are strongly sweet scented. The leaves are long and narrow, the blossom stalk rising about two feet high carries from four to six "lilies" enclosed in curious spidery bracts. They are commonly found in open woods. *H. caroliniana* [*H. occidentalis*] is found in South Carolina. *H. galvestonia* is widely distributed in Texas. *H. caribaea* is native in Florida and the West Indies. They flower in summer.

Hypericum ascyron. A tall perennial weed found from Quebec to Pennsylvania and westward, the leaves of which have a rank unwholesome smell. *H. scouleri* is a handsome yellow-flowered plant growing from one to two feet high and bearing bright yellow resin-scented flowers in an open branched cluster. Copses and hillsides of the West and Northwest.

Iris verna. This small southern iris, which grows in great mats over the sand hills of North Carolina, is pretty enough to pay its way anywhere, but it has in addition to beauty a most delightful perfume. A good patch of it has the sweetness of a whole bunch of hothouse violets. It is the most fragrant of our native species. Occasionally I find a specimen of *Iris cristata* that is fragrant but it is not invariable or even very usual. *I. macrosiphon,* the ground iris, a lovely species found in brushy places and slopes of the Coast Ranges of Central and Northern California, bears bright purplish blue flowers that are very sweet scented.

Itea virginica. Sweetspire. Tassle-white. Virginia willow. A pretty little native shrub, hardy in Massachusetts, growing three to five feet tall and producing numerous downy racemes of pure white flowers, during the early summer, that have a fragrance very like that of the ordinary pondlily. The foliage colours nicely in the autumn. Good for a shaded situation.

Jacquinia keyensis. Joeweed. A shrub with yellow-green foliage and fragrant creamy flowers borne in short racemes, found along the extreme southern coast of Florida, blossoming in winter.

Jamesia americana. A deciduous shrub four to seven feet tall from the Rocky Mountains, bearing slightly fragrant white flowers in terminal clusters in May.

Juglans nigra. Black walnut. All parts of the walnut tree are richly and pungently aromatic.

Juniperus sabina. All the junipers have a pleasant aromatic smell but the above is the strongest and most agreeable.

Krameria grayi. Crimson beak. A desert shrub with a pleasant scent like balsam and curious reddish flowers in spring. Arizona.

Larrea tridentata [*Covillea glutinosa*]. Creosote-bush. An attractive and graceful evergreen bush that, according to Margaret Armstrong, is a characteristic feature of the desert landscape, filling the air with its peculiar balsamic odour. The leaflets are small and resinous, the flowers bright yellow.

Lappula floribunda. False forget-me-not. Lovely little plant that greets the summer wayfarer on bushy hillsides from Manitoba to New Mexico, from British Columbia to California. The light blue flowers have much the appearance of forget-me-nots but besides their pleasant colour they have also a delicate fragrance which is not the portion of the true forget-me-not. It is annual or biennial.

Lathyrus torreyi. A plant of the shaded woods of Central and Northern California with pea-shaped flowers and herbage that is lastingly fragrant.

Layia platyglossa. Tidy tips. A little hairy glandular plant of the valleys and foothills of California, with yellow rayed flowers tipped with white that are delicately fragrant.

Ledum palustre. Wild rosemary. Crystal tea. This attractive member of the heath family is a low evergreen shrub bearing small white flowers in terminal clusters in spring. The woolly leaves have a powerful odour when bruised, something like rosemary. It is a denizen of sphagnum bogs in cold parts of the northern hemisphere in both the New and the Old Worlds. *L. glandulosum*, Trupper's tea, is similar but the foliage is less woolly. The flowers and leaves have both a bitter-sweet fragrance. It is found in wet mountain meadows in California. These plants are considered poisonous. *L. groenlandicum.* Labrador tea. This lovely plant usually haunts low-lying flats or marshy places in the North. The evergreen leaves are densely woolly beneath and the scaly buds are covered with a sticky exudation. The flowers appear in large terminal clusters, and are pure white and highly aromatic, as are the leaves.

Leonurus cardiaca. Motherwort. A coarse weedy plant naturalized from Europe and found principally in the neighbourhood of dwellings. Like most strong-smelling plants it was formerly important in domestic medical practice.

Leptosyne maritima. Sea dahlia. A curious prostrate plant with yellow dahlialike flowers that flourishes on the cliffs overlooking the Pacific in California. The leathery gummy leaves are not attractive but the flowers have an odour that is liked by some.

Liatris odoratissima (*Trilisa odoratissima*). Carolina vanilla. A herbaceous plant native in the Southern States, found in lowlying situations and pine woods, growing two to four feet high. The purplish flower heads and the foliage smell of vanilla when dried. It is said that they retain this fragrance for many years and that a damp day will cause it to develop after all activity has apparently ceased. Southern planters were said at one time to mix the leaves with their tobacco to impart a pleasant fragrance.

Limonium carolinianum (*Statice latifolia*). Sea lavender. A plant of our sea marshes whose clouds of tiny mauve flowers drift like puffs of mist above the grasses. They are delicately fragrant. Often dried for winter bouquets.

Linanthus dichotomus (*Gilia*). Evening snow. Exceedingly pretty little plants found in hot sandy or gravelly places in Central and Southern California, blooming in spring. The flowers are large, salverform, white and of satin texture. They open only in the evening, remaining open all night and repeating the performance several times. They give out an odour which is sweet but not to all persons agreeable.

Linaria canadensis. Old-field toadflax. This common and pretty little weed which is found throughout the country has a faint sweet odour.

Linnaea borealis var. *americana.* Twinflower. Diminutive and indescribably dainty member of the honeysuckle family found in our deep cool northern woods. The nodding white flowers have the fragrance of almonds. Mr. Edward St. John writes me, "Just now our forests (in New Hampshire) are richly perfumed with the odour of the twinflower. A few days ago I noticed it along the trails before I could find a single blossom and was reminded of an experience of several years ago in Western New York where it is a rare plant. I noticed and recognized the odour as I was wandering through a swampy forest and following it up the breeze traced it to a large colony which was fully fifteen rods away from the point where I first noticed the odour."

Liquidambar styraciflua. Sweet gum. Red gum. A large tree common from Connecticut to Florida and Mexico, with beautiful leaves that turn a superb colour in the autumn. The leaves and buds have an agreeable odour when crushed and the sap, the liquid amber, hardens into a fragrant resin.

Ludwigia peploides [*Jussiaea repens*]. Primrose willow. An aquatic plant with a creeping stem that roots at the nodes. It is frequently seen cultivated among collections of aquatics. The flowers are fragrant and as they lift their heads above shallow water "look like exquisite pale yellow cups or even like poppies that have lost their way." It blossoms in May and June and its range is through South Carolina and westward.

Lupinus arboreus. Tree lupine. A conspicuous shrubby plant of California, growing four to six feet in height with "a thick trunk, gnarled and twisted below, with purplish downy branches, silvery twigs and dull bluish green leaves, downy on the undersides, with about nine leaflets. The fine flower clusters are sometimes a foot long, composed of beautiful canary-yellow flowers deliciously sweet scented." Common in sandy soil near the sea. It is much grown in gardens abroad and is the parent of many fine garden varieties. Nearly all lupins are honey-scented, among them *L. nanus,* hills and foothills of California; *L. stiversii* of the Yosemite; *L. paynei* of California. One of the finest floral shows our country has to offer is the sandy hillsides blue with the rare colour of the wild lupine, *L. perennis,* in various parts of the East and

South to Texas, where it is known as Texas blue bonnet.

Lycopus americanus. Sweet bugleweed. Water hoarhound. A small perennial herb growing in moist ground from Newfoundland to Florida and westward. The little purple flowers are of no account but the whole plant has a pleasant mintlike odour.

Lyonia ferruginea (*xolisma ferruginea*). Called locally in Florida, myrtle. A shrub or small tree with evergreen leathery leaves and tiny globose white flowers that are sometimes fragrant, when they fill the air with a honeylike scent. Found in sandy soil from Florida to South Carolina, blossoming in winter and early spring.

Lysichitum camtschatcensis. Yellow skunk cabbage. A stemless ill-scented herb found in swamps in Northeastern America and Eastern Asia.

Lysimachia ciliata [*Steironema ciliatum*]. Fringed loosestrife. An erect plant found in low ground in thickets blossoming in summer. The clear yellow flowers are sweet scented. Wide distribution.

Madia elegans. Common showy madia. A plant found from Southern California to Oregon and east to Nevada, growing profusely on hillsides. Although the blossoms are much like those of coreopsis they make little show, because they remain closed during sunshine, opening only on cloudy days or in the evening. The stems are stout and sticky and the plant gives off a strong odour of turpentine which, borne on the breeze to a little distance, however, has a refreshing spicy tang.

Magnolia tripetala. Umbrella tree. Tree indigenous from Pennsylvania to Alabama growing forty feet tall. The large white flowers have an unpleasant odour. *M. macrophylla,* large-leaved cucumber tree. This is a rare species from the swampy forests of the South. It grows to a height of forty feet, having exceedingly large and handsome leaves and immense widely spreading waxen white flowers with some basal purplish suffusion. Slightly fragrant.

Maianthemum canadense. Two-leaved solomon's seal. A charming plant with a slender creeping rootstock and flexuous stem. The delicate white, sweet scented flowers are borne in May in dense erect spikes. Commonly found growing in moist woods from Labrador to North Carolina and out through the West.

Malacothamnus fasciculatus [*Sphaeralcea fasciculata*]. False mallow. Pretty little plant of the hill slopes of Central and Southern California with delicately perfumed flowers.

Malvastrum thurberi. False mallow. A handsome shrub common in Southern California, with bluish green leaves and pink-lilac flowers that have an agreeable scent. *Malacothamnus fasciculatus* [*Malvastrum fasciculatum*]. Bush mallow. This tall shrub is a distinctive feature of the hillsides and canyons of Southern California. The wandlike branches are clothed in grey leaves with charming mallow-pink blossoms, fragrant and not unlike garden hollyhocks, nestling among them. It blooms in spring and summer.

Manfreda virginica (*Agrave virginica*). False aloe. A fleshy bulbous herb with basal leaves and large white flowers in terminal racemes that flower at night. They are sweet scented. It is found in sterile or dry soil in Florida, Texas, and as far north as Maryland.

Marrubium vulgare. Horehound. The leaves of this once popular medicinal plant when fresh have a strong aromatic odour. It is naturalized sparingly in this country in old rural neighbourhoods.

Matricaria recutita [*M. chamomilla*]. Sweet false chamomile. An annual herb introduced from the Old World, with strongly scented, finely dissected foliage and small white-rayed flowers. It is found along roadsides and in waste places all along the Atlantic Coast and west as far as Ohio. In old fashioned gardens a row of chamomile was one of its attractions and was much in demand as a remedy for colds, while the pretty fragrant foliage was used in bouquets. *M. matricarioides* is a little weed common along highways in California. It has feather foliage that exhales a strong pleasant fruity smell when crushed, from which is taken its name of pineapple weed. It is also called manzanilla.

Medicago sativa. Alfalfa. Chilean clover. Lucerne. A valuable forage plant that is generally becoming naturalized in various parts of the country. It has come to us from Chile and is widely grown as a fodder plant. The fragrance from a field of alfalfa is delicious. In Chile bunches of the plant are laid about the rooms to drive away fleas.

Melilotus alba. Sweet or bokara clover. Melilot. A tall and weedy adornment of our dusty summer roadsides along which it crowds closely, as does the yellow-flowered *M. offficinalis*, but both were originally introduced to this country from Europe. The latter is much valued in Switzerland as a fodder plant where it is supposed to give the Gruyère cheese its peculiar flavour. In this country the melilots are used by country people to put among clothes to keep away moths as well as to perfume them. They are important bee plants. They are sweeter when dried and then keep their fragrance for a long time. *M. indica* is sometimes used as a cover crop in California, where it is found throughout the state. Both flowers and foliage are fragrant.

Mentha pulgium [*Hedeoma pulegioides*]. American pennyroyal. An annual herb giving off spontaneously a powerful but agreeable and pungent odour noticeable at some distance from the plant. It was once of great importance in domestic medical practice. The expressed juice mixed with a little sugar candy was a popular remedy in whooping cough.

Mentzelia decapetala (*M. ornata*). A very beautiful American plant found from South Dakota to Texas. The flowers are white or yellowish and sometimes five inches across, seemingly made of the finest silk crepe. They open towards evening and are then very fragrant. *M. Lindleyi* or *Bartonia aurea* is an annual, opening fragrant golden yellow flowers in the late afternoon. Southern California. These make delightful garden plants in the East.

Menyanthes trifoliata. Buck bean or bog bean. Perennial herb with creeping rootstock found in ponds and ditches and spongy boggy ground in the cooler parts of the Northern Hemisphere. The white flowers borne in racemes are fragrant. Sometimes grown in bog gardens.

Mertensia lanceolata. The graceful western lungwort has a pleasing, refreshing aroma, though not strong. *M. bakeri* is also mildly fragrant as doubtless are a number of others of the genus.

Mesosphaerum spicatum. Swamp basil. A mintlike plant of Florida and Alabama, blooming from March to December, found in waste places and along roadsides.

Micromeria brownii. This creeping plant, most of whose family dwells along the shores of the Mediterranean, grows on the banks of muddy streams in Florida. The flowers are unimportant but the foliage is very aromatic. *M. chamissonis* [*M. douglasii*]. Yerba buena, or tea vine, is a low creeping plant of the Coastal woods of Northern and Central California to Washington, the leaves of which are employed medicinally by the Indians of California and are said to have been used as a tea by the Spanish Californians. The whole plant is richly aromatic. This little plant is as beloved in California as is the trailing arbutus in the East.

Mimulus moschatus. Musk plant. A sticky little plant of streamsides in California and other parts of the West. It smells of musk in all its parts.

Mirabilis longiflora. A clammy Mexican plant two to three feet high with black turnip-like roots and large leaves from among which arise terminal clusters of sweet scented funnel-shaped flowers about two inches long and variously colored red, white or yellow.

Mitchella repens. Partridgeberry. Checkerberry. Oneberry. Winter clover. Squaw vine. Small evergreen procumbent creeper covering the forest floor in broad areas with small shining leaves. The small white flowers are followed by bright red berries. The scent of the flowers is refreshing and agreeable and according to Thoreau "between the mayflower and cherry bark, or like peachstone meats." The checkerberry was formerly highly esteemed as a remedy in many ills both by the Indians and for many years by the white settlers.

Monarda. Bergamot or bee balm. American herbs with delightfully sweet scented leaves. The familiar *M. didyma* and its varieties is frequently grown for garden decoration. *M. fistulosa* is the charming pale wild bergamot that scrambles along roadsides and at the edges of fields from Maine to Florida. *M. pectinata,* plain's lemon monarda, horse mint, is a plant of sandy-dry plains in Arizona and Utah, with flowers in clustery heads, light lilac in colour. *M. russeliana* [*M. bradburiana*] is a handsome Central Western species, sometimes grown in gardens, and besides these are *M. punctata* ssp. *villicaulis* [*M. lasiodonta*], the hairy bee balm of Oklahoma and Arizona, and *M. media, M. fistulosa* [*M. mollis*], *M. menthifolia* [*M. ramaleyi*], and *M. punctata.* The Indians of the Winnebago tribes used a decoction of monarda leaves as a cure for pimples, and the young braves of the Omaha made a pomade of them for the hair.

Monardella macrantha. A delightful and highly aromatic plant from pine covered slopes of Southern California mountains, that blooms in the autumn making bright spots of red colour where it grows in quantity. It is a creeping plant of tufted growth, the flowering branches reaching a height of about six inches, the blossoms are about an inch in length and are shaped like those of a salvia. *M. Lanceolata,* mustang mint, with small bright pinkish lilac flowers and fragrant leaves, is found in the mountains and foothills throughout California. *M. odoratissima* is a fragrant species from the mountains of Northern California, and *M. villosa,* coyote mint, with purple, pink or white flowers, is found in dry rocky hillsides of Central and Northern parts of the State.

Moneses uniflora. Single beauty. Low growing evergreen perennial plant with a tuft of shining leaves from the center of which arises a slender stem topped by a single drooping waxen flower that is very richly scented. Northwest United States of America.

Monotropa uniflora. Indian pipe. These strange parasitic ghost flowers never fail to give us a sort of shock when we come upon them, clustered in seemingly sinister gregariousness, deep in some somber forest. Emanating from the waxen white or palely flushed flowers at certain periods of their development is a "delicate and wholly sweet scent" – the odour of sanctity perhaps, for these flowers, if such they be, seem wholly of another sphere. They are found all across the continent as well as in Asia. *M. hypopithys*, pinesap or false beechdrops, is a somewhat similar parasitic plant but considerably less ghostly in appearance. The stems are slightly downy, whitish or yellowish, and the curious drooping vase-shaped flowers are quite noticeably fragrant. They are found in dry woods usually beneath pine or beech trees. It is more common than the Indian pipe.

Muilla maritima. A fragile pretty little bulbous plant native in California and Nevada, with clusters of fragrant flowers striped with green on the outside. "This grows in alkaline fields, on sea cliffs and mesas."

Myrica californica. California wax myrtle. California bayberry. A tall shrub found on coastal dunes and wooded slopes throughout California, Washington and Oregon. The leaves are highly aromatic. It is valuable for use in dry sterile places but it is not hardy in the East.

Navarretia squarrosa or *Gilia squarrosa.* Skunkweed. Ill-scented annual plant found from British Columbia to California.

Nelumbo luteum. This is the "American lotus" or water chinquapin of the United States, found from Southern Ontario to Florida and Louisiana. Gray says probably of Indian introduction. The leaves are blue green and held well above the water and the creamy-yellow flowers, ten inches across when fully expanded, exhale a delicious magnolia-like fragrance. I know a pond near Swampscott, Mass. where it is naturalized. Hardier than *N. nucifera* [*N. speciosum*], the sacred lotus.

Nepeta cataria. Catnip. Catmint. A weedy aromatic plant naturalized from Europe and widely distributed in this country. It was formerly of great importance in domestic medical practice but is now chiefly fancied by cats. Its odour is very strong and resembles both mint and pennyroyal.

Nicotiana bigelovii. Indian tobacco. An annual herb growing two feet high with white fragrant salver-shaped flowers, found in Colorado, Nevada and Arizona. *N. attenuata.* Coyote tobacco. An annual plant bearing greenish salver-form flowers that open at night. The whole plant is strong smelling. Found in dry stream beds throughout California and in many other parts of the West and Southwest.

Nothoscordum bivalve. False garlic. A little plant three to twelve inches high with narrow grasslike leaves and an umbel of white flowers on a slender stem that just tops the foliage. The stem has a strong taste and smells of garlic. It is found in sandy soil in Florida, Texas and west to Nebraska. It is hardy in my garden and is quite pretty in a modest way. *N. gracile* [*N. fragrans*], naturalized in Bermuda and the Southern States, has pinkish fragrant flowers. It is reported from England as a most dangerous and pestiferous weed.

Nymphaea odorata. This is the lovely white pond lily of the Northeastern States. Its fragrance is exquisite, as pure and cool and sweet as its appearance. In sheltered ponds in the neighbourhood of New York and Philadelphia it comes into bloom as early as the middle of May. Thoreau loved the white pond lily and never failed to commemorate its unfolding. "Tomorrow," he wrote in his journal, "will be the first Sabbath when the young men, having bathed, will walk slowly and soberly to church, in their best clothes, each with a lily in his hand or bosom, and as long a stem as he could get." A quaint picture this of bygone rural America. There are several forms of *N. odorata* all having the same delicious fragrance. *N. odorata* var. *rosea* is the famous Cape Cod pink pond lily, and there is *N. odorata* var. *gigantea* the great white pond lily of the Southern States, and *N. odorata* var. *minor*, a small form with delightfully sweet flowers. Fine cultivars of the type are the following: 'W. B. Shaw', large rose-pink flowers; 'Helen Fowler', pink and exquisitely fragrant and borne well above the water; 'Rose Arey', deep carmine pink and very large; *N. sulphurea* 'Sulphurea grandiflora', a yellow lily of lovely habit, carrying its fragrant flowers high above the water; 'Eugene de Land' with deep rose-pink star-shaped flowers that float upon the surface of the water. *N. tuberosa* is a native species from the West and Northwest. It is too vigorous for cultivation in tubs or small pools and does not blossom as freely as the Eastern species, nor is it as fragrant, but its great white broad-petalled flower is often nine inches across. There are pink and rose forms of this, the best of which for fragrance is *N. tuberosa* [*Nymphaea polysepala*]. The yellow pond lily. Less beautiful than the white pond lily, this mountain species has handsome floating foliage and the golden flowers are quite fragrant. Lakes and slow streams in Montana, Dakota (the Black Hills), Colorado, California and Alaska.

Oemleria cerasiformis [*Osmaronia cerasiformis*]. Osoberry. A deciduous shrub growing fifteen feet high, found from British Columbia to California in shady canyons, bearing short clusters of greenish white flowers with a delicious bitter fragrance, in drooping racemes in April and May. Sometimes grown for ornament and hardy in the North Central States. The flowers are followed by plumlike fruits.

Oenothera speciosa. White evening primrose. A charming plant of the West, with large tissue-paperlike white flowers that in my garden remain open both day and night. Their fragrance is light and pleasing. In a poor warm soil this plant runs about freely and may even become a nuisance, but its flowers are so altogether engaging that one is tolerant of its colonizing. *O. pallida* ssp. *trichocalyx* is a fine species native in Colorado, Utah and Wyoming, that has lately made its appearance in seed catalogs. I am not sure if it is a reliable perennial. It grows about twelve inches high, has hairy leaves and nodding buds, which open into wide white salvers of lovely texture and nice perfume.

Orchids—wild and naturalized. See the orchids section at the end of this chapter.

Orthocarpus erianthus. Popcorn flower. Dainty little plant found in dry places in California, growing ten inches high with leafy stems and small pink flowers said to be scented of violet. *Aristolochia grandiflora* [*O. luteus*]. Pelican flower. A plant of the plains and bench lands of the Northwest, uninteresting and insignificant, but the curious little beaked flowers possess a very pleasing sweetness. *O. versicolor.* White owl's clover. During the spring the owl's clover makes its appearance in the meadows about San Francisco in great quantities, making patches white as snow here and there. The flowers are said to be delightfully fragrant, which is not true of all the owl's clovers.

Osmorhiza longistylis. Smooth sweet cicely. Aniseroot. A rather weedy plant with a wide range north and south, east and west. The roots are thick and smell strongly of anise. There are numerous other species.

Oxalis acetosella (*O. montana*). Wood sorrel. Cuckoo bread. Alleluia. This dainty woodland plant is common in damp situations from Maine to the mountains of North Carolina. The clustering leaves composed of three pale-green leaflets shaped like hearts and the fragile five-petalled, white flowers so brightly etched with crimson, combine to make a charming whole, and the faint delicate fragrance that belongs to the flowers is a wholly gratuitous gift. The leaves have the pretty habit of folding up and drooping their heads with the coming of nightfall.

Pachysandra procumbens. Allegheny mountain spurge. This low growing plant is found in dense shady woods in Florida and Louisiana and as far north as Virginia. It makes a fine ground cover, far handsomer than its alien relative that is in such general use. It blooms very early in the spring, the purplish or greenish flowers with thick white stamens exhaling a curious aroma. They are partly hidden by the leaves.

Paeonia brownii. Wild peony. The wild peony has a wide range in the Northwest, growing on brushy hillsides. The flowers are rather thick in texture, nodding, and of a rich deep red colour streaked with a darker hue and flashed with yellow. They are quite sweet scented but the plant has a disagreeable odour rather like skunk cabbage when bruised. It blooms in early spring or in mild climates in winter.

Pedicularis groenlandica. Elephant's head. A handsome plant of damp mountain meadows of California and other parts of the far West. The slightly fragrant flowers are pink and the corollas are shaped amusingly like the head of an elephant.

Peniocereus greggii. This is the desert night blooming cereus, called by the Mexicans *reina de noche.* Its spectacular blossoming used to be the occasion for festivity and merry-making around the old Spanish haciendas and Indian pueblos in Mexico and Southern Arizona. This strange plant opens its flowers during the hottest and dryest part of the year and at the period of the longest days, from June fifteenth to June twenty-fifth. Usually all the flowers in a community of plants come into bloom at the same time, opening with clocklike regularity with the sunset and closing again about seven-thirty in the morning. The flowers fill the air for a considerable distance round about the ungainly plants with a heavy but delicious odour, described as between that of magnolia and jasmine, which usually persists until they close in the morning.

Pentachaeta aurea. A plant with narrow leaves and pretty yellow flowers like miniature suns that is found only in the southernmost counties of California. The flowers remain open only until afternoon and do not open at all in chill weather. The plant has a fragrance not unlike that of goldenrod.

Petasites palamatus. Sweet coltsfoot. A plant of woods and swamps and recent clearings from Labrador to Alabama and westward, with broad kidney-shaped leaves and whitish flowers borne early that are quite fragrant.

Phacelia crenulata. Wild heliotrope. A showy spring-flowering plant found in Arizona and on the plateau in the Grand Canyon of the Colorado. The foliage is coarse and hairy and very sticky and has an unpleasant odour when bruised, but the flowers which are not unlike heliotrope are pleasantly fragrant. *P. sericea.* Mountain phacelia. This showy and beautiful plant with rich purple-blue flowers, borne in long spikelike panicles, is found at very high altitudes in Colorado, Nevada, Washington and British Columbia. Unhappily it has a strong and very disagreeable odour.

Phlox douglasii. A delightful low alpine of the Northwest, forming cushion-like mats of needle-like leaves, starred all over in early summer with charming lilac-coloured flowers that are faintly but sweetly scented. *Phlox multiflora* of the Rocky Mountains has a delicious scent and, according to Mr. Andrews, most of the Rocky Mountain phloxes are agreeably perfumed. *P. divaricata,* wild sweet william, blue phlox, when grown in masses is very sweet scented and *P. stolonifera* [*P. reptans*] is quite powerfully sweet, especially the form with creamy-lilac flowers.

Physaria [*Isomeris arborea*]. Burrofat. Bladderpod. A rather attractive little plant that seems to flit over the hills and cliffs of Southern California, making bright patches of yellow colour amidst the sober grey of coastal sage brush. The flowers themselves have little odour but unfortunately the foliage when bruised retaliates with a quite dreadful odour. The flowers are followed by large leathery inflated pods, containing two rows of bitter pealike seeds.

Physocarpus malvaceus [*Opulaster malvaceus*]. A tall handsome shrub of the Northwest and Utah, bearing large clusters of sweet smelling white flowers. Mountainsides in rich soil.

Phyllodoce breweri. Brewer's mountain heather. Purple heather. A delightful heathlike shrub of the Northwest blossoming in summer. It makes heathery patches on high mountain slopes up to twelve thousand feet in the Sierra Nevadas. The gay little reddish flowers are sweet scented.

Picea glauca (*P. canadensis*). The white spruce of the Northwest is a beautiful tree with branches sweeping out in fine curves to form a pyramid, but its foliage, unlike the majority of evergreens, has a very disagreeable smell. Engelman's spruce, *P. engelmannii* with thin aromatic leaves and inconspicuous flowers. It is said that the foliage was used as a tea by the first settlers. Common in woods of a widely distributed, high mountain tree, also has this unattractive characteristic.

Plagiobothrys nothofulvus. Popcorn flower. A quaint little plant that whitens the valleys and foothills of parts of the Northwest with its small fragrant flowers.

Pluchea camphorata. Salt marsh fleabane. Inconspicuous little composite with lavender flowers found in the marshes along the eastern coast. Its odour is somewhat suggestive of camphor.

Podophyllum peltatum. Mandrake. May apple. The little may apple flower hidden under its broad green umbrella has an odour spicy but not pleasant to all. It is found in rich woods from Quebec southward.

Polemonium brandegei ssp. *mellitum* [*P. mellitum*]. Beautiful plant of the Rockies with white fragrant flowers carried on eight-inch stems. *P. viscosum* [*P. confertum*], though as lovely to look at, has the telltale name of skunkweed to its disadvantage. Both these plants make fine ornaments in the rock garden, when they can be induced to accept lowland conditions, but I have found them very difficult though they come readily from seed.

Polygonum fagopyrum [*Fagopyrum esculentum*]. Buckwheat. This plant is a native of Northern Asia and is widely cultivated in this country. It has become naturalized in certain sections, reappearing in old fields and along roadsides after cultivation. At the time of its blossoming, when the short dense racemes of white fragrant flowers wave above a forest of coral-coloured stems, whole areas of the countryside are perfumed with it. It is a tender annual of easy culture under many conditions. The flour that furnishes our historic breakfast cakes is ground from the seeds.

Polygala Senega. Seneca snakeroot. Senga root. A perennial plant growing about a foot high, found through the Northwestern and Central States. The American Indians used the plant as a remedy for snake bite. The leaves smell and taste much like wintergreen. *P. cruciata* is intermittently fragrant.

Polygonum bistortoides. Alpine smartweed. An inconspicuous but comely little plant found in grassy alpine meadows in the Northwest. The slender stem carries a head of small creamy flowers, pink in the bud, that smell deliciously of honey.

Polypteris integrifolia. A member of the thistle family indigenous to Florida and Georgia, bearing ragged sweet scented white or purplish flower heads in the late summer.

Populus trichocarpa. Black cottonwood. Western balsam poplar. This is a tall tree found from Alaska to Southern California. "A young tree fills the air around it with a strong fragrance commonly described as balsamic." The young shoots of *P. balsamifera* are covered with a fragrant viscid yellowish resin. The young leaves and buds of *P.* x *canadensis* also have an agreeable balsamic odour.

Primula angustifolia. A high alpine primula of very small size bearing a loose cluster of large pink blossoms with a delicate fragrance. My specimens came to me from high places in the Rockies through the kindness of Mr. D. M. Andrews. Mr. Andrews writes me that *P. parryi,* another western mountain species, has a powerful odour, rather too heavy and cloying. "Most persons find it pleasant if diluted."

Prunus. P. americana is a small native round-topped tree bearing in spring a wealth of hawthorn scented blossoms. It is found from New England to Manitoba. The fruit is edible, reddish or yellowish in colour. In early May shore districts along the Atlantic are sweet with the keen fragrance of the beech plum, *Prunus maritima.* It is a low shrub with crooked, picturesque branches. The fruit makes a good preserve. *P. nigra,* the Canadian plum, is a small tree, perhaps thirty to forty feet in height, with pale pink scented blossoms in spring. It is found as far south as New York. *P. serotina,* the wild black cherry or rum cherry, is a large forest tree found from Nova Scotia to Dakota and south to Florida and Texas. Its masses of white flowers are exceedingly fragrant, the fruit is purplish black and edible. *P. virginiana,* the choke cherry, is a bushy shrub widely distributed in the Eastern States, north and south. The racemes of creamy flowers have some odour but it is usually thought to be of a rather sickening character.

Psilostrophe tagetina. A yellowish wall flower-like plant of the Southwest. Its clusters of lemon-yellow flowers appear in spring and are delicately scented. It is found in arid places in Arizona and Utah.

Psoralea physodes. California tea. A pretty little plant of the Northwest with thin aromatic leaves and inconspicuous flowers. It is said that the foliage was used as tea by the first settlers. Common in the woods of the Coast Ranges.

Ptelea. Hop tree. The leaves of the native hop trees, *P. baldwinii* and *P. trifoliata,* are aromatic, though there seems to be a difference of opinion as to their agreeableness. Professor Hottes quotes C. C. Dream as saying, "The odour is akin to that of a polecat."

Purshia tridentata. Antelope brush. A low shrub found on the prairies, in the Rocky Mountains, the Pacific Northwest and the dry hills of the Southwest. It bears fragrant yellow flowers in spring that yield both nectar and pollen for the bees.

Pycnanthemum. Mountain mint. North American perennial herbs with small white or purplish flowers in heads or cymes in late summer. *P. virginianum* is the best scented.

Pycnothymus rigidus [*Satureja*]. Wild savory. This fragrant shrubby mint found only in Florida is abundant in damp pinelands in many localities, and is readily recognized by its low growth of woody stems, evergreen needlelike leaves, and dense oblong silky heads of little pale purple flowers spotted with darker colour on the lower lip. The odour of the whole plant when crushed or brushed against is something like pennyroyal.

Pyrola. Wintergreen. Shinleaf. Low, mostly evergreen woodland plants with thick shining rounded leaves and fragrant nodding waxen flowers, white or pale pink, strung along a slender scape. *P. americana* is perhaps the showiest species. It is found in dry woods from Nova Scotia to South Dakota and south to Georgia and Ohio. The waxen flowers are creamy white and very fragrant, the leaves rounded and evergreen. *P. elliptica,* the shinleaf of our rich woods has thin longish leaves, not evergreen, and the flowers are perhaps the most fragrant of any of the species. *P. chlorantha,* green-flowered wintergreen, found in many parts of the country east and west, has greenish flowers that are only slightly odorous. Other species are *P. asarifolia* var. *purpurea* [*P. uliginosa*], a species inhabiting cold northern woods, west and east, with pink or magenta flowers; *Orthilia secunda* [*Pyrola secunda*], a plant of rich woods whose flowers are in a one-sided scape, and *P. minor,* a small species found in mossy places at high altitudes as far west as the Rockies. The flowers are pale pink. *Pyrola asarifolia* ssp. *bracteata* [*Pyrola bracteata*] is a far western member of the wintergreen family with handsome leathery leaves and creamy blossoms, pink in the bud, that are very richly scented.

Ramona incana. Desert ramona. A rather odd and beautiful desert shrub with grey-green aromatic leaves and bright blue flowers set in variously tinted bracts.

Rhus trilobata [*Petiveria alliacea*]. Skunk bush. A plant growing from one to four feet tall inhabiting parts of tropical America. The small greenish flowers are borne in a wandlike spike. The whole plant emits a rank smell of garlic. Thickets in Florida.

Ribes hudsonianum. Northern black currant. An attractive shrub of the Northwest with close erect clusters of white flowers and ill-smelling leaves. The berry also has an evil odour. *R. glutinosum.* Incense shrub of the Coast Ranges is so called because of the strong pungent odour emanating from it. *R. laxiflorum* has earned the name of skunk currant for obvious reasons. It belongs to the woods of Alaska, Idaho and Northern California. *R. nevadense,* the Sierra currant, is a tall sturdy mountain shrub with scalloped leaves and pink fragrant flowers, followed by sweet-tasting black berries. *R. malvaceum,* Chaparral currant, of dry hills of Central and Southern California, has fragrant flowers and foliage, and the leaves of *R. viburnifolium,* a wild shrub of California, give off the clean odour of turpentine.

Romneya coulteri. Matilija poppy. Mission poppy. This is one of the most beautiful of all American wild flowers and looks not wild at all but as if it were the result of years of careful cultivation and hybridization. It is not hardy in the Northeastern States, though I kept a fine specimen in my Rockland County garden against a south-facing wall for three years with careful winter protection. It is abundant in parts of California. The blossoms are immense, white, silken, filled with golden stamens and exhale a pleasant fragrance. The plant is shrubby in character, growing from two to fifteen feet high. The blue-green leaves are just what is needed to set off the great shining blossoms.

Rubus. Many kinds of blackberries have exquisitely fragrant blossoms. Thoreau wrote, "How agreeable and wholesome the fragrance of the low blackberry blossoms, reminding one of all the rosaceus, fruit-bearing plants, so near and dear to our humanity. It is one of the most deliciously fragrant flowers, reminding one of wholesome fruits." *R. parviflorus* [*R. nutkanus*], the thimble-berry found in far western woods from Monterey to Alaska, spreads a fair canopy of green. Its canes grow from three to eight feet in height and the large white deliciously fragrant blossoms are followed by red fruit, large and "like an inverted saucer" in shape.

Salix alba var. *vitellina.* Golden willow. This is perhaps the first honey plant sought by the bees. The blossoms send out a wild sweet fragrance very early in the year, even before the blossoms of the sugar maple. *S. pyrifolia* [*S. balsamifera*] is a much branched shrub found from Canada and the Northern States all across the continent. The leaves have a balsamic sweetness. *S. pentandra* is a European species, long naturalized in parts of this country. It is called the bay or laurel willow and the fragrant leaves are shaped like those of the laurel.

Salvia. Many members of this large and pungent family decorate various parts of our country. *S. carduacea,* the thistle sage, is a fantastically beautiful and decorative plant found growing on dry open plains in Southern California. The plant when crushed gives out a strong odour of sage with a dash of lemon verbena. *S. columbariae,* known as chia, is a plant of curious appearance, growing on dry hillsides in California, with a stout purplish stem that springs from a cluster of "rough leaves sometimes so wrinkled as to look like the back of a toad." The Mission Fathers use the strongly sage-scented leaves as a poultice in certain ailments.

Salvia apiana [*Hyptis emoryi*]. Bee sage. A shrub belonging to the mint family, growing from two to five feet tall, with small dense clusters of flowers and strongly sage-scented leaves. The flowers are much enjoyed by bees. Arizona and deserts of Southern California.

Salvia spathacea [*Audibertia grandiflora*]. Hummingbird sage. This is the largest flowered of all the audibertias. Found in the Coast Ranges from San Mateo southward, blossoming in woodlands in April and May. The inflorescence is over a foot long and made up of whorls of crimson flowers. The leaves and bracts are quite viscid and have a rank unpleasant odour. *Salvia apiana* [*Audibertia polystachya*]. White sage. Greasewood. A famous honey plant of Southern California which covers extensive reaches of valley and hillside. The whitish stems have a greasy feel and a rank, rather unpleasant odour. *A. nivea*, the white ball sage has lilac flowers and a strong sagelike odour. The black ball sage is *Salvia brandegei* [*Audibertia stachyoides*]. All are sought by bees.

Sambucus pubens. Red-berried elder. Stinking elder. This is a shrub found in field and forest and by the wayside "thriving with undaunted hardihood amid the most barren surroundings" over a vast part of the country and often at very high elevations. The creamy flowers are fragrant as are those of *S. melanocarpa*, the blackberried elder, found from British Columbia to California. *S. caerulea* (*S. glauca*), blue elder, is also of the far West, British Columbia to California and Utah. It has somewhat bluish leaves and the characteristic lacy heads of fragrant creamy flowers. Pies and preserves are made from the berries. *S. canadensis* is the common elder of waysides and thickets from Nova Scotia to Florida. It is sometimes called sweet elder though all do not consider its fragrance sweet.

Saponaria officinalis. Bouncing bet. Lady-by-the-gate. Chimney pink. Soapwort. A pretty old-fashioned plant that has escaped from gardens and haunts our country roadsides. The blush coloured blossoms have a rather insipid scent though in the evening it strengthens and it is then, too, that the spreads of pale flowers show at their best. A double flowered form is a plant of greater consequence.

Saururus cernuus. Swamp lily. Lizard's tail. This curious plant of our eastern marshes, with its spikes of feathery white flowers is attractive chiefly for its very agreeable fragrance. It whitens whole swamps in certain districts at midsummer.

Schinus molle. Pepper tree. Peruvian mastic tree. Lovely and graceful Peruvian tree widely grown for ornament in California. Its great bunches of currantlike fruit make it a highly decorative object. The whole tree is fragrant.

Schrankia. Sensitive brier. Two perennial herbs, *S. uncinata* and *S. angustata*, related to the true sensitive plants (*Mimosa*) with prickle-armed procumbent stems and dense heads of small pea-shaped yellow flowers that hide amidst the grass. When picked the leaflets fold together and cling tightly. The flowers are fragrant of hyacinths, and John Muir, in an account of a walking trip through the Cumberland Mountains, reports the pleasure of finding it. Virginia southwards and west to Illinois and Idaho.

Scoliopsis bigelovii. Fetid adder's tongue. A curious little California plant of the lily family that begins to bloom early in March. Numerous flower stalks spring from between two shining green leaves, each carrying a solitary purplish brown flower that is very unpleasantly scented. Deep cool woods or redwood forests in Central and Northern California.

Selenicereus pteranthus (*Cereus nycticallus*). A Mexican species of night-blooming cactus with very fragrant white flowers.

Solanum xantii. The violet nightshade of the mountains and foothills of Southern California is a much handsomer plant than its Eastern prototype. The flowers are beautiful, each about an inch across and hang in graceful clusters. They often have the fragrance of the wild rose.

Solidago odora. Sweet scented goldenrod. Common North American herb with aromatic leaves from which an essential oil, possessing a powerful odour a good deal like anise, is expressed. *S. pallida* (*S. speciosa*), and others of the goldenrods are characteristically fragrant.

Sorbus aucuparia [*Pyrus sambucifolia*]. Western mountain ash. The rowan tree of the mountainous regions is a handsome large shrub, or small tree, with dark leaves, pale on the undersides, and "huge clustered cymes of soft-tinted flowers which diffuse an extremely pungent odour." It is frequently found growing close to the edge of perpetual snows.

Sophora secundiflora. Mescal bean. Frijolito. Texas mountain laurel. Found in Texas and Mexico. Bears long honey-scented racemes of violet-blue flowers that are attractive to bees.

Sphacele calycina. Pitcher sage. A strongly aromatic low shrub that grows on dry hills in Central California.

Stachys chamissonis. A strongly odorous plant found in damp places in Coastal Central and Northern California. *S. bullata,* the wood mint, is considered a troublesome weed in parts of California and Oregon, but the slender straight little plant, with its whorls of rosy-lipped flowers, is pleasing to the eye of the casual wanderer afield, and the soft wrinkled leaves give off a spicy fragrance when bruised.

Stenanthium gramineum var. *robustum* [*S. robustum*]. Feather fleece. A tall perennial plant of the Alleghenies and the Highlands of North Carolina, bearing in the late summer panicles of fleecy greenish white blooms that look crisp and cool in the summer motley, and have a pleasant fragrance. It is good for garden cultivation.

Strombocarpa odorata. Screwbean. Tornillo. A spreading spiny shrub or small tree native in the Southwest, with fragrant greenish flowers in spikes followed by long pods.

Styrax grandifolium. A shrub or small tree found from Virginia to Florida, bearing white fragrant flowers in loose racemes. They have somewhat the appearance of orange blossoms and more than a slight whiff is said to be an embarrassment of sweetness. *S. officinale* var. *californicum* called snowdrop bush, grows on dry foothills throughout California. The blossoms are sweet scented.

Symplocos tinctoria. Sweet leaf. Horse sugar. This is a small tree whose leaves in the South persist through the winter. The flowers are yellow and very fragrant in clusters, and appear very early in the spring. The leaves, as the common name implies, are sweet to the taste. Its range is through Florida to Louisiana, and as far north as Delaware.

Tanacetum parthenium [*Chrysanthemum parthenium*]. Feverfew. Featherfew. A plant not unlike the chamomile, but erect instead of procumbent and with larger flowers. The whole plant has a strong bitter odour and bees are said to particularly dislike it. It was at one time important in domestic medicine. A double form is sometimes found in old gardens. Naturalized from Eurasia.

Thalictrum dasycarpum. A meadow rue found from New Jersey to Saskatchewan and southwestwards. The mature fruits were used as a perfume by the Indians, who broke them off and scattered them among their clothing. Dampness enhanced the effect. "This, like all other perfumes used by the Indians, is of slight evanescent quality; they used no heavy scents." *T. revolutum,* common in rocky upland woods in the Eastern States, emits a heavy odour.

Thlaspi arvense [*Galinsoga parvilsora*]. French weed.

This is an annual weed imported from Peru and now widely naturalized in all parts of North America. It is found in door yards, along waysides, and in waste places, a lowly pestiferous thing with mean blossoms of minute size. In the autumn it becomes important to bee keepers for it suddenly gives off an alluring odour, rather spicy, like allspice, or the smell of sweet preserves being cooked, especially in very dry weather. Then its existence is justified for the bees swarm upon it for a few days.

Thlaspi glaucum. Wild candytuft. Pennycress. An inconspicuous plant of moist mountain slopes in the Northwest with heads of small white flowers in clusters that are slightly sweet scented.

Thuja occidentalis. American arbor vitae. If you pass along an arbor vitae hedge when the sun is shining hot upon it you will be amazed at the rich fragrance that arises from it, something like that of wild strawberries with a hint of resin. *T. plicata* of the far West is also very fragrant.

Torreya taxifolia. Stinking cedar. An evergreen tree native in Florida of fetid odour when bruised.

Trichostema lanatum. Wooly blue curls. California romero. A pretty shrubby plant that grows on dry hills of the Northwest with blue flowers and aromatic leaves. It is used medicinally by the Spanish Californians and is an important bee plant. *T. Lanceolatum.* Turpentine camphor weed, is a weedy plant of low dry hills throughout California. The whole plant is unpleasantly strong-scented.

Trifolium pratense. Red clover. This is the common red clover of our summer meadows so beloved by bees. As a child I thought the scent of this and of the white clover, *T. repens,* the best of all perfumes, and would carry a thick wad of the soft blossoms done up in a none too clean handkerchief to regale me as I went about childhood's engrossing affairs. Both were originally introduced from Europe but are extensively cultivated and have become permanent wanderers along our roadsides.

Trillium ovatum. The wood lily of California and the Northwest has a very pleasant fragrance and *T. sessile* var. *giganteum* is faintly scented. This species belongs to wooded hillsides of Coastal, Central and Northern California and Oregon.

Triteleia grandiflora (Brodiaea douglasii). Indian hyacinth. A charming bulbous spring and summer flowering plant of the Northwest. The flower stalk sometimes reaches a height of two feet and bears at the top a loose cluster of hyacinthlike bells. They are delicately scented.

Tsuga canadensis. Eastern hemlock. When the sun shines hot upon this most noble of our evergreen trees it gives off a peculiar and almost flowery odour. A hemlock hedge in the garden insures pleasant odours the year round. A tea made from the leaves and boughs was once famed for producing perspiration. A volatile oil is produced from the bark.

Ulmus rubra [U. fulva]. Slippery elm. A small tree abundant in various parts of the country. It is characterized by rough branches, unevenly toothed leaves, hairy on the undersides. The inner bark has medicinal value and is official in the United States Pharmacopoeia. It has the odour of fenugreek. Country children like the mawkish taste and enjoy chewing it.

Utricularia cornuta. Horned bladderwort. This lowly plant, which John Burroughs says is perhaps the most fragrant of our wild flowers, is found in peat bogs. On a slender pedicel it bears from two to four bright yellow flowers which have a helmet shaped lower lip and long curved spur. It may be found from Newfoundland to Florida, flowering from June to August, according to locality.

Smilacina racemosa [*Vagnera amplexicaulis*]. Wild spikenard. A graceful plant common in moist rich woods, growing from one to three feet tall, the slender leafy curving stalk tipped with a cluster of lightly scented cream-white flowers.

Valeriana sitchensis. Wild valerian. A delightful plant much like the familiar garden heliotrope, with heads of strongly sweet scented, pinkish white flowers. It belongs to Washington and Oregon. *V. arizonica* is considerably dwarfer in stature and bears small pretty clusters of fragrant lilac-pink flowers. It grows in crevices in the rocks in moist places and blossoms in spring. *V. septentrionalis.* Northern heliotrope. The flowers of this species are white and exceedingly sweet scented. They are borne in large clusters on the top of succulent stalks nearly two feet tall. The roots of all valerians have a strong and extremely offensive odour.

Venegasia carpensioides. This large leafy plant with its green-gold flowers is a handsome feature in the California woods and mountains in June, but unfortunately the whole plant has a most objectionable odour.

Viola blanda. Our little native sweet white violet or wildenow violet, which we find in low places in many parts of the East, is delicately but definitely scented. *V. canadensis,* the Canada violet, has a faint lemonlike odour and its leaves are faintly sweet scented when crushed.

Vitis. Grape. "The vine flower's scent impalpable and sweet" is one of the most precious perfumes of the year, though it is surprising to find Thoreau writing in his diary on June 19, "The grape is in bloom, an agreeable perfume to many; not to me." The flowers of the vine are tiny, wholly unnoticeable, yet as you walk or ride along the early summer roads, especially at night, you are suddenly enveloped, caught up so to speak, among tendrils of exquisite fragrance, indescribably gentle yet searching. It searches out old memories, old scenes, old loves, and brings them before you without warning, between two breaths, sometimes with cruel clarity. Someone has called the box the most memory stirring of all fragrances, but to us, in this country, I think it is the scent of the vine that has power to disarm us and leave us unprotected before memory's shrewd attack. Often old walls along country roadsides are draped with the beautiful foliage of the vine, and the cedars and low trees are festooned with it. This is usually *Vitis riparia* (*V. vulpina*), known as the river-bank grape, found from Nova Scotia to Manitoba and south to Tennessee and Texas. *V. cordifolia,* the frost or chicken grape, a very tall climber, has also highly scented blossoms. It is found from Pennsylvania to Florida, Kansas and Texas. The Western species, *V. californica,* is also very fragrant when in bloom. And there are doubtless others.

Whipplea modesta. Modesty. Yerba de selva. A woody little trailing plant found in Coast Range forests and moist Redwood canyons. The branches are clothed with slightly hairy leaves and the clusters of white flowers have a honeylike fragrance.

Wisteria frutescens. American wisteria. A vigorous scrambling climber found climbing over high trees, festooning them with a deep lilac fragrant fringe at their time of blossoming. It is one of our most beautiful native vines, found growing from Florida to Virginia and westward, but it is perfectly hardy at least as far north as Northern New York.

Wizlizenia refracta. Jackass clover. Stinkweed. A rank-smelling annual plant with yellow flowers, growing sometimes as high as six feet. It is an important honey plant in the interior valleys of California, where it is said to bloom only every other year.

Wyethia mollis. Indian wheat. A coarse plant abundant in the Sierras, growing in open woods, with woolly leaves and small yellow "sunflowers." F"It has a strong odour and gives a characteristic smell to the region where it grows." It is called indian wheat because the Indians gather the seeds and grind them into flour.

Xerophyllum tenax. Squaw grass. Elk grass. Bear grass. Indian basket grass. Spectacular plant of the district about Mount Rainier, growing three to six feet tall, with strong leafy stems springing from a large tuft of wiry grasslike leaves. The great flower cluster, borne at the top of the stem, is a foot in length and is composed of hundreds of fragrant white flowers, each about a half inch across, closely crowded together. It is said that this plant blossoms only every five or seven years and then dies.

Yucca whipplei [*Hesperoyucca whipplei*]. Our Lord's candle. A handsome plant from the warmer sections of California with a woody caudex and large rosette of narrow leaves from which arises the scape, twelve feet high, hung with nodding creamy fragrant flowers.

Ximenia americana. Hog plum. Tallow wood. A small thorny shrub common in many places in Florida, especially in dry soil along the coast. The flowers are yellow and very sweet scented and are followed by an edible yellow drupe.

Yucca. Many yuccas have sweet scented flowers, especially towards evening, and some are rather unpleasantly scented. Among the latter is the grotesque tree yucca, *Y. brevifolia,* called on the desert mesas where it towers, joshua tree. Its flowers appear from March to May, but are not attractive because of their soiled whitish colour & disagreeable fetid odour. Among the fragrant species is *Y. aloifolia,* Spanish bayonet, dagger plant, a species found on the sand dunes of the Southern Atlantic States, and also on the banks of the St. Johns River. The blossoms are white, slightly tinged with purple.

Zanthoxylum americanum. Prickly ash. A shrub or small tree, growing finally to a height of twenty-five feet, beset with thorns and bearing small polygamous creamy flowers in panicles, and leaves that are exceedingly sweet scented. Planted as a hedge it makes an impenetrable barrier, even against small animals. Perfectly hardy. The young men of the Omaha used the fruits of this shrub as a perfume.

Zephyranthes drummondii [*Cooperia drummondii*]. Rain or prairie lily. A pretty little night-blooming plant of the amaryllis family, native in Texas and Mexico. It has narrow leaves about a foot long and white starry fragrant blossoms on slender stalks during the summer months.

Zizia cordata. Alexanders. Meadow parsnip. An attractive and showy plant spoiled by its offensive odour. It is found in wet meadows and open woods over a large portion of the country, west and east. The minute flowers are carried in a bright golden umbel and the leaves are a lovely shining green.

ORCHIDS

Calypso bulbosa [*C. borealis*]. The exquisite little orchid whose name literally translated means nymph of the north (for the flower was dedicated to the goddess Calypso) is found only in cold mountain shades, and then not often, though it is commoner in the far West, in Oregon, than in our Eastern woods. "The sunset would need to stock a painter's palette if he would represent the little blossom as it hangs from its jointed stalk some six inches above the ground. The flowers are purple, varied with pink and shading to yellow. Deep purple lines accentuate the colour in the crimson petals and a brush of yellow woolly hairs bristles up under the column on the two-pointed yellowish tip of the shoelike pouch." Mr. St. John writes me, "I have found it but once, among the mosses close beside Bierstadt Lake, but I have kept for fourteen years a vivid memory of its fragrance."

Cypripedium acaule. The lovely pink moccasin flower of our pine and oak woods is fragrant in its own way. Mr. Edward St. John of Conway, N. H., writes me this: "The odour is slightly spicy and very musky, somewhat like the smell of the roots when one handles the plants. It differs from the ordinary flower scents as does that of the witch hazel, which seems to me like a sublimation of the odour of the mouldering leaves of autumn." *C. arietinum,* the ram's head orchid, the rarest of our native cypripediums, is a small species found growing shyly in cold damp woods of New England, New York and Minnesota, beneath pines and cedars. The plant grows only a few inches high and bears a single fragrant blossom, a curious green-brown in colour. *C. calceolus* var. *parviflorum* [*C. parviflorum*], the yellow moccasin flower, has fragrant flowers. Other Cypripediums that should be mentioned here are the lovely white *C. candidum, C. montanum* and *C. passerinum,* a Canadian species.

Epipactis gigantea [*Serapias gigantea*]. Stream orchid. Chatter box. An interesting member of this ever intriguing clan, growing from one to four feet tall, found along streams and in wet places in the West and in Colorado and Texas, blossoming in summer. The handsome pinkish and reddish pouched flowers have a light sweet scent.

Habenaria albida. The Newfoundland orchid is found along the Straits of Belle Isle. The plants stand from six to nine inches tall and bear a crowded cylindrical spike of creamy flowers that smell strongly of vanilla. *H. dilatata,* the tall leafy white orchid, is found in temperate and sub-Arctic America in moist meadows, bogs and woods. She is "one of the most stately children of the forest and her velvety spike, springing out of rank sedges and ferns, catches the eye at once, or where the plant grows profusely so perfumes the air as to need no other sign of its presence." It is thought to have the finest fragrance of any orchid, "a blending of *Syringa* and clove pinks." *H. blephariglottis,* the white fringed orchid, is perhaps the loveliest of the orchids and its charms are augmented by a delightful fragrance. Its choice of a home is in cool sphagnum swamps. *H. psycodes,* the small purple fringed orchid blooms earlier than its taller sister flower, the large purple fringed orchid, or plume royal, *H. fimbriata.* The fragrance of both is spicy, that of the latter especially so and towards night carrying to a considerable distance. *H. unalascensis,* the Alaska orchid, has small greenish white flowers that give off an unpleasant smell of pollen. *H. leucophaea,* the beautiful and conspicuous prairie orchid bears large white or greenish flowers that are very sweet scented. *H. elegans,* found in the woods of the Coastal Ranges is another fragrant kind.

Limnorchis fragrans. Fragrant bog orchid. This pretty little orchid is found in more or less shaded bogs throughout the Rockies, flowering in July. The pure white blossoms are borne along a little spike and are gifted with a spicy scent. *L. lceucostachys (Habenaria).* Lovely member of the orchid tribe with leafy stalks, sometimes three feet tall, finished with a spike of delicate white blossoms that are very finely scented. This is the sierra rein orchid, found in damp mountain meadows.

Orchis spectabilis. Showy orchid. A charming orchid that makes an early appearance in the spring woods. The flowers are purplish pink and very fragrant. New York to Georgia and westward.

Pogonia ophioglossoides. Rose pogonia. This lovely wild flower is known to many persons who fare afield in summer days. It is a grasslike plant with brightly coloured flowers that flutter like butterflies above the surrounding grasses. When fresh these flowers smell like ripe red raspberries but as they wither the odour becomes vaguely disagreeable. Found in sphagnum swamps. *P. trianthophora,* the nodding pogonia, or three birds, is a fragile form of the above with delicate faint rose-coloured nodding flowers, slightly fragrant and carried on a weak stem, usually three to the stem which accounts for its quaint name of three birds. Flowers in the late summer.

Spiranthes cernua. Nodding lady's tresses. A quaint little orchid found in grassy places through the Northern States with waxen flowers along a little spike, white and fragrant. *S. odorata,* the fragrant lady's tresses, has spikes of very sweet scented creamy flowers. This is a Southern species found from Maryland southwards to the Gulf States. It is the largest of all the lady's tresses. *S. romanzoffiana,* a Northern species, found from Newfoundland to Alaska and in Oregon in swampy places, has flowers much like the foregoing, scented of almonds. It is the last orchid of the season.

CHAPTER XX

Fragrant Miscellany

The gift of perfume to a flower is a special grace like genius or like beauty, and never becomes common or cheap.

— JOHN BURROUGHS

Abelmoschus moschatus [*Hibiscus abelmoschus*]. Musk mallow. Annual or biennial growing six feet tall, with large lobed leaves and yellow flowers, with a crimson center four inches across. The seeds have a musky odour and are sometimes used in perfumery. Native in India.

Abobra tenuifolia (*A. viridiflora*). Cranberry gourd. Tuberous-rooted herbaceous climber belonging to South America, with dark green, shining foliage and small green fragrant flowers, followed by bright little oval scarlet fruits. Grown under glass in the North for the sake of its gay fruits. In its native land it is a rapid grower much used for covering trellises and arbours.

Achillea erba-rota ssp. *moschata* [*A. moschata*]. This is a small plant found in the Swiss Alps at rather high elevations. The flowers yield an essential oil of musklike quality that is used to perfume and flavour the liqueur known in Switzerland as Iva. *A. odorata* is a dwarf plant with woolly, warm-scented leaves. The leaves of nearly all plants from the genus *Achillea* have a pleasant rough scent, among them *A. erba-rota* [*A. herba-rota*], *A. macrophylla*, *A. nana* and *A. erba-rota* ssp. *rupestris* [*A. rupestris*].

Aciphylla squarrosa. A New Zealand plant yielding a semi-transparent resinous gum, which affords the most prized scent used by the Maoris. A Maori lullaby has been thus translated:

> My little neck sachet of sweet-scented moss, / My little neck sachet of fragrant fern, / My little neck sachet of odoriferous gum, / My sweet smelling neck locket of sharp-pointed tamarea.

"The gum of the tamarea was collected at early dawn, and with it were mixed the fronds of the moki-moki (the fern *Doodia caudata*) and of

piri-piri (certain species of *Hepaticae*), the oil of miro *Prumnopitys ferruginea* [*Podocarpus ferrugineus*] and the flowers of pa-totara (species of *Leucopogon* and *Gaultheria*). The mixture was subjected to heat for some days, then strained through a sieve made of the plumes of the toe-toe *Chionochloa conspicua* [*Arundo conspicua*]. It was afterwards placed in carved boxes, where the mats of the chiefs were kept, or was used as a sachet by girls in the way described in the poem."[1]

Acokanthera. Bushman's poison. Poison bush. Poison tree. Shrubs or small trees with poisonous properties, native in Africa. Scarlet scented lilylike flowers. From the large bulbs of this plant the Bushmen of South Africa express a very poisonous juice. Sometimes grown under glass for the sake of their handsome white or pink fragrant flowers. *A. oblongifolia* [*A. spectabilis*], the winter sweet, grows eight to ten feet tall and bears clusters of starry white flowers that have the perfume of jasmine.

Acrocomia mexicana. Coyoli palm. A species of feather-palm with a thick trunk ten to fourteen feet high, with long prickles and yellow fragrant flowers. Mexico and Guatemala.

Adenandra fragrans. Breath of heaven. Small shrub native of the Cape of Good Hope, bearing rosy fragrant flowers. It is a favourite plant in California.

Ageratina ligustrina [*Eupatorium weinmannianum*]. An autumn flowering shrub useful in mild localities, free-flowering, growing from six to ten feet tall, and nearly covering itself with fragrant white flowers succeeded by fluffy seed-vessels which are decorative for several weeks. It makes an effective greenhouseplant. Mexico to Central America.

[1] *"Plants of New Zealand," Laing and Blackwell.*

Ajuga chamaepitys. Yellow bugle. A low plant common in many parts of Europe, the Levant and North Africa, as well as in certain parts of Britain. The whole plant is hairy and has a strong pungent odour, something like that of turpentine.

Albizia julibrissin. Silk tree. A small tree growing from thirty to forty feet high, bearing pink, very fragrant flowers crowded in heads at the ends of the branches, followed by long pods. It may be grown as far north as Washington. *A. lophantha* belongs to Australia and is there called the plume acacia. The flowers are yellow. It blooms in May. Nicholson mentions it as a good greenhouse species.

Albuca nelsonii. A bulbous plant related to *Galtonia,* native of Natal suitable to grow in a cool greenhouse. The flowers are white, tinted with red on the outer sides and borne in a spike. Very fragrant of almonds.

Allamanda cathartica 'Nobilis'. A strong tall growing climber native in Brazil with clear yellow flowers that give out a magnolia-like fragrance.

Allium. Numerous members of the onion tribe have sweet scented flowers and if we do not bruise the stem the characteristic and objectionable odour is not released. *A. carinatum,* a European species growing two feet tall and bearing rose-coloured flowers in drooping umbels, has an agreeable fragrance as also have *A. ramosun* [*A. odorum*] of Siberia and *A. naocissitolium.* The author of "Odorographia" thinks there must be some connecting link between the apparently antipathetic odours of violet and onion. A number of plants that have normally a sweet odour of violets, curiously enough smell strongly of onions when crushed. Cassia flowers that smell of violets make the breath smell of garlic, and the lily of Buenos Aires is exquisitely scented of violets but when crushed is rank of onions. In my garden is an unidentified *Allium* (it may be *A. denudatum* [*A. albidum*]) with heads of white flowers that smell like violets until you press them against the nose, then the onion odour is only too apparent.

Alocasia odora. A noble Asiatic herbiferous plant of the arum tribe bearing greenish yellow flowers said to have the fragrance of mignonette.

Alpinia. Perennial herbs grown for their ornamental foliage and frequently bright flowers. *A. officinarum.* Galingale. In Russia the root of this species was used at one time to flavour a popular liqueur called Nastoika, and in India it was added to the Bazar Spirit to make it more intoxicating. The flower is white with deep red veins. *A. nutans* (*A. speciosa*) shell flower. This is a tall Asiatic species with fragrant pink and yellow orchidlike flowers. In the East the gingerlike roots of several species are used as a perfume.

Alseuosmia macrophylla. New Zealand honeysuckle. A tender shrub bearing fragrant flowers in axillary clusters, white streaked with red, followed by a purple many-seeded berry.

Alstroemeria. Peruvian lily. A large genus of plants native of tropical South America, with thickish roots from which arise leafy stems bearing clusters of richly coloured flowers. Some species are hardy as far north as Massachusetts in very sheltered locations, as against a south-facing wall. *A. caryophyllaea.* A low Brazilian species bearing sweetly scented scarlet flowers in February. It is not hardy North. According to Donald McDonald, it bears white and scarlet flowers that smell strongly of mignonette.

Alyxia olivaeformis. Maile. Somewhat twining shrub with shining evergreen leaves and yellowish very fragrant flowers. It is a native of Hawaii, where it is much prized for use in garlands. *A. buxifolia* is the scentwood, an evergreen shrubby tree, native of Australia. The flowers are pale in colour and have the scent of jasmine.

X *Amarcrinum memoria-corsii* [*A. howardii*]. A hybrid between *Amaryllis* and *Crinum.* The flowers are pink and somewhat fragrant. Blooms in California in summer and autumn and is also suitable for pot culture.

Amaryllis belladonna. Not many of the stiff and gorgeous members of this lily-like race add sweetness to their somewhat flamboyant charms. The belladonna lily of the West Indies, however, has a fine fragrance, something like that of ripe apricots. It blooms in summer before the foliage appears.

Amomum compactum [*A. cardamon*]. A decorative foliage plant with thick leathery leaves, native of the East Indies. When crushed the leaves give out a pleasing gingery odour.

Amomyrtus luma [*Eugenia apiculata*]. A Chilean evergreen shrub with white, deliciously fragrant flowers.

Anacardium occidentale. Cashew. A large spreading tree native in the American tropics and grown to some extent in the southernmost part of Florida. Produces the popular cashew nuts. The panicles of rosy blossoms are very fragrant.

Andira inermis. Angelin tree. A tall tree native in tropical Africa, bearing fragrant pea-shaped purple flowers followed by drupe-like pods.

Anredera cordifolia [*Boussingaultia baselloides*]. Madeira vine. Mignonette vine. Perennial tuberous-rooted climber from tropical America, grown out of doors in mild climate and under glass in cold regions. Tall vigorous twiner with small white hawthorn-scented flowers.

Angelica archangelica. A stately biennial umbelliferous plant growing six feet tall, native of Northern Europe. The whole plant is pleasantly aromatic with a mild musky scent and it was at one time in great demand for its leaf stalks which were blanched and eaten like celery. The stems today are candied and used as a decoration on sweets and in cakes. The essential oil, that is distilled chiefly from the seeds, is used as a flavouring in certain liqueurs and in perfumery. "Angelica is peculiar in its distribution, for almost alone among scented plants, it is a northerner and reaches up to the Arctic Circle and beyond."

Angelonia salicariifolia 'Grandiflora' [*A. grandiflora*]. A small herbaceous tropical plant with sticky leaves and spikes of blue flowers that have the odour of pineapple. Pernambuco.

Anisotome latifolia. Aromatic shrubby plant from New Zealand with thick leathery leaves and small white or red flowers in umbels.

Annona purpurea. Cabeza de negro. A small tropical tree that bears a curious fruit having pyramidal protuberances, the flesh of which is edible and very fragrant. Mexico and Panama. *A. glabra,* pond apple. alligator Apple. Corkwood. Medium sized tree with fragrant flowers followed by an apple-like fruit that is not edible. Everglades of Florida. West Indies and Galapagos.

Aponogeton distachyus. Cape pondweed. Water hawthorn. Cape of Good Hope. An interesting and attractive aquatic often cultivated in tanks in greenhouses and in mild climates out of doors. The lance-shaped leaves lie flat upon the water and among them appear in summer and autumn spikes of delicate fragrant white waxen flowers, whose odour is much like that of hawthorn. "In its native habitat it appears almost spontaneously at certain seasons when the heavy rains collect in shallow places and here it blooms profusely, filling the air with a dainty fragrance. With the return of the drought it dies away as quickly as it came."

Ardisia crenulata. A compact and neat shrub with long wavy leaves and sweet scented flowers, followed by coral-scarlet berries. It is in much demand as a Christmas plant. East Indies and China.

Areca. A graceful and well known group of spineless palms, native in the Asiatic and Australian tropics. The male flowers are white and sweet scented.

Argyreia [*Lettsomia bona-nox*]. The odour of cloves is strongly developed in the flowers of certain plants. This is notably so of the clove-scented bindweed, a twining vine of the forests of Bengal, that bears large white flowers expanding at night and perfuming the air to a considerable distance with the odour of the finest cloves.

Aristolochia odoratissima. A sweet scented climber of Jamaica and Central America, with purple flowers.

Arnica. Composites with large yellow flowers and leaves that are somewhat glandular and aromatic. The best known is the handsome *A. montana.*

Artemisia. A large genus of mostly hardy perennial herbs or small shrubs usually having an aromatic or bitter scent and feathery or much dissected foliage. They are found in both the Old and the New Worlds and are grown for ornaments as well as for medicinal purposes. Among them are some common weeds. *Artemisia dracunculus,* tarragon, is well known. The taste has been described by an early writer as "not unpleasant which is somewhat austere with the sweetness." It is from wormwood, *Artemisia absinthium,* that absinthe is made. This is an attractive species to grow in the garden but the leaves have a bitter and somewhat acrid smell. *A. alba* [*A. camphorata*], a shrubby species growing about two feet tall, has camphor scented leaves. It belongs to Southern Europe. *A. pontica,* Roman wormwood, has an especially delicate and pleasing aroma. And besides these are *A. pedemontana, A. chamaelelifolia, A. eriantha, A. gallica, A. glacialis, A. granatensis, A. umbelliformis* [*A. mutellina*], *A. nitida, A. roezli, A. genipi* [*A. spicata*].

Arum palaestinum (*A. sanctum*). Black calla. A liliaceous plant native of Palestine. "In spring it produced one large sweet scented flower rising on a vigorous stalk, brown red at the lower part and green at the top, giving the whole plant a stately and elegant appearance."

Ascarina lucida. Aromatic shrub or small tree native in New Zealand, with aromatic leaves and minute unisexual flowers. Sometimes grown in California.

Asphodelus luteus [*Asphodeline lutea*]. Jacob's-rod. A herbaceous plant native in Southern Europe, growing four feet tall, its stems covered with light green awl-shaped leaves. The highly fragrant yellow flowers are borne in summer in a long dense raceme, each blossom springing from the axil of a buff-coloured bract. There is a very pretty double-flowered variety. The plants from this genus are good for the border.

Astelia. A noticeable genus of New Zealand herbs with swordlike leaves and spreading panicles of sweet creamy or purplish blossoms.

Aster linosyris [*Linosyris vulgaris*]. Goldilocks. Old World plant flowering in late autumn in heads or corymbs of soft yellow blossoms. When slightly bruised a pleasant spicy odour is given forth. In Parkinson's day it was "laid in chests and wardrobes to preserve vestments from moths."

Astrantia major. Masterwort. A perennial plant growing three feet tall with deeply lobed leaves and heads of pinkish flowers in umbels. To be seen at its best it should be grown in broad masses in semi-wild places when it reveals a quiet beauty and sends off a scent like honey. It flowers in summer.

Averrhoa. Evergreen trees with alternate pinnate leaves and small fragrant yellow flowers. *A. bilimbi,* growing fifty feet high, is known only in cultivation. *A. carambola* is native in Malaysian regions and is rather widespread in the tropics. The fruit is an edible fleshy berry. *A. nitida* is the honey mangrove tree of tropical America.

Babiana. A genus of bulbous-rooted plants from South Africa producing brilliant flowers, many of which possess scented attractions. Donald McDonald gives the following: *B. disticha*] with pale purple flowers smelling like hyacinth; *B. plicata,* light violet with a scent resembling the clove carnation; *B. sambucina,* purple flowers that are elder-scented, and *B. angustifolia* with blue flowers slightly fragrant. The plants from this genus are sometimes grown in pots under glass, or out of doors in warm climates.

Backhousia citriodora. Queensland myrtle. An Australian shrub with foliage strongly lemon-scented.

Ballota. Hairy herbs of the Old World belonging to Labiatae. *B. foetida* is very ill-scented, and *B. nigra,* black hoarhound, has also a rank unpleasant smell.

Barosma. A genus of small evergreen shrubs with

aromatic leathery leaves, native of the Cape of Good Hope. The highly aromatic leaves are used by the Hottentots to perfume themselves with.

Bauhinia corymbosa. A climbing plant of Eastern Asia bearing pinkish fragrant fluted flowers in loose racemes.

Beaumontia grandiflora. Herald's trumpet. A magnificent plant from the Himalayas with large trumpet-shaped white flowers that are lily scented. Grown in greenhouses. A tall climber. *B. fragrans* from Cochin China is an evergreen shrub with sweet scented, white, shallow, bell-shaped flowers.

Begonia picta. A low growing species with large curiously spotted leaves and hairy stalks. The flowers are large and light pink and have a sweet scent. *B. suaveolens* is another scented species. *B. minor* [*B. nitida*] of Jamaica has clusters of pink or rose fragrant flowers. *B. odorata* is a variety of the above. *B. nancy* is highly scented. *B. fulgens* is a handsome species of Bolivia with bright rose-red fragrant flowers, and there are doubtless other sweet scented begonias.

Betula pubescens [*B. alba*]. White birch. The agreeable odour of so-called Russia leather is due to the employment in the dressing of the leather of an oil made from the bark of the white birch.

Bouvardia. Shrubs native to Mexico and Central America, with opposite whorled leaves and terminal cymes of tubular flowers that have the delicious scent of jasmine. Grown in greenhouses and much used by florists in winter bouquets. The flowers range in colour from pure white to bright scarlet. First introduced to cultivation by Baron Humboldt, for whom one species is named.

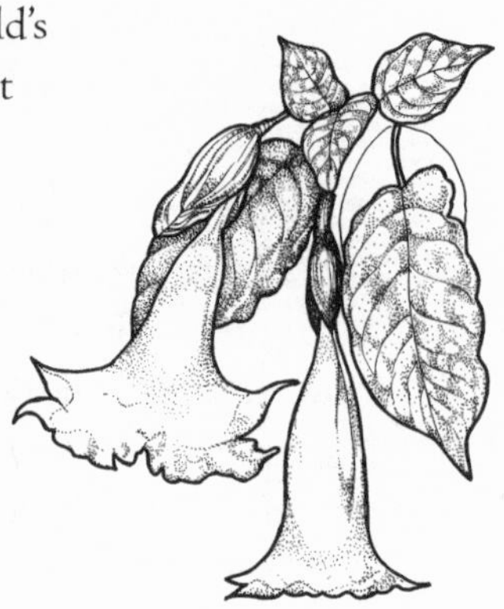

ANGEL'S TRUMPET
(*Brugmansia arborea*)

Brugmansia suaveolens (*Datura*). A beautiful shrubby tree from Brazil bearing many white trumpet flowers that give out a rich scent, especially toward night. Cultivated in greenhouses.

Brunfelsia americana. Lady of the night. A tall shrub native in the West Indies, bearing white flowers fading to yellow that are very fragrant at night. Sometimes grown in conservatories or greenhouses.

Brunsvigia. Plants of the *Amaryllis* tribe, native in South Africa whose funnel-like flowers are said to be powerfully scented of orange.

Bulbine suavis. A half hardy South African plant with yellow flowers arranged in a long raceme. They are said to smell like mignonette.

Bursaria spinosa. Australian spiny shrub, or small tree, bearing small sweet scented white flowers in panicles in June.

Caesalpinia paniculata. A handsome tropical climber with dark glossy leaves and showy racemes of fragrant orange-coloured flowers. *C. coriaria,* the divi-divi of tropical America, is said to have paler flowers of a most delicious aromatic odour. *C. decapetala* [*C. sepiaria*] of India is also fragrant.

Calamintha nepeta ssp. *glandulosa* [*C. officinalis*]. Old World medicinal plant sometimes found in old gardens in this country. It has long ascending branches, one to three feet high and inconspicuous flowers in cymes. The foliage has an aromatic somewhat mintlike odour. *Acinos arvensis* [*Calaminth acinos*] is the basil thyme of Great Britain, an annual plant, very aromatic throughout, with purple flowers in summer. There are numerous other kinds all fragrant and all at some time esteemed for medicinal purposes.

Callisia fragrans [*Spironema fragrans*]. A Mexican perennial creeping herb with white fragrant flowers in dense headlike cymes. Sometimes grown in hanging baskets.

Callistemon. Bottle-brush. Australian shrubs belonging to the myrtle family. The leaves of some of them have a pleasant odour when bruised. A few of the species are suitable for cultivation in Southern California.

Calomeria amaranthoides [*Humea elegans*]. Amaranth feathers. A pretty half hardy biennial from Australia used for pots and bedding in this country. It grows five feet high and the long wrinkled leaves give off a delightful odour, something like that of Russia leather. The flowers are borne in gracefully drooping panicles and are ruby-red, rose coloured or pink.

Calophyllum calaba (*C. antilanum*). A West Indian tree growing ninety feet high that bears short racemes of sweet scented white flowers.

Campanula thyrsoides. Yellow bellflower. This yellow flowered European plant is one of the few members of the *Campanula* tribe that is fragrant. *C. lactiflora* has a pleasant warm scent also.

Camphorosma monspeliacum. Low hairy subshrub native in Southern Europe, with whitish flowers and leaves that smell of camphor.

Cananga odorata. Ilang-Ilang. The common name of the tree yielding the important oil of this name means "flower of flowers." It is a tree native in Malaysia, growing eighty feet tall and bearing handsome flowers in clusters of three or four, from the axils of the leaves. They are large, bell-shaped and pale or greenish yellow, drooping, and possess a most exquisite fragrance which has been compared to a mixture of hyacinth, narcissus and clove, and again to a mixture of jasmine and lilac.

Canthium parviflorum. A spiny Indian plant with white fragrant flowers and pungent leaves that are used in flavouring curries.

Capparis spinosa. Common caper. The unopened buds of the caper plant preserved in salt and vinegar provide the aromatic and spicy delicacy so indispensable to many sauces and salads.

Carduus nutans. Musk thistle. Annual plant found in waste land, fallow fields and barren pastures in Great Britain, where the soil is gravelly and somewhat calcareous. The drooping flowers borne in July are not ornamental but smell strongly of musk in warm weather.

Carica papaya. Papaya. Pawpaw. Tree twenty-five feet tall with deeply lobed leaves, bearing edible fruits. The flowers of the male trees are sweet scented. Tropical America.

Carissa. Spiny, much branched evergreen shrub of tropical countries, bearing pink or white fragrant flowers followed by showy edible fruits. Popular as hedge plants in hot countries. *C. carandas* belongs to India, *C. macrocarpa* [*C. grandiflora*], natal plum or amatungula, to South Africa.

Carmichaelia. Perhaps the most characteristic genus of New Zealand shrubs, with flattened or cylindrical branches and fragrant pea-shaped flowers. *C. arborea* [*C. australis*] grows from three to nine feet high and has small lilac flowers striped with deeper colour. *C. odorata* has pendulous branches with white or pale lilac, sweet scented flowers in drooping racemes.

Carpodetus serratus. Putputawheta. A curious flat-topped shrub or small tree of New Zealand, with veined and marbled leaves and small very fragrant white flowers borne in broad cymes, followed by black fruit about the size of a pea. Introduced to cultivation in California.

Carum carvi. Caraway. Annual or biennial with white flowers and leaves cut into fine segments. The seeds are used for flavouring. Native in Europe but naturalized in the United States. The unripe fruits have an exceedingly unpleasant odour so that it is necessary to wait until they are quite dry before harvesting them.

Cassia fistula. Golden shower. An Indian tree with drooping racemes of yellow flowers, not unlike those of the laburnum, appearing in spring before the leaves. "We are told by Alpinus, when he was in Egypt in the latter part of the sixteenth century, that the natives took great delight in walking early in the morning at certain seasons near plantations of this *cassia,* regaling themselves with the fragrance of its flowers."

Cassinia fulvida. A New Zealand shrub growing six feet high, with crowded leaves and white flowers in dense corymbs, that have a strong honey scent. Suitable for Southern gardens.

Cedrela odorata. West Indian or Spanish cedar. Cigar-box cedar. A tree belonging to the West Indies and tropical America, growing to a height of one hundred feet, the highly aromatic and coloured wood of which is used for cigar boxes. *Toona sinensis* [*C. toona*] is a tall tree, nearly evergreen, native in the Himalayas and planted in Southern Florida, that bears white flowers in fragrant panicles.

Cedrus libani. Cedar of Lebanon. Both the leaves and the wood are curiously but pleasantly scented.

Celsia cretica. Cretan mullein. A stout hairy biennial or annual plant, native of the Mediterranean region, with spikes of soft yellow flowers with maroon centers, that emit a fragrance said to be much sweeter than that of the common furze.

Cerinthe. Honeywort. Members of Boraginaceae and beloved of bees, which are said to obtain wax from the tubular, drooping flowers. *C. minor* is said to be especially sweet scented.

Cestrum. Shrubs and small trees grown in hot countries and under glass in northern latitudes. The flowers are tubular, red, yellow or greenish white and very fragrant. *C. aurantiacum* is a half climbing species from Guatemala, with panicles of orange-yellow flowers. *C. laurifolium* [*C. diurnum*], the day jasmine, is a shrub growing to fifteen feet, native in the West Indies. The fragrant white flowers are open during the day while *C. nocturnum,* the night jasmine, native in the same region, blooms and is scented only at night. *C. parqui* of Chile, the willow-leaved jasmine, a low shrub, also blooms and is fragrant at night. The flowers are greenish white and borne in full terminal clusters.

Chamaebatiaria millefolium. An aromatic alpine shrub with finely divided leaves and creamy flowers.

Chamaedorea fragrans. A tropical American palm with white flowers said to smell like 'Maréchal Niel' roses.

Chlidanthus fragrans. Allied to *Sternbergia.* Native in the Andes of Peru and not hardy save in mild localities. The yellow funnel-shaped flowers appear in late spring and have an agreeable perfume.

Chloranthus inconspicuous. A Chinese shrub with minute fragrant flowers that are employed, when dried, in scenting the more expensive teas.

Cinchona. Quinine. Sacred bark. Jesuit's bark. Evergreen forest trees and shrubs native in the Andes, the bark yielding quinine for which they are cultivated in tropical countries. The pink flowers are very fragrant.

Cineraria. The showy flowers of these popular greenhouse plants have an agreeable fragrance.

Cinnamomum. Evergreen aromatic trees and shrubs from Asia and Australia grown for ornament in warm climates as well as for the medicaments and spices yielded by the various species. *C. camphora* is the camphor tree of China and Japan that yields the commercial camphor. It thrives in Southern California and in the far Southern States where it is used as a street tree. *C. aromaticum* [*C. cassia*] is the cassia-bark tree, the bark of which is used as a substitute for cinnamon. True cinnamon is the bark of *C. zeylanicum,* native in India and Malaysia where it is widely distributed in the forests. It is a small tree with beautiful shining leaves, bearing panicles of greenish flowers that are said to have rather an unpleasant odour.

Cladanthus arabicus (*Anthemis arabica*). A strong smelling annual, native of Spain and Morocco, sometimes grown in flower gardens. Flowers yellow.

Clavija longifolia. A small tropical tree found in Trinidad and South America, with fragrant orange-coloured flowers in drooping racemes.

Clematis foetida. A New Zealand species that produces, in spite of its specific name, fragrant greenish flowers in long sprays.

Clusia odorata. A shrubby South American plant, one of the many called balsam tree, from its pleasant fragrance. Sometimes used as a stove evergreen. The pink flowers are fragrant.

Coffea arabica. Common or Arabian coffee. Shrub growing to fifteen feet with dark shining oval leaves and flat white fragrant flowers in clusters. Tropical Africa.

Coprosma x *cunninghamii* [*C. foetidissima*]. A common New Zealand shrub that forms dense thickets. When brushed against, it gives out an odour that is so fulsome and unpleasant as to be almost insupportable.

Cordyline australis (*Dracaena australis*). New Zealand cabbage tree, or palm lily. A tree growing to forty feet that forms one of the most striking features of the New Zealand bush. It bears white fragrant flowers, smelling of lily of the valley, in pointed spikes that are very attractive to bees. A preparation of the roots is eaten and from them also an intoxicating drink is made. The leaves are used in thatching.

Coronilla valentina ssp. *glauca* [*C. glauca*]. Shrub native in Southern Europe growing four feet tall and bearing clusters of fragrant yellow flowers. Sometimes grown under glass. *C. emerus,* the scorpion senna, growing taller than the foregoing, also has sweet scented yellow flowers. It is said to be hardy in the North.

Correa. Australian fuchsia. Australian shrubs with bell-shaped or tubular flowers that have a curious fragrance. Sometimes grown under glass.

Corypha umbraculifera. Talipot palm. Fan palm. Tall tree native in the East Indies, bearing handsome yellow blossoms "so powerfully scented that it is necessary to cut them away from near dwelling houses."

Cotoneaster multiflorus. An Asiatic member of this family, which unlike the majority of its relatives is more remarkable for its show of flowers than for its gay fruits, though these are handsome enough. It is a hardy shrub, growing ten feet high with "a thousand long and elegant whiplash branches wreathed from base to tip with the bold clusters of the white blossoms" which last in beauty for a long period. Unfortunately the odour of these blossoms is not wholly agreeable and has suggested to various noses the stink of frying fish or that of "sheepskins whose visit to the refinery has been delayed."

Crinum. Beautiful subtropical bulbous plants of Amaryllidaceae, many of which have fragrant flowers. Of these are *C. moorei, C. bracteatum* [*C. brevifolium*], *C. americanum, C. bulbispermum* [*C. longifolium*], *C. augustum* [*C. amabile*] (powerfully fragrant), *C. zeylanicum, C. amoenum.*

Croton eluteria. Cascarilla. Sweet bark. A small tree of the Bahamas, bearing very fragrant white flowers early in the spring. The bark is also highly scented and the oil extracted from it is used medicinally.

Cuminum cyminum. Cumin. An annual herb native in Mediterranean regions. It is an old-fashioned medicinal plant "which was in the Middle Ages one of the commonest spices of European growth." The plant grows a foot tall or less, with feathered foliage and small white or rose-coloured flowers in compound umbels. The odour resembles caraway but is more bitter.

Curcuma. A genus of robust herbaceous plants with tuberous roots, native in hot countries. *C. zedoaria* is found in Bengal and China. Native women make an important cosmetic from the fragrant tubers. The flowers are borne in the hot season and the plant is then highly ornamental and emits a delicate aromatic fragrance. *C. rubescens,* whose bright sweet scented flowers appear in April and May is also a native of Bengal. The whole plant gives off a pleasant aromatic odour when crushed.

Cyanella odoratissima. South African plant growing from a corm and bearing deep rose-coloured sweet scented blossoms.

Cybistetes longifolia [*Ammocharis falcata*]. A bulbous plant native of the Cape of Good Hope where it is found at high elevations. The narrow leaves appear in summer or autumn and attain a length of one to two feet. During the winter the fragrant bright red flowers make a spectacular appearance with twenty to forty in an umbel, carried on a scape about twelve inches long. Not hardy, but may be grown in pots in a greenhouse.

Cyclanthus bipartitus. Stemless milky-juiced herb resembling palms, the flowers of which are fragrant. Guyana.

Cyrtanthus mackenii. A South African bulbous plant requiring greenhouse treatment. "The flowers are pendulous in heads rather like a hyacinth but the individual flowers are very much longer and narrower." They are white and sweet scented.

Dalbergia latifolia. Indian rosewood. A tall deciduous tree of Indian forests, having scented wood and a profusion of fragrant white flowers, that fill the evening air with sweetness for a considerable distance from the tree. The wood has commercial value.

Daphniphyllum macropodum. China and Japan. Evergreen. A low shrub or tree with leaves like those of a rhododendron and small inconspicuous pale green flowers borne in the axils of the leaves that have a strong pungent scent.

Davidia involucrata. Dove tree. Western China. A pyramidal tree growing forty to sixty feet tall with strongly scented leaves.

Delphinium. It is said that the species of *Delphinium* generally give off a musky odour, if they are scented at all. This is true of *D. brunonianum, D. glaciale, D. moschatum,* all growing at very high altitudes in the mountains of Tibet. Stephen Hamblin speaks of a species, *Delphinium pictum* var. *miscodorum,* as possessing a strong musklike odour.

Detarium senegalense. Tallow tree. Dattock tree. tropical African trees with small fragrant petalless flowers borne in clusters. Grown in Florida for ornament.

Deutzia. The flowers of this genus are not commonly gifted with fragrance but *D. corymbosa,* a deciduous shrub from the Himalayas, growing six to eight feet tall, bears crowded corymbs of small white flowers in summer, that have the scent of hawthorn.

Dianthus. Additional sweet-scented species. *D. virgineus,* Western and Southern France and the Mediterranean region; *D. libanotis,* a species close to superbus and powerfully fragrant; *D. ciliatus,* Sicily, Egypt, etc.; *D. fruticosus* [*D. arboreus*], Greece and Macedonia; *D. serotinus,* near *plumarius,* Eastern Europe; *D. nitidus,* Carpathian Mountains of Macedonia; *D. petraeus,* Balkans, etc.

Dillenia indica. Chulta. A handsome evergreen tropical tree that loses its foliage in the dry season. The flowers are white with a mass of yellow stamens and are highly fragrant.

Dipelta floribunda. Chinese deciduous shrub related to *Diervilla* and bearing in May fragrant tubular pink flowers with yellow throats. Hardy in the North and thriving in any good soil.

Dipteryx odorata. The fragrant bean called tonka or tonquin bean is the product of this tree. Native in Cayenne, Martinique, etc. Used in snuff.

Discaria serratifolia. Spiny South American shrub, with drooping branches and sweet scented greenish white flowers.

Dombeya tiliacea [*D. natalensis*]. Shrub or small tree native in Natal with poplar-like leaves and sweet scented white flowers in umbels.

Dracaena fragrans. Handsome member of a tribe of subtropical plants commonly grown as greenhouse subjects. The species here mentioned bears sprays of finely scented yellowish flowers. Upper Guinea.

Dracocephalum moldavicum. Moldavian balm. An annual plant growing two feet tall, native in Europe and Northern Asia, remarkable chiefly for its aromatic leaves. Flowering blue or white in long leafy racemes. Summer.

Echites caryophyllata. A tropical climbing plant bearing white flowers that smell strongly of cloves.

Edgeworthia papyrifera. Paperbush. A small shrub with tough branches, from China and Japan. The fragrant flowers are clear yellow in rounded clusters at the ends of the shoots. Not hardy save in southern gardens. Flowers in late winter. *E. gardneri* from the Himalayas also bears sweet scented yellow flowers.

Ehretia acuminata. Kodd wood. Himalayas. Japan. A small deciduous tree of open spreading habit bearing white honey-scented flowers in terminal pyramidal clusters in August. Fairly hardy north.

Elettaria cardamomum. Cardamon. An Indian tree that produces the cardamon of commerce. The leaves have a highly aromatic odour and are used for scenting clothing and in bouquets. The seeds also are aromatic and are used to perfume the breath. The white flowers resemble orchids. A lovely tree.

Elsholtzia stauntonii. China. A semiwoody plant

that dies back in winter. The flowers are scentless but when crushed the leaves give forth a strong scent of mint.

Epacris pulchella. An Australian shrub grown in greenhouses, with pink tubular flowers that are sweet scented.

Epilobium hirsutum. Codlins and cream. A perennial herbaceous plant common in damp places in Great Britain. It is somewhat sticky to the touch, hairy, and has rather an acrid though agreeable odour, suggestive of apples – hence its common name. The magenta flowers appear in July.

Epiphyllum crenatum. A species of cactus, native in Honduras and Guatemala, bearing strongly fragrant cream coloured or greenish flowers.

Eremocitrus glauca. Australian desert kumquat. This small spiny tree bears very fragrant white flowers, solitary or two or three together in the axils of the leaves.

Eremurus. Desert candle. Magnificent members of the Liliaceae [Asphodelaceae] tribe some of which are sweet scented.

Erica arborea. Tree heath. Mediterranean regions and Caucasus. The tree heath is evergreen and of shrubby bushy habit, growing sometimes to a height of fifteen feet. The small delicately tinted flowers emit a most penetrating sweetness. *E. australis,* the Spanish heath, is one of the most beautiful of the species but unfortunately it is not very hardy. The flowers, borne in April and May, are pitcher-shaped and exceedingly fragrant, and they are said to wear a deeper rose colour than any other heath. It is a tall evergreen species. *E. odorata* is a small low heather with white tubular blossoms exhaling a scent that has been compared to that of honeysuckle. Other heathers with scented attractions are *E. lusitanica,* Spain and Portugal; *E. regerminans, E. melanthera* and *E.* × *veitchii.*

Eriocephalus. Kapok bush. A genus of aromatic South African composites. *E. africanus* has been introduced into California.

Erlangea tomentosa. An African shrub growing five feet high with lilac disc-flowers and scented leaves woolly on the undersides.

Erysimum cheiri [*Cheiranthus senoneri*]. A woody, much branched wall flower from Greece, with fragrant orange flowers. Most wall flowers are sweet in greater or lesser degree.

Eucalyptus. A genus of immense fast growing trees, native in Australia, called gum trees, because of the quantity of gum that exudes from their trunks. The thick leathery leaves give off balsamic odours supposed to increase the healthfulness of districts where they thrive. Some of the most fragrant species are *E. globulus,* the blue gum; *E. citriodora,* the lemon-scented gum; *E. bridgesiana* [*E. stuartiana*], the apple-scented gum, and *E. maculata,* the spotted gum.

Eucharis × *grandiflora.* The Amazon lily. Grown out of doors in warm countries or in greenhouses north. It is a beautiful bulbous plant of Amaryllidaceae, native in the Andes of Colombia. The white tubular flowers are very fragrant. There are several other species all possessing fragrant flowers.

Eucomis comosa [*E. punctata*]. Pineapple flower. Lily-like South African bulbous plants with large leaves and creamy or yellowish star-shaped fragrant flowers that appear in dense cylindrical trusses from July to September.

Euonymus europaeus. Spindle tree. A low tree forming part of the hedge-row tangle in Britain and naturalized in parts of this country near the coast. It is notable in September for its pinkish scarlet ear-droplike fruits which hang in profusion from the dark branches until late in the autumn, making the little tree a very gay spectacle indeed. The odour of the small greenish flowers, as of the leaves when crushed, is extremely disagreeable.

Evodia. A genus of mostly Chinese trees and shrubs, somewhat like sumacs, with aromatic leaves. *E. officinalis* is used by the Chinese to give a bitter tang to certain drinks.

Exacum affine. Pretty little biennial from Socotra sometimes grown for greenhouse decoration. The flowers are lavender-blue with bright yellow stamens and very fragrant.

Faramea odoratissima. A sweet scented greenhouse shrub, native in the West Indies, with white flowers. Allied to the coffee tree.

Ferula assa-foetida [*F. foetida*]. Asafoetida. Devil's dung. A coarse umbelliferous plant, growing often seven feet tall, and bearing greenish yellow flowers in umbles. The whole plant has an abominable odour. Afghanistan and Persia.

Ficus. Fig. The leaves of the fig tree have a delicious odour which they keep for years when dried. There was an old fig tree growing on an island in Chesapeake Bay from which I gathered a leaf when I was a child. The leaf was pressed between the pages of a small Testament and retains a strange haunting fragrance after all these years.

Foeniculum vulgare (*F. officinale*). Common fennel. A common plant in the south of Europe and according to Gray, a frequent escape from gardens in this country, often found naturalized in Maryland and Virginia. It has a stately beauty and might be put to good use in gardens, with its tall stems, delicately dissected leaves and wide umbels of yellow flowers. It was once in great requisition as a dressing for all sorts of sea food. Sweet fennel, *F. dulce,* called also Roman fennel, is considered a form of the above; it differs, however, in the plant being smaller throughout.

Franseria artemisioides. A tall ornamental plant, probably a biennial, from the Andes of Chile and Peru. The foliage has a pleasant aromatic odour.

Freesia refracta. Lovely South African plant growing from a bulblike corm and bearing deliciously fragrant white or pale yellow tubular flowers. There are many cultivars with exquisitely coloured blossoms, pink, rose, lavender, brownish, orange, with the same delightful fragrance. These are favourite winter-flowering greenhouse plants.

Furcraea foetida [*F. gigantea*]. Large succulent plant belonging to the Agavaceae. Brazil. The flower scape is ten feet high and bears an immense number of white flowers, greenish on the exterior and exhaling a perfume said to be much like that of the tuberose, though as its name indicates, it apparently does not always appeal as agreeable.

Galipea odoratissima. An evergreen tree native in South America with fragrant white flowers and odorous leaves. The angostura bark of commerce is produced from *G. trifoliata,* a tree of Guyana.

Galium triflorum. A pretty little bedstraw found over most of Northern Europe. The flowers are white and sweet with a delicate hay scent.

Gaultheria fragrantissima (*Arbutus laurifolia*). Indian wintergreen. A ramous shrub found in the hills of India, Burma and Sri Lanka, etc. The oil from the plant has an odour much like that of our native wintergreen, *G. procumbens.*

Geonoma pumila. Scented palm. A reedlike palm whose natural habitat is confined to the tropics of the Western Hemisphere, where it grows in dense forests. The young shoots are said to exude a perceptible odour of violets.

Geranium macrorrhizum. The leaves of many geraniums are odoriferous but those of this Southern European species are unusually warmly and pleasantly scented when bruised. The flowers that come in early June are undoubtedly magenta but the plant is handsome and good to have if only for the sake of the fragrant leaves.

Gethyllis. A genus of small bulbous plants from the Cape of Good Hope, allied to *Sternbergia.* The white flowers are deliciously fragrant.

Ginseng. Two species of woodland plants are known by this name and are valued for the same reputed medicinal properties by the Chinese. *Panax ginseng* is the Asiatic ginseng and *Aralia quinquefolium* is the American ginseng. The American species is exported in large quantities and brings a good price. Ginseng has a peculiar but rather pleasant smell with a slight degree of aromatic bitterness.

Gladiolus callianthus [*Acidanthera bicolor*]. Magpie gladiolus. Tender summerblooming plant belonging to the Iridaceae, intermediate between *Gladiolus* and *Ixia.* Slender stems furnished with stiff narrow leaves and white, sweet scented flowers with a dark center that are good for cutting. Eighteen inches. Tropical Africa.

Glaucium flavum. Yellow horned poppy. Beautiful seagreen plant, bearing in great profusion evanescent yellow flowers, shaped like corn poppies, found growing by the sea in Britain. Old writers claim that to eat of this plant causes madness. The scent of it when bruised is fetid.

Glycosmis pentaphylla. Small spineless evergreen shrub bearing white fragrant flowers in panicles. Native in India, Malaysia and the Philippines.

Guarea grandiflora. An evergreen tree native in French Guyana. The flowers are white or reddish, borne in elongated racemes and the tree in all its parts, but especially the bark, has a strong musklike perfume.

Gynoxis fragrans. A Central American climber with pale yellow scented flowers, used as a greenhouse evergreen.

Habranthus tubispathus [*Zephyranthes tubispatha*]. Pretty little bulbous plant from Jamaica, flowering in early summer. The frosted white "lilies" are delicately sweet scented.

Haematoxylum campeachianum. Logwood. Bloodwood tree. A charming graceful tree of the American tropics bearing bright yellow flowers that emit a strange but delicious and pervading fragrance. When approaching the Islands of the West Indies, if the wind is off shore, the fragrance of the logwood greets one far out at sea.

Hakea suaveolens. Australian evergreen shrub, ten feet tall, with needlelike leaves, bearing delicately sweet white flowers in sessile clusters.

Hebenstretia comosa. A perennial plant of South Africa, bearing in long spikes yellow flowers, blotched with orange. Very fragrant at night.

Hedychium. Ginger lily. Rather large genus of robust tropical herbs. The generic name means sweet snow, in reference to the fragrant white flowers. In warm countries they are grown out of doors and in the North are recommended for greenhouse culture. They require a great deal of water. The fragrance of the flowers is sweetest towards evening. *H. spicatum* is much valued by the Arabs and Persians as a perfume and is used by the Hindus as an incense in religious ceremonies. *H. coronarium* is found in various parts of Bengal and is cultivated for the sake of its large very fragrant white blossoms. The white sweet scented blossoms of *H. chrysoleucum* are blotched with orange.

Yellow-flowered *Hedychium* with fragrant flowers are *H. gardnerianum, H. flavum, H. flavescens* and *H. villosum.* The flowers of the last named delightful Indian species keep their fragrance even when dry. *H. gracile,* a Brazilian species, is used by the native women to perfume and decorate their hair.

Helichrysum fragrans. An evergreen shrub from South Africa with small pink agreeably scented flowers that have everlasting qualities. *Ozothamnus antennaria* [*H. antennaria*] is a rare shrub from Australia with white fragrant flowers.

Helleborus odorus. Scented hellebore. A sweetly scented species that bears its greenish blossoms throughout the winter in mild climates. It is found wild over the wooded regions of eastern Central Europe, usually on limestone formation. It should be given a sheltered and shady situation in rich loam of a calcareous nature.

Hermannia verticillata [*Mahernia verticillata*]. Honey bells. Straggly subshrub with much cut fragrant leaves. Native in Africa. Used in greenhouses in northern latitudes for the sake of the sweet leaves. The yellow flowers are also pleasantly fragrant.

Hemidesmus indica. Indian sarsaparilla. A slender climbing plant with a long rigid little-branched aromatic root, that has been used in India as a substitute for sarsaparilla. Its fragrance is not unlike that of new-mown hay.

Herreria sarsaparilla. A tuberous-rooted plant from Brazil, with climbing stems about eight feet long, and small scented yellow flowers in whorls.

Hesperantha. Evening flower. A genus of dwarf plants growing from corms, with narrow leaves and loose spikes of sweetly scented flowers which open in the evening. Native in South Africa.

Hesperethusa crenulata. A small spiny bush of India and IndoChina, evergreen and bearing small white fragrant flowers. A good pot plant.

Holboellia latifolia. A graceful climber belonging to the barberry family, native in the Himalayas. It is often grown under glass for the sake of its very fragrant greenish flowers which appear in March.

Idesia polycarpa. A tall tree native in Japan and China, bearing sweet scented yellowish flowers in drooping panicles, followed by orange-red berries.

Ilex yunnanensis. Yunnan holly. An attractive evergreen shrub with small neat leaves and clusters of agreeably fragrant purplish flowers.

Itea ilicifolia. A Chinese relative of the little Virginian willow, an evergreen, growing ten feet tall, with toothed holly-like leaves and long tails of creamy white fragrant flowers. Must be grown in a pot under glass if wanted in the North.

Ixora acuminata. A tropical evergreen shrub, native in India, with oval leaves and sweet scented white flowers. *I. hookeri* [*I. odorata*] is a sweet scented species from Madagascar. There are other fragrant members of this family.

Jaborosa integrifolia. A rare plant from the neighbourhood of Buenos Aires with tuberous roots and handsome foliage. The very fragrant white flowers are borne in June. It is sometimes grown in rock gardens on the continent and in Britain.

Kaempferia galanga. A well-known economic plant in the West Indies, cultivated for its clusters of ovoid tubercules which are employed medicinally and in the manufacture of perfumes. The flowers are white and appear in summer. *K. rotunda* is extensively cultivated in gardens in India for the sake of its beautiful white and purple flowers which appear in early spring before the leaves, and diffuse a most enchanting perfume for some yards in the neighbourhood. The flowers open in the morning and fade away towards evening.

Kerria japonica. The blossoms of the single Jew's mallow have a pleasing but indefinite fragrance. It is one of the best of yellow-flowered shrubs.

Laburnum anagyroides [*L. vulgare*]. Though Mary Webb in the "Golden Arrow" speaks of "the curious sharp scent of the laburnum," the common form, usually seen in gardens, seems to me to be almost scentless. There is, however, a variety of *L. alpinum,* known as *fragrans,* that has more perfume.

Lachenalia. Cape cowslip. A genus of small African bulbous plants, grown in greenhouses North. The flowers appear in May and have a very delicate perfume; they continue long in perfection.

Lactuca virosa (*L. integrata*). Strong scented lettuce. A British weed with long thin leaves and unprepossessing yellow flowers. "The whole plant," says Gerard, "is full of clammy, milky juice which hath a very strong and grievous smell of opium." Gray calls it an abundant and pernicious weed introduced from Europe, and naturalized all across the continent, in waste places and along roadsides.

Lantana. Shrubby plants of the verbena family, native in warm regions. They are much used for bedding and for greenhouse culture. The gay-hued flowers, borne in close heads, have a curious oily pungent odour that is disliked by some persons.

Laserpitium. Big aromatic umbellifers with more or less divided foliage, white or pink flowers in large umbels or coarse panicles. They are European mountain plants.

Lathyrus tuberosus. A common plant in Europe, Western Asia and Northern Africa. From the tuberous roots arise lax climbing stems two to four feet long bearing sweet scented bright pink flowers in early summer, three to six on a peduncle. The root is edible.

Laurelia novae-zealandiae. Tall tree native of New Zealand. The leaves when crushed emit a powerful aromatic fragrance. *L. sempervirens* [*L. aromatica*] is from Chile. Sometimes grown under glass.

Lavandula. Lavender. Shrubs with fragrant leaves. *L. angustifolia* ssp. *angustifolia* [*L. delphinensis*], *L. dentata, L. lanata, L. multifida, L. angustifolia* ssp. *pyrenaica* [*L. pyrenaica*], *L. spica, L. stoechas, L. vera.*

Lavanga scandens. An evergreen, spiny, climbing shrub, native in India, Malaysia, etc., bearing white fragrant flowers in axillary clusters. Sometimes grown for ornament in the far South.

Leptospermum scoparium [*L. ericoides*]. The tree manuka. A tall tree native of New Zealand bearing profusely very fragrant white flowers. The wood is much used for fuel and manuka logs have a pleasant odour when burned.

Leucocoryne ixioides. Glory of the sun. A bulbous plant native in Chile requiring greenhouse treatment in the North. The flowers resemble those of a *Brodiaea* and are clear lavender paling to white at the center, borne in loose clusters on long wiry stems. They have a very pleasant fragrance, something like that of heliotrope, but the plant when bruised gives out a strong scent of garlic. The flowers last over two weeks in water and keep their fragrance until the end. *L. alliacea,* with pale lavender flowers and a strong garlic scent, is also a native of Chile.

Leucojum autumnale. Fragrant bell-shaped drooping flowers, red tinted, one to three carried on a slender stem. Portugal.

Levisticum officinale. Lovage. A tall old-fashioned perennial herb with celery-scented leaves grown for its aromatic seeds. It is a plant of Southern Europe, but is naturalized in this country in the neighbourhood of old gardens. It was once of great importance in domestic medicine.

Libertia. Interesting irids having rich evergreen foliage and spikes of flowers as delicate as orchids, possessing a lovely and distinctive perfume. The finest is *L. magellanica,* growing eighteen inches tall and bearing pure white flowers in closely packed heads, a little after the manner of the old double rocket. *L. formosa* [*L. ixioides*] is taller, perhaps four feet in height, and the flowers are white with masses of yellow stamens. New Zealand. These flowers are grown out of doors in the Southern States.

Limonia acidissima [*Feronia limonia*]. Elephant apple. A tree of the East Indies with anise scented leaves used medicinally by the natives. The pulp of the "apples" is acid and is made into jellies.

Lippia dulcis. Yerba dulce. A tall evergreen branching shrub native in Mexico, the leaves of which have an agreeable and exceedingly pungent scent and taste. Other odorous lippias are *L. cymbosa,* of Jamaica, that smells like pennyroyal; *L. ligustrina,* a tall shrub found from Texas to Argentina with fragrant violet coloured flowers in spikes; *L. urticoides,* a South American shrub bearing sweet scented white flowers in panicled spikes. The popular lemon verbena is properly *Aloysia triphylla* [*Lippia citriodora*]. The lippias are used medicinally and in the manufacture of perfumes.

Lyperia fragrans. A compact South African evergreen shrub of little ornamental value, but bearing racemes of pale fragrant flowers in early summer. *L. tristis* is of even less consequence but at night the inconspicuous purplish flowers are said to give off a delicious perfume.

Lysimachia vulgaris. Yellow loosestrife. A somewhat downy herb with leaves generally in whorls and yellow flowers in showy branching clusters in summer. Found in damp shaded places and along reedy marshes and streamsides in Britain and other parts of Europe. It is naturalized in the United States. The peculiar odour of the plant is said to keep away flies, and the Romans are reported to have put the leaves under the yokes of their oxen in the belief that if they were kept free of flies they would be less quarrelsome. Lyte, writing in 1578, says, "The perfume of this herbe dried driveth away all serpents and venomous beastes, and killeth flies and gnattes."

Magnolia. M. championii. Island of Hong Kong. Flowers globular, cream-colored and very fragrant at night. *M. coco.* Evergreen shrub native in Canton, with nodding rounded flowers, very fragrant at night. *M. cubensis.* An evergreen tree found in Cuba with very sweet scented flowers. *M. dealbata.* A deciduous tree found in Southern Mexico. The yellowish white flowers appear after the leaves and are "heavily, or rather, narcotically fragrant." *M. diva.* Western Hupeh. White flowers, rose-colour on the outer petals and saucer-shaped, appearing before the leaves. Very sweet scented. *M. sieboldii* ssp. *sinensis* [*M. globosa* var. *sinensis*]. A shrub with slender branches bearing white fragrant flowers after the leaves have developed. China. *M. hypoleuca.* Large, erect, deciduous tree from China, bearing immense flowers somewhat like a waterlily in appearance in early June. They are creamy white but turn yellow as they mature, and are highly fragrant. *M. kobus.* A deciduous tree whose young bark and twigs give off an aromatic scent when bruised. *M. nitida.* An evergreen species of Western China, bearing creamy white fragrant flowers. *M. officinalis.* A deciduous tree, the white sweet scented, cupped flowers of which appear with the leaves. Rare in cultivation. Hupeh. *M. portoricensis.* Evergreen tree with white perfumed flowers. Puerto Rico. *M. salicifolia.* Slender deciduous tree with white flowers. The bark and young shoots when bruised give off a scent like lemon verbena. *M. globosa* [*M. sarogensis*]. A shrub bearing yellowish white sweet scented flowers. Yunnan. *M. wilsonii.* A spreading shrub, slender and deciduous. The flowers appear with the leaves and are white with red stamens and very fragrant. Common in the woods of Szechuan.

HONEY BELL
(*Mahernia vertcillata*)

Mammea americana. Mamey. Mammee-apple. Tropical tree bearing an edible fruit from which an aromatic liqueur called Eau de Creole is distilled. The blossoms are white and fragrant. Tropical America.

Neomarica northiana [*Marica northiana*]. An attractive irid, native in Brazil. The flowers are white and very fragrant and a good deal like an iris in appearance. Grown in Florida.

Matthiola odoratissima is a somewhat hoary or downy plant native in Persia. The flowers are a rather dirty cream-colour or sometimes purplish and are very fragrant at night. *M. sinuata,* the great sea stock, is a biennial growing freely along Mediterranean shores. The flowers are pale lilac and give out a most lovely fragrance, but only at night. *M. vallesiaca.* A rare and charming little cliff dweller found occasionally on Mt. Cenis and sometimes in the southern Alps. It is a perennial, with a tuft of narrow grey foliage from which arise several stems six inches or so tall carrying mauve stock-like flowers that exhale, especially towards evening, a most delicious sweetness. It is a difficult subject but worth any amount of trouble to induce it to settle down in the rock garden. Many *Matthiola* species are distinguished by their fine fragrance.

Mazus radicans is a not uncommon plant in boggy localities in New Zealand. It is a pretty little creeper with stems that root as they go and fragrant white flowers with yellow centers.

Meconopsis. Species reputed to be fragrant. *M. speciosa* and *M. latifolia.* The pretty little Welsh poppy, *M. cambrica* as omnipresent, in British gardens as it is absent from ours, has a faint pleasing aroma.

Melaleuca. Bottle brush. A genus of shrubs and trees of the myrtle family, native in Australia, that have been freely planted in California. The leaves of some of the species are very fragrant.

Melianthus. Honey bush. South African shrubs, evergreen, with herb-like stems and bearing large showy flowers in racemes in late summer and autumn. "The plants are very strong scented and in

Africa are valued as medicine. They do well in Southern California."

Melicoccus bijuga. Mamoncillo. Spanish lime. Honey berry. Tropical American tree grown in warm regions for its sweet jet black edible fruit. The flowers are small, greenish white and fragrant in racemes. West Indies.

Meliosma dilleniifolia ssp. *cuneifolia* [*M. cuneifolia*]. A deciduous shrub, or small tree, growing in pyramidal form to a height of twenty feet, with spikes of yellowish white flowers that are strongly fragrant. West China. *M. myriantha* bears yellowish white sweet scented flowers. Japan.

Melittis melissophyllum. Bastard balm. Honey balm. A handsome perennial herb native in Europe, belonging to the sage family, found growing in low moist places. It forms dense tufts of square stems bearing whorls of large blossoms of the most vivid white and pink with ample lip and showy helmet. The whole plant is said to have rather a fulsome odour when fresh but when dried has the sweetness of new-mown hay. A good plant to grow in half shaded herbaceous borders or along the edges of ponds.

Mentha cunninghami. A slender prostrate fragrant herb with matted stems, called in New Zealand, where it is very common, Maori mint. Other mints found for the most part in Europe are *M. alopecuroides, M.* ×*gracilis* [*M. gentilis*], *M. longifolia* and *M.* ×*smithiana* [*M. rubra*]. All of these are naturalized in the United States. *M. pulegium* is the strong scented European pennyroyal. "Mint ottos have more power than any other aromatics to overcome the smell of tobacco."

Mesua ferrea. A handsome hardwood tree native in Eastern Bengal, Eastern Himalaya, and Andaman Islands, etc., noted for its richly fragrant beautiful large white flowers that have a globe of golden stamens at the heart, appearing in summer. "The anthers retain the fragrance in a dried state and are sold in the Indian bazaars under the name of nag-kesur, for the making of sachets and stuffing pillows."

Meum athamanticum. Bawd-money. Aromatic umbellifers of low growth with umbels of white flowers. Mountains of Europe. Suitable for borders and rock gardens.

Micromeria. Fragrant species. *M. cremophyla, M. cristata, M. croatica, M. filiformis, M. marginata* [*M. piperella*], *M. thymifolia* [*M. rupestris*]. These are all small aromatic labiates inhabiting mild regions, chiefly about the Mediterranean.

Mikania suaveolens (*M. cordifolia*). An evergreen twining plant from Central America with heart shaped leaves and panicles of white sweet scented flowers.

Moluccella laevis. Bells of Ireland. Molucca balm. A hardy annual plant native in Southern Europe, the leaves of which when bruised give off a pleasant fragrance. The flowers are white.

Monodora myristica. Jamaica nutmeg. Calabash nutmeg. A small tropical African tree rarely seen outside botanical collections. Flowers are yellow blotched with purple & somewhat fragrant. "The seeds abound in an aromatic oil of nutmeg flavor and the entire fruit is not unlike a small calabash."

Moraea spathulata [*M. spathacea*]. A South African irid with bright yellow sweet scented flowers with purple lines on the claws, not unlike an iris in appearance.

Morina longifolia. Whorl flower. Perennial thistle-like plant found in the Himalayas, with prickly acanthus-like foliage, scented of lemon and spikes of pale pink and white flowers in whorls. Two to four feet high.

Moringa oleifera. Horseradish tree. Deciduous tree found in the East Indies and naturalized in tropical America. The flowers are white and fragrant. The roots are "hot" and used as horseradish.

Moscharia pinnatifida. A musk-scented, erect, annual herb from Chile, growing two feet high and bearing white or rose ray and disc flowers in long racemes.

Murraya paniculata [*M. exotica*]. Orange jasmine. Satin-wood. Cosmetic bark tree. Chinese box. A lovely evergreen shrub or small tree native in Malaysia but grown for ornament in Florida and Southern California. The foliage is handsome and shining and the white flowers are deliciously fragrant. It blooms several times a year and the flowers are followed by clusters of red fruit.

Muscari. Fragrant species are *M. conicum, M. campagna; M. moscarimi* [*M. moschatum*], Asia Minor; *M. neglectum,* France, Italy, etc.; *M. armeniacum* [*M. szovitsianum*], Persia, Caucasus, etc.

Myoporum sandwicense. Bastard sandalwood. Hawaiian Island tree growing sixty feet tall, the wood of which has the smell of true sandalwood.

Myristica fragrans (*M. moschata* or *M. officinalis*). Beautiful tree with a straight trunk and horizontal branches. The leaves are dark, shining and aromatic. The pale yellow flowers are small and clustered in the axils of the leaves. The fruit looks like a small rounded pear; when ripe it bursts into halves disclosing the single seed covered by a false "aril" or "arillode," which constitutes the spice known as mace. "The seed itself has a thick hard outer shell enclosing the nucleus of nutmeg. The shrub is especially luxuriant in the Banda Islands, which are sometimes called the Nutmeg Islands."

Myroxylon balsamum var. *pereirae* [*M. pereirae*]. Balsam of Peru. A large handsome tree that grows in the forests of Mexico and Central America. It contains a resin that is richly balsamic in odour. There are several other species with like properties. One of these is *M. balsamum* [*M. toluiferum*], balsam of Tolu. This is native in Northern South America. "The balsam flows from incisions made in the bark during the hot season; its smell is extremely fragrant, somewhat resembling that of lemon and its taste is warm and rather sweet." Nicholson.

Nardostachys jatamansi. Spikenard. A low herbaceous plant found at high altitudes in the Himalayas and hardy in England. The whole plant is odoriferous but not agreeably so to all. It was "used as a perfume as far back as Sumerian times. The scent is contained in the roots, which smell of patchouli, though their scent is rather softer and sweeter, the leaves have the unpleasant mangy-dog smell of the nearly related valerians, and the flowers smell rather like the alpine poppy." (Dr. Hampton.) It is stated by some authorities to be the spikenard of the ancients.

Nelumbo nucifera [*Nelumbium speciosum*]. Sacred bean of India. Egyptian lotus. These beautiful water plants should be in every garden where conditions may be made to suit them. The flowers are large, exquisitely tinted from creamy white to deep rose and are borne well above the decorative blue-green foliage and they are deliciously though delicately fragrant. Summer. Not hardy North but suitable for growth in tubs.

Nepeta. A large genus of perennial mostly strong scented herbs some of which are cultivated in gardens. Desirable kinds are *N. cyanea, N. grandiflora, N. racemosa* [*N. mussini*], *N. sibirica* [*N. macrantha*] and *N. nuda. N. cataria* is the catnip which is widely naturalized in the United States from the Old World. *Glechoma hederacea* [*N. hederacea*] is the little ground ivy, or gill-over-the-ground. It is naturalized near old gardens. Before hops were made use of for clarifying and flavouring ale, the leaves of the ground ivy, or alehoof, were used for the purpose.

Nicotiana. Besides the sweet scented tobaccos enumerated in other parts of the book the following should have some notice. *N. longiflora,* an annual found in Chile and Argentina and sometimes in Texas; *N. noctiflora,* a perennial species native in Argentina and Chile, open and fragrant at night; *N. plumbaginifolia,* West Indies; *N. suaveolens,* annual or biennial, white, night blooming and fragrant, Australia, and *N. sylvestris,* a tall perennial of Argentina.

Nigella sativa. Black cumin, Roman coriander, nutmeg flower. An Asiatic annual with greyish leaves and blue flowers. It is sparingly cultivated for the sake of its seeds which smell and taste like nutmeg and are employed as a spice by the French. "This plant is supposed by some persons to be the Fitches mentioned in Isaiah XXVIII, 25, 27."

Notholaspi rosulatum. A rather common plant in New Zealand in sub-alpine districts. The leaves are arranged in a curiously shaped rosette and the flowers have a delicious orange-like fragrance.

Nymphaea. Waterlily. While some *Nymphaea* species are among the sweetest of flowers others are quite without fragrance, and it would seem the simple part of wisdom, when beauty need not be sacrificed, to make choice among the scented varieties, for when they are sweet few flowers can compare with them. Besides the fragrant American species and varieties mentioned in Chapter II, here is a list of hardy exotic varieties that are both fragrant and beautiful: *N. marliacea* 'Albida', pure white with sepals tinted pink; *N. marliacea* 'Carnea' exhales the pleasant odour of vanilla; *N.* x *somptuosa* of French origin, pink double flowers of waxen texture touched with lavender; 'Mary Exquisita' (morning glory), very beautiful; Loose, large white flower with peculiarly delicate fragrance.

Nymphaea, tender or tropical. Of these there are two distinct classes, the day flowering and the night flowering. The tropical lilies are amazingly beautiful but of course cannot be left out of doors over the winter in the North. Fragrant sorts are the following: 'Henry Shaw', 'Campanula-blue'; 'Mrs. George H. Pring', white with pointed petals; 'Jupiter', curiously bell-shaped flowers, deep blue shaded purple; 'Pennsylvania', rich blue – also known as 'Blue Beauty' and 'Pulcherrima'; 'General Pershing', a charming sweet scented pink flower that opens very early in the morning. Interesting and beautiful tropical species are: *N. caerulea,* the blue lotus of the Nile, pale blue star shaped flowers four to six inches across; *N. amazonium,* yellowish white and sweet, Jamaica; *N.* x *daubenyana,* large pale blue; *N. flavoirens* (*N. gracilis*), a star shaped Mexican species with white, only slightly fragrant flowers; *N. elegans,* yellowish white tinged with blue, Mexico; *N. parkeriana,* large white, British Guyana; *N. tetragona* [*N. pygmaea*], lovely North Asiatic species that next to *N. baumi* is the smallest; *N. scutifolia,* South African species, with sweet bright blue flowers; *N. stellata,* blue, very delicately scented, tropical Africa; *N. thermalis,* Hungarian lotus, pure white flowers with the odour of wine; *N. capensis* var. *zanzibariensis* [*N. zanzibariensis*], the royal purple water lily of Africa, said to be the best dark blue in cultivation and very free flowering.

Of the beautiful night blooming water lilies, Mrs. Helen Fowler, of the Shaw Waterlily Gardens, near Washington, writes me that they can hardly be classed as fragrant flowers. "They do have, however, a rather spicy odor, oriental in effect but only noticeable when you have them in your hand, in contradistinction to the wonderful fragrance of the tropical day lilies whose sweet odor pervades the room in which they are placed, and is lovely, even when one comes near them in the open air."

Ocimum. Basil. Aromatic annual or perennial herbs long in favor with herbalists and cooks. They are native in warm countries. *O. basilicum,* sweet basil, is the species best known to cooks and especially appreciated in France, where many a good dish owes its special gust to this little annual herb. It is native in tropical Asia, Africa, and the Pacific Isles. A pot of sweet basil makes a very welcome gift to a friend and many uses are found for the fragrant leaves. *O. basilicum* 'Minimum' *O. minimum,* or bush basil, comes from Chile, near Valparaiso. It is an annual, fragrant thymelike plant. *O. gratissimum* is the strongest scented of the basils, it smells and tastes of lemon. It is a woody shrub growing eight feet tall and is very popular with the Bengalese who plant it in their gardens and about their temples.

Olearia. Daisy bush. A genus of Australian shrubs, the leaves of which have a decided musky odour. Sometimes called musk trees. *O. fragrantissima, O. ilicifolia, O. moschata, O. odorata,* are all fragrant. *O.* 'Waikariensis' [*O. oleifolia*] is smothered with white flowers that are pleasantly scented. *O. argophylla* blooms very early and the silvery leaves are pleasantly scented.

Origanum. Marjoram. A genus of subshrubs or herbaceous perennials mostly native about the Mediterranean, famous for their aromatic leaves. *O. vulgare* is the hardy sweet herb well known in kitchens for its sweet and aromatic scent and savour. Other varieties good to have because of their aromatic leaves are *O. dictamnus,* dittany of Crete; *O. libanoticum,* Lebanon; *O. pulchrum,* Greece; *O. sipyleum,* Levant; *O. calcaratum* [*O. tournefortii*], Grecian Archipelago; *O. maru,* Mastic, Syria and Arabia, *O. marjorana* is the knotted or sweet marjoram of gardens. North Africa.

Ornithogalum arabicum. This cousin of the star of Bethlehem found about Mediterranean shores has fragrant flowers and is useful as a greenhouse plant. It grows nearly two feet tall and the flowers are white with black pistil. They have a decidedly aromatic perfume .

Osmanthus x *burkwoodii* [*Osmaria burkwoodii*] is a new shrub, the result of a cross between *Osmanthus delavayi* and *Phyllyrea decora.* It is an evergreen, quite hardy and the blossoms are exquisitely sweet.

Oxalis enneaphylla. Scurvy grass. A pretty species from the Falkland Islands, with tuberous roots and glaucous leaves. The flowers are solitary, waxen white with lavender veins and scented of almonds. The plant grows two inches high and blooms in June. Good for the rock garden.

Pancratium illyricum. Bulbous plant allied to *Hymenocallis,* native of the Mediterranean region. Evergreen leaves six to twelve inches long and white sweetly scented flowers in an umbel in June. *P. maritimum* has narrow grey-green leaves and very sweet scented white flowers. *P. verecundum,* a tender species from Bengal with fragrant green and white flowers. These plants make good greenhouse subjects.

There are numerous other fragrant plants of this genus.

Pandanus odoratissimus. A fragrant-flowered species of the screw pine found in marshy places in the warmest parts of the tropics, Hawaiian Islands, Tahiti, etc. It grows ten to twelve feet high and creates an impenetrable jungle. The male and female flowers are on separate trees and are produced in the rainy season, the tender white floral leaves of the male tree being the most fragrant. The perfume has been described as the "most delightful, the richest and the most powerful" of floral odours; it is also long lasting, being retained by the flower after almost complete desiccation. In Tahiti the natives make a wine called Pandanus wine from the pulp of the fruit.

Parsonia (*Cuphea*). A small genus of climbing plants with sweet scented flowers in panicles. *P. capsularis* is a fine New Zealand species with white or red, jasmine-like flowers, extremely fragrant, that are much sought after by visitors to the bush. Leaves are narrow and leathery and red-brown in colour.

Paulownia tomentosa [*P. imperialis*]. A tall ornamental tree from Japan. Bears showy large purple blossoms in terminal panicles in June, the scent of which is distinguishable at some distance from the tree.

Pennantia corymbosa. An interesting little tree common in many parts of New Zealand, Norfolk Island and Australia. It bears in profusion fragrant white flowers followed by black fruit.

Pergularia odoratissima. West coast creeper. A twining plant with very sweetly scented greenish yellow blossoms. The flowers of *P. minor* are also exceedingly fragrant and they are of a warmer colour than those of the foregoing. India and China.

Perovskia atriplicifolia. Silver sage. A deciduous semi-woody plant, three to four feet high, the leaves of which have a pleasant aromatic odour. The flowers are violet-blue in whorled spikes and the whole inflorescence is covered with a white down. Native of the Himalayas and Afghanistan. Hardy in Massachusetts and a most effective plant as to colouring. Fine for borders but seldom seen in this country.

Petasites hybridus. Butter-burr. Bog rhubarb. A coarse creeping plant, native in Europe and Asia and naturalized in the United States. The leaves, according to Gerard, "are of such a wideness as is big and large enough to keep a man's head from rain, and from the heat of the sun." The stout hollow stem carries purple, fragrant blossoms in an elongated raceme in April. It is used medicinally.

Peucedanum officinale. Sulphurwort or hog's fennel. A fennel-like plant related to the parsnip, with clusters of yellow flowers, a rare inhabitant of salt marshes in certain parts of Britain. The root has a fetid smell and the plant is said to be poisonous.

Peumus boldus [*P. fragrans*]. An evergreen deciduous tree from Chile, the leaves and young shoots of which smell a good deal like the sweet gale (*Myrica*). It is sometimes grown in California for the sake of its fragrant foliage and handsome greenish yellow, sweet scented flowers that appear in the autumn. It grows ten to twenty feet.

Phebalium nudum. One of the most beautiful of New Zealand shrubs and highly aromatic in all its parts. A perfume has been made from the flowers.

Phellodendron amurense. Chinese cork tree. This tree bears black fruit emitting a strong odour of turpentine when crushed. Said to be hardy in the North.

Phillyrea. Jasmine box. Mock privet. Evergreen shrubs native in the south of Europe where they are frequently grown as standards in gardens. The flowers are of small account but those of *Osmanthus decorus,* formerly *P. decora* are said to be sweet scented.

Phlomis fruticosa. Jerusalem sage. A low shrub of the Mediterranean region, the leaves of which are lined with soft hairs and which, when crushed, emit a sagelike odour. Showy yellow flowers in whorls. It makes a good border plant where the climate is not too cold.

Pimelea suaveolens. Sweet rice flower. A fragrant member of a large genus of greenhouse shrubs from Australia and New Zealand. The leaves are narrow and the yellow flowers are borne in round terminal heads. Grown out of doors in mild climates.

Pimenta dioica [*P. officinalis*]. Allspice. The flavour and odour of allspice is midway between cinnamon and cloves. It is the product of a small tropical American tree with a slender upright trunk, much branched at the top and covered with grey aromatic bark. The leaves also are sweet scented. In July the little tree is covered with very small fragrant flowers, the perfume of which is carried to a great distance by the wind. The berries, which are aromatic only when green, are therefore harvested as soon as they have reached their full size and while still unripe are dried on mats placed on terraced wooden floors. *P. acris,* known as the bay rum tree, or black cinnamon, is grown for the oil which is extracted from the berries and used in the preparation of bay rum. The fragrance from the leaves is said to permeate the air for a great distance. West Indies.

Piper cubeba. Tailed pepper. Cubeb. Cubeb pepper. A climbing perennial plant of the East Indies, extensively grown in the coffee plantations where it is shaded and supported by the coffee trees. The fruit is aromatic and used medicinally. *P. nigrum* is a climbing plant bearing reddish berries that when dried and ground furnish the black and white pepper of the kitchen. Old World tropics.

Pitcairnia suaveolens. A sweet scented yellow flowered herbaceous perennial, native in Brazil.

Pittosporum eugenioides. Lemonwood. Tarata. A beautiful New Zealand tree whose pale green leaves emit when bruised a lemonlike odour. In October the tree produces masses of yellowish green flowers whose heavy honeyed odour is almost sickening in its intensity. *P. tenuifolium,* tawhiwhi, kohuhu, is another New Zealand species, a small tree, the bark of which gives off a pungent odour when crushed. This species is used for the formation of ornamental hedges. The fragrant gum taken from it is collected and hung around the neck in a sachet by the natives. At night the dark colored flowers diffuse a sweet odour that fills the air for many yards around.

Plectranthus foetidus. Stinking cockspur flower. A deciduous Australian plant blossoming in summer.

Plumieria alba. Frangipani. West Indian jasmine. Pagoda tree. Nosegay. Temple tree. A tree with white, strongly fragrant flowers discovered by Frangipani, the botanist, when he landed in Antigua with the Columbus expedition. The species are trees or shrubs with fleshy leaves growing in tufts at the ends of the branches. They are native in Peru and other parts of South America and the West Indian Islands. *P. rubra,* sometimes called red jasmine, is used by the native women to adorn themselves and to put among linen to scent it. *P. lutea* belongs to Peru and has exceedingly sweet scented flowers. We are told that the sailors with Columbus smelled a delicious flowery fragrance as they approached one of the islands of the West Indies. This was the scent of *P. alba.*

Pogostemon patchouli. An herbaceous shrub found in parts of India which furnishes the famous perfume of the Hindus, patchouli or pucha-hat. The odoriferous part of the plant is the leaves. Valuable India shawls used to be distinguished by their odour of patchouli and it is one of the commonest perfumes found in the bazaars, a most peculiar fragrance, very disagreeable to some persons.

SEA DAFFODIL
(*Pancratium maritimum*)

Polygala chamaebuxus. A low evergreen shrubby plant seldom rising more than two to three inches from the ground. It is a native of the Alps of Switzerland and Austria and has long been cultivated in gardens. During the spring, summer, and sometimes in autumn, it bears many delicate creamy flowers that possess a peculiarly mild and delicious fragrance, much like that of ripe apricots. Stands out in southern New England and is ideal for rock gardens.

Polyscias. Aromatic shrubs and trees from the Old World planted for ornament in the far South and in greenhouses in northern latitudes. *P. scutellaria* 'Balfourii' [*P. balfouriana*], *P. filicifolia, P. fruticosa, P. guilfoylei,* and *P. obtusa.*

Pomaderris elliptica. A branching shrub growing from two to ten feet tall, bearing cymes of pale yellow fragrant flowers. It is much cultivated in New Zealand gardens.

Poncirus trifoliata (*Citrus trifoliata*). Hardy orange. Trifoliate orange. Bitter orange. China. Deciduous, very spiny shrub eight to twelve feet tall and often as much through, with crooked angular branches and flowers, pure white and sweet, borne in the axils of the spines before the leaves appear. Fruit like small oranges. Probably hardy as far north as Philadelphia in sheltered locations. Valuable hedge plant for the South. The greenish yellow fruits have a hard shell and fragrant edible pulp.

Pongamia pinnata. Karum tree. Indian beech. Karanja. Thinwin. Poonga oil tree. A tree growing forty feet high found in tropical Asia and Australia, bearing pink or rose, pea-shaped flowers. The leaves are strong smelling.

Populus x *jackii* 'Gileadensis' [*Commiphora opobalsamum*]. Balm of Gilead. A small tree native in the countries on both sides of the Red Sea. It is the source of the true balm of Gilead and has been cherished as such for countless ages. Mrs. Grieve ("A Modern Herbal") says: "It is both rare, and difficult to rear, and is so much valued by the Turks that its importation is prohibited. They have grown the trees in guarded gardens at Matarie, near Cairo, from the days of Prosper Alpin, who wrote the Dialogue of Balm, and the balsam is valued as a cosmetic by the royal ladies. In the Bible, and in the writings of Bruce, Theophrastus, Galen and Dioscorides, it is lauded."

Porana paniculata. Snow-in-the-jungle. Snow creeper. Christ vine. Bridal-bouquet. White corallita. A profuse blooming twining plant sometimes grown for ornament in the Southern States. The flowers are white and in shape something like a morning glory. Very sweetly scented. India and Malaysia.

Posoqueria fragrantissima. A shrubby tree from Brazil, bearing large white tubular flowers that are exceedingly fragrant. Allied to gardenia. *P. longiflora* belongs to French Guyana; *P. coriacea* ssp. *formosa* [*P. formosa*] to Caracas; *P. multiflora* to Brazil; all are deliciously fragrant.

Poterium sanguisorba. Salad burnet. An old fashioned salad herb, the pretty deeply toothed leaflets of which smell and taste like the fresh rind of cucumber. Our ancestors were fond of it but it is little used today. Burnet wine is made in rural neighbourhoods in England and was once very popular. "This is a homely drink to which the reddish brown flowers of the burnet impart a colour of port wine and a faint, earthy bouquet."

Premna odorata. Tree or shrub native in the Philippines with terminal corymbs of dark purple flowers.

Protea mellifera. Cape honey flower. African shrub from the Cape region known as sugarbush on account of the honey secreted by the flowers.

Prunus dulcis [*Amygdalus communis*]. Almond. Anyone who has inhaled the airs from the pink-clouded almond plantations in California or Europe cherishes a memory of their sweetness. There are two kinds, the sweet and the bitter, *Prunus dulcis* and *Prunus amara.* The almond tree is a native of Africa and the warmer parts of Asia, but it has long been cultivated in gardens. Poets of all ages have sung of it, inspired by its fragile and precocious beauty. In the Scriptures there are many allusions to it by its Hebrew name of 'Shaked', apparently with reference to its early awakening. In Palestine it flowers in January. "Almonds, as well as the oil pressed from them, were well known in Greece and Italy long before the Christian era."

Prunus padus (*Padus racemosa*). Common bird cherry. A tree growing thirty feet tall, bearing small fragrant white flowers in drooping racemes. Often planted for ornament. The bark when bruised gives out a strong odour.

Pseudopanax colensoi [*Nothopanax colensoi*]. Ornamental shrub growing to twenty feet. Small flowers in umbels, heavily scented. New Zealand.

Psidium. Guava. An extensive genus of tropical trees and shrubs of Myrtaceae, nearly all bearing large white fragrant flowers. They are grown in Florida for the sake of their fruits from which jellies are made.

Psoralea. Scurvy-pea. A large genus of strongly scented herbs or shrubs with pinnate leaves and pea-shaped flowers in spikes. South Africa.

Pterospermum lancaefolium. A shrubby sub-tropical tree of Asia, with dense handsome foliage and large fragrant white flowers. Said to be a popular roadside tree in parts of India. *P. acerifolium,* maple-leaved bayur, which also has fragrant white flowers, is sparingly grown in California. East Indies.

Pterostyrax hispida (*Halesia hispida*). Fragrant tree. Deciduous tree from China and Japan, growing fifty feet tall and bearing drooping panicles, ten inches long, of white fragrant flowers in June and July. It is hardy in the North.

Pulicaria odora (*Inula odora*). Old World herb of Asteraceae, rather weedy, but with some claims to fragrance in both leaves and flowers. *P. dysenterica* has yellow flowers and the whole plant emits a soapy smell when bruised.

Pyracantha coccinea 'Lalandei'. The firethorn is better known for its spectacular display of orange-scarlet berries in the autumn than for the small flowers that crowd the shoots in spring and which have the scent of new-mown hay. One of the finest of all shrubs. Evergreen.

Pyrus sorbus (*Sorbus domestica*). Service tree. The service tree of England is very ornamental though not often seen in gardens. Its flowers are white, in panicles, resembling those of the hawthorn. They open in May and are sweet scented. Others of this genus have scented attractions.

Quisqualis indica. Rangoon creeper. A climbing shrub without tendrils. The charming sweet scented flowers are first white then change to pink and rose. They hang from the bush in drooping terminal spikes. A delightful climber. Philippines, Burma and Malaysia.

Ranunculus buchananii. McDonald mentions this as a rare New Zealand buttercup with delicately scented creamy flowers.

Reineckia carnea. An attractive perennial plant from China and Japan with creeping rootstock and tufts of narrow leaves, six to twelve inches long, and spikes of sweet scented flesh coloured flowers in April and May. Sometimes grown as a pot plant and in the open in mild climates.

Reseda glauca. Hardy mignonette. This little plant is a native of the Pyrenees, where it is found in rocky places at high altitudes and by streamsides. It has not the fine fragrance of its garden relatives but the yellowish flowers have some claim to sweetness. The leaves of the plant are its chief fortune for they turn bright red in late summer, making it a conspicuous object late into the autumn. Sometimes grown in rock gardens.

Retama monosperma [*Genista monosperma*]. Southern Europe. North Africa. "This splendid Spaniard I first saw at San Remo where its fragrance filled a large garden and its silver green graces were almost concealed under a shower of white flowers. There is a touch of pale chocolate in the heart of each blossom, and the fragrance, so fresh and clean, is not exceeded by any growing thing." (Phillpotts). A deciduous species native in Southern Europe and frequently employed as a greenhouse shrub.

Rhodorhiza florida (*Convolvulus floridus*). "A convolvulus-like plant from the Canary Islands possessing in its stems and leaves the scent of roses and from which a powerfully odorous oil is extracted. Largely employed to adulterate Attar of roses." –McDonald.

Rondeletia odorata. A shrub found in Cuba and Mexico, growing on rocks by the coast. The flowers are bright vermilion with the projecting ring of the tube orange coloured. They are so sweet scented that McDonald says a popular perfume has been named after them. It is grown out of doors in warm climates and in greenhouses north. There are several other fragrant species, among them, *R. gratissima,* Mexico; *R. laurifolia,* Jamaica; *R. purdiei,* Colombia.

Roupellia grata. Cream-fruit tree. A vigorous greenhouse climber native of South Africa and bearing a profusion of pale pink and white very fragrant flowers in dense sessile cymes. The fruit, called cream-fruit, is eaten by the natives.

Ruta graveolens. Rue. Herb of grace. Very bitter tasting herb with grey leaves, strongly aromatic, native of the Mediterranean region. Once very important in domestic medical practice and believed to ward off witches and contagion. It was one of the important strewing herbs of old times. A few sprigs of rue hung in the room will drive out flies. *R. suaveolens,* with yellow flowers having the smell of cowslips, is native in Taurea and blossoms in June.

Salvia. Sage. Many sages have aromatic leaves besides the well known garden sage, *S. officinalis.* Of these are *S. cadmica, S. candelabrum, S. cretica, S. fulgens* [*S. grandiflora*], *S. greggii,* one of the hardiest of the shrubby salvias, the leaves of which smell somewhat like rosemary; *S. ringens, S. rutilans,* pineapple-scented sage, an old fashioned greenhouse subshrub, the leaves of which smell like pineapple, *S. scabiosaefolia, S. sclarea,* etc.

COMMON RUE
(*Ruta graveolens*)

Sambucus ebulus. Dwarf elder. Danewort. Dane's elder. Wallwort. Gerard says of this plant "it is not a shrub, neither is it altogether an herby plant." It grows about four feet tall with narrow serrated leaves and bears pinkish flowers in irregular heads. It "has a most disagreeable odour, being nauseous, fetid, and noxious. . . . The foliage is not eaten by cattle, nor will moles come where the leaves of this, or those of any of the species are laid. They drive away mice from granaries and the Silesians strew them where pigs lie, under the belief that they prevent diseases to which they are liable."

Sansevieria hyacinthoides [*S. thyrsiflora*]. A South African plant of the lily family, grown under glass in the North. The leaves are long and narrow and margined with yellow. The flowers are greenish white and fragrant.

Satureja. A genus of small fragrant herbs of which *S. hortensis* and *S. montana,* the summer and winter savory of the garden, are important in the kitchen. Summer savory is naturalized in the eastern part of our country and may often be met with by the wayside, or in the fields. The savories are native in warm countries and are related to *Micromeria.* Good kinds to grow, especially in the rock garden, are *S. boissieri, S. diffusa, S. spicigera* [*S. intermedia*], *S. montana* [*S. pygmaea*], *Micromeria thymifolia* [*S. rupestris*] (very aromatic) and *S. stenophylla.* All these little plants have small inconspicuous flowers, not fragrant but greatly appreciated by bees. The sweetness is in the leaves.

Schima wallichii. Tall evergreen tree belonging to India and Sumatra, sometimes grown in Southern California. The flowers are white, very sweet scented and borne in terminal racemes.

Schisandra chinensis. A twining shrub reaching a height of twenty-five feet. It bears in May and June white or pinkish sweet scented flowers, followed by scarlet berries. Japan.

Scilla verna. The vernal squill. Charming little bulbous plant found wild in Western Europe, in Britain and Ireland, and in the Orkney and Shetland Islands. A slender stem rises between narrow leaves, carrying in early spring a head of bright blue very fragrant flowers.

Selago serrata. One of the most attractive species of a large genus of little known South African plants. A shrubby evergreen not more than two feet high, bearing flat corymbs of light blue flowers at the extremities of the numerous stems. They are pleasantly aromatic. The plant is at its best in August and continues to bloom until October.

Serissa foetida (*S. japonica*). A shrub of Southeastern Asia, the leaves of which have an exceedingly unpleasant odour when bruised.

Sicana odorifera. Curuba. Coroa. Curua. Cassabanana. A tall South American climber grown as an annual in the Southern States for the sake of its long orange-crimson scented fruit.

Sisyrinchium odoratissimum. A rush-leaved species introduced by Clarence Elliott from Elizabeth Island in the straits of Magellan. It may be grown as a pot plant or out of doors in the milder parts of the country. The characteristic flowers are creamy-white lightly penciled with purple and said to possess the delightful fragrance of *Daphne cneorum.*

Solandra. Chalice vine. Tall woody plants, erect or climbing, sometimes grown in greenhouses and frequently in the open in the Southern States and in California. *S. grandiflora* (*Swartzia grandiflora*) has cream-colored sweet scented flowers in March and April and greenish slightly acid fruits. Native of the West Indies. *S. guttata* (*Swartzia guttata*) a Mexican species, is half climbing and bears creamy purple-spotted flowers that are exceedingly fragrant. *S. longiflora* [*S. laevis*] bears green and white flowers that are sweet scented. South America.

Spermadictyon suaveolens [*Hamiltonia suaveolens*]. An ornamental evergreen shrub found from India to China. White flowers borne in corymbs in the autumn are very sweet scented. Grown in greenhouses.

Spiranthera odoratissima. An evergreen shrub found in the tropics of America that bears red and white sweet scented flowers.

Sysygium aromaticum [*Eucomis aromatica*]. The clove tree is native in the Moluccas and grows to a height of about thirty feet. From the dried unexpanded buds the clove of commerce is derived. The clove tree is a charming evergreen, bearing quantities of pale purple flowers in terminal cymes. A young plantation just coming into bloom is said to be a most attractive sight, the leaves of various tones of green setting off the clusters of dull red clove buds. In the Moluccas, according to Mrs. Leyel, no one is allowed to approach the orchard wearing a hat, lest the tree should become alarmed and bear no fruit. *E. uniflora,* Surinam cherry, is a tall shrub or small tree of Brazil, evergreen, and bearing quantities of white fragrant flowers, followed by deep crimson edible fruit.

Tabernaemontana. A large genus of ornamental tropical shrubs and subshrubs, many of which have exceedingly fragrant flowers, usually pale yellow in colour. *T. amygdalifolia* is very sweet scented, and other fragrant kinds are *T. dichotoma, T. recurva* and *T. citrifolia.*

Tabernaemontana divaricata [*Ervatamia coronaria*]. Moonbeam. Clavel de la India. A much-branched Indian evergreen shrub planted in the far South for ornament. It bears large white gardenia-like blossoms that give out a delicious fragrance at night. There is a double-flowered variety.

Tagetes lucida. Sweet-scented Mexican marigold. A Mexican perennial cultivated as an annual in northern countries but not common in cultivation. The flowers are golden or orange-yellow.

Tamarindus indica. Tamarind. Indian date. A picturesque evergreen tree, native in India and tropical Africa, and widely grown in the tropics for the sake of its long brown pods which follow the fragrant yellow flowers and which are eaten in various ways and made into pleasant drinks. The tamarind fruits are also well known for their medicinal properties.

Tchihatchewia isatidea. "This is a marvelous crucifer with pink flowers much like those of *Daphne cneorum* 'Major' and exceedingly fragrant." This quotation is from the writings of M. Correvon, who says further that this plant, which was introduced by Mr. E. Boissier, from the Valley of the Euphrates, is now lost to cultivation.

Tecophilaea cyanocrocus. Chilean crocus. A charming Chilean bulbous plant, six to eight inches high, having fibrous-coated corms and narrow channeled leaves. The crocus-like flowers appear in March and are bright or dark blue with white throats and pleasantly fragrant. McDonald says the scent is similar to that of violet. It makes a good pot plant in the North.

Teucrium chamaedrys. Wild or wall germander. A half shrubby little plant native in Europe, Syria and the Greek Islands. The plant is hairy and the small rose-garnet flowers are borne in summer. The whole plant is bitter and slightly aromatic and the leaves when rubbed emit an odour of garlic. *T. fruticans,* tree germander, is a half hardy evergreen shrub from the regions of the Mediterranean, the leaves of which when crushed are pleasantly aromatic. *T. marum,* cat thyme, is so called because cats have a strange liking for this little southern shrub. The leaves are somewhat downy and very aromatic when bruised. *T. scorodonia,* the water germander, is an unattractive plant with wide woolly leaves, a weak hairy stem and nondescript rose-pink flowers. The whole plant has a rank pungent odour and, according to "A Modern Herbal," when eaten by cows, gives the milk the odour of garlic.

Thalictrum foetidum. A strong smelling species native in the mountains of Europe.

Thevetia peruviana [*T. nereifolia*]. Yellow oleander. A small evergreen tree native of Tropical South America but grown outside in the Southern States. Will stand a degree or two of frost. The tubular yellow flowers are very fragrant. June. Brazil.

Thunbergia fragrans. A woody twiner, native of India, bearing lovely white scented flowers.

Tigridia pavonia 'Lutea'. Peruvian bulbous plant with sweet scented yellow flowers, spotted.

Toddalia aculeata. Lopez root. A shrub widely distributed through Asia. It is of moderate growth, has trifoliate leaves and a weakly almost climbing habit. The flowers are white and strongly fragrant.

Trigonella foenum-graecum. Fenugreek. Strongly odorous annual herbs belonging to Southern Europe and Asia. The seeds were in ancient times held in great repute for medicinal & culinary purposes.

Triphasia trifolia. Lime berry. Myrtle lime. A spiny evergreen shrub bearing white fragrant flowers followed by dull red berries. It is native in Malaysia but is grown in the far South for ornament. In Manila the fruits are found preserved in syrup.

Tulbaghia alliacea. A South African rhizomatous perennial plant smelling of garlic.

Ursinia. Strongly scented South African annual herbs grown for ornament, with daisy-like flowers.

Valeriana celtica. A hardy perennial plant native of the Swiss Alps and the Tyrol (the country of the ancient Celts). This is said to be the famous spikenard known from antiquity for its perfume which pervades the whole plant but especially the root, and is still used in the East for perfuming clothes, the bath, and as a disinfectant. The flowers are white. The odour is said to resemble a mixture of Roman chamomile and patchouli.

Verbena teucroides [*V. tridens*]. Mate negre. Attractive dwarf shrub from South America, with heath-like foliage and small fragrant lilac flowers. It is found in Patagonia.

Vicia faba. Field bean. Vetch. Broad bean. A native of Persia but now widely naturalized in Europe. It has been cultivated for countless ages. The white and black flowers have a delicate honeylike fragrance with a hint of cinnamon, hardly perceptible in a garden bed but quite powerful and most delicious when grown over a large area. The scent of the bean flowers is famous and many poets have sung of it, Shenstone for one.

The tangled vetches purple bloom,
The odour of the Bean's perfume,
Be theirs alone who cultivate the soil,
And drink the cup of thirst and eat the
bread of toil.

Virgilia oroboides [*V. capensis*]. A South African tree named in honor of the poet Virgil. The leaves are somewhat leathery and it bears with prodigal profusion terminal racemes of pinkish purple pea-shaped blossoms. It has been introduced into Southern California and is sometimes grown under glass in the North.

Xylopia. A genus of trees or shrubs widely distributed throughout tropical America. The leaves, wood and flowers of certain species are sweet scented. *X. glabra.* The wood pigeons feed upon the berries of this species and the delicate bitter flavour peculiar to them is wholly owing to this part of their food. The wood, bark and berries of this species all have an agreeable bitter taste. Bedsteads and linen presses made of it are proof against insects. It is called the bitterwood of Jamaica.

Zaluzianskya capensis [*Nycterinia capensis*]. Charming South African annual having a long period of bloom. The nine-inch tufts are bushy and covered with pure white blossoms that open in the evening only and smell strongly of vanilla. A pretty edging for a border of night-scented flowers.

Ziziphora tenuior. A dwarf mint-like plant native of Persia and Baluchistan, with square stems and small purple flowers. It is sold in Indian bazaars as a sweet herb, having a strong mint-like taste and scent. *Z. serpyllacea* is a sweet scented species from the Caucasus.

ORCHIDS, TERRESTRIAL

Cypripedium calceolus. This is the lady's slipper of Europe, a handsome flower with bright yellow pouch and rich purple-brown streamers, and a fine fragrance. This fine plant needs protective measures in England for it is almost extinct there, though still plentiful on the continent.

Gastrodia cunninghamii. A terrestrial orchid of New Zealand, growing two feet tall. The flowers are a soiled greenish colour spotted white and give off an aromatic but objectionable odour.

Gymnadenia albida (*Orchis albida*), which takes refuge upon alpine slopes among bushes of rhododendron and huckleberry, "is very tiny in its flower, very delicate, absolutely charming, its little whitish corolla exhales a sweet odour of honey."

Habenaria bifolia. A sweet scented species found in beech woods in England, the flowers of which are greenish and not very effective. *Gymnadenia conopsea* [*H. conopsea*]. Fragrant orchid. A European species with flowers of a uniform crimson without spots, borne on a slender spike and exhaling a powerful and delicious odour, resembling that of a clove pink. *H. odoratissima* is similar to the above but much smaller. The flowers are a deep purple-red and exceedingly fragrant. *Orchis papilionacea* [*H. chlorantha*], the butterfly orchid, is a form of *H. bifolia.* It is said to give off a rich aromatic scent at night.

Herminium monorchis. Musk orchid. A small European species found on humid chalky banks in Britain (also in Siberia and Himalaya), bearing a dense spike of small greenish yellow flowers with a musky odour. (M. Correvon describes it as a strong formic acid odour.)

Himantoglossum hircinum [*Orchis hircina*]. Lizard orchid. A not very attractive species. The flowers are a soiled greenish colour and their unattractiveness is further accentuated by a disagreeable fulsome odour which is said to carry on the breeze for many yards. Europe and North Africa. *Dactylorhiza foliosa* [*O. maculata*], the spotted orchid, common in Europe and Asia Minor, has pale purplish or white flowers that are powerfully scented in the evening. *O. mascula,* the early purple orchid, found in Britain, as well as in North Africa, "has ordinarily a scent of vanilla but from a bunch of flowers, especially when they are fading, there is a distinct suggestion of cats." *O. morio,* the green-winged orchid, when first opened has a pleasing scent but later develops the curious catty odour of the foregoing species. Both the root and leaves of *O. fusca* have a sweet hay-like fragrance, and *O. pyramidalis* smells sweetly by day but gives off a foxy odour at night. *O. sancta* [*O. coriophora*], of Central and Southern Europe, a rare and curious species, has, according to M. Correvon, "the odour of bedbugs and flowers of a livid red and purple."

Nigritella nigra [*N. angustifolia*]. The deliciously sweet vanilla orchid which haunts the mountain pastures of Europe and parts of Siberia. "It has produced with *Gymnadenia odoratissima* a charming hybrid, *N. suaveolens,* with even more delicate perfume, longer spike and a dark carmine flower, which is found occasionally in the Alps." Correvon.

Spiranthes spiralis. European lady's tresses. Small spikes of waxen creamy white flowers that are very fragrant.

ORCHIDS, EPIPHYTES

Among these are some of the strangest as well as the most beautiful of flowers. They are to be found clinging to the trunks or branches of trees in humid tropical forests where the perfume of some of the species, as strange and complicated in many of them as is the structure of the flowers, fills the air. There is the most surprising variability in the perfumes of the different orchids, some reproducing the scent of violets, some of wallflowers, of honey, of hay, elder, wild grape, vanilla, lilac, tuberose, and of several fruits, while others are endowed with a horrid stench. In Donald McDonald's "Fragrant Flowers and Leaves" he gives an exhaustive list of odorous orchids. The list presented here has been furnished me by Mr. T. H. Everett.

Aerides odorata. White flowers with purple tip, flowers smelling like apples. Philippine Islands. *A. fieldingii,* sweet odour of pansies in the early morning and at evening. India. *A. angustifolium* and *A. expansum* have also scented flowers.

Angraecum sesquipedale (*Macroplectrum sesquidelale*). Flowers ivory white and smelling like those of the gardenia. Madagascar.

Bifrenaria atropurpurea. Wine red, very fragrant flowers. Brazil. *B. harrisoniae* (*Lycaste harrisoniae*) also from Brazil, has a delicate fragrance.

× *Brassocattleya.* Hybrids between the genera *Brassavola, Laelia* and *Cattleya.* Nearly all are sweet and some powerfully so.

Bulbophyllum virescens (*Moluccas*) and *B. becharii* have the odour of putrid fish. *B. fletcherianum* smells like putrid meat. *B. odoratissimum,* an Indian and Chinese species, has a delicate sweetness and *B. suavissimum,* Burma, has the perfume of new-mown hay.

LIZARD ORCHID
(*Himantoglossum hircinum*)

Catasetum scurra. A species found in Guyana, has pale straw-coloured fragrant flowers in drooping racemes.

Cattleya. Nearly all the species of this beautiful genera are fragrant but some more so than others, and though there is much variety in the odours of these flowers there seems an underlying spiciness in them all. Some are sweet only towards evening, like *C. eldorado,* which then gives off a delicious rose perfume. *C. trianaei* smells of 'Green Gage' plums only in the morning. *C. schroederae* is fragrant of hawthorn. *C. violacea* is said to smell deliciously of violets.

Coelogyne cristata. Snow-white flowers with yellow keels in drooping racemes. The scent is heavy, something like that of banana. Himalayas.

Crassula fascicularis [*Rochea odoratissima*]. A succulent greenhouse plant from South Africa, bearing pale yellow or creamy white flowers that have a pleasing fragrance.

Cycnoches ventricosum var. *chlorochilon* [*C. chlorochilon*]. Swan orchid. A species with yellow-green flowers darker spotted and exceedingly fragrant. Venezuela and Colombia.

Cymbidium eburneum. A fragrant white flowered species from the Himalayas. *C. mastersii* is a late flowering species also from the Himalayas with white petals tinged with brownish rose that smell strongly of almonds at night. The fragrance of *C. ensifolium* is much liked by the Chinese.

Dendrobium heterocarpum (*D. aureum*). A species found in the Philippines and in the Himalayas, has creamy flowers marked on the lip with brown and gives off the scent of violets. *D. moschatum,* with reddish yellow flowers, is musk scented. *D. nobile,* a Himalayan species with rosy-purple flowers is reported as giving off the odour of hay in the evening, of honey at noon, and of primrose in the morning. *D. chrysoloxum* [*D. suavissimum*] from Burma and China, has golden yellow, honey scented flowers. *D. scabrilingue* has the fragrance of wallflowers. *D. nobile* has pure white sweet scented flowers.

Dendrochilum glumaceum. A Philippine species, white, greenish yellow at the tip and powerfully sweet.

Earina mucronata. A charming New Zealand orchid bearing white very sweet scented flowers.

Encyclia aromatica (*Epidendrum aromaticum*). Primrose-yellow fragrant flowers. Mexico and Guatemala. *E. odoratissima* (*Epidendrum odoratissimum*). A species found in Brazil with greenish very fragrant flowers.

Encyclia fragrans [*Epidendrum fragrans*]. Sweet scented species from Brazil and the West Indies with yellowish white flowers with purple lined lip.

Gongora scaphephorus. Fragrant yellowish white flowers spotted with purple-brown. Peru.

Houlletia odoratissima. Deliciously sweet scented chocolate-brown flowers with white lip. Colombia.

Laelia albida. Dainty Mexican species with white flowers sometimes tinged with rose. Fragrance light and delicate. *L. anceps,* a species with yellow-throated, violet-rose flowers, is said to have the fragrance of primroses in the morning. *Schomburgkia superbiens* [*L. superbiens*] is a sweet scented species from Mexico and Guatemala.

Lycaste aromatica. Fragrant Mexican species with orange-yellow flowers, the lip spotted with rose.

Masdevallia gargantua. Curious species from high places in Colombia that has an unpleasant gamy odour.

Maxillaria luteoalba. Fragrant species, found in Venezuela, with large flowers yellow tinged with brown. *M. picta* smells of hawthorn.

Miltoniopsis roezlii [*Miltonia roezlii*]. Species of epiphytes from Colombia with white flowers spotted purple that have an odour something like that of the rose.

Odontoglossum. Several of these have scented flowers, including *O. edwardii,* a purple flowered species from Ecuador, scented like violets; *Cuitlauzina pendula* [*O. citrosmum*] with rose scented flowers.

Osmoglossum pulchellum, from Costa Rica and Guatemala, with white flowers scented of vanilla in the morning; *O. triumphans* from Colombia, with dark yellow flowers having the warm fragrance of pansies.

Oncidium incurvum. A Mexican species with white flowers spotted violet-rose that smell of lilac and primrose. *O. ornithorhynchum,* very fragrant, rose or rarely white flowers with golden crests that are said to smell of lilac in the morning and of elder at night. *O. tigrinum,* a Mexican species, has yellow flowers spotted with brown that have somewhat the odour of violets.

Peristeria elata. Holy ghost flower. Dove flower. Very fragrant species with waxen white flowers. Panama.

Pescatorea. Several of these tropical American species have sweet scented flowers, among them *P. dayana* of Colombia, and *P. klabochorum* of Ecuador.

Phalaenopsis schilleriana. Philippine species with rose-purple fragrant flowers, said to smell of roses in the morning and lily of the valley at evening.

Rodriguezia venusta (*Burlingtonia fragrans*). South American orchid with narrow leaves and white fragrant flowers, spotted yellow on the lip, in pendulous racemes. Brazil.

Trichopilia suavis. White or creamy flowers spotted with rose, and with the scent of hawthorn. Central America.

Vanda parishii. Indian species with yellow flowers spotted with brown that have a strong characteristic fragrance. *V. tricolor,* native in Java, has brown-spotted yellow flowers that smell of carnation in the morning and of vanilla in the evening.

Vanilla planifolia [*V. fragrans*]. Common vanilla. A climbing orchid of Tropical America which yields the vanilla bean of commerce.

Warscewiczella aromatica. White very fragrant flowers with azure lip. *Zygopetalum wendlandii* [*W. wendlandi*] has yellowish green violet-edged flowers. Panama and Costa Rica.

Xylobium hyacinthinum (*Maxillaria hyacinthinum*). White flowers with the fragrance of hyacinths. Venezuela.

CHAPTER XX

Odorous Grasses, Ferns and Mushrooms

GRASSES

EVEN THE HUMBLE GRASSES contribute their mete of sweetness to the summer air and some of them are used in the composition of perfumes. The grass to which our hay fields chiefly owe their delightful and peculiar fragrance is the sweet vernal grass, *Anthoxanthum odoratum.* The scent of this species is secreted mainly in the stems and it is less powerful when growing than when cut or in a dried state. The sweet vernal grass is a perennial species introduced from Europe and naturalized in this country from coast to coast. It is most luxuriant and highly perfumed in damp situations.

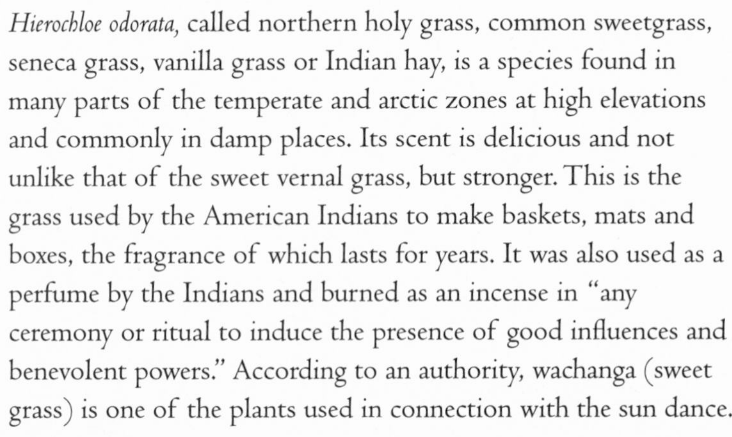

> *Hierochloe odorata,* called northern holy grass, common sweetgrass, seneca grass, vanilla grass or Indian hay, is a species found in many parts of the temperate and arctic zones at high elevations and commonly in damp places. Its scent is delicious and not unlike that of the sweet vernal grass, but stronger. This is the grass used by the American Indians to make baskets, mats and boxes, the fragrance of which lasts for years. It was also used as a perfume by the Indians and burned as an incense in "any ceremony or ritual to induce the presence of good influences and benevolent powers." According to an authority, wachanga (sweet grass) is one of the plants used in connection with the sun dance.

It is interesting to read that "On Palm Sundays old Dakotas, members of the church, when they have received palms at the church, carry them home and tie sweet grass with them when they put them up in their houses.... it is said, some of the old people still carry sweet grass to church for the Palm Sunday service. This is from the old-time association of sweet grass with sacred ceremonies and things holy."[1] Its name of holy grass arose from the custom in Europe of strewing it in the aisles of churches and about the doors on festival days. It gives out a strong sweet odour when trodden upon. In Iceland where it grows abundantly it is laid in sheafs among linen and hung up in rooms for the sake of the refreshing perfume it imparts to the air. In Sweden it is sold in bundles to be hung over beds, in the belief that it induces sleep. There are several species of *Hierochloe*, all with scented attributes.

Other odorous grasses found in America are the following: *Cinna arundinacea*, wood reed grass, a rather common species in moist woods and shaded swamps in the cooler parts of the country. It has hay-scented foliage. *Eragrostis megastachya*, snake grass or stink grass, common along sandy waysides, makes itself known when trodden upon by a sharp disagreeable odour. *E. cilianensis*, known in California where it is widely naturalized along roadsides and in waste places as snake grass, is strong smelling when fresh. *Poa annua*, low spear grass, which, according to McDonald, is one of the sweetest of grasses, is found, says Gray, on cultivated and waste ground everywhere in this country, but was introduced originally from Europe. It is sweetest when dried. Mrs. Rowntree writes me of the California vanilla grass, *Torresia macrophylla*, found throughout the Redwood belt of Central and Northern California. The whole of this plant is sweet scented.

[1] *"Uses of Plants by the Indians in the Missouri River Region." Melvin Randolph Gilmore.*

Other fragrant grasses are:

Ataxia horsfieldi, a grass from Java that emits when crushed the same fragrance as the sweet vernal grass.

Cymbopogon citratus, lemon grass, is a large bluish-leaved grass, cultivated in Jamaica and elsewhere for the sake of the oil which is extracted from its leaves and which is called lemon grass oil, verbena oil, or Indian melissa oil. *Vetiveria zizanoides* [*C. muricatus*], vetiver, or khus khus grass, is very common in moist soil throughout India, Sri Lanka, Burma, and the Philippine Islands, and is also abundant in the Antilles, Puerto Rico, Jamaica, Brazil, etc. The leaves are without odour but the roots possess a strong peculiar scent "somewhat like myrrh combined with some flower of the mignonette type." From these roots is extracted an oil very valuable in the composition of several perfumes. It formed the basis of two scents that enjoyed great popularity in the last century – Mousseline des Indes and Bouquet du Roi. In India, especially in the neighbourhood of Sri Lanka, the roots of this grass are woven into sun blinds and on hot days are sprinkled with water which evaporates and gives off a fragrant and refreshing odour. *C. nardus*, citronella grass, is very common on the plains of Punjab and the Northwest Provinces. It is extensively cultivated in Sri Lanka, Java and Burma, and at Singapore, for the manufacture of the oil we know as citronella oil, which is extracted from the leaves. This is distilled in enormous quantities and used for perfuming the cheaper soaps and scents. *C. schoenanthus*, palmarosa, is the source of Indian geranium oil. "It is grown in India and was formerly known as 'Turkish Geranium Oil' because it was imported into Europe via Turkey and Bulgaria as an adulterant to Otto of roses. It has a strong geranium-like odour."

Cyperus is a large genus of plants of the sedge family some of which are sweet scented. *C. articulatus* is a tall sedge found in Jamaica and on the banks of the Nile. The tuberous roots have much the same fragrance as *Calamus aromaticus;* they are the source of the drug Adrue. *C. longus,* a British species, which Gerard called the English galingale, is said to exhale the scent of violets from its joints. The roots of *C. rotundus* and *C. scariosus,* Indian species, are largely employed in the manipulation of Eastern perfumes, and besides being popular as a scent for the hair, the roots are used in dyeing and imparting an agreeable perfume to fabrics.

Oplismenus hirtellus 'Varegatus' [*Panicum variegatum*] is a variegated form of a sub-tropical grass. "When in full bloom the flowers smell strongly, giving off an odour like that of certain orchids."

FERNS

"Give me the strong, rank scent of ferns in the spring for vigor," wrote Thoreau, and many of us catch this haunting odour in the damp spring woods without ascribing it to its true source. Thoreau also noted the odour of dying fern fronds and especially those of the dicksonia, *Dennstaedtia punctilobula.* "Going along the old Carlisle road," he wrote in his journal, "I perceive the grateful scent of the dicksonia fern now partly decayed. It reminds me of all up-country with its springy mountain sides and unexhausted vigor. When I wade through my narrow cow-paths it is as if I had strayed into an ancient and decayed herb garden. Nature perfumes her garments with this essence now especially. The very scent of it, if you have a decayed frond in your chamber, will take you far up country in a twinkling. You would think you had gone after the cows there or were lost in the mountains."

Willard Clute writes that during the haying season whole counties in eastern Pennsylvania are thoroughly perfumed by the fronds of this fern, which have been cut with the hay. It is commonly known as the hay-scented fern.

The maidenhair fern, *Adiantum pedatum,* has a delicate haylike scent when dried. *Aspidium fragrans* is another native fern that deserves to be celebrated here because of its agreeable odour. It is a rare and uncommon little species found on a lucky day "growing in clefts in the face of precipices in the northern part of the country and yields only to the enduring and persistent fern hunter." (Clute). The fragrance of this small fern has been likened to that of strawberries, raspberries and primroses. It is said to cling long to a handkerchief in which the plant has been wrapped and to last for many years in dried herbarium specimens.

The New York fern, *Parathelypteris novae-boracensis* [*Aspidium noveboracense*], so abundant in rural sections about New York City, gives off a pleasant breath when the fronds are crushed, a strong sweet odour somewhat reminiscent of fresh turned earth with something sweet mingled with it. Several others of this genus have scented attractions, among them a greenhouse fern, listed by McDonald, *P. nevadense, A. trapezioides* and *A. peruvianum.* They are all said to smell like new-mown hay when crushed.

The dying fronds of the dainty maidenhair spleenwort, *Asplenium trichomanes,* have a faint sweetish aroma, and the ebony spleenwort, *A. platyneuron* [*A. ebeneum*], is also slightly fragrant when dried. The crushed fronds of the beech ferns, *Thelypteris polypodioides* [*Phegopteria polypodioides*] and *Phegopteris hexagonoptera,* according to Willard Clute, emit a peculiar earthy odour from the minute glands scattered over their blades, and this is true also of *P. roboertiana,* the scented oak fern, or limestone polypody. And the lovely bladder fern, *Cystopteris bulbifera,* found on dripping cliffs in limestone regions, is often exceedingly fragrant. The rhizome of the common polypody is sweet scented.

Miss Jekyll speaks somewhere of the scent of the bracken, *Pteridium aquilinum* (*Pteris aquilina*), as being "so like the smell of the sea as you come near it after a long absence." This odour is particularly strong in the autumn. One would like always to have the bracken near for this reason, if for no other, but it is a grasping plant and must be entertained with caution, and only where there is plenty of space.

Other ferns with claims to notice here are *Adiantum raddianum* 'Fragrantissimum' [*A. fragrantissimum*] a scented maidenhair from Brazil; *Cheilanthes pteridioides* [*C. fragrans*], a greenhouse species from Southern Europe, whose fronds when handled emit a pleasant scent of new-mown hay, which is retained when they are dried for some time; *C. suaveolens* and *C. odora* are other fragrant species listed by McDonald, but they are probably synonymous with *Cheilanthes pteridioides.*

Lindsaea cultrata is a species from Guyana whose fronds are said to have very much the same fragrance as sweet vernal grass, and which retain the odour when dried. A small African fern, *Mohria tutifraga,* has won the local name of frankincense, because of its agreeable scent. *Drynaria wildenovi is* an Indian species with hay scented leaves.

Nephrodium is a genus of ferns belonging to warm countries and related to *Aspidium.* They are said to yield sweet odours especially in warm weather. *Dryopteris aemula* [*Nephrodium aemulum*], the hay-scented buckler fern, from Southern and Western Europe, is one of these. *Dryopteris fragrans* [*N. fragrans*] belongs to Asia and America, and has rather leathery leaves. *Oreopteris limbosperma* [*N. monthanum*], the mountain buckler fern, a beautiful species of the mountains of Europe, from the Arctic regions to the Pyrenees and also of Japan, has a strong apple scent, as has *N. rigidum,* the rigid fern, "characteristic of limestone piles on calcareous mountains in Southern Europe."

MUSHROOMS

We are not accustomed to look for odour in the flowerless plants yet some of them have a pleasant fragrance while the stinkhorns exhale the most terrible stench perhaps of any growing thing. Among odorous mushrooms are the following:

Cantharellus cibarius. A gold-colored mushroom called in France chanterelle. It is found in many parts of this country and its pleasant odour has been compared to that of ripe apricots.

Clitocybe fragrans. Highly scented with anise. Margaret McKenny[1] wrote of this – "At one of my

[1] *"Mushrooms of Field and Wood."*

mushroom exhibits a timber cruiser saw and smelled the little *Clitocybe fragrans.* He had spent his life in the deep western woods always seeking to learn more of the secrets of the wilderness. 'Why' he exclaimed, 'this is the flower I have smelled and tried to find for years in the winter woods'. *C. odora,* the anise funnelcap, is also a fragrant species with a less strong odour of anise.

Clitopilus prunulus. This species is said to have the odour of new meal, bread dough or cucumber.

Helvella lacunosa. Elfin saddle. Small species with rather offensive odour.

Hygrophorus eburneus. Ivory waxycap. Odour and flesh agreeable.

Inocybe. Most of the numerous kinds of *Inocybe* have an unpleasant odour.

Lactarius piperatus. Pepper milkcap. Flesh quite aromatic.

Marasmius scorodonius. "Sometimes as you are sitting in the woods, you may notice an odour of garlic. If you look about you will find, perhaps at your feet, a little twig and on it a prim row of tiny mushrooms. That more than likely is the way in which you will find your first garlic mushrooms."

Mycena pura. Lilac fairy helmet. Flesh has a distinct odour of radishes.

Phallus impudicus. Common stinkhorn. Probably the most evil smelling of all plants. "An overpowering fetid odour suddenly evident upon the premises has many times filled with consternation the guests at summer resorts." This upon investigation proves to be a sudden uprising of the terrible stinkhorn mushrooms.

Pholiota squarrosa. Shaggy scalecap. Old plants are said to smell like stale lard. Sometimes garlicky or onion-like.

Polyporus sulphureus. In a letter Miss McKenny sends me the following:

"The lower slopes of Mount Rainier are clothed with a forest of virgin growth. Moss carpets the ground, disguises the form of every fallen snag, drapes all the boughs with curtains green throughout the year. And here from the rich damp leaf mould and from the immense fallen trees grow innumerable mushrooms of varied tints and odors. Once on a still warm day in September as we explored the woods near Elbe, we came on a log thirty feet long covered with a marvelous growth of *Polyporus sulphureus,* the sulphur polypore. The woods were deep and shadowy yet so vivid was the orange and yellow coloring of the fungus that it was as if the boughs of the cedars and Douglas firs had parted and let in a blaze of sunlight. Suddenly we perceived a mysterious odor and could not place the source. But as we stood, our eyes fixed on the glowing mushrooms, shell superimposed over shell, in intricate fluted patterns, we became conscious of a mist rising above the log, and then again caught the odor, wave on wave. Gradually we realized that we were seeing what few had seen, the fungus, as Fabre says, at the nuptual moment, for rhythmically, through the damp, still air, rose the almost invisible mist of spores, and each time the puff arose, the voluptuous odor floated toward us, sweet and heady, combination of yeast and musk."

Russula foetans. Stinking russula. "This ill-smelling russula is common in woods of the east. At first suggesting bitter almonds, the odor becomes intensely disagreeable, resembling that of burnt milk."

BIBLIOGRAPHY

Bach, Rene. *Growing Roses for Perfumery.* The Puritan, April, 1900.

Bardswell, Frances. *The Herb Garden,* Chapter XII. 1911. Adam & Charles Black. London.

Burbidge, F. W. *The Book of the Scented Garden.* 1905. John Lane. London and New York.

Burbidge, F. W. *Fragrant Leaves v. Sweet-Scented Flowers.* 1898. The Journal of the Royal Horticultural Society, Vol. XXII, part 2.

Burbidge, F. W. *A B C List of Perfumes, Essential Oils, etc. and the plants that afford them.* 1898. The Journal of the Royal Horticultural Society, Vol. XXII.

Burroughs, John. *Pepatcon and Other Sketches.* Chapter VII. 1881. Houghton Mifflin Company. Boston and New York.

Brown, Charlotte Cowdry. *Gardens to Color.* Chapter IX. 1917. The Knickerbocker Press. New York.

Ellacombe, Canon. *In My Vicarage Garden.* Chapter XIII. 1902. John Lane. London and New York.

Earl, Florence Morse. *Old Time Gardens.* Chapter XIII. 1922. The Macmillan Company. New York.

Fox, Helen Morgenthau. *Patio Gardens.* Chapter XI. 1929. The Macmillan Company. New York.

Grayson, David. *Great Possessions.* 1927. Doubleday, Page and Co. New York.

Hampton, Dr. F. A. *Flower Scent.* 1925. Dulau and Co., I,td. London.

Hampton, Dr. F. A. *The Scent of Flowers.* 1929. The Journal of the Royal Horticultural Society.

Jekyll, Gertrude. *Wood and Garden.* Chapter XIX. 1904. Longmarns, Green and Co. London, New York and Bombay.

Leyel, Mrs. C. F. *The Magic of Herbs.* Chapters XI and XIII. Jonathan Cape. London.

McKenzie, Dan, M.D. *Aromatics and the Soul.* Paul B. Hoeber, Inc. New York City.

McDonald, Donald. *Fragrant Flowers and Leaves.* Frederick Warne and Co. London and New York.

Mott, Frederick T. *Flora Odorata.* 1843. Orr and Co. London

Peck, Harry Thurston. *The Morality of Perfumes.* September 1898, Cosmopolitan.

Peckham, Ethel Anson. *The Perfume of Narcissi.* Journal of the New York Botanical Garden.

Peckham, Ethel Anson. *Farming for Bouquets on the Côte D'Azure.* Journal of the New York Botanical Garden.

Pellett, Frank C. *American Honey Plants.* 1923. American Bee Journal, Hamilton, Ill.

Piesse, G. W. Septimus. *The art of Perfumery,* 3rd edition. 1862.

Pemberton, J. H. *Rose Perfumes.* 1917. Rose Annual (English).

Rimmel, Eugene. *The Book of Perfumes.* 1864. Chapman and Hall. London.

Rohde, Eleanour Sinclaire. *The Scented Garden.* 1931. The Medici Society. London.

Saltus, Edgar. *The Toilet of Venus.* The Smart Set.

Sawyer, J. Ch. F.L.S. *Odorographia.* 1894. Gurney and Jackson. London.

Theophrastus. (Translation by Sir Arthur Hort) *Enquiry Into Plants. Concerning Odours.*

Schimmel & Co.'s *Reports on Essential Oils, Synthetic Perfumes, Etc.*

Thompson, C. J. S. *The Mystery and the Lure of Perfume.* 1927. John Lane. The Bodley Head Limited. London.

Thonger, Charles. *The Book of the Cottage Garden.* Chapter VIII. 1909. John Lane. The Bodley Head. London.

INDEX

Index

Index

Index

Index

Index

Index

Index

Index

Index

Index

Index

Index

Index

Index